Liberty's Captives

LIBERTY'S CAPTIVES

Narratives of Confinement
in the Print Culture
of the Early Republic

THE JEFFERSON CITY EDITORIAL PROJECT

Editor Daniel E. Williams

Associate Editors Christina Riley Brown,
Salita S. Bryant, Dixon Bynum, Randy Jasmine

Consulting Editor Boyd Childress

Technical Consultant Austin Lingerfelt

The University of Georgia Press *Athens and London*

© 2006 by the University of Georgia Press
Athens, Georgia 30602
All rights reserved
Designed by Louise OFarrell
Set in 11/13 Bulmer by Bookcomp, Inc.

Printed digitally

Library of Congress Cataloging-in-Publication Data
Liberty's captives : narratives of confinement in the print culture of
the early republic : the jefferson city editorial project / editor, Daniel
E. Williams ; associate editors, Christina Riley Brown . . . [et al.] ;
consulting editor, Boyd Childress ; technical consultant, Austin Lingerfelt.
p. cm.
Includes bibliographical references and index.
ISBN-13: 978-0-8203-2800-3 (cloth : alk. paper)
ISBN-10: 0-8203-2800-6 (cloth : alk. paper)
ISBN-13: 978-0-8203-2801-0 (pbk. : alk. paper)
ISBN-10: 0-8203-2801-4 (pbk. : alk. paper)
1. Captivity narratives—United States.   2. American prose
literature—1783–1850.   3. American prose literature—Revolutionary
period, 1775–1783.   I. Williams, Daniel E.   II. Brown, Christina Riley.
PS651.L53 2006
818'.20808—dc22   2005028386
British Library Cataloging-in-Publication Data available

CONTENTS

ILLUSTRATIONS

PREFACE

The Jefferson City Editorial Project began six years ago in a small classroom in the west wing of Bondurant Hall on the University of Mississippi campus. I had decided to teach a graduate seminar on historical editing and had planned to give the students an opportunity to work individually with one or two narratives taken from early American print culture. I wanted to have the students gain hands-on experience working with original documents, as I had gained a decade before when I had attended the National Historical Publications and Records Commission's Institute for the Editing of Historical Documents in 1989. I had learned a lot from the institute and especially from John Kaminsky and Gaspare Saladino, and I wanted to pass along what I had learned in a graduate seminar.

Quite early in the semester, however, it became apparent to the eight original students and I that we had a book instead of a class project. Instead of merely editing for the sake of an academic exercise, I realized that we could combine our efforts and actually produce an anthology, which I at once thought could make a valuable contribution. In my own research I had been working on various types of popular narratives published in the print culture of the early Republic, and I had found what I thought were an astonishing number of non–Native American captivity narratives. I had already been working on the Barbary narratives of James Riley and Archibald Robbins when I began to trace the remarkable print history of the Maria Martin narrative. About the same time I had found half a dozen impressment narratives, which I thought were as unique and relevant as they were unknown. I had also recently worked on an essay discussing several pirate captivity and slave narratives, which I thought were equally unique and relevant. From previous work I knew that most Revolutionary narratives incorporated captivity themes and experiences and that most criminal narratives incorporated prison scenes, if not direct comments on liberty and captivity. Thus it seemed clear to me that the discussion of captivity narratives should be widened to include these texts. Moreover, it also seemed clear that the cultural and political exploration into the meaning of liberty during the early Republic was much greater than had previously been acknowledged, as the popularity of these texts suggested. I discussed the possibility of focusing on various types of captivity texts with my students, and we agreed to narrow our search to such texts published in the United States and produced for American readers from, roughly, the Revolution to the Missouri Compromise (1820–21). We further agreed to narrow our criteria of selection to complete texts of seventy-five pages or less that had been published by themselves. We wanted texts that demonstrated the variety of captivity narratives, that were interesting, that held some historical significance, and that in some way contributed to our understanding of liberty's cultural significance during the early Republic.

When we began our selection process, we had no idea how long and comprehensive this process would be. My students read far more primary texts than students in other seminars and certainly far more than they had anticipated at the outset. We read and discussed hundreds of narratives. A few weeks into the semester I realized that my students were learning far more about early American print culture than I could ever have hoped to teach them in a more conventional seminar. From this process, which was broken down into three different stages of discussion and selection, we finally settled on a list of twenty-five titles, which we later narrowed down to seventeen with the able help of editors and readers. Each student chose two or three texts with which to work, and that student was responsible for editing, proofing, annotating, and introducing his or her own text. Since I had become as much a participant and collaborator as a seminar leader, I chose my own texts and worked alongside the students. Thus, by the end of the 2001 spring semester, the students and I produced roughly a third of the copy material included in the present volume. Since we were convinced of the project's relevance and viability, we continued working together, although marriages and moves reduced our number and increased our workloads. After the tragedy of 9/11 we renewed our effort to explore the significance of liberty in early American culture in an effort to understand how the nation's new citizens interpreted and responded to their rights of life, liberty, and the pursuit of happiness—and how captivity narratives aided their interpretations and responses. Although further relocations and disruptions slowed our progress, we continued to collaborate during the last couple of years, during which time we were greatly aided by the responses we received from the readers who read the manuscript for the University of Georgia Press.

I am extremely grateful to the core of four students who worked with me from the beginning to produce this anthology. They became more than graduate students—they became my colleagues. They certainly have earned their title as associate editors. Although his primary area of interest somehow remains entrenched in southern literature, Randy Jasmine has contributed much to this project. He is an excellent editor and has produced exceptional work, even if he still leans toward Faulkner. Dixon Bynum, Salita Bryant, and Christina Riley-Brown have all become outstanding early Americanists, and I am thoroughly impressed with the quality of their work and their potential as scholars. I cannot thank these four individuals enough. But I also must express my gratitude to the other four seminar participants who, although personal and professional activities redirected their attention elsewhere, also contributed much to this project: Tiffany Griffin (who got married during the seminar), Lauren McNeill (who got engaged during the seminar), Julie Coris (who moved to Alaska shortly after the seminar), and Katherine Todd (who directed her energy toward completing her degree). Also, I must thank Boyd Childress, who at the last hour has become an honorary member of the Jefferson City Editorial Project. An old friend and coeditor, Boyd generously began to answer so many of my numerous questions about printers and print histories that he truly earned recognition for his efforts. I am grateful for his help and his expertise. Finally, after making a move of my own, I have to acknowledge the generous, tireless work of Austin Lingerfelt. After arriving at TCU with a partially finished manuscript, Austin helped reformat and paginate in successive stages, and his help was invaluable.

No book is ever written alone, and in addition to the editors this book has had numerous contributors along the way. Nancy Grayson has been a wonderful editor to work with, and I appreciate her suggestions and support. My good friends at the American Antiquarian Society also deserve special recognition for their generous help and for always making me feel so welcome in Worcester. I would particularly like to thank Nancy H. Burkett, Joanne D. Chaison, John B. Hench, Marie Lamoureux, and Denis R. Laurie for supporting my work and aiding my visits. I am also deeply grateful to my new TCU family. Dr. Mary Volcansek, Dean of the AddRan College of Humanities and Social Sciences, Dr. Nowell Donovan, Provost and Vice Chancellor for Academic Affairs, and Dr. Victor Boschini, Chancellor of TCU, have been supportive and helpful since the first day I stepped on campus.

We believe that *Liberty's Captives* is a valuable and important project. These texts, all carefully edited and proofed, demonstrate a remarkable richness in range and type in the captivity genre that hitherto has gone unnoticed. At the same time, these texts contribute to our understanding of how dynamic a concept liberty was during America's first decades. By dramatizing the loss of liberty, these narratives stressed its necessity.

Daniel E. Williams
Texas Christian University

INTRODUCTION

It's a Free Country

We hold these truths to be self evident: that all men are created equal;
that they are endowed by their Creator with CERTAIN inalienable
rights; that among these are life, liberty, and the pursuit of happiness.

The known propensity of a democracy is to licentiousness, which
the ambitious call, and the ignorant believe to be, liberty.

—Fisher Ames, "The Dangers of American Liberty" (1809)

During the first half century after the Revolutionary War, an astonishing variety
of captivity narratives were published in American print culture. In hundreds of
narratives, readers of the early Republic encountered sensational accounts of individuals who struggled to escape hostile confinement and regain their liberty. In
the explosion of print that took place in the late eighteenth and early nineteenth
centuries, captivity texts were constantly published to compete in the literary
marketplace, and in this steady flow of print commodities readers could choose
to engage themselves imaginatively with a variety of captive voices. In addition
to the popular tales of Americans held captive by Native Americans, readers
could also immerse themselves in the textual experiences of American prisoners
of war, Americans enslaved by North Africans, Africans enslaved by Americans,
Americans imprisoned by other Americans, American mariners forced to sail
on British warships, Americans taken by pirates, and Americans shipwrecked
on desolate, hostile shores. Whether abducted on the western frontier or subjugated on the Barbary Coast, whether chained in prison or left to die on a prison
ship, the accounts of captives offered readers similarly striking dramatizations
depicting an individual's movement from freedom to confinement and his or her
subsequent struggle to maintain identity without autonomy in an inimical environment. Through imaginative immersion, readers became involved in the lives
of individuals who, despite all manner of degradation and deprivation and despite
all manner of confinement and coercion, dreamed of regaining their liberty.

That an astonishing number of captivity narratives were published during
the early Republic should not be surprising. In a post-Revolutionary culture

1

that celebrated individual freedom, tales of individuals denied their freedom were of intense interest to readers politically sanctioned and socially empowered to explore their newly acquired rights and privileges. Without a doubt, *liberty* was the most pervasive political term used by English-speaking people in the eighteenth century; certainly it was the most popular political concept of English-speaking people in the eighteenth century.[1] Yet it was also the most contested and volatile term in the new republican discourse that evolved during the early national period.[2] No matter the party or agenda, politicians invariably made use of the term, and political disputants often used the term simultaneously as they argued against one another. Moreover, as political participation increased and as political factionalism developed, politicians found it increasingly necessary to appeal for popular support, and in so doing they encouraged all manner of Americans to conceive of themselves as citizens of a republic entitled to explore their liberties.

Decades before the Revolution, American colonists had inherited the British belief that individuals had certain rights and that liberty was an essential condition of these rights.[3] During the period before and after the Revolution, both liberty and its antithesis, slavery, were central to political discourse on both sides of the Atlantic. To justify their rebellion, colonial patriots continually decried British attacks on what they viewed as their rights and liberties. Although an elusive and contradictory term, liberty became a popular cause of the Revolution and in some way touched all English-speaking people.[4] One way or another, all Revolutionary leaders made use of the term, and as a form of rhetoric both the concept and the word became "a way of arguing" (Reid 98). As a means of combating arbitrary power and enslavement, liberty was used as a call to action, as a means of arousing passion and expectation, and its popular appeal was universal. After the Revolution liberty and slavery remained central to political discourse, and politicians, whether Federalist or Republican, whether arguing for an expansion or a curtailment of individual rights, had to make use of similar rhetoric. One way or another, all political discourse during the formative decades of the United States explored the meaning of liberty.

Yet politicians were not the only ones to utilize the rhetoric of liberty; in the coffeehouses as well as in Congress, individuals declared their rights and defined themselves as being free. American freedom became the nation's founding myth and most cherished ideal.[5] The rhetoric of the Revolution had been disseminated, at least on a general level, to all ranks and regions of the population, and once the idea of liberty was unleashed, individuals—at least those who were empowered—embraced the notion of self-determination as the defining tenet of liberty. What had begun as a social and political concept was gradually but inevitably viewed as a personal right, and citizens of the new nation, at least those who were white and male, perceived of themselves as living in a free country, which they took to mean that they were free to pursue personal happiness. The Revolutionary rhetoric that was used to justify the rebellion was taken to heart by those who became the new nation's first citizens—often to the dismay of the Revolutionary elite who had employed that very rhetoric. Once the Declaration of Independence became popularized as socially and politically sanctioned declarations of individual independence, "it's a free country" became an often-heard pronouncement used to justify acts of free will.[6] Liberty came to mean much more than living in a country governed by laws and free of arbitrary power; as a powerful ideological force it came to mean that individuals were free to unleash their private ambitions.

Neither in 1776 nor in 1787 was there a clear understanding of what the new nation would become. Those who attended the Continental Congresses and those who later attended the Constitutional Convention did not share a single vision of what the new nation should be. There were perhaps as many visions as there were delegates, yet they were all guided by an abiding veneration of liberty—though the term was neither precise nor well defined. The early Republic was a remarkable experiment, and its history must be told, not by the codes and conventions it developed to give itself structure and continuity, but by the instability that existed before it developed codes and conventions. For centuries the concept of government had been dominated by monarchical and aristocratic notions of a common people serving an elite, but the Revolutionary concept of popular sovereignty reversed the order, and within an extraordinarily short period of time the concept of a government by the people and for the people was universally accepted. Such radical change resulted in entirely new concepts of authority as the old order of deference was shattered and as an egalitarian ideology became pervasive. The phrase "it's a free country" came to mean not only that individuals were free to pursue their private interests but also that no one individual was better than anyone else, and thus all individuals were equally entitled to pursue their private interests. Rights, privileges, and advantages were to be taken—not inherited. Never before had so many people been empowered to assert themselves politically, socially, and economically. Once "popular consent . . . became the exclusive justification for the exercise of authority by all parts of government," politicians had to appeal to people for their support, thus encouraging people to take sides, and decision-making processes—once the secretive property of the elite—were opened up to the public (Wood 187).

With equally astonishing speed, the early Republic quickly developed a public sphere characterized by an entirely new political dynamic. On a popular level people—at least those who were privileged and franchised—were encouraged not only to participate but also to arbitrate. Promotion and publicity became the primary forces in the public realm. In such a context print culture quickly became a vibrant arena in which issues and ideas were contested.[7] In newspapers, pamphlets, broadsides, and even novels, partisan politicians attacked their opponents and promoted their agendas. To gain popular support, writers, editors, and printers adopted a variety of rhetorical styles and strategies intended to incite and instigate readers, and almost inevitably they cloaked their agendas under the Revolutionary rhetoric of liberty. Yet as both Federalists and Republicans equally claimed the same rhetoric and equally pronounced themselves as the proper heirs of the Revolution, readers often encountered "a babel of conflicting voices," and, ironically, the confidence Revolutionary leaders had first placed in the power of republican discourse to articulate laws and rights eroded into partisan controversies over meaning (Howe 75). To protect political and personal liberties, there had to be a rule of law rather than rule by arbitrary power, and laws required a language that necessarily had to be clear and exact. As meanings and interpretations began to be contested in public debates, particularly during the 1790s, there was far less certainty in the clarity and exactness of the language used in republican discourse than there had been two decades earlier when Thomas Paine appealed to the common sense of American readers.[8] Instead of disseminating truth, early national print culture offered readers possibilities of truth.

In the narratives of captives, readers of the early Republic encountered individuals who resembled themselves, despite drastic differences in environments and capacity. Both captive characters and American readers had been powerfully shaped by the ideology of liberty and had accepted—if not fully embraced—the right to individual self-fulfillment. In some way both were confronted with the need to experience and explore liberty on a personal level as it was being contested on a national level. Once the Constitution had been ratified and the government formed, citizens of the new Republic had no clear definitions or models for either personal or political liberty. As a free people, Americans of the post-Revolutionary period were thus left to define and discover their rights through personal enactments. Much of the factional turmoil of the 1790s is related to a widespread uncertainty concerning how liberty would be understood and how personal autonomy and political authority would be balanced. In depicting the loss of liberty, captivity texts touched some of the deepest fears and desires of American readers, particularly fears concerning tyranny and slavery. Significantly, as the new nation struggled to establish its autonomy and explore its identity as a free country, captivity texts presented readers with dramatic spectacles not only of tyrants and slaves but also of individuals forced to live without any measure of self-autonomy.[9] The parallels between the national and the personal are obvious. Certain texts, such as prisoner-of-war accounts from both the Revolution and the War of 1812, offered dramatic microcosms of the greater political struggles, merging self and nation. In recounting scenes of arbitrary rule imposed ruthlessly on helpless individuals, captivity narratives inculcated powerful political lessons of what the loss of liberty would mean, and thus all such texts in some way reiterated the Revolutionary drama of the struggle for self-sovereignty. No wonder that captivity narratives were among the most popular and affective of all print commodities during the nation's early decades. As the nation collectively sorted out the various meanings of its Revolutionary rhetoric, captivity narratives textually enacted graphic scenes of repression and defiance. Given their movement from the familiar into the unfamiliar and from independence to dependence, captives were compelled to examine their most basic assumptions concerning race, culture, and identity in dialogical binaries of self and other. At a time when political factions were making competing claims for truth, such texts vividly dramatized individual battles for truth. [10]

Still, what does cause wonder is how little read such texts are today. Traditionally, the discussion of captivity narratives has been limited to those texts relating the experiences of individuals taken captive by Native Americans. Such discussions have been immensely rich and have contributed much to the general understanding of significant issues in both print and culture, particularly the ideologies of race and gender. [11] But such discussions have not accounted for either the wide variety of captivity texts or the pervasive contradistinction between liberty and captivity in American print culture. Although there are consistent similarities in rhetoric and scene, only a handful of recent scholars have looked at Native American captivity narratives alongside other types of captivity texts, and few have commented on the explosive ideology of liberty themes in the print culture of the early Republic. In her excellent analysis, *Captivity and Sentiment: Cultural Exchange in American Literature, 1682–1861*, Michelle Burnham has traced the development of sentimentality in Native American captivity narratives, novels, and slave narratives. In his valuable anthology *American Captivity Narratives*, Gordon M. Sayre also stresses the connections between Native American captivity narratives, novels, and slave narratives and suggests how all such texts might be read as prisoner-of-war accounts. This perspective is forcefully argued in Robert C. Doyle's *Voices from Captivity: Interpreting the American POW Narrative*, which discusses a wide range of captivity texts—from King Philip's War to the Vietnam War—as prisoner-of-war accounts. One of the more intriguing recent discussions is Joe Snader's *Caught Between Worlds: British Captivity Narratives in Fact and Fiction*. While arguing against American exceptionalism in favor of British exceptionalism, Snader discusses how the captivity genre developed in Europe and England long before Mary Rowlandson was abducted from her home in 1676. American captivity texts, he argues, must be examined as having developed out of such earlier British texts as Barbary captivity narratives and religious persecution narratives. Using a similar approach in her recent study *Captives*, Linda Colley insightfully analyzes English captivity accounts spanning three centuries and covering three continents. According to Colley, captivity texts ranging from seventeenth-century Mediterranean narratives to nineteenth-century narratives from India and Afghanistan are a "mode of writing rather than a genre" and serve as an accurate reflection of the British imperial enterprise (13). Also making use of a helpful transatlantic approach, Rebecca Blevins Faery analyzes the archetypal figures of both Mary Rowlandson and Pocahontas in her study *Cartographies of Desire: Captivity, Race, and Sex in the Shaping of an American Nation*. Another helpful study that broadens the discussion of captivity narratives is James D. Hartman's *Providence Tales and the Birth of American Literature*, which discusses captivity texts in the context of seventeenth-century English prose narratives. Finally, although they were some of the most popular of all captivity narratives and were the first to depict the inhumanity of slavery graphically in print, Barbary narratives remain relatively unknown, despite the welcome appearance of Paul Baepler's *White Slaves, African Masters*.

Liberty's Captives intends to contribute to the discussion of captivity narratives in American print culture in two areas, by introducing new and significant texts and by proposing that these texts be read as part of a dynamic enactment of national and personal selfhood. To accomplish the first endeavor, the anthology presents a variety of captivity texts published in American print culture during the early Republic, during the period of time when citizens of the nascent nation sorted out the possibilities of liberty. With one or two exceptions, these texts are little known if not entirely unknown, and because they functioned effectively as popular texts and as political tracts, they deserve to be included in current discussions of captivity and liberty, autonomy and authority. They are discursive artifacts of a general national debate—a debate that still has not been settled. In addition to Native American captivity accounts, *Liberty's Captives* includes prisoner-of-war narratives both from the Revolution and the War of 1812, slave narratives, Barbary narratives, maritime impressment narratives, a pirate captivity narrative, a shipwreck narrative, and one mob riot narrative. Yet these genre distinctions, while initially helpful, are flexible and in no way meant to imprison the texts in structural patterns or paradigms. The variety of texts in *Liberty's Captives* suggests the rich capacity for variance in captivity texts, not their similitude. All the texts are published in complete form, and all of them are first-person narratives with the exception of the one narrative in which the captive—the slave Betty—was not allowed a voice.[12]

The process of selection was exhaustive and, we hope, comprehensive. Hundreds of titles published in American print culture between 1770 and 1820 were researched and read, and from this arduous first selection a middle list of ninety titles was chosen, which were then closely read and discussed by the editors. After a final round of reading and discussion, the anthology's list of seventeen titles was then chosen based on several criteria: length, representational types, reader interest, contemporary relevance, popularity or frequency of publication, depiction of historically significant themes or scenes, and rhetorical patterns, particularly concerning references to liberty, captivity, tyranny, and slavery. Once chosen, the process of editing was equally exhaustive. In order to replicate the original narratives as much as possible, special care was taken not only to reproduce the texts but also to examine all textual variants and inconsistencies. Other than standardizing the spacing and adding a letter or two where a type misstruck, no changes have been made to the original texts; all of the original spelling, punctuation, capitalization, and textual irregularities remain. Much care was taken to approach the original print artifact as much as was humanly and technologically possible.

By presenting a rich variety of unfamiliar yet relevant captivity texts, *Liberty's Captives* proposes to focus new attention on the contradistinction between liberty and captivity and how this contradistinction helped to define both the new American nation and its citizens as freedom loving. Most obviously, captivity narratives served potent ideological functions in fostering feelings of outrage against all those who suppressed liberty. Certain narratives effectively aroused anti-British sentiment, anti–Native American sentiment, and anti-Muslim sentiment (among a host of other prejudices). As Bakhtin and his adherents have cogently argued, however, the depiction of otherness is essential in self-definition.[13] This sense of the dialogical formation of self is important in understanding how captivity narratives helped to strengthen national and personal conceptions of self-identity. Bakhtin maintains that self-consciousness is only possible through acts of self-revelation. By examining captivity narratives, it is apparent that the development of self-consciousness takes place not only in social utterance but also in textual dissemination, that the dialogical process takes place on both national and individual levels. For both the new nation and its citizens, self-conception was developed through acts of narration.[14]

Such acts of narration are diverse. There is no single formula, whether structural or thematic, that connects all the captivity texts included in *Liberty's Captives*. Yet what does connect the narratives is the rhetorical perspective of outrage at the loss of liberty. Although scholars have tended to characterize the captivity genre as a body of texts in which contact is made between unfamiliar peoples, *Liberty's Captives* intends to widen the concept of the genre to include a broader range of contact. All the narratives can be perceived as zones of contact where cultural work is transacted, but such contact is best seen as the hostile engagement between oppressor and oppressed.[15] Certainly part of the cultural work transacted in these texts was the promotion of national and racial prejudice, which in turn promoted national pride and nationalist agendas, but on a deeper level the texts also served to support the formation of national identity. Self-formation and self-narration are inextricably linked. All the narratives connect deprivation and degradation with the loss of liberty, and, inversely, all the narratives connect happiness and self-fulfillment with the preservation of liberty. For readers of the early Republic, who were diverse from one another, who were suspicious of both external and internal threats, and who were uncertain about what freedom meant, captivity narratives provided a significant form of cultural exploration into American selfhood.

In the last lines of his captivity narrative, John Dodge urges readers to affirm his "right to revolt" against tyranny. Rather than remain a helpless captive, he declares that he is duty bound to "exert every faculty God has given me to seek satisfaction for the ill usage I received." All acts of oppression are unjust and undeserved, but individuals who passively accept tyranny—according to Dodge—deserve their fate. He concludes his narrative by stating that "if I had ten thousand lives, and was sure to lose them all, I think, should I not attempt to gain satisfaction, I should deserve to be a slave the remainder of my life."

These are remarkable lines, and they represent a far different notion of both liberty and seekers of liberty than colonial Americans had generally perceived just a decade or so earlier. Published in 1779, Dodge's lines demonstrate that the Revolution was not only political but also millennial. Not only were the colonists breaking with a corrupt and tyrannical government, they were also breaking with traditional configurations of power and conventional patterns of sociopolitical behavior. Rather than defer to figures of authority, and rather than accept providential disposition, liberty gave them the right to "seek satisfaction."

Traditionally, and somewhat paradoxically, liberty was previously understood in terms of religious submission. The early Puritans in New England arrived with a conception of liberty as the individual's capacity to submit to God's will. Individuals were free to surrender their souls to divine power, and only by surrendering themselves could they become free from original sin. In this sense, liberty required a denial of self and an acceptance of dependence. Selfhood in all its manifestations, whether self-love, self-reliance, self-determination, or self-sufficiency, was an indication of sinful pride.[16] In general, and despite its emphasis on the necessity of the individual to stand alone before God, Christianity traditionally encouraged submission to all forms of authority, secular as well as sacred. Christian duty required individuals to deny the impulses of the self and to accept their place in the world. For the colonists to revolt against a king who claimed divine sanction, a new conception of liberty had to be developed, one that accepted—rather than deprecated—self-interest.[17]

The right to "seek satisfaction," to satisfy the self, was always present, even when the early Puritan ministers denounced it from their pulpits. Indeed, perhaps far more people came to the New World on selfish—rather than selfless—errands. The same Puritans who struggled to repress their impulses of self were also proud of their inherited traditions of English civil liberties and natural rights. Yet certainly the Revolution gave great impetus to seekers of satisfaction, allowing them the freedom to act upon their desires without spiritual censure or social restriction. Political independence could not be conceived of without the development of larger spheres of personal independence.[18] Civil liberty could not be realized without opening up unprecedented possibilities for personal liberty. While both sacred and secular leaders carefully distinguished between license and liberty, they continually privileged "the primacy of individual judgment" (Dworetz 177).[19] Individuals—at least those who were white and male—were expected to think and act for themselves. By the time the first shots were fired at Lexington and Concord, Adam Smith had clearly articulated his revolutionary doctrine that "man's self-interest was God's Providence," a doctrine entirely antithetical to the Puritans who first settled in New England a hundred and fifty years earlier.[20]

Certainly most of the individuals depicted in post-Revolutionary captivity narratives thought and acted for themselves in their private pursuits of self-interest. Unlike Mary Rowlandson, they tended not to accept their captivities passively as providential fate. Whether overtly or covertly, all the captives who relate their experiences in this anthology defied their captors, and nearly all of them attempted to escape. Embracing individual agency, they struggled, at times violently, to maintain their self-sovereignty, and they expressed outrage at those who denied them their natural rights. In more than a third of the narratives included here, the captives successfully eluded their captors, and in one quarter of the narratives that follow, the captives killed their captors. Philip M'Donald and Alexander M'Leod, for example, reenacted the story of Hannah Dustan by taking up tomahawks and bashing in the heads of their six sleeping captors. Although she at times echoed (and repeated) Rowlandson's language, Eunice Barber similarly dispatched her captor. During a battle between two hostile tribes, she picked up a hatchet, and, "discovering her captor wounded on the ground," she did not hesitate: "I instantly aimed a blow at his head, and continued to repeat them until I was sure that he was quite dead."

As they were related, Barber's experiences offer an interesting contrast to those of Rowlandson, despite her obvious borrowings. Rather than take up a sewing needle, she took up a hatchet. Yet killing her captor did not free her. Once the battle had ended, she was taken into captivity by the victorious tribe, who soon demonstrated their "most diabolical cruelty" in torturing their captives. "These unfeeling monsters" constantly raided the settlements and returned "loaded with human scalps, and dragging into captivity more or less of their defenceless inhabitants." Thus surrounded by savagery and cruelty, she took advantage of "the most favourable opportunity" to escape, preferring "certain death, either by hunger or wild beasts" rather than remain a captive in "awful barbarity." After journeying seven days through swamps and "craggy mountains," and after eating nothing but "the roots and bark of trees," she finally heard "the pleasing sound of a woodman's ax." Feeling "inexpressible joy," she followed the sound until she discovered a "Christian friend," who then led her back to a settlement. In mimicry of Rowlandson, Barber concludes her relation by commenting on affliction. Although her husband and children "fell victims to savage barbarity," and although she had "experienced every hardship and cruelty which it was in the power of the inhuman monsters to inflict," she acknowledges that it was "right and just, that I have been afflicted," and—rephrasing Rowlandson's passage from Hebrews—she adds that "God chastiseth him whom he loveth." While thanking God for saving her "from the tomahawk and scalping knife," and then later "from the ravenous jaws of wild beasts," Barber concludes her narrative repenting her "manifold sins": "May I improve the remaining precious moments of my life in such a way as will insure me permanent and uninterrupted happiness in the world to come."

Clearly, Barber was not passive in her pursuit of happiness. Refusing to resign herself to her fate, she took up a hatchet and then later took the opportunity to escape. Moreover, a number of indications also show that her "inexpressible joy" was situated more in worldly affairs than in spiritual matters. Although she clearly models her conclusion on Rowlandson's eloquent final passage, Barber was not a model of Calvinist self-abnegation. Until she invokes the spirit of Rowlandson in the final paragraph, she does not once make any sort of sacred reference. Although she witnessed "the awful butchery" of her husband and seven children, and although she had repeatedly witnessed other "instances of barbarity," she never mentions God, Providence, or affliction until her final lines. Her narrative was produced not to delineate divine benevolence but to market human malevolence. Beginning with the murdering and scalping of her husband and seven children, including one child who—she declares—"was tomahawked in my arms," there are bloody scenes of cruelty and atrocity throughout the narrative, and the scalpings are too numerous to count.

There is an obvious nationalist, racist agenda in such depictions. Toward the end of the narrative, Barber attends a "Council of War" and listens while the warriors plot to capture and butcher "their much dreaded enemy, General JACKSON." Such references are obviously intended to excite readers into adopting a politically convenient antithesis of Native American savagery versus American civility. How Barber—a captive of six weeks—understood the bloodthirsty orations is less important than the exultation of American virtues personified in "this distinguished Commander." Yet the Barber narrative is by no means merely a representation of national and racial ideologies, a political text produced to advance an obvious agenda of self-entitlement and self-justification. Rather, it is an entrepreneurial text marketed as a print commodity that represents a different sort of self-interest. Its use of nationalist and racist ideologies, along with its graphic use of bloody savagery, functions primarily as a promotional strategy. Despite its concluding claims, the depiction of Barber's sensationalized captivity experiences is not offered as an indication of her "uninterrupted happiness in the world to come" but as an expression of more worldly mercantile interests. Rather than spiritual profits, the narrative represents the printer's desire for commercial profits. The text was created as print merchandise.

Eunice Barber is a fictional character. She did not witness the deaths and scalpings of her husband and seven children on January 26, 1818. She was not carried into captivity in southeastern Georgia. She did not kill her captor with a hatchet. She did not observe "the most diabolical cruelty" of captives being tortured. And she did not escape by crossing "dismal swamps" and "craggy mountains." As a textual representation, she was created to narrate a highly sensational, marketable story. David Hazen, a Boston printer far removed from southeastern Georgia, either created the text or had it created for him. The printer's promotional strategy is evident on the title page. Although 90 percent or more of the narrative relates Eunice Barber's captivity, the title page prominently announces "The Tragical Death of Mr. Darius Barber, and His Seven Children, Who Were Inhumanly Butchered by the Indians." Eight engraved coffins, clearly the most conspicuous representations on the cover, follow this grisly announcement. Only after the symbolic coffins were lined up across the page were the "Captivity and Sufferings of Mrs. Barber" mentioned. Ironically, although he is no more than a reference in the narrative, Andrew Jackson occupies more space on the title page than Eunice Barber. Merging national ideology and individual tragedy, the title page also announces: "It may be a gratification to the reader, to learn that the said tribe of SAVAGES have been since exterminated by the Brave and Intrepid GEN. JACKSON."

Thus the Barber narrative was marketed in order to provoke and arouse readers of the early Republic. Liberty is extolled while a racist ideology of extermination is justified. Still, it is important to consider that the propaganda was used as an early type of marketing ploy. While they certainly endorsed a national policy of replacing what they transparently perceived as Native American savagery with American civility, those involved in the production of the Barber narrative were more interested in selling their print commodity than they were in promoting a nationalist agenda. The readers they wanted to capture in New England would have felt little direct connection with Camden County, Georgia. Ideology and atrocity were as much components in creating the text as were the engravings, the typeface, or even the stitching used to bind the pages. The Barber narrative, like many other captivity narratives from the early nineteenth century, equally reflects the commercialization of the print trade and the popularization of the public sphere. As the literary marketplace developed rapidly in the decades after the Revolution, printers increasingly appealed to popular taste in order to turn a profit.

In 1816, two years before Boston readers encountered Eunice Barber, a different sort of captivity narrative was published, *A Journal of the Shipwreck and Sufferings of Daniel Foss*. Like Barber, Foss was an imaginative creation produced to sell a print commodity. The lone survivor of a shipwreck, Foss supposedly spent five years as a castaway marooned on a barren island. Such a fictional formula was apparently successful, as there were four separate editions of the Foss text by Boston printers in the same year. The protagonist's triumph over adversity, along with his constant desire for deliverance, dramatized deeply felt American values of self-determination and stoic fortitude. In one passage of philosophical reflection, Foss comments on the nature of happiness. After the famished castaway feasted on the raw carcass of a dead seal ("in quite a putrid state") and drank plentifully from rainwater, he exclaimed:

> "What a strange thing (as once said an object of wretchedness) is that called happiness." How shall I express my extreme joy, when after being for three days deprived of a draught of sweet water, I was unexpectedly blessed with a sufficient quantity to last me, at least, ten days—"the fond lover (indeed) never rushed more eagerly to the arms of his bride; the famished tyger more ravenously on his prey, than I to partake of the reviving draught; I drank, rested, surveyed the precious liquid, drank again, and absolutely shed tears of pleasure!"

Interestingly, Foss introduces a relativity of values. What is worthless in one context can become invaluable in another context. Happiness is contingent upon the subjective perceptions of condition and situation. Depending on the context, rainwater and the rotting flesh of a dead seal can be more valuable than gold and silver. Yet what is most interesting about this passage is that Foss—the fictional narrator—quotes "an object of wretchedness" who is actually another fictional narrator.

A decade before the Foss text appeared in print, the narrative of Maria Martin was widely published. Truly an "object of wretchedness," Martin—as she was presented—spent six years as a slave in Algiers, and for two of those years was "confined in a dark and dismal dungeon, loaded with irons." During this period of misery, after nearly expiring from her sufferings, the narrator first remarks on the subjective nature of her happiness: "What strange thing is that called happiness! How shall I express my extreme joy, when after eleven months of intolerable hunger, I was indulged with a sweet loaf of bread free from mould? The fond lover never rushed more eagerly into the arms of his bride; the famished tiger more ravenously on his prey[,] than I upon this loaf; I eat, rested, surveyed the precious morsel, eat again, and absolutely shed tears of pleasure." Despite her sufferings, despite her heavy chains and dismal conditions, Martin experiences "extreme joy," which leads her to discover that happiness was contextual. A loaf of ordinary bread, unexceptional in most settings, became invaluable in the context of Martin's extraordinary setting. Shaped by immediate circumstances, the act of perception inevitably assigns value.

Yet this lesson on the relativity of values and the subjectivity of happiness is, by itself, not all that exceptional. Readers of the Martin narrative, and later those of the Foss narrative, would probably not have been startled by such a perception, particularly those who were familiar with the volatile fluctuations of paper currencies and the self-righteous declarations of rogues and counterfeiters.[21] What makes these words exceptional, however, is the connection they demonstrate between the two narratives. Ironically, having one fictional narrator borrow the words of another fictional narrator suggests a value system far less relative and subjective than the narrators seem to embrace. Both voices are used to animate textual commodities that were created for exchange in a market that necessarily assumed a foundation of stable values, a market in which gold and silver could never be replaced with bread and water. Having Foss appropriate Martin's words not only connects the narratives but also their writers, printers, and readers, all of whom shared a basic belief in enterprise and profit.

By the turn of the century, as the new nation struggled to establish its political and cultural identity, American print culture had clearly demonstrated the profitability of catering to popular taste. By tapping into the deeply held values of the early Republic, by providing readers with graphic dramatizations of captivity and liberty, savagery and suffering, writers and printers validated their right to pursue decidedly pecuniary forms of happiness. Scenes of atrocity were undoubtedly used to help sell the narratives, but such gory marketing techniques were less important than the ideologically symbolic dramatization of the individual's journey from confinement to liberation. As free citizens of the new Republic, Americans generally believed that they had an inherent right to seek satisfaction, and as commercial products captivity narratives provided popular illustrations of individual captives seeking to regain their autonomy and reclaim their inalienable rights to seek satisfaction for themselves. Both directly and indirectly, captivity narratives of the early Republic exemplified the link between freedom and profit.

Entrepreneurial printers made use of the national ideology of liberty as a marketing scheme to facilitate the exchange between producers and consumers of print. Lured by marketing devices promoting individual representations of national beliefs, readers sought imaginative satisfaction through an engagement in shock dramas of captivity and liberty, while those involved in creating the texts sought commercial satisfaction in a system of production and profit. Still, this exchange was never equal. As demand outstripped supply, and as the literary marketplace rapidly expanded and extended, printers turned increasingly to fiction and fictive techniques in order to produce enough commodity to meet the needs of their market, and as print culture increasingly became commercially competitive, printers developed extravagant strategies of fictionalization for embellishing narratives of liberty with spectacle and sensation. Before the codes and conventions separating fiction and nonfiction were firmly established, before narrative texts were separated into the oppositional categories of literature and history, and before genres, styles, and structures were used to define how a text should be read, entrepreneurial printers believed that they were free to take liberty with the truth. During the volatile decades of the early Republic, printers claimed fiction as a means to facilitate their pursuit of happiness.

Notes

1. My discussion on liberty here and throughout is indebted to John Phillip Reid's *The Concept of Liberty in the Age of the American Revolution* (1998). In his recent study *Reading the Early Republic* (2004), Robert A. Ferguson provides a particularly insightful chapter on both the concept and rhetoric of liberty, "The Dialectic of Liberty." For further helpful discussions of liberty and early national political ideologies, see Appleby, Clark, Hatch, Kramnick, Looby, Rogers, and Wood.

2. While discussing semantic confusions concerning liberty, Ferguson notes that Samuel Johnson's range of meanings went from the antithesis of slavery to licentiousness (52–53). Ferguson concludes that part of the American confusion over the term resulted from "two main competing sources" of meaning—religion and law (52).

3. In discussing the tradition of liberty the colonists inherited, Wood states: "Liberty: Englishmen everywhere of every social rank and of every political persuasion could not celebrate it enough. Every cause, even repression itself, was wrapped in the language of English liberty. No people in the history of the world had ever made so much of it" (*Radicalism* 13). For a still insightful discussion of America's ideological origins, see Bailyn, particularly his final chapter, "The Contagion of Liberty."

4. Overstating liberty's popular appeal is impossible, despite its semantic confusions. For an informative discussion of liberty's popular iconography, see Silverman, particularly his discussion of liberty songs. On the subject of the Revolution in memory and commemoration, see Purcell.

5. There are a number of excellent discussions analyzing the historical developments of the period, particularly relating to the popularization of political ideologies and issues. In addition to the excellent work of Appleby, Bailyn, and Wood, see also Stanley Elkins and Eric McKittrick's *The Age of Federalism: The Early American Republic, 1788–1800* (1993), Edmund S. Morgan's *Inventing the People: The Rise of Popular Sovereignty in England and America* (1988), and Robert H. Wiebe's *The Opening of American Society* (1984). As overviews of social, cultural, and political developments during the early

Republic, both Richard D. Brown's *Modernization: The Transformation of American Life, 1600–1865* (1976) and James A. Henretta's *The Evolution of American Society, 1700–1815* (1973) remain helpful and informative. For works discussing developments in print culture, see Brown, Buell, Gilmore, and Zboray.

6. For an informative discussion of how a national and political declaration of independence was used to justify personal declarations of independence, see Imbarrato.

7. Still the best discussions of early national print culture and the development of the public sphere are Warner and Rice, both of whom extend the work of Habermas.

8. For a helpful discussion of early national attitudes toward republican discourse, see Howe, particularly his chapter "Language Contested." According to Howe, the period began with an "extraordinary trust" in the capacity of political language to be clear, exact, and permanent, but "within a decade that confidence began to wane" as political factions fought over language and meaning (91).

9. In examining the rhetoric of liberty, Reid notes that "slave was probably the most frequent word used by both American Whigs and their British supporters" (92). While historians and political scientists have remarked on the pervasive use of *slave* and *slavery* in public discourse during the Revolution and the decades that followed, literary scholars have not fully examined the equally pervasive use of the terms in print culture. With a few exceptions, which in certain cases might be problematical designations, the term *slave narrative* is most often applied to abolitionist texts of the 1830s and 1840s. Yet *slave* and *slavery* are oft-repeated words in captivity narratives, particularly in Barbary narratives and impressment narratives. For a highly informative discussion of slavery during the early Republic, see Winthrop Jordan's *White over Black: American Attitudes Towards the Negro, 1550–1812* (1968).

10. According to Hartman, the "battle over truth" dominates captivity narratives (26). Colley similarly declares that "captivity narratives were always disturbing texts at some level" because all captives were dragged across culturally, socially, and politically defining lines (16). Thus all captives somehow "were compelled by the nature of their predicament to re-examine—and often question for the first time—conventional wisdoms about nationality, race, religion, allegiance, appropriate modes of behavior, and location of power." Although not all texts depict confrontations between the alien and the familiar, captivity narratives inherently involve contrasts of empowerment and disempowerment.

11. Recent work in the captivity genre has been exceptionally useful and interesting. In addition to the texts mentioned, see also Christopher Castiglia's *Bound and Determined: Captivity, Culture-Crossing, and White Womanhood from Mary Rowlandson to Patty Hearst* (1996), Derounian-Stodola and Levernier's *The Indian Captivity Narrative, 1550–1900* (1993), Gary L. Ebersole's *Captured by Texts: Puritan to Postmodern Images of Indian Captivity* (1995), and June Namias's *White Captives: Gender and Ethnicity on the American Frontier* (1993). Two essays should also be noted for their cogent discussions of captivity texts: Armstrong and Tennenhouse's "The American Origins of the English Novel" (1992) and Tara Fitzpatrick's "The Figure of Captivity: The Cultural Work of the Puritan Captivity Narrative" (1991).

12. There are a number of relevant and interesting narratives whose length precluded their inclusion in *Liberty's Captives*. Two particularly interesting texts from the War of

1812 period are Charles Andrews's *The Prisoner's Memoir, or, Dartmoor Prison* (which recounts the infamous and quite sensational "massacre" that took place at Dartmoor Prison on April 6, 1815) and Benjamin Waterhouse's *A Journal of a Young Man of Massachusetts* (which also relates prisoner-of-war experiences at Dartmoor). Published about the same time are the two most popular and influential Barbary narratives: James Riley's *Loss of the Brig Commerce* (1816) and—describing the same wreck and Barbary captivity—Archibald Robbins's *Journal, Comprising an Account of the Loss of the Brig Commerce* (1817).

13. Still the best place to begin with Bakhtin is Emerson and Holquist's *The Dialogic Imagination* (1981), especially Bakhtin's "Discourse in the Novel." For valuable discussions of Bakhtin's theories, see David K. Danow's *The Thought of Mikhail Bakhtin* (1991), Michael Holquist's *Dialogism: Bakhtin and His World* (1990), and Morson and Emerson's *Mikhail Bakhtin* (1990).

14. Edward Said's discussion of orientalism offers a similar view concerning the importance of otherness in national mythmaking. In his seminal study *Orientalism* (1979), Said proposes that Orientalism was not merely a broad subject or geographical area but also a discourse used by Europeans to strengthen their cultural and political self-conceptions.

15. Both "zones of contact" and "cultural work" are borrowed from the invaluable work of Mary Pratt (*Imperialist Eyes: Travel Writing and Transculturation* [1992]) and Jane Tompkins (*Sensational Designs: The Cultural Work of American Fiction, 1790–1860* [1985]).

16. For elucidating discussions of early New England Puritan attitudes toward self-conception, see Bercovitch's *Origins* and *Jeremiad*.

17. For a discussion of the distinctions between divine and civil liberty, see Fliegelman's excellent *Prodigals and Pilgrims*, particularly his chapter "Filial Freedom and American Protestantism."

18. For an invaluable discussion of the connections between civil liberty and personal liberty, see Appleby's *Inheriting the Revolution*, particularly her introduction, "Responding to a Revolutionary Tradition," and "A New National Identity."

19. For an insightful discussion of "theistic liberalism," see Dworetz's *The Unvarnished Doctrine: Locke, Liberalism, and the American Revolution*. Dworetz argues that "Lockean individualism is actually derived from the theistic doctrine of individual responsibility" and that throughout the Revolutionary period "Christian liberty" stressed "the primacy of the individual" (176, 177).

20. For an insightful analysis of Adam Smith's *The Wealth of Nations*, see Fleischaker. I have used the 1981 Liberty Classics edition of Smith.

21. For the period's most popular self-righteous declarations of unrighteous actions, see Stephen Burroughs's *Memoirs*. In one of the more outrageous passages, Burroughs—in the voice of Lysander—argues that he is committing selfless acts of public good by counterfeiting. Interestingly, in the beginning Burroughs declares that as a republican he believes that happiness results from internal consciousness and not external conditions.

A Narrative

of the

Capture and Treatment of

John Dodge,

by the English at Detroit

The narrative of John Dodge (1779) is one of the earliest appearances of an American Revolutionary captivity narrative, and it is also an early example of a frontier narrative. A historical figure who lived in the Ohio Valley and Great Lakes region, Dodge traded among the various Native American tribes residing in the area. He is mentioned in Thomas Jefferson's *Notes on the State of Virginia* as a cataloger of aboriginal tribes. Despite this proximity to Native Americans, Dodge's captivity came not at the hands of "Indians" or "Savages," as he alternately refers to them throughout his narrative, but at the hands of the British. Demonstrating the profound influence of Enlightenment thinking, his narrative is vitally concerned with the property rights and political freedoms of those living in America, as well as with the license he and his fellow traders and merchants took in defying the power of the British, which he saw as arbitrary and corrupt.

Dodge spoke several of the Native American languages used by the tribes in the Great Lakes region, and he was clearly a sympathizer with the Continental Congress and the cause of American liberty. For these reasons he became the target of the British commandant of Fort Detroit, Henry Hamilton, and his henchman, prison warden Phillip De Jeane. Both are historical figures, and both were indeed high-ranking British officials at Detroit in the 1770s, when Dodge was taken prisoner. Dodge's narrative recounts and condemns not only his suffering while imprisoned but also the loss of his property, confiscated by the British on two separate occasions, ultimately causing him to lose several thousand pounds sterling.

Dodge's attitude toward Native Americans was remarkably ambivalent. He established a cordial working relationship with many tribes. In his narrative, he clearly vilifies the British rather than the Native Americans, who were manipulated by men like Hamilton and stirred up to violence, despite the fact that they

sometimes did not agree with the British orders. When ordered to slaughter a
group of settlers, including women and children, Dodge reveals that the Indians
refused: "To this cruel mandate even some of the Savages made an objection." Yet
throughout the narrative Dodge constantly refers to Native Americans as "Savages" and depicts them as childlike and impressionable. Although, contrary to
the conventions of most early captivity narratives, the Native Americans are not
presented as the primary aggressors, Dodge still describes them, ultimately, as
bloodthirsty and pagan.

The cause that Dodge champions by the end of the narrative is American
liberty. Upon returning to America after captivity on a prison ship in Canada,
Dodge met up with several key figures in the Revolution, including General
Washington, and by the end of the narrative, his rhetoric has changed from that
of a man who cares most about the recovery of his wealth and property to that
of a man who sounds a forceful cry for American independence. He closes his
narrative with the following words, stronger by far for the cause of the Revolution
than any he has written to this point:

> Had the love of my country no ways prompted me to act against the tyranny of
> Britain, I leave it to the world to judge, whether I have not a right to revolt from
> under the domination of such tyrants, and exert every faculty God has given me
> to seek satisfaction for the ill usage I received; that if I had ten thousand lives,
> and was sure to lose them all, I think, should I not attempt to gain satisfaction,
> I should deserve to be a slave the remainder of my life.

Dodge concludes his narrative with this endorsement of a selfless fight for freedom. Such an uncompromising call for liberty and political independence clearly
echoed the sentiments of many of his countrymen and helps to explain the popularity of this early American captivity narrative.

The narrative included here is the 1779 first edition, published by T. Bradford
in Philadelphia; where words were missing or unreadable in this version, the 1780
second edition, published by Russell in Salem, was consulted. These two editions
are understandably similar, with the second edition primarily boasting updated
grammatical changes and the inclusion of several engravings. The second edition
further contains a remarkable publisher's advertisement for the recently printed
captivity narrative of Ethan Allen, who, like Dodge, found himself a prisoner
of the British. Between 1779 and 1780 the Allen text was reprinted five times,
suggesting great popularity and a substantial readership for the time. The Dodge
narrative was also twice published in newspapers; the first ran in the *Continental
Journal* (December 30, 1779, and January 6 and 13, 1780), and the second ran
in the *Connecticut Gazette* (February 2, 9, and 16, 1780).

RJ

NARRATIVE

OF THE

CAPTURE and TREATMENT

OF

JOHN DODGE,

By the ENGLISH at DETROIT.

WRITTEN BY HIMSELF.

PHILADELPHIA,

P:n:ed by T. BRADFORD, at the COFFEE-HOUSE.

MDCCLXXIX.

Title page of *A Narrative of the Capture and Treatment of John Dodge* (1779 edition; the Library Company of Philadelphia)

NARRATIVE

Of his SUFFERINGS among the

BRITISH

AT DETROIT.

LETTER to CONGRESS.

Illustration from *An Entertaining Narrative of the Cruel and Barbarous Treatment and Extreme Sufferings of John Dodge*, "John Dodge" (1780 edition; courtesy of the American Antiquarian Society)

I some time since left the place of my nativity in Connecticut, and, in the year 1770, settled in Sandusky, an Indian village, about half way between Pittsburgh and Detroit, where I carried on a very beneficial trade with the natives, til the unhappy Dispute between Great-Britain and America reached those pathless wilds, and roused to war Savages no ways interested in it.[1]

In July, 1775, Captain James Woods called at my house in his way to the different Indian towns, where he was going to invite them, in the name of the Congress,[2] to a treaty to be held at Fort-Pitt the ensuing fall; I attended him to their villages, and the Savages promised him they would be there. Capt. Woods also invited me to go with the Indians to the treaty, as they were in want of an interpreter, which I readily agreed to.

Soon after the departure of Capt. Woods, the Commander of Fort Detroit sent for the Savages in and about Sandusky, and told them that he heard they were invited by the Americans to a treaty at Pittsburgh, which they told him was true; on which he delivered them a talk to the following purport: "That he was their father, and as such he would advise them as his own children; that the Colonists who were to meet them at Pittsburgh were a bad people, that by the indulgence of their Protector, they had grown a numerous and saucy people; that the great King[3] not thinking they would have the assurance to oppose his just laws, had kept but few troops in America for some years past; that those men being ignorant of their incapacity to go through with what they intend, propose to cut off the few regulars in this country, and then you indians, and have all America to themselves; and all they want is, under the shew of friendship, to get you into their hands as hostages, and there hold you, until your nations shall comply with their terms, which if they refuse, you will be all massacred. Therefore do not go by any means; but if you will join me, and keep them at bay a little while, the King, our father, will send large fleets and armies to our assistance, and we will soon subdue them, and have their plantations to ourselves."

This talk so dismayed the Indians, that they came to me and said they would not go to the treaty, at the same time telling me what the Governor of Detroit had said to them. On this Mr. James Heron and myself, having the cause of our country at heart,[4] affected that what the Governor had said was false, and told them that the Colonists would not hurt a hair on their heads, and if they would go to the treaty, that I, with Mr. Heron, would be security, and pledge our property, to the amount of 4000£.[5] for their safe return. This, with the arrival of Mr. Richard Butler with fresh invitations, induced some of them to go with me to the treaty.

In the fall I attended a number of them to the treaty, where we were politely received by the Commissioners sent by Congress. The council commenced; the

Indians, who are always fond of fishing in troubled water, offered their assistance, which was refused, with a request that they would remain in peace, and not take up the hatchet on either side. On the whole, these Indians were well pleased with the talk from the Congress, and promised to remain quiet.

The Commissioners thinking it proper, sent the continental belt and talk by some to the Chiefs to the Savages who resided about the lakes. These Chiefs being obliged to pass Sandusky in their rout, Mr. John Gibson, Agent for Indian affairs, requested us to accompany them, and furnish them with what they stood in need of; on which I took them home.

On my arrival at the village I found the Savages in confusion, and preparing for war, on which I called a Council and rehearsed the Continental talk, which, with a present of goods to the amount of twenty-five pounds, quieted them. This I informed Congress of, agreeable to their request, by express, and that the Governor of Detroit was still urging the Indians to war.

Soon after this, a party of Savages from the neighborhood of the lakes, came to my house on their way to the frontiers to strike a blow; I asked them the reason they took up the hatchet; they replied, that the Governor of Detroit had told them, that the Americans were going to murder them all and take their lands; but if they would join him, they would be able to drive them off, and that he would give them twenty dollars a scalp. On this I rehearsed the Continental talk, and making them a small present they returned home, believing as I had told them, that the Governor was a liar and meant to deceive them.

On this I thought proper to write the Governor of Detroit, what he was to expect should he continue to persuade the Indians to take up the hatchet. He was so enraged at the receipt of this letter, that he offered 100£. for my scalp or body; he sent out several parties to take me without effect, till having spread an evil report of me among the Indians, on the 15th of Jan. 1776, my house was surrounded by about 20 soldiers and savages, who broke into the house, made me a prisoner, and then marched me for Detroit.

It was about the dusk of the evening when, after a fatiguing march, I arrived at Detroit, and was carried before Henry Hamilton, late a captain in the 15th regt. but now Governor and Commandant of Detroit; he ordered me to close confinement, telling me to spend that night in making my peace with God, as it was the last night I should live; I was then hurried to a loathsome dungeon, ironed and thrown in with three criminals, being allowed neither bedding, straw, or fire, although it was in the depth of Winter, and so exceeding cold, that my toes were froze before morning.

About 10 o'clock the next morning, I was taken out and carried before the Governor, who produced a number of letters with my name signed to them, and asked me if they were my hand writing? to which I replied, they were not; he then said, it was a matter of indifference to him whether I owned it or not, as he understood that I had been carrying on a correspondence with Congress, taking the Savages to their treaties, and preventing their taking up the hatchet in favour of his majesty, to defend his crown and dignity; that I was a rebel and a traitor, and he would hang me. I asked him whether he intended to try me by the civil or military law, or give me any trial at all? to which he replied, that he was not obliged to give any damn'd rebel a trial unless he thought proper, that he would hang every one he caught, and that he would begin with me first. I told him if he took my life, to beware of the consequence, as he might depend on it that it would be looked into. What, says he, do you threaten me you damn'd rebel, I will soon alter your tone, here take the damn'd rebel to the dungeon again, and let him pray to God to have mercy on his soul, for I will soon fix his body between heaven and earth, and every scoundrel like him.

I was then re-delivered to the hands of Phillip De Jeane,[6] who acted in the capacity of judge, sheriff, and jailor, and carried back to my dungeon, where I was soon waited on by the missionary to read prayers with me; but it was so extremely cold, he could not stand it but a few minutes at a time. In conversation with him, I told him I thought it was very hard to lose my life without a trial, as I was innocent of the charge aledged against me; he said it was very true, but that the Governor had charged him not to give me the least hopes of life, as he would absolutely hang me.

I remained in this dismal situation three days, when De Jeane came and took out one of the criminals who was in the dungeon with me, and held a short conference with him, then came and told me, the governor had sent him to tell me to prepare for another world, as I had not long to live, and then withdrew. I enquired of the criminal, who was a Frenchman, what De Jeane wanted with him, but he would not tell me.

The evening following he told his brother in distress, that De Jeane had offered him 20£. to hang Mr. Dodge (meaning me) but that he had refused unless he had his liberty; De Jeane then said, that we should both be shot under the gallows.

Being at last drove almost to despair, I told De Jeane to inform the Governor I was readier to die at that time that I should ever be, and that I would much rather undergo his sentence, than be tortured in the dreadful manner I then was; he returned for answer, that I need not hurry them, but prepare myself, as I should not know my time till half an hour before I was turned off.

Thus did I languish on in my dungeon, without a friend being allowed to visit me, denied the necessaries of life, and must have perished with the cold, it being in the depth of Winter, had not my fellow prisoners spared me a blanket from their scanty stock. Thus denied the least comfort in life, together with the unjust and savage threatening I received every day, brought me so very low, that my inability to answer De Jeane's unreasonable questions, with which he daily tormented me respecting innocent men, obliged him to notice my situation, and no doubt thinking I should die in their hands, they thought proper to remove me to the barracks, and ordered a Doctor to attend me. The weather had been so extreem cold, and my legs had been bolted in such a manner, that they were so benumbed and the sinews contracted, that I had not the least use of them; and the severity of my usage had brought on a fever, which had nigh saved them any further troubel.

After I had lain some time ill, and my recovery was dispaired of, De Jeane called and told me that the Governor had altered his mind with respect to executing me, and bid me be of good cheer, as he believed the Governor would give me my liberty when I got better; I replied, that it was a matter of indifference to me whether he gave me my liberty or not, as I had much rather die than remain at their mercy; on which, he said, "You may die and be damn'd," and bounced out of the room.

When I had so far recovered as to be able to sit up in my bed, my nurse being afraid I should inform her husband of her tricks in his absence, told the Governor that I was going to make my escape with a party of soldiers, that I was well and could walk as well as she could; tho' at the time my legs were still so cramped and benumbed with the irons and cold, that had kingdoms been at stake, I could not walk.

On this information, De Jeane came and told me to get up and walk to the dungeon, from whence I came; I told him I was unable, "Crawl then, you damn'd rebel, or I will make you"; I told him he might do as he pleased, but I could not stand, much more walk; on this he called a party of soldiers, who tossed me into a cart and carried me to the Dungeon: here, by the persuasion of the Doctor, who was very kind and attentive, I was allowed a bed and not ironed. By his care and the weather growing milder, I got rid of my fever and began to walk about my dungeon, which was only eight feet square; but even this was a pleasure too great for me to enjoy long, for in a few days I was put into irons. The weather now growing warm and the place offensive, from the filth of the poor fellows I had left there, and who were afterwards executed, I relapsed. By persuasion of the Doctor, who told them unless I had air I should die, a hole, about seven inches square, was cut to let in some air.

I remained ill till June, altho' the Doctor had done all that lay in his power; he then let the Governor know, that it was impossible for me to recover unless I was removed from the dungeon, on which he sent De Jeane to inform me, if I would give security for my good behavior, that he would let me out of prison. Being, by my usage and fever, reduced to a state of despondence, I told him that it was a matter of indifference what he did with me, and that his absence was better than his company: he then published it abroad, and several gentlemen voluntarily entered into 2000£. security for me, and I once more was allowed to breath the fresh air, after six months confinement in a loathsome dungeon, except eight or nine weeks that I lay sick at the barracks.

On my going abroad, I learned that all the property I left in the woods, to the amount of 15 or 1600£. was taken in the King's name, and divided among the Indians. As I had but little to attend to but the recovery of my health, I mended apace. As soon as I could walk abroad, Gov. Hamilton sent for me and said, he was sorry for my misfortunes, and hoped I would think as little as possible of them; that as I was in a low state, he thought I had best not think of business, or think of what I had left, as he would lend me a hand to recover my losses. This smooth discourse gave me but little satisfaction for the ill usage I had received at his hands; however, I was determined to rest as easy I could, till I had an opportunity of obtaining redress.

As soon as I found myself so far recovered as to be able to do business, which was in September, I applied to the Governor to go down the country, but he put me off with fine words, a permission to do business there, and a promise of his assistance. I now settled my accounts with the persons with whom I was connected in trade, and found myself 700£. in debt. My credit being pretty good, I set up a retail store, and as many of the inhabitants pitied my case, they all seemed willing to spend their money with me. My being master of the different Indian languages, about Detroit was also of service to me, so that in a short time I paid off all my debts, and began to add to my stock.

In the spring of 1777, I heard there was like to be a good trade at Machili-makanac,[7] on which I applied to the Governor, and, with a great deal of trouble, got a pass, went, and met with good trade. On my return Gov. Hamilton, by several low arts, attempted to *pick* my cargo, which as it would spoil the sale of the remainder, I could not allow. As he had no pretence for taking them from me by force, it once more provoked him to wrath against me; he greatly retarded my sales by denying me a permit to draw my powder out of the magazine; also ordered myself and two servants to be ready at a moment's warning to march under Capt. Le Mote on a scouting party with Savages: I told him it was against my inclination to take up arms against my own flesh and blood, and much more so to go with Savages to butcher and scalp defenceless women and children, that were not interested in the present dispute: He said it was not any of my business whether they were interested in the dispute or not; and added if you are not ready when called for, I will fix you. Lucky for me he was soon after called down the country, and succeeded by Capt. Mountpresent as Commander, who ordered Le Mote to strike my name out of his books; but my servants with their pay, I lost entirely.

The party of Savages under Le Mote went out with orders not to spare man, woman, or child. To this cruel mandate even some of the Savages made an objection, respecting the butchering of women and children, but they were told the children would make soldiers, and the women would keep up the stock.— Those sons of Britain offered no reward for Prisoners, but they gave the Indians twenty dollars a scalp, by which means they induced the Savages to make the poor inhabitants, who they had torn from their peaceable homes, carry their baggage till within a short distance of the fort, where, in cold blood, they murdered them, and delivered their green scalps in a few hours after to those British barbarians, who, on the first yell of the Savages, flew to meet and hug them to their breasts reeking with the blood of innocence, and shewed them every mark of joy and approbation, by firing of cannon, &c.

One of these parties returning with a number of women and children's scalps, and three prisoners, they were met by the Commander of the fort, and after the usual demonstrations of joy, delivered their scalps, for which they were paid; the Indians then made the Commandant a present of two of the prisoners, reserving the third as a sacrifice to the manes of one of them that had fell in the expedition. Being shocked at the idea of one of my fellow creatures being tortured and burnt alive by those inhuman Savages, I sought out the Indian who had lost his relative, and to whom, according to the Indian custom, this unhappy man belonged; I found him, took him home with me, and by the assistance of some of my friends, and twenty-five pounds worth of goods, I persuaded the inhuman wretch to sell his life to me. As the rest of the gang had taken the prisoner about two leagues distance, and were making merry over him, we were obliged to lay a scheme to deliver him from their hands, which we did in the following manner,—It being midnight and very dark, the Indian, myself, and two servants, crossed the river in a batteaux to where they were carousing around this unhappy victim. The Indian then went to his companion, and under pretence of taking the prisoner out to answer a call of nature, he delivered him to me who lay at some distance, and I carried him to the batteaux. As soon as he found himself in the hands of his deliverer, his transport was too great for his tender frame; three different times he sunk lifeless in my arms, and as often, by the help of water, the only remedy at hand, I prevented his going to the land of spirits in a transport of joy. None but those who have experienced it, can have an idea of the thoughts that must have agitated the breast of a man, who but a few minutes before saw himself surrounded by Savages, whose dismal yell, and frightful figures, heightened by the glare of a large fire in a dismal wood, which must have harrowed up the soul of an uninterested bystander, much more one who knew that very fire was prepared for his execution, and that every moment the executioner was expected to arrive.—The executioner arrives; he advances towards him; he loosens this unhappy victim from the tree to which he was bound, no doubt, as this young man imagined, to be led to the stake; but as it were in an instant, he finds himself in the hands of his deliverer and fellow-countryman. This, as I said before, was too much for him to bear; however I got his almost lifeless corpse to my house, where I kept him hid. The Indian, according to our agreement, in an hour or two after I was gone, returned seemingly much fatigued, and told his fellow Savages, who were impatiently waiting to begin their brutal sacrifice, that the prisoner had escaped, and that he had in vain pursued him.

Some time after this I found an opportunity, and made an agreement with the Captain of a vessel going to Michilimakanac, to take my unhappy inmate with him, but one of my servants being tempted, by a large reward that was offered for retaking the above prisoner, informed De Jeane that he was hid in my house, on which my habitation was soon surrounded by a party of soldiers under the command of said De Jeane, and myself, the young man and four servants were made prisoners, and having demanded my keys, which I delivered, we were hurried to goal and confined in different rooms. Here this unhappy young fellow, in high expectations of seeing his friends, was once more plunged into the horrors of imprisonment.

I was sent for and carried before the Commandant, where, on being examined who was the person in my house, I frankly told him it was a young man whom I had bought of the Indians when they were going to burn him, and that I meant to send him to Canada to be out of the way of the Savages, but De Jeane, like other men of bad principles, thinking no man could do a good action without sinister views, said that he believed I had purchased him to serve my own ends, and that he would find them out, which the Commandant ordered him to do as soon as possible, and I was ordered to prison.

De Jeane then took my servant, who was his informant, ironed him, put him in the dungeon, and, after keeping him three days on bread and water, the lad almost frightened out of his senses, sent for De Jeane, and told him that the day before I was taken up I had wrote several letters, and, on his bringing a candle to seal them, that I said, if he told any one that I was writing to Pitsburg, that I would blow his brains out. This suiting De Jeane's purpose, he made the lad swear to it, and then set him, with the rest of my servants, at liberty.

I was now once more called before the Commandant, who told me he understood I was going to send an express to his Majesty's enemies, in consequence of which he had taken an inventory of my effects, and meant to send me to Canada. I told him he was certainly misinformed, he then taxed me with what De Jeane had forced from my servant; asked me where I was writing the day before I was taken. I told him to my correspondents in Montreal; and luckily for me a neighbour of mine, having been at my house, was produced, who declared the truth of what I said, and that, I being hurried, had given him the letters to carry on board the vessel: This, with some other false accusations, being cleared up, I was once more released on giving fresh security.

Though myself and servants were, for want of a pretence for detaining us, set

at liberty, it was not so with the unfortunate young man whom I had purchased
from the Indian; he still remained in prison, daily tormented with the threats
of De Jeane, that he would deliver him to the Indians, which so preyed on his
spirits, that in a short time it threw him into a fever. I then applied to Captain
Montpresent, the Commandant, who gave me permission, and I removed him
to sick Quarters, where I hired Jacob Pue, of Virginia, his fellow prisoner, to
attend to him: I also, when leisure would permit, attended him myself; but De
Jeane, who still haunted him, had so great an effect on him, that one day when
I visited him, he called me to his bed side and said to me, that De Jeane had
just left him, that he told him to make haste and get well, as the Indians were
waiting for him.—Pray Sir, (said the young man to De Jeane) for God's sake try
to keep me from the Indians, for if they get me they will burn me. Keep you
from them, said De Jeane, you damn'd Rebel you deserve to be burned, and all
your damned countrymen with you, so you need not think Dodge can save you;
General Hamilton is now come up, and he will fix you all. I tried to comfort him,
and told him to be of good courage;—Oh! replied he, I am almost distracted with
the idea of being burnt by the Savages; I had much rather die where I am, than
be delivered into the hands of those horrid wretches, from whom I so lately, by
your hands, escaped, the recollection of which, makes me shudder with horror.
He could say no more; he sank under it, and in a few hours after, death, more
kind than his cruel tormentors, released him from his troubles. I paid the last
tribute to this my unhappy countryman, and had his corpse decently interred,
attended by the Missionary and most of the principal Merchants of the town.

As Hamilton was arrived, I had every thing to expect that his malice could
invent, more especially as De Jeane, to whom his ear was always open, had told
him (as I was informed) all and more than what had happened during his absence. About a month after the death of the unhappy young man above related,
I had occasion for some of my powder out of the Magazine; I wrote an order
to the conductor, according to custom, and waited on the Governor to have it
signed; on presenting it to him, he looked at it, and then looking at me with a
sarcastic smile, said, It is powder you want, you damn'd rascal, is it? at the same
time tearing my order and throwing it in my face; you have behaved yourself
very well, have you not? after my granting you your life, you would not go with
Le Mote, would you not? says he, and starting up in a great passion, as though
he would strike me, put himself between me and the door. What, says he, you
have a damn'd deal of influence with the Indians; you can purchase prisoners
without my approbation, can you? you damned rascal. Sir, says I, I am no rascal;
not a word out of your mouth, says Hamilton, go about your business and take
care of me or I will fix you: I replied, it had always been my study to take care of
him; not a word, says he, go about your business, and bless your stars I was not
here instead of Captain Montpresent, for I would have fixed you, you damned

scoundrel. Here I took my leave, went home, and determined to think as little of Mr. Hamilton and his usage as possible, till I had an opportunity for getting redress.

Notwithstanding the hatred of Hamilton and De Jeane, I spent the forepart of the Winter very happily, till the 25th of January, 1778, when several of the Merchants of the town, got permission to go to Sandusky to trade, and as they proposed encamping about two leagues from the town, myself and several others, in a friendly manner, proposed and did accompany them in our sleighs to their first stage; but on our return, I being a head, was challenged by De Jeane, at the head of thirty or forty soldiers, by asking who came there? to which I replied, John Dodge; he then ordered the soldiers to seize me and the two Gentlemen in the sleigh with me, and forced us to return to the encampment we had just left, where he seized the whole of the Gentlemen, who were going, by permission, to Sandusky, with their goods, sleighs, &c. and carried the whole of us, the next morning, back to the Fort, and charged us with sending out goods to supply (as he politely termed it) the Rebels.

After being detained three days in prison, I was taken to De Jeane's house, to see my papers, books, desks, &c. examined. They broke open my desk, pretending to have lost the key. On searching, they could not find any thing worth their notice, or what they expected to find. De Jeane then gave me my keys, and told me to send for my desk and take care of myself, as he would watch me; I told him, as he had taken it from my house and broke it, he should mend it and send it home, before I would receive it: Stop a little, said he, I will speak to the Governor, and fix you yet if I can; he then gave me into the care of the guard, and ordered me to goal. About the fifth day after this, not hearing any thing from him, I sent for my violin, and was diverting myself, when Governor Hamilton passed by, and enquired who was playing on the violin, to which the Corporal of the guard answered, it was me. The next day, De Jeane waited on me with a Blacksmith, who soon clapped on a pair of hand-bolts; and now, says De Jeane, I have fixed you, you may play the violin till you are tired; I asked him what I had done to be treated thus; for that you must apply to the Governor, replied he, for it is his pleasure that you are so: He then threatened to put on leg-bolts; on which I told him, I did not value his irons, but if he kept me prisoner, I should look to him for my property, (about 3000£.) Yes, says he, we will fix you and your property too, and then left me. About six days after, I was taken to my own house, where two English and two Frenchmen, by order of the Governor, took an inventory of my goods, and soon after sold the whole at vendue, for about 1900£. New-York currency.[8] Thus being a second time robbed of my property, I lay a prisoner as contented as possible, without any thing material happening, until the first of May.

On the first of May, 1778, I was put on board a vessel to go down to Quebec, and by some of my friends furnished with provision and necessaries for the voyage; but of these I was robbed by De Jeane, and had it not been for some Gentlemen, passengers in the same vessel, I must have suffered with hunger. On the first of June I arrived at Quebec, where I was conducted to Mr. Printices, the Provost Marshal: Ha, ha, says he, Mr. Dodge, Are you here? I have often been told you were a damn'd rascal, doing all you could against government; it is a pity Gov. Hamilton did not hang you when he was about it, as he would have saved government a great deal of trouble. From hence I was conducted on board the prison ship, *Meriah* with a number of farmers, taken off their plantations by the Savages.

Two days after I was put on board the prison ship, we were visited by Mr. Murray, Commissary of Prisoners, to whom I gave an account of my capture and ill usage; he told me, he would speak to the General, and give me an answer. Two days after, he again came on board, and told me, as it was very difficult times, I could not have a hearing at present; I told him I wanted nothing but what the English constitution allowed, and if I could not get that in Quebec, I would apply to England; to which he replied, I had better be easy, for if I did not, he would put me in irons again.

I remained on board the prison ship till the beginning of August, when Mr. Murray came on board, and informed me that I was not to go with the prisoners; but if I would give my parole, I should be allowed the liberty of Quebec. I asked him the occasion I could not be sent with the other prisoners; he replied, it was the Governor's orders: I asked him if I was to be allowed any support; he said, not any. I told him it was very hard to be dragged from my house, robbed of my property, deprived of my liberty, sent 1200 miles in irons, and still be held a prisoner in the town of Quebec, without any allowance for support: All my applications were in vain, I was set on shore under parole the fourth of August, and the ship sailed with the other prisoners soon after.

The cause of my detention, as I was afterwards told by Mr. Murray, was, that Governor Hamilton, of Detroit, had wrote the General not to send me round with the other prisoners; for if I got into the United States, he knew I would come immediately upon him, and as I knew the country, was well acquainted with the languages of the different Indians about the lakes, and had great influence among them, should be the means of their losing the fort, which would be much against the crown.

On my enlargement, I soon got acquainted with a number of gentlemen, who were friends of the United States, and the cause in which they were engaged. Some days after, going on shore, I fell in company with a Mr. Jones, who happened at that time to be reading a letter sent by General Montgomery, while he lay before Quebec, to Gov. Carlton, and on concluding it, said he hoped General Montgomery was in hell, and that all the rebels would soon be with him; to this

I made a reply, words ensued, and then blows; he drew on me, but I parried his thrust with my cane, so that I only got a small wound in my knee: He then made a complaint, and I was sent for by the General, who threatened to put me in confinement if I did not find security; this I soon found, and bonds were given for me for two months; at the end of which, as they neglected renewing them, and left me without parole or security, I hired an Indian guide, and on the ninth of October, quitted Quebec. After a fatiguing march through the woods, on the 20th of November, I arrived at Boston, where I was kindly received, and politely treated by General Gates, who supplied my wants and forwarded me to his Excellency General Washington; I waited on him, was politely received, and sent on to Congress, having some matters relating to Canada worthy of their hearing.

Had the love of my country no ways prompted me to act against the tyranny of Britain, I leave it to the world to judge, whether I have not a right to revolt from under the domination of such tyrants, and exert every faculty God has given me to seek satisfaction for the ill usage I received; that if I had ten thousand lives, and was sure to lose them all, I think, should I not attempt to gain satisfaction, I should deserve to be a slave the remainder of my life.

Finis.

Notes

1. Dodge is making reference to the American Revolution and the numerous Native American tribes in the Ohio Valley region.

2. The Continental Congress.

3. King George III of England.

4. The cause to which Dodge refers is the independence of the American colonies from Great Britain.

5. The references in the narrative to currency all represent the unit pounds, but the pound in the American colonies was not the same as the English pound.

6. Phillip De Jeane was the jailor at Fort Detroit.

7. Michilimackinac was a former French fur-trading post in northern Michigan eventually occupied by the British.

8. In the colonies, the value of the pound fluctuated significantly from state to state.

A Surprising Account,

of the

Captivity and Escape of

Philip M'Donald,

and

Alexander M'Leod,

of Virginia, from the

Chickkemogga Indians

Two years after John Filson's Daniel Boone narrative (1784) was published, thrilling readers with exploits of the daring backwoodsman and descriptions of the new country westward, another tale of adventure was issued to a public hungry for such fare. Its full title is *A Surprising Account, of the Captivity and Escape of Philip M'Donald, and Alexander M'Leod, of Virginia. From the Chickkemogga Indians and Their Great Discoveries in the Western World.* The 1786 edition reproduced here was first printed by Anthony Haswell and David Russell in Bennington, Vermont. The popularity of the text is evident from the numerous editions that appeared; five others were published in the next eleven years, all in New England, by Alden Spooner in Windsor, Vermont; Roger Storrs in Pittfield, Massachusetts; Henry Blake in Keene, New Hampshire; Nathaniel Coverly and Son in Haverhill, New Hampshire; and Josiah Fay in Rutland, Vermont. All five publishers reprinted M'Donald and M'Leod's narrative between 1786 and 1797, in chronological order. Something from the story appealed to early American readers, especially those in the Northeast. Two modern-day editions have also been published. Ye Galleon Press of Fairfield, Washington, produced a limited run of the Haswell and Russell edition in 1973; additionally, the Garland Library of Narratives of North American Indian Captivities reprinted the Haswell and Russell as well as the Blake text in 1978.

M'Donald and M'Leod present a fantastic tale to the reader. Beginning as a familiar captivity narrative, the protagonists are captured by the "Chickkemogga" Indians and describe a horrid scene of torture and death, including an inventive and gruesome method of scalping, for which they too are destined. However, the two enact a brave escape, and henceforth the narrative depicts a journey westward into a fabulous world. They enter an Edenic country where fruit that tastes like bread grows in abundance and "a variety of animals passed us, seemingly inoffensive, within a few rods of us and would stop and graise near us." A wide river prevents them from traveling any further, but the voyagers find a canoe, which they paddle for fifteen days before reaching an immense island in the middle of the continent. There, they discover a race of giants, who curiously speak Hebrew, and their story becomes an ethnological report until their speedy and convenient return to the new American nation.

Contemporary readers will surely be entertained by M'Donald and M'Leod's journey. The text itself is highly readable, although it includes several period spellings and references. One "Dr. Stiles of New-Haven College" is an example. This would be Ezra Stiles, then president of Yale, whose research interests included both Hebrew and the ten lost tribes of Israel. As well, Dr. Stiles encouraged the study of natural science and history and was a close friend and correspondent of Benjamin Franklin, whose famous letter to Stiles has been widely anthologized. Missing punctuation and wording was corroborated with the Coverly edition, which differs slightly from the Haswell and Russell.

A Surprising Account would have fulfilled several psychological needs and desires of its early American readership. The island-dwelling giants answered with their size the charge of American "degeneracy" leveled by Europeans. Like the "ancient fortifications, and the jaw-teeth, thigh bones, &c." of the narrative's introductory comments, the antiquity and gentleness of the sun-worshipping culture discovered by the two protagonists assuages American concerns of heritage while reinforcing the importance of nature. Their society is peacefully utopian—no war, murder, or infidelity—and the residents are shocked at tales of Christian wars. Temperance and vegetarianism are also high virtues; it is explained that "people are strangers to the use of flesh, and all kinds of spirituous liquors." Readers of eighteenth-century America must have been enthralled by the promise of the West as well as the promise of their own new nation. Not only does the Hebrew spoken by the giants authenticate an American antiquity, it also proves the presence of the divine at the heart of the American experiment. Out of the familiar theme of captivity, M'Donald and M'Leod fashion an adventure narrative that points toward the possibilities of the expanding country.

Marketing was definitely a consideration in the construction of *A Surprising Account*. Readers would have recognized the inclusion of the "Chickkemogga" Indians in the title as an immediate and hostile enemy of the young nation. Also, the few but significant changes made in the text over time would reflect an attempt to further vilify Native Americans. The giants are described in later editions as "Patagonians" whose "aspect [is] open, and free from that savage fierceness so conspicuous of American Indians." Further, this report from the frontier would have supported the enduring myth that lost Israelites were located in the New World, as evidenced by the Hebrew-speaking residents. Finally, the fantastic nature of the material must have titillated audiences—tame woodland creatures, trees ever in bloom, hairy giants, and gigantic rivers. The American myth of potential was never so hyperbolically expressed in such a short narrative.

DB

It has been a matter of observation, that whatever is out of the commen line of human occurrences, though credibly attested to, it is generally passed over very slightly, and treated as empty chimeras by a respectable part of mankind.

The accounts received from the Ohio, of the discovery of ancient fortifications, and the jaw-teeth, thigh bones, &c. of certain animals, though recorded by a Parsons,[1] v. Sullivan, and other esteemed personages, and some of these curiosities deposited in the custody of Dr. Stiles of New-Haven college, yet the truth of the matter is doubted by many, and the veracity of the writers called in question. Probably the truth of this little narrative may be doubted, but as the narrators are well known by many, and the reality of their sufferings evident from the marks on their mutilated bodies, they doubt not that the account of their extraordinary discoveries will be highly pleasing to the public in general, and pay the expense of printing, &c.

It was early in the month of May in the year 1779, that the narrators, Philip M'Donald, of Edinburgh, lately resident in Virginia, and Alexander M'Leod, of Scotch descent, born in Williamsburg, Virginia, and educated as well as that part of the continent could afford; left the place of their residence to join the American army, as volunteers, against the indians. Our offer was graciously accepted, and we soon had an opportunity, not only to shew our courage in combating those brutal enemies, the indians, but, almost fatally, to be made acquainted with their most horrid cruelty. We were detached with a small party, to make discoveries, and re-connoitre the situation of a number of indians supposed to be in the vicinity; after a tedious scout of three or four days, we were almost worn out with fatigue, and being destitute of necessaries, we determined to return to the main body, but were soon convinced of the impracticabilty of our scheme. It was just about eight o'clock in the evening of the 17th of June, when, not being apprehensive of danger, we were sat down to supper on a quarter of a buck, which one of our company had killed about two hours before; our arms and

A

Surprising Account,

OF THE

Captivity and Escape

OF

Philip M'Donald,

AND

Alexander M'Leod,

OF VIRGINIA.

FROM THE

Chickkemogga Indians,

AND OF THEIR

Great Discoveries

IN THE

Western World.

From June 1779, to January 1786, when
they returned in health to their Friends,

After an Absence of six Years and a half.

WRITTEN by THEMSELVES.

THE SECOND EDITION.

Printed in BENNINGTON : In the Year
M DCC, LXXXVI.
By HASWELL & RUSSELL.

Title page of *A Surprising Account of the Captivity and
Escape of Philip M'Donald and Alexander M'Leod* (1786 edition;
Rare Books Division, the New York Public Library, Astor,
Lenox and Tilden Foundations)

ammunition were about thirty rods distant; our little company as happy in their repast as good food and keen appetites could make them; and the fear of an enemy entirely banished from our minds, when we were fired on by a party of about twenty indians of the Chickkemogga nation,[2] and four out of ten, of which number our company combined were killed instantly, and two others so badly wounded as to be unable to move. It may easily be conceived how astonished we were at this salute, but no time for consideration was given, for the savages, rising from their ambush, had nearly surrounded us, at the distance of about thirty rods. An opening towards the place where our arms were deposited, was left which we eagerly took the advantage of, and got safe to the spot: By this time we were totally surrounded, but determining to sell our lives as dear as we could, we discharged all our pieces at the enemy. The surviving indians, now rushed on and disarmed us in a moment, and from their behaviour we had every reason to expect a horrid and immediate death, but Providence had otherwise decreed.

The dead indians, nearly double our number, were no sooner buried, than the state of the surviving part of our little company was examined, and from the looks and gestures of the indians, we could easily perceive a massacre was intended, and one of their party, who could speak English, insultingly asked us if we would not have a little more roast meat, & which of us would choose to be roasted. As we well knew that no humiliation would move them to pity, we offered them every insult in our power, to induce them to dispatch us instantly, but all in vain; their horrid thirst for cruelty and torture, was not to be so easily disappointed.

A great fire was now made, and the two unfortunate creatures, who, as before related, were badly wounded, named Thomas Hudslip, and William Gradnew, of Pennsylvania, were stript naked, and bound fast to the tops of two saplings, previously cleared of limbs and bark for the horrid business. There saplings were just strong enough to keep the enfeebled bodies of the unfortunate sufferers in an erect position. Another sapling, rather larger was now pruned of the limbs and bent down so as to reach the heads of the victims, by the weight of two indians, who, having with their knives cut round the skin of each of the victim's heads, from the forehead to the back of the neck, and skinned it a little way, fastened their hair to the tree, and jumping from the tree it tore the whole scalp off in an instant. They then threw hot coals and embers on their heads, after this they pierced their bodies all over, and stuck them full of pitch pine splinters, dipt in turpentine, even in their very eyes some of these instruments of torture were placed, and set on fire. The poor unfortunate creatures, under these dreadful tortures, were suffered to remain about half an hour, when the split pieces of pitch pine before mentioned being wholly consumed, or extinguished by their blood, the infernal savages brought fire and placed under their feet, burning them by degrees till their entrails dropped into the fire, the fire was then renewed, about them and the whole carcases consumed to ashes.

After this most horrid and unnatural tragedy, we were carried on for six days through the woods into the Ohio country, without making any stop, here our other two companions, were unable to proceed any farther, by reason of their wounds, they were therefore massacred in a manner equally cruel as the others, being roasted to death by such slow degrees, as to be nearly twenty four hours in the extremity of torture.

After six days further very severe travel, we arrived at a large indian town. Here we were met by a great number of indians, men, women and children, who were no sooner acquainted with the loss they had sustained by our means, than they determined on putting us to the torture for revenge: We were both accordingly stripped, and whipped by every indian present, till at length we fainted with anguish and loss of blood. After remaining some time in this distrest situation, we were removed into a wigwam, under a strong guard of indians, to be kept a few days till the arrival of another party expected from the westward, who were going to war against the Americans, when we were to be sacrificed. But this horrid scene we providentially escaped in the following remarkable manner.

The sixth night after our dreadful punishment, we awoke, and perceiving that four out of six of our guard were asleep, and the others in a defenceless posture, as our soreness made them think we could do them no harm: being both unbound, and two or three tomahawks lying within our reach, we determined to make an attempt to escape, we communicated our intention by signs to each other, and seizing the tomahawks sunk them in an instant in the heads of the waking indians. We killed the others likewise without any noise, and snatching up our own knapsacks and clothes that lay in one corner of the wigwam, and taking each of us a knife, tomahawk and musket, we issued forth and traveling all night, reached the top of a high mountain; here we tarried near a week, feeding on roots, &c. till our wounds began to heal, and then pursued our rout along the mountain, fearing to descend into the vallies, least we should fall into the hands of the inhuman savages, which we dreaded worse than death itself. It was now, according to our calculation, about the middle of August, and we had travelled near twelve days, improving every hour we could in a due west direction. We were arrived at a part of the country beautiful to view, the air was serene, the trees at so great a distance as almost to bear the appearance of a cleared up country, for a considerable distance round, and a variety of animals passed us, seemingly inoffensive, within a few rods of us and would stop and graise near us. Our surprise at these matters was very great: It was sometime since we had tasted flesh, and appetite prompted us to desire it; we had gathered a variety of fruits that answered very well for bread, but we felt a reluctance at the thoughts of destroying creatures feeding peaceably around us. We had ranged about for some time in search of a spring, when we at last came to one, on the side of a hill, that laid open to the sun. We dipped up a cupfull and tasted it, when we were surprised to find it salter than brine, and observing the channel in which it flowed, we perceived the margin was covered with a thin crust of pure white salt, of which we scraped up a considerable quantity, returning grateful thanks to providence for so great a favour.

We now determined to make use of our newly acquired treasure, to prepare a little food for prosecuting our journey westward, as we were not yet freed from our fear of the indians. With this view we shot one of the peaceful tenants of the wood, whose body was about the size of a sheep, and most delicious food. We corned our meat, and should have stayed in this beautiful place a long time, but our fear of the Indians prevented. We found in this pleasant retreat trees that bore a sort of fruit that tasted sweet and much like a good pear, when first gathered but after being dried a few days, tasted like new bread.

We began to gather and prepare our bread, and in about four days set forward again with all the expedition we could, being still haunted with the dread of the savages. We traveled at a great rate, for a long time finding such a plenty of delicious wild fruits, that we scarcely ever eat more than one meal a day of our preserved food.

We reckoned now that it must be about the latter part of September, and as we had traveled at a great rate, we thought ourselves out of the reach of the hostile indians, and thinking so beautiful a country must be designed for the sustenence of some favored beings, we determined to descend into the vallies, and make what discoveries we could.

We had passed several small rivers on logs, and trunks of trees, &c. which we found blown down and lying near their banks, but after travelling in the low lands about three weeks longer, in our old due west course, we arrived at the bank of a large river or sea. We thought now that all our journeying westward, was at an end, however after travelling along the bank of the river a few days we discovered a large canoe with paddles in it; this circumstance made us fear we were near some nation of indians, and as we were afraid of falling into the hands of savages, we determined, to embark, although the wind blew high from the east, and accordingly jumping into the canoe, we soon rigged up a sort of a mast, and committed ourselves to the mercy of the winds and waves.

We had when we went on board, about ten days provision, which we determined to husband to the best advantage as we were uncertain what provision we should find on the western shore.

It was about the middle of the afternoon when we embarked, and as we sailed at a great rate we were soon out of sight of land, however as the wind seemed rather to fall than rise, and the weather was clear, we apprehended no danger, but put on before the wind in cheerful expectation of reaching the western shore next morning. But alas! how uncertain are all human prospects; about midnight, we were hurried away by a swift south-west current, at an inconceivable swift rate, without any prospect of release from it, and without any appearance of a western shore.

After being carried at a surprizing rate for fifteen days, towards evening we perceived the current gradually changed its course, and set towards the shore, and that its force abated considerably. Our provisions were now exhausted to the last morsel, but we had some hopes of relief, as we had worked our boat into the eddy, and were got into a creek, with a pleasant shore on each side, on which to our inexpressible joy we soon effected a landing, and feasted on the spontaneous luxuries of nature, with which the shore abounded.

Here we must mention with admiration, the surprizing beneficence of Deity, in replenishing the earth with every necessary and even luxurious growth of nature, for the sustenance of his dependent creatures. Here we found a fine well watered country, beautiful to behold, the trees were exceeding high and large, at a great distance from each other, and so little underbrush that a man may easily have cleared an acre in two days. The wild fruits were excellent, and the spontaneous growths of the earth were beyond all description luxuriant. We had not travelled far in the level country, before we reached a large plain kind of track, free from every sort of vegitation, and resembling a road in America: on seeing this, we concluded we must be near some sort of inhabitants, but as we were uncertain of what sort they may be it made us tremble with apprehension. We lifted up our hearts and voices to heaven for protection, and relying on the mercyful care of providence determined to prosecute our journey along the beaten path untill we arrived at some place of dwelling for human beings; we had not been long traveling, in the road before mentioned, when we distinctly heard a human voice at a small distance from us, and by the sound, we were led to conclude, the speaker was not of the indian tribes with whom we had been acquainted. We stopped for some time, irresolute and undetermined whether to proceed or to retire; when a tremendous voice assailed our ears, and suddenly a monstrous creature in human shape, but nearly twelve feet in height, jumped from a rock into the road, and taking us both up, almost dead with fear, into his hand, exclaimed, in the Hebrew language, what creatures can these be!

We were now partly recovered from our fright, and seeing no appearance of malignity in the aspect of our possessor, we carefully turned ourselves round & took hold of the long shaggy hair of his outside garment to keep us from falling, and then ventured to address him in the language of his exclamation, and beg him not to kill us. He was pleased beyond measure to hear us speak, and told us to apprehend no danger from him, for he belonged to a race of beings that never intentionally did harm to any creature.

We were greatly relieved from our fears by this declaration, and after about an hour's travel, upon rising a high hill we discovered a large regular built city before us, in appearance, but when we came to it our astonishment was greatly encreased. The houses were exceedingly beautiful and lofty though consisting of but two stories, and the people appeared exceedingly loving and tractable.

It was only a little village as they informed us, about ten English miles in length, and the same in breadth, and contained about five hundred families.

Mr. M'Donnald having been educated at the University of Edinburgh, could understand their language perfectly well, and communicated to them the history of Europe, at which they were much surprised. In return they informed us, that they had ancient records which we might see, if we pleased.

In examining the records, we discovered that they were originally from Asia, and most probably seperated from that continent soon after the flood. They have a tradition among them that a long time ago, their progenitors were miraculously, planted by the being they adore, on the happy spot they at present possess, (which is a fertile island according to our computation, two thousand miles in circumference. That they were prohibited by their religion from war, and that murder and infidelity were equally unknown among them.

They address their praises to the sun, as the representative of the being they adore; for which purpose the whole village were summoned together at the rising and setting of that planet. When with united voices, and a solemn attention beyond what we had ever seen before, they performed their ceremonies.

These people are strangers to the use of flesh, and all kinds of spirituous liquors; they live to a great age, and though vastly numerous, they populate so slow that it is very rare three children belong to one family. We saw some people among them above an hundred years old, according to their reckoning, and their days are nearly twice the length of ours.

We were sent soon after we were found, to the high priest or king of their nation, who attended with great pleasure the recital of our principles of religion, and the divine precepts of the scripture, but when we informed him of the quarrels among christians, and their shedding so much blood to support their different sectaries, his astonishment was greater than can be conceived, and in his public declamations he often took occasion to return thanks that the vices of christians were unknown to them as to practice.

We could have spent our lives among this people contentedly, and never should have thought of seeking for another home, but Providence had ordered otherwise, and our return to our native home after a long absance was effected by accident as follows.

On a little uninhabited island, about three leagues from the main, grows a sort of fruit of which the inhabitants of the main are exceeding fond, and which, when dried, in taste, nearly resembles rich cake: the produce of this island is collected annually by the king's orders, and distributed throughout his dominions. The water craft made use of in this business, is very large and strong built boats, conveniently fixed for the purpose, & covered with a deck to prevent the fruit from getting wet. The annual produce of this island is computed to be equal to one half the bread consumed by the inhabitants in a year. And as the inhabitants are exceeding fond of milk with their cake, (of which they have great plenty) it forms a very considerable part of their living.

We had been among these hospitable people so long that all their cares became ours, and we partook of all their amusements. We were with the party employed on the island business, and had nearly completed our lading, when a violent storm arose, which occasioned some of the boats to break their landfasts, and as none of the natives were in the boat with us, we were driven at the mercy of the winds and waves, and were soon out of sight of land. The storm beginning to encrease, we lashed our helm down, and went below. The wind now raged with great violence, and the rain poured from the clouds in [. . .] [. . .] to oblige us to fast ourselves up close, the storm continuing with unremitted fury for several days, during which we lost our rudder and mast.

We were driven in this situation twenty eight days without any prospect of relief. We put up our earnest supplications to heaven for assurance, and returned unfeigned thanks for the signal interpositions of providence in our behalf. It was early in the morning of the twenty ninth day, while we were at our devotions, that we discovered a ship to the south of us, and steering towards us. Tho, we had never hoped to see Europeans again our joy at this discovery cannot be easily conceived or described. The ship proved to be a Russian frigate, just returning from a voyage of discoveries in the South Sea, who took us on board and treated us with great humanity. Our fruit was of a kind they had not seen in their voyage, and on our arrival at St. Petersburgh, we received a handsome price for our cargo, and a strong invitation to sail in Her Imperial Majesty's service in quest on the land we described, but our impatience to see our friends prompted us to equip ourselves for our voyage to America. We accordingly left Petersburgh on board an English vessel bound to London, from whence we set sail for America, a few days after, and by the blessing of Heaven arrived in Virginia on the 4th of January 1786, after an absence of above six years and a half.

Finis

Notes

1. Possibly Samuel Holden Parsons, a major general who served in the Revolutionary War and author of *Antiquities of Western States*.

2. The "Chickkemogga," or in the modern spelling "Chickamauga," split from the Cherokee nation after substantial land cessions, preferring war rather than the loss of more territory.

A Very Surprising
Narrative
of a Young Woman,
Who Was Discovered
in a Rocky Cave

When Thomas Jefferson was elected president in the "Revolution of 1800," he was not particularly interested in expanding the American West. In his inaugural address he claimed that the country had enough land "for a thousand generations," thereby indicating that the vast expanse between the Mississippi River and the Rocky Mountains was outside the concern of his administration. Jefferson soon changed his mind—and with good reason. Even before he had the good fortune to double the country's size with the Louisiana Purchase, his countrymen were interested in the remote West. Americans sought ownership of this "unclaimed" western land for financial gain from the exploitation of its abundant natural resources, for information about the pristine natural world, and for the possibility of adventure in unknown territory. Even Americans who did not, and would not, venture into the remote wilderness were fascinated with its possibilities. The following narrative, generally known as *The Panther Narrative* or *The Panther Captivity*, was written in 1787 under the pseudonym of Abraham Panther and gave voice to the possibilities and apprehensions Americans felt about the mysterious West. The enormously popular tale helped mark the immense, unbounded world then outside the perimeter of America as a locus of both wondrous potential and menacing dangers.

The Panther Captivity is a fictitious epistle from a pseudonymous Abraham Panther to an unnamed friend. In it Panther writes about his recent journey into "the Western wilderness," where he and his companion come across a woman who lives alone in a cave, described as "a most beautiful young Lady!" When the men ask her how she came to live in such a remote place, she tells them her story, which Panther claims he has recorded in her own words. In 1777, she tells the men, she and her lover eloped and ran away into the wilderness. The lovers were captured by Indians, and her lover was killed. She escaped from the Indians, but after wandering in the woods for days, she was found by a man "of gigantic proportion." He threatened to force her to share his bed, so while he slept, she beheaded, quartered, and buried him in the woods. She tells Panther and his traveling companion that she has spent nine years in the giant's cave, living off the land.

After five days, the men decide to go home, and they ask her to go with them. She refuses at first, but she eventually decides to go back to her home. When she returns to civilization, she reconciles with her aged father. He is in poor health and dies shortly after their reunion. However, he bequeaths to his long-lost daughter enormous wealth. Panther ends the letter by calling the event "the most singular and extraordinary of my life."

The Panther Captivity was a popular, if enigmatic, early American captivity narrative. As much as it appears to have delighted its contemporary readership, it challenges present-day critics and readers. To begin with, an examination of the narrative turns up subtle, but not unremarkable, changes to the text over the course of its print history. The narrative was first published in *Bickerstaff's Almanack* (1788). It was reprinted over twenty times between 1787 and 1814, with at least three notable alterations to the text. For example, between the 1799 and 1824 editions, the lady's description of the man who sexually threatened her while she was alone in the wilderness changes. In the 1787 edition the lady describes him as "a man of gigantic figure." In the 1799 edition (reprinted here) he is described as "an Indian, of gigantic figure," and finally in the last, popularly read edition, he is called "a black man." These additions, while only amounting to about eight hundred words, also explain more of the lady's life before she goes into the woods, provide a more sympathetic depiction of her lover, and portray her father as more stern and disagreeable. Interestingly, the lady is also less responsible for her own freedom in this revised edition, being accidentally left alone by her Indian captors rather than planning and executing an escape as in the previous edition.

The manipulation of the text is not the only challenging point in this narrative. In matters of content, the work's themes and characters remain in an uneasy, unresolved tension. This narrative combines elements of the (male) adventure narrative, the (female) captivity narrative, the sentimental seduction novel, and the oral tradition of Indian fertility myths. However, at the heart of the work, these conventions are overturned in a genre that Annette Kolodny describes as the female adventure narrative. In addition to Kolodny's examination of the text, readers should also note Richard Slotkin's provocative archetypal reading of *The Panther Captivity* in *Regeneration through Violence*.

While *The Panther Captivity* presents challenges to the modern critic in terms of defining its genre or specifying its themes, it is easy to understand the numerous forces that made it appealing to early American readers. Captivity narratives were the most enduring popular narrative form in early America. While many men were protagonists of these works, women were also moving westward at the close of the eighteenth century. As they did so, Native American culture came into more intimate contact with white culture, and the mythology of the frontier experience may have changed the nature of the captivity narrative's purpose. Additionally, as readers after the Revolution were steeped in the language of change, citizens increasingly challenged authority and criticized the limitations of equality. Undoubtedly, the shocking scenes recounted in the narrative were a form of great entertainment, and the allure of the strange was undeniable. And while rewards for defiance of authority were not new for male adventurers, such defiance, obviously, was also an attraction for women readers as well.

CRB

Sir,

Having returned from the Westward—I now sit down, agreeable to your request, to give you an account of my journey.—

Two days after you left my house Mr. *Camber* and myself, after providing ourselves with provisions, began our journey, determining to penetrate the Western Wilderness as far as prudence and safety would permit. We travelled for thirteen days in a westerly direction, without meeting any thing uncommon or worthy description, except a very great variety of birds and wild beasts, which would frequently start before us—and, as we had our muskets, contributed not a little to our amusement and support. The land we found exceeding rich and fertile, every where well watered, and the variety of berries, nuts, ground-nuts, &c. afforded us very comfortable living.

On the 14th day of our travels, while we were observing a high hill, at the foot of which, ran a beautiful stream, which passing through a small plain, after a few windings, lost itself in a thicket,—and observing the agreeable picturesque prospect, which presented itself on all sides, we were surprised at the sound of a voice, which seemed at no great distance.

At first we were uncertain whether the voice was a human one or that of some bird; as many extraordinary ones inhabited these wilds. After listening some time, the voice ceased, and we then determined to proceed up the hill, from whence, we judged, the sound to come; that we might, if possible, discover what voice it was that so much astonished us. Accordingly, crossing the brook, we proceeded up the hill; and having arrived near the summit, we again distinctly heard a voice singing in our own language, a mournful Song.—When the voice ceased, we observed a small foot path we followed; and arriving at the top of the hill, passed round a large rock, then through a thicket of bushes, at the end of which, was a large opening: Upon our arrival here, to our inexpressible amazement, we

A VERY
SURPRISING NARRATIVE
OF A
YOUNG WOMAN,
DISCOVERED IN

A Rocky-Cave;

AFTER HAVING BEEN TAKEN BY THE
SAVAGE INDIANS of the Wilderness,
in the Year 1777,
And seeing no human being for the space of nine years.

In a Letter from a Gentleman to his Friend.

SECOND WINDSOR EDITION.

Printed by ALDEN SPOONER, at his Office, and sold
Wholesale and Retail.
M,DCC,XXIX.

Title page of *A Very Surprising Narrative of a Young Woman,
Discovered in a Rocky Cave* (1799 edition; courtesy
of the American Antiquarian Society)

beheld a most beautiful young Lady! sitting near the mouth of a cave!—She, not observing us, began again to sing. We now attempted to approach her; when a dog, which we had not before observed, sprung up and began to bark at us: at which she started up and seeing us, gave a scream and swooned away. We ran to her assistance and having lifted her up, she soon recovered; and looking wildly at us exclaimed, Heavens! Where am I?—And who and from whence are you?—We desired her to be under no uneasiness,—told her we were travellers,—that we came only to view the country: but that in all our travels, we had not met with any thing that had surprised us so much, as her extraordinary appearance, in a place which we imagined totally unfrequented.

After a little conversation, having convinced her of our peaceable dispositions, and that we intended her no injury she invited us into the cave, when she refreshed us with some ground-nuts, a kind of apples, some Indian cake, and excellent water.—We found her to be an agreeable, sensible Lady; and after some conversation, we requested to know who she was, and how she came to this place.—She very readily complied with this request, and begun her story as follows:—

"Strangers, your appearance and conversation, entitle you to my confidence; and though my story cannot be very interesting or entertaining,—yet it may possibly excite your pity, while it gratifies your curiosity."

"I was born near Albany, in the year 1760—My father was a man of some consequence, and of considerable estate in the place where he lived.—I was his only child, and had I continued with him, possibly, I might have been happy. In the fifteenth year of my age, my father received into his family a young Gentleman of education, as his clerk. This young man, by his easy politeness—his good sense and agreeable manners, soon gained the esteem of all the family.—He had not been long with us, before he conceived an unfortunate passion for me; and, as he had frequent opportunities of conversion with me,—his insinuating address, added to a sensible, engaging conversation, soon found way to my heart. He quickly perceived that I was not indifferent to him—and took occasion to declare his passion, which he did with so much ardour; and yet, with so much modesty, that I readily acknowledged a mutual attachment.

After this, we spent many happy evenings, vowing unalterable love, and fondly anticipating future happiness. We were however obliged to conceal our attachment from my father, who as he was excessively eager in pursuit of riches, we had no reason to suppose he would countenance our loves, or consent to my marriage with a man destitute of fortune.

It happened, one evening while we were discoursing by ourselves in a little garden, adjoining our house, that we were overheard by my father; who, either suspected our attachment to each other, or from some other motives, had purposely concealed himself in this place, where he knew we usually walked.

Next morning, my father, with, an angry countenance, upbraided my lover with treacherously engaging his daughter's affections—and after calling him many hard names, dismissed him, with peremptory order never again to enter his house. It was in vain to remonstrate; he insisted on being obeyed—and ordered me to my chamber where he confined me.—My lover then wrote my father, stating to him our situation; requesting leave to address me, and informed him of our mutual engagements, with the reason for not sooner consulting him.—To this, my father ordered the young Gentleman to trouble him no further with his impertinence, nor ever to think of further connection with me. By means, however, of an old servant, long attached to my lover, we found means to carry on a correspondence; and, in about a month after, we contrived matters, that I had an interview with my lover: I then agreed to quit my father's house, and retire into the country, to see whether my absence would not soften his heart, and induce him to consent to my happiness: I therefore packed up some clothes, and other things, and left my father's house in the evening of the 10th of May, 1777, and retired several miles into the country, to a little hut, where my lover left me, and went in disguise, to see what effect my absence had upon my father. In five days he returned, and informed me, that, my father, enraged at my elopement, had hired several men to search the country, in pursuit of us; that he threatened vengeance to us both, and declared that he would be the death of the man who carried off his daughter. Thunder-struck at this account, I knew not what to do; to attempt reconciliation with my father was vain; or if possible to be effected, my lover must be sacrificed to it, which would make me insupportably unhappy.—In order to elude the search of those who were in pursuit of us, we proposed to move further into the country, and there to wait till time should calm my father's rage, or effectually cool his resentment.

We accordingly left the hut, and traveled at an easy rate, for four days, determining to avoid being taken.—But O! how shall I relate the horred scene that followed?—Towards the evening of the 4th day we were surrounded and made prisoners, by a party of Indians! who led us about two miles and then barbarously murdered my lover! cutting and mangling him in a most inhuman manner! Then, after tying him to a stake, they kindled a fire round him! and, while he burnt, they run round, singing and dancing, rejoicing in their Brutal cruelty! I was at a few rods distance during this transaction! and this scene had well nigh deprived me of life.—I fainted away, and lay some time motionless on the ground:—When I recovered my senses, I perceived that my guard had joined his companions, some of whom were seated round in rings, and others continued singing and dancing.—Seeing them all engaged, I got up and stood for about an hour:—I then sat down by the side of a tree, and being overcome by fatigue, and the sight I had seen, I either fainted or fell asleep, and knew nothing till the next morning, about 7 o'clock—. Tis impossible for me to describe my feelings; or for you to

conceive a situation more wretched than mine at this time.—Surrounded, as I
supposed, on all sides with danger—I knew not what to do, without a guide to
direct, or friend to protect me. Often I was upon the point of returning, and
endeavoring to find, and deliver myself a prisoner to those Indians, to whose
cruelty I had lately been a witness; and, had I then seen them, I certainly should
have delivered myself into their powers. At length I got up, and after walking
some time I resolved to seek some place of shelter, where I might be secure from
storms by day and from beasts by night, where I might dwell till a period should
be put to my miserable existence.

—With this view I wandered about for fourteen days, without knowing whither
I went. By day, the spontaneous produce of the earth supplied me with food; by
night the ground was my couch, and the canopy of heaven my only covering.—In
the afternoon of the fifteenth day I was surprized at seeing an Indian, of a gigantic
figure walking towards me:—to run I knew would be vain, and no less vain to
attempt to hide. He soon came up with me, and accosted me in a language I did
not understand, and after surveying me for some time, he took me by the hand,
and led me to his cave; having entered, pointed to a stone seat on which I sat
down; he then gave me to eat some nuts and some Indian cake, after which, he
stretched himself out on a long stone, covered with skins which he used as a
bed, and several times motioned to me to lay myself beside him. I declined his
offer, and at length he rose in a passion, and went into another apartment of the
cave, and brought forth a sword and hatchet. He then motioned to me, that I
must either accept of his bed, or expect death for my obstinacy. I still declined
his offer, and was resolved to die rather than comply with his desire. He then
brought a walnut bark, and having bound me pointed to the east, intimating that
he left me till next morning to consider his proposal; he then returned to his
bed, and, happily for me, he soon fell asleep. Having the liberty of my teeth I
soon made out to bite the bark in two, with which he bound me, by which I
found means to liberate myself while he continued sleeping. I considered this
as the only opportunity I should have of freeing myself from him—as I expected
that he would use violence when he awoke, to make me partake of his bed, and
as I knew I could not escape him by flight, I did not long deliberate,—but took
up the hatchet he had brought, and summoning resolution, I, with three blows,
effectually put an end to his existence.

I then cut off his head, and next day, having cut him in quarters, drew him out
of the cave, about half a mile distance; when, after covering him with leaves and
bushes returned to this place. I now found myself alone, in possession of this
cave, in which are several apartments. I here found a kind of Indian corn, which
I planted, and have yearly raised a small quantity. I here contented myself as well
as my wretched situation would permit—here have I existed for nine long years,
in all which time this faithful Dog, which I found in the cave, has been my only
companion, and you are the only human beings, who ever heard me tell my tale."

Here she finished her narration, and, after shedding a plentiful shower of tears, and a little conversation, she requested us to take rest, which request we willingly complied with.

Next morning she conducted us through the cave in which were four apartments, one of which appeared pretty deep in the earth; in which was a spring of excellent water—in the other three were nothing very remarkable, except four skulls, which we supposed were of persons murdered by the owner of the cave, or of his former companions. We found also three hatchets, four bows, and several arrows, one large tinder box, one sword, one old gun, and a number of skins of dead beasts, and a few clothes. The bows, some arrows, the sword, and one hatchet, we brought away, which are now in my possession.

After continuing in the cave five days we proposed returning home, and requested the Lady to accompany us. At first she refused to quit her cave; but after some persuasion she consented.

"Gentlemen, said she, I trust myself to your good Protection—I have no reason to question your good intentions, and willingly believe, from my small acquaintance with you, that you would not seek to heap affliction upon a weak woman, already borne down with misery and sorrow."

We together left the cave, on the morning of the sixth day after our arrival in it, and travelling the way we went, arrived at my house in seventeen days. After resting about a week, we accompanied the Lady, agreeable to her desire, to her father's house. The old man did not at first recognize his daughter, but being told who she was—he looked at her for some time, and then tenderly embraced her, crying, *"O! my child, my long lost child! do I once more fold thee in my arms!"*— He then fainted away. We with difficulty brought him to life; but the scene had overcome him; he opened his eyes and being a little recovered, requested to know where she had lived so long, and what had happened to her, since her leaving his house. We desired him to wait till he should be better recovered; but he begged to be satisfied immediately, observing that he had but a few moments to live. She then briefly related what had happened to her and the tragical death of her lover. He seemed much affected, and when she had finished, he took her by the hand, and affectionately squeezed it, and asked her forgiveness, and attempted to say something more but immediately fainted; all our endeavours to recover him were in vain, he lay about seven hours, and then expired.

He left a handsome fortune to his daughter, who, notwithstanding his cruelty, was deeply affected at his sudden death. This adventure, the most singular and extraordinary of my life, I have communicated, agreeable to your desire, as it really happened, without addition or diminution, and am Sir, yours, &c.

ABRAHAM PANTHER.

Finis

Narrative

of the

Remarkable Occurrences,

in the Life of

John Blatchford

of Cape-Ann

John Blatchford's account (1788) of his voyages is one of the most extraordinary sea narratives from the American Revolution. According to the text, Blatchford sailed out of Boston harbor in 1777 as a fifteen-year-old cabin boy on an American privateer but was soon taken captive when his ship was captured, and for the next six years he journeyed on various British ships throughout the world, including Nova Scotia, the West Indies, England, France, Gibraltar, and even Java and Sumatra. A nautical microcosm of the Revolution, the text relates Blatchford's persistent efforts to regain his freedom.

The *National Union Catalogue* lists seven entries under John Blatchford (ca. 1762–ca. 1794). The original printer, Timothy Green of New London, Connecticut, secured a copyright for the narrative and printed the first and second editions. Under the title *Narrative of remarkable occurrences, in the life of John Blatchford, Of Cape-Ann, Commonwealth of Massachusetts. Containing, his treatment in Nova-Scotia—the West-Indies—Great-Britain—France, and the East-Indies, as a prisoner in the late war. Taken from his own mouth*, the text was first published by Green in 1788. The second edition, with a slightly changed title and several minor emendations, was printed by Green in 1794.

In 1865 Charles I. Bushnell reprinted the 1794 edition of the text, although he claims it as the 1788 edition. He published the reprinting, accompanied by his own extensive notes, twice in 1865, the first time on its own, and the second as volume 2, number 3, as part of Bushnell's *Crumbs for Antiquarians*. Both were privately printed in New York.

There are three other early cataloged printings. One is incomplete, listing no printer or date and containing only pages 1–4 and 9–22. The second was published in the *Stevens Addenda*, no. 41, about which little information is available, and lists New London as the original place of publication but contains the erroneous date of 1768. The third printing is also vague; supposedly published in Leominster, Massachusetts, by Adams and Wilder in 1800, the place of publication, printer, and year are all questionable. The narrative also appeared in part or entire in three newspapers: the *Vermont Journal* (November 1791), Freneau's New York City paper, *Time Piece*, in 1797, and twice in 1860 in the *Cape Ann Gazette* (July and October). More recently, the narrative has been published in 1941, 1963, and 1980; it was also included in the bicentennial series "Eyewitness Accounts of the Revolution," which reprints the 1865 Bushnell edition.

John Blatchford was born in Cape Ann, Massachusetts, around 1762, and in June 1777 sailed on the ship *Hancock*, commanded by Captain John Manley (spelled "Manly" in Blatchford's narrative). Manley is noted at length in *Rebels under Sail: The American Navy during the Revolution*, and Blatchford's description of the *Hancock*'s capture corresponds with what is known about Manley. During the next six years, Blatchford sailed on over ten different ships, mostly as a prisoner of the British, spent time in several prisons, and was set to work on a Sumatran pepper plantation run by the East India Company. He returned home on May 9, 1783, shortly after the end of the Revolutionary War.

According to Bushnell, Blatchford married Anna Grover of Rockport, Massachusetts, and together they had four children, Nancy, Rachel, William, and John. Rachel and John were still alive at the time of Bushnell's publication, and he dedicated his edition "to Capt. John Blatchford, of Rockport, Mass., Eldest surviving son of the hero of this narrative." According to Bushnell, the elder Blatchford spent a few years as a fisherman and coastal sailor before venturing to Port-au-Prince, where he died around 1794 and was buried (iii–vi).

Bushnell thoroughly annotated his edition of the Blatchford narrative. Most of his notes focus on the various ships that Blatchford mentions and include basic statistics, such as size, place of origin, and captain, as well as a detailed history of each ship. Aside from a brief mention of the East India Company and speculation regarding a poisonous fruit Blatchford attempted to eat, Bushnell made almost no comments about Blatchford's experience in Indonesia.

Still, many of the details concerning Blatchford's experiences in Sumatra seem, at least on a general level, to be accurate. For example, he mentions many animals that he and his companions encounter: "buffaloes, tigers, jackanapes, leopards, lions, baboons and monkies." A list of mammals both "extant and extinct" in *The Ecology of Sumatra*, published in 1984 by the Gadjah Mada, includes almost all of these animals, with the exclusion of lions. The fruit he describes also grows in Indonesia. Beyond the indigenous animals and plants, Blatchford is less specific. He describes a visit to a native village, but his story lacks enough detail to allow identification of the ethnic group he encounters or its location. Also, his trip around the Sumatran coast is so vague that it is impossible to trace. He mentions finally reaching a Dutch port, which he identifies as Croy. The closest approximation of this name to be found on a modern map is Krui, located about 200 miles down the coastline from Bengkulu (formerly known as the Bencoolen, which Blatchford mentions). This location, however, does not fit the narrator's description of his incredible eight-hundred-mile-long trek along the coastline to reach the port of Croy.

Blatchford's narrative, then, is an entertaining mixture of fact and fiction and reflects the American determination at the time to escape from British rule and to establish liberty. His descriptions of the treatment that he and his companions received at British hands, as well as his repeated attempts to flee from his British captors, would have stirred up strong feelings of nationalism in his readers so soon after the end of the war. With the exception of the fantastic experiences in Sumatra, many of the aspects of Blatchford's story are likely to have occurred, if not to one person, then to several. His will to survive helped him fit the mold of an American hero and thus made this narrative a popular commodity in American print culture. It seems likely that both Blatchford and Green anticipated a market and collaborated on the text.

DW & JC

In June, 1777, I shipped myself as a cabin-boy on board in the Continental ship Hancock, John Manly, Esq. commander, being then in the 15th year of my age, and a few days after sailed on a cruize. Being out some days we fell in with and took the Fox, a British frigate of 28 guns, after an engagement of four glasses.[1] Our captain sent on board the prize as many men as we could spare, and both ships kept company several days, till on the 8th of July we fell in with the British ships Rainbow of 40 guns, and Flora with 32 guns (who had in company the brig Cabot of 16 guns, which had just before been taken by Milford British frigate) by whom we were both taken and carried into Halifax.

I was kept prisoner, among a number of my countrymen, on board the Rainbow, until we arrived at Halifax. On our arrival there we were taken on shore and confined in a prison which had formerly been a sugar house.—The large number of prisoners confined in this house (near 300) together with a scanty allowance of provisions, occasioned it to be very sickly. So irksome a situation put us upon meditating an escape—but we could form no plan that was likely to be attended with success, till George Barnard, who had been a midshipman in the Hancock, and who was confined in the same room with myself, concerted a plan to release us, which was to be effected by digging a small passage under ground, to extend to a garden that was behind the prison and without the prison

NARRATIVE

OF

Remarkable Occurrences,

IN THE LIFE OF

JOHN BLATCHFORD,

Of *Cape-Ann*, Commonwealth of *Massachusetts.*

CONTAINING,

An account of his treatment and sufferings, while a prisoner in the late war, in *Nova-Scotia*---the *West-Indies---Great-Britain----France*, and the *East-Indies.*

Taken from his own mouth.

SECOND EDITION.

New-London : Printed by Timothy Green.

M,DCC,XC,IV.

[With the privilege of Copy-Right.]

Title page of *Narrative of the Remarkable Occurrences, in the Life of John Blatchford* (1788 edition; courtesy of Wellesley College Library, Special Collections)

wall, where we might make a breach in the night with safety, and probably all
obtain our liberty.—This plan greatly elated our spirits, and we were all anxious
to proceed immediately in executing of it.

Our cabins were built one above another, from the floor to the height of a
man's head; and mine being one of those built on the floor, was pitched upon
to be taken up:—this being done, six of us agreed to do the work, whose names
were, George Barnard and William Atkins of Boston, (late midshipmen in the
Hancock), Lemuel Fowle of Cape-Ann, Isaiah Churchill of Plimouth, Asa Cole
of Weathersfield, and myself. We took up the cabin and cut a hole in the plank
underneath.

The sugar-house stood upon a foundation of stone which raised the floor
four feet above the ground, and gave us sufficient room to work, and to convey
away the dirt that we dug up. The instruments which we had to work with were
one scraper, one long spike, and some sharp sticks; with these we proceeded in
our difficult undertaking. As the hole was too small to admit of more than one
person to work at a time, we dug by turns ten or twelve days, and carried the
dirt in our bosoms to another end of the cellar; by this time we supposed we
had dug far enough, and word was given out among the prisoners to prepare
themselves for flight. But while we were in the midst of gaiety, congratulating
each other upon our happy prospects, we were basely betrayed by one of our own
countrymen whose name was Knowles: he had been a midshipman on board the
Boston frigate, and was put on board the Fox when she was taken by the Hancock
and Boston.—What could have induced him to commit so vile an action cannot
be conceived, as no advantage could accrue to him from our detection, and
death was the certain consequence to many of his miserable countrymen—that
it was so, is all I can say. A few hours before we were to have attempted our
escape, Knowles informed the sergeant of the guard (Mr. Bible) of our design;
and by this treachery lost his country the lives of more than a hundred valuable
citizens—fathers and husbands—whose return would have rejoiced the hearts
of now weeping fatherless children, and called forth tears of joy from wives,
now helpless and disconsolate widows.—When we were discovered, the whole
guard was ordered into the room; and being informed by Knowles who it was that
performed the work, we were all six confined in irons—the hole was filled up, and
a centinel constantly placed in the room, to prevent any further attempt.—We
were all kept in close confinement till two of my fellow-sufferers Barnard and
Cole, died; one of which was put into the ground with his irons on his hands.
I was afterward permitted to walk the yard. But as my irons were too small and
caused my hands to swell, and made them very sore, I asked the sergeant to
take them off and give me larger ones,—he being a person of humanity, and
compassionating my sufferings, changed my irons for others that were larger,
and more easy to my hands.

Knowles, who was likewise permitted to walk the yard, for his perfidy, would take every opportunity to insult and mortify me, by asking me whether I wanted to run away again? and when I was going home, &c?—His daily affronts, together with his conduct in betraying of his countrymen, so exasperated me, that I wished for nothing more than an opportunity to convince him that I did not love him. One day as he was tantalizing over me as usual, I suddenly drew one hand out of my irons, flew at him and struck him in the face, knocked out two or three of his teeth, and bruised his mouth very much. He cried out, that the prisoner had got loose,—but before any assistance came, I had put my hand again into the hand-cuff, and was walking about the yard as usual. When the guard came, they demanded of me in what manner I struck him? I told them with both my hands. They then tried to pull my hands out, but could not, and concluded it must be as I had said;—some laughed and some were angry—but in the end I was ordered again into prison. The next day I was sent on board the Greyhound frigate, capt. Dickson, bound on a cruize in Boston-bay. After being out a few days, we met with a severe gale of wind, in which we sprung our main-mast and received considerable other damage. We were then obliged to bear away for the West-Indies, and on our passage fell in with and took a brig from Norwich, laden with stock, &c. The captain and hands were put on board a Danish vessel the same day. We carried the brig into Antigua, where we immediately repaired, and were ordered in company with the Vulture sloop of war to convoy a fleet of merchantmen to New-York. We left the fleet off Sandy-Hook, and sailed for Philadelphia, where we lay till we were made a packet and ordered for Halifax with dispatches. We had a quick passage, and arrived safe. While we lay in the road, admiral Byron arrived in the Princess Royal from England, who being short of men, and we having surplusage for a packet, many of our men were ordered on board the Princess-Royal, and among them most of our boat's crew.

Soon after, some of the officers going on shore, I was ordered into the boat.—We landed at the Governor's-slip—it being then near night. This was the first time since I had been on board the Greyhound that I had had an opportunity to escape from here, as they were before this particularly careful of me; therefore I was determined to get away then if possible, and to effect it I waded round a wharf and went up a by-way, (fearing I should meet the officers): I soon got into the street and made the best of my way towards Irishtown, where I expected to be safe;—but unfortunately while running, I was met and stopped by an emissary, who demanded of me my business, and where I was going? I endeavoured to deceive him, that he might let me pass; but it was in vain—he ordered me to follow him:—I offered him what money I had (about 7£6 sterl.) to let me go—this too was ineffectual. I then told him I was an American and making my escape from a long confinement, and was determin'd to pass, and took up a stone. He immediately drew his bayonet and ordered me to go back with him.—I refused, and told him to keep his distance.—He then run upon me, and pushing his bayonet into my side, it came out near my navel; but the wound was not very deep;—he then made a second pass, and stabbed me through my arm: he was about to stab me a third time, when I struck him with the stone and knocked him down. I then run, but the guard which had been alarmed, immediately took me, and carried me before the governor (Hughes), where I understood the man was dead. I was threatened with every kind of death, and ordered out of the governor's presence.

Whilst in confinement I was informed by a young gentleman (who was to be sent to England and tried for killing a man in a duel) that it was not in the power of the governor to try me; but that I should be sent to England; which I found to be true. The next day I was sent on board the Greyhound, the ship I had run from, and we sailed for England. Our captain being a humane man, ordered my irons off, a few days after we sailed, and permitted me to do duty as formerly. Being out thirteen days we spoke the Hazard sloop of war, who inform'd that the French fleet was then cruising in the English channel:—for this reason we put into Cork, and the dispatches were forwarded to England.—While we lay in the Cove of Cork, I jumped overboard, with intention of getting away; but unfortunately I was discovered and fired at by the marines: the boat was immediately sent after me, took me up and carried me on board again. At this time almost all the officers were on shore, and the ship was left in charge of the sailing-master, one Drummond, who beat me most cruelly;—to get out of his way I run forward—he followed me, and as I was running back he came up with me and threw me down the main hold. The fall, together with the beating, was so severe that I was deprived of my senses for a considerable time; when I recovered them I found myself in the carpenter's birth, placed upon some old canvass, between two chests, having my right thigh, leg and arm broke, and several parts of my body severely bruised. In this situation I lay eighteen days, till our officers (who had been on business to Dublin) came on board. The captain enquired for the prisoner, and being informed of my situation, came down with the doctor to set my bones, but finding them calluss'd they concluded not to meddle with me.

The ship lay at Cork till the French fleet left the channel, and then sailed for Spithead.—On our arrival there I was sent in irons on board the Princess-Amelia, and the next day was carried on board the Britannia, in Portsmouth harbour, to be tried before Sir Thomas Pye, lord high admiral of England, and president of the court-martial.

Before the officers had collected, I was put under the care of a centinel; and the seamen and women who came on board compassionated my sufferings, which rather heightened than diminished my distress. I was sitting under the awning, almost overpowered by the reflection of my unhappy situation, every moment expecting to be summoned for my trial, when I heard somebody enquiring for the prisoner—supposing to be an officer, I rose up and answered, that I was there. The gentleman came to me, told me to be of good chear, and taking out a bottle of cordial bid me drink, which I did:—he then enquired where I belonged—I informed him—he asked me if I had parents living, and if I had any friends in England?—I answered I had neither: he then assured me he was my friend, and would render me all the assistance in his power.—He then enquired of me every circumstance relative to my fray with the man at Halifax, for whose death I was now to be tried;—and instructed me what to say on my trial,—told me if it was asked in court "if I had any friend or attorney to speak for me," to look at such a corner of the state-room, where I should see him, and to answer the court "Yes, Mr. Thomas," for that was the gentleman's name. All this was spoken in so friendly a manner, that I could not distrust him, although what he had instructed me to say, appeared to me, would be against myself.

The court having assembled, I was called in and examined partly, and on being asked "If I had any friend to speak in my behalf," I looked round, and saw Mr. Thomas, and answered, "Yes, Mr. Thomas," who then came forward.—The court asked him what he had to say in behalf of the prisoner?—On which he desired them to question the prisoner; and if he could not answer sufficiently, he would speak for him. I was then asked if I meant to kill the man. I answered as instructed (tho' loth) that I did. The court seemed surpriz'd, and asked me the question again; and I again answered, Yes. I was then asked if I should have hurt the man had he not molested me? I replied, No.—I was then asked many other questions, and if I was not sorry I had undertaken in the rebellion against my king?—Mr. Thomas then spoke, and said it was hardly fair to ask me such a question upon this occasion; and that considering my youth, I had given as fair an account of myself as could be expected.—He spoke a considerable time on the subject, and concluded with comparing our combat to a field battle between two armies—expatiated largely and explained the subject so clearly that no answer was made to his arguments.—I was ordered to withdraw, and waited with painful impatience to know my destiny.—This was repeated two or three times, till at last I was called in and acquitted of the murder, and was informed that I was to be sent back to Halifax, to be exchanged as a prisoner of war. I cannot express my feelings on this occasion, and no one can know them, but by experiencing the same reverse of fortune.

I immediately found my benefactor and returned him thanks, with gratitude for his friendly and benevolent assistance. Mr. Thomas then asked the liberty of taking me on shore with him, engaging to return me the next day—and liberty was granted him.—He told a young lad, his son, to walk with me about Portsmouth, and show me the town, and then carry me home to his house; which he did. In the evening Mr. Thomas came into the kitchin and asked me to walk into the parlour, to satisfy the curiosity of some ladies, who had never seen a Yankee, as they called me: I went in, and they seemed greatly surprized to see me look like an Englishman; they said they were sure I was no Yankee, but like themselves. The idea they had formed of the Americans was nearly the same as we have of the natives of this country. When the ladies had satisfied with curiosity, Mr. Thomas put a guinea into his hat, and carrying it round asked the ladies to contribute for the poor Yankee; he then gave me the money, (about four guineas.)

The next morning I was sent on board the Princess-Amelia, where I spent a joyful day; expecting soon to be sent on board the Greyhound, which was bound to Halifax.

In the evening I heard a boat coming along-side, and supposing it to belong to the Greyhound, (as the people in the boat enquired for me)—I made haste and jumped into the boat; but to my extreme disappointment and grief, I was carried on board an Indiaman, and immediately put down into the run, where I was confined seven days. I begged that I might send word on shore to my former benefactor, and inform him of my situation, but they would not grant it. On the seventh day I heard the boatswain pipe all hands, and about noon I was called up on deck, when I found myself on board the Princess-Royal indiaman, captain Robert Kerr;—we were then off the Isle of Wight, bound to the East-Indies, in company with six others, viz. the Ceres, Hawke, Prince, Sandwich, Walpole and True-Briton, all large ships, belonging to the East-India company. Our captain told me, if I behaved well and did my duty, I should receive as good usage as any man on board:—this gave me great encouragement. I now found my destiny was fixed—that whatever I could do, would not in the least alter my situation, and therefore was determined to do the best I could, and make myself as contented as my unfortunate situation would admit.

After being on board several days, I found there were in the Princess-Royal, eighty-two Americans, all destined to the East-Indies, for being what they called Rebels.

We had a passage of seventeen weeks to St. Helena, where we put in and landed part of our cargo, (which consisted wholly of provisions), and some of the soldiers who were brought out for that island. The ship lay here about three weeks; we then sailed for Batavia—and on the passage touched at the Cape of Good-Hope, where we found the whole of the fleet that sailed with us from England—we took in some provisions and necessaries and set sail for Batavia, where we arrived in ten weeks. Here we purchased a large quantity of arrack and remained a considerable time.

We then sailed for Bencoolen, in the island of Sumatria, and after a passage of about six weeks arrived there, (this was in June 1780). At this place the Americans were all carried on shore; and I found that I was no longer to remain on board the ship, but condemned to serve as a soldier for five years.—I offered to bind myself to the captain for five years, or any longer term, if I might serve on board the ship;—he told me it was impossible for me to be released from acting as a soldier, unless I could pay fifty pounds sterling. As I was unable to do this, I was obliged to go through the manual exercise with the other prisoners; among whom was William Randall of Boston, and Josiah Folgier of Nantucket; both young men, and one of them an old ship-mate of mine;—these two and myself agreed to behave as ignorant and awkward as possible; and what motions we learned one day we were to forget the next.—We pursued this conduct near a fortnight, and were beaten every day by the drill-sergeant, who exercised us; and when he found we were determined in our obstinacy, and that it was not possible for him to learn us any thing, we were all three sent into the pepper gardens belonging to the East-India company, and continued picking peppers from morning till night, and allowed but two scanty meals a day;—this, together with the amazing heat of the sun, (the island lying under the equator) was too much for an American constitution, unused to a hot climate, and we expected that we should soon end our misery and our lives;—but Providence still preserved us for greater hardships.*

The Americans died daily with heat and hard fare, which determined my two companions and myself in an endeavour to make our escape.—We had been in the pepper gardens four months when an opportunity offered, and we resolved upon trying our fortune;—Folgier, Randall and myself sat out with an intention of reaching Croy, (a small harbour where the Dutch often touch at to water) on the opposite side of the island.—Folgier had by some means got a bayonet, which he fixed on the end of a stick—Randall and myself had nothing but staves, which were all the weapons we carried with us. We provided ourselves with fire-works for our journey, which we pursued unmolested till the fourth day just at night, when we heard a rustling in the bushes, and discovered nine seapoys, (country-born soldiers in the British service) who suddenly rushed out upon us. Folgier being the most resolute of us, run at one of them and pushed his bayonet through his body into a tree; Randall knocked down another;—but they overpowered us, bound us, and carried us back to the fort, which we reached in one day and half, though we had been four days travelling from it, owing to the circle we made by going round the shore; and they came across the woods, being acquainted with the way. Immediately on our arrival at the fort the governor called a court-martial, to have us tried.—We were soon all condemned to be shot the next morning at seven o'clock, and ordered to be sent into the dungeon and confined in irons, where we were attended by an adjutant who brought a priest with him to pray and converse with us;—but Folgier, who hated the name and sight of an Englishman, desired that we might be left alone, and not be troubled with any company:—the clergyman reprimanded him, and told him he made very light of his situation,

---

* Sumatria is an island on the Indian ocean, situated between 93 and 104 degrees of East longitude, and between 5 degrees and 30 minutes North and 5 degrees and 30 minutes South latitude; extending from N.W. to S.E. 900 miles long, and from 100 to 150 broad, separated from the continent of the Further India by the straits of Malacca on the N.E. and from the island of Java by the straits of Sunda on the S.E. This island lying under the equater, and the low grounds near the sea-coast being flooded one half of the year, is very unhealthful. The natives build most of their houses upon pillars, to secure them against the annual inundations

on supposition that he would be reprieved; but if he expected it he deceived himself:—Folgier still persisted in the clergyman's leaving of us, if he would have us make our peace with God; for, said he, the sight of Englishmen, from whom we have received such treatment, is more disagreeable than the evil spirits of whom you have spoken:—that if he could have his choice, he would choose death in preference to life, if he must have it on conditions of such barbarous usage as he had received from their hands; and that the thoughts of death did not seem so hideous to him as his past sufferings. He visited us again about midnight, but finding his company was not acceptable, he soon left us to our own melancholy reflections.

Before sun-rise we heard the drum beat, and soon after heard the direful noise of the door grating on its iron hinges—we were all taken out, our irons taken off, and we conducted by a strong guard of soldiers to the parade, surrounded by a circle of armed men, and let into the midst of them, where three white coffins were placed by our side:—silence was then commanded, and the adjutant taking a paper out of his pocket read our sentence:—and now I cannot describe my feelings upon this occasion, nor can it be felt by any one but those who have experienced some remarkable deliverance from the grim hand of death, when surrounded on all sides, and nothing but death expected from every quarter, and by Divine Providence there is some way found out for escape—so it seemed to me when the adjutant pulled out another paper from his pocket and read, "that the governor and council, in consideration of the youth of Randall and myself, (supposing us to be led on by Folgier, who was the eldest) thought fit to pardon us from death, and that instead we were to receive eight hundred lashes each,"—although this last sentence appeared terrible to me, yet in comparison with death, it seemed to be light.—Poor Folgier was shot in our presence— previous to which we were told we might go and converse with him—Randall went and talked with him first, and after him I went up to take my leave, but my feelings were such at the time that I had not power to utter a single word to my departing friend, who seemed as undaunted and seemingly as willing to die as I was willing to be released—and told me not to forget the promises we had formerly made each other, which was, to embrace the first opportunity to escape:—we parted, and he was immediately after shot dead. We were next taken and tied; and the adjutant brought a small whip made of cotton, which consisted of a number of strands and knotted at the ends; but these knots were all cut off by the adjutant before the drummer took it, which made it not worse than to have been whipt with cotton yarn. After being whipped 800 lashes we were sent to the company hospital, where we had been about three weeks, when Randall told me he intended very soon to make his escape:—this somewhat surprized me, as I had lost all hopes of regaining my liberty, and supposed he had:—I told him I had hoped he would never mention it again; but however, if that was his design,

I would accompany him. He advised me (if I was fearful) to tarry behind;—but finding he was determined on going, I resolved to run the risque once more; and as we were then in the hospital we were not suspected of such a design.

Having provided ourselves with fire-works and knives about the first of December 1780, we sat out, with intention of reaching the Dutch settlement of Croy, which is but about two or three hundred miles distance upon a direct line, but as we were obliged to travel along the sea coast, (fearing to risque the nearest way) it was a journey of eight hundred miles. We took each a stick and hung round our neck, and every day cut a notch, which was the method we took to keep time.—In this manner we travelled, living on fruit, turtle-eggs and some turtle, which we cooked every night, with the fire we built to sleep by to secure us from wild beasts—they being here in great plenty, such as buffaloes, tigers, jackanapes, leopards, lions, baboons and monkies. On the 30th day of our travelling we met with nothing we could eat, and found no water—at night we found some fruit which appeared to the eye to be very delicious, (different from any we had seen in our travel), it resembles a fruit which grows in the West-Indies, called a Jack, about the size of an orange:—we being very dry and hungry immediately gathered some of this fruit—but finding it of a sweet sickish taste I eat but two—Randall eat freely:—in the evening we found we were poisoned: I was sick and puked considerably:—Randall was sick and began to swell all round his body: he grew worse all night, but continued to have his senses till the next day, when he died, and left me to mourn my greater wretchedness,—more than 400 miles from any settlement—no companion—the wide ocean on one side and a prowling wilderness on the other—liable to many kinds of deaths, more terrible than being shot. I laid down by Randall's body, wishing if possible that he might return to tell me what course to take.—My thoughts almost distracted me, so that I was unable to do any thing till the next day; during all which time I continued by the side of Randall—I then got up and made a hole in the sand and buried him.

I now continued my journey as well as my weak state of body would permit; the weather being at this time extreme hot and rainy.—I frequently lay down and would wish that I might never rise again:—despair had almost wholly possessed me; and sometimes in a kind of delirium would fancy I heard my mother's voice, and my friends calling me, and I would answer them:—at other times my wild imagination would paint to my view scenes which I was well acquainted with, then supposing myself near home I would run as fast as my feeble legs could carry me:—frequently I fancied that I heard dogs bark, men cutting wood, and every noise which I have heard in my native country.

One day as I was travelling, a small dog, as I thought it to be, came fawning round me and followed me, but I soon discovered it to be a young lion;—I supposed that its dam must be nigh, and therefore run; it followed me sometimes and then left me;—I proceeded on, but had not got far from it before it began to cry;

I looked round and saw a lioness making towards it—she yelled most frightfully, which greatly terrified me; but she laid down something from her mouth for her young one, and then with another yell turned and went off from me.

Some days after, I was travelling by the edge of a woods, (which from its appearance had felt severely the effects of a tornado or hurricane, the trees being all torn up by the roots) and I heard a cracking noise in the bushes—looking about I saw a monstrous large tiger making slowly towards me, which frightened me exceedingly; when he had approached within a few rods of me, in my surprize I suddenly lifted up my hands and hollowed very loud: this sudden noise frightened him, seemingly as much as I had been, and he immediately turned and run into the woods, and I saw him no more. After this I continued travelling on without molestation, only from the monkies, who were here so plenty that oftentimes I saw them in large droves: some times I run from them as if afraid of them; they would then follow, grin and chatter at me, and when they got near I would turn, and they would run back into the woods, and climb the trees to get out of my way.

It was now fifteen weeks since I had left the hospital—I had travelled most all the day without any water, and began to be very thirsty, when I heard the sound of running water, as it were down a fall of rocks—I had heard it a considerable time, and at last began to suspect it was nothing but imaginary, as many other noises I had before thought to have heard. I however went on as fast as I could, and at length discovered a brook—on approaching of it I was not a little surprized and rejoiced at the sight of a Female Indian, who was fishing at the brook:—she had no other dress on than that which mother nature affords impartially to all her children, except a small cloth which she wore round her waist.—I knew not how to address myself to her:—I was afraid if I spoke she would run—and therefore I made a small noise; upon which she looked round and, seeing me, run across the brook, seemingly much frightened, leaving her fishing-line. I went up to her basket, which contained five or six fish that looked much like our trout. I took up the basket and attempted to wade across where she had passed, but was too weak to wade across in that place, and went further up the stream, where I passed over—and then looking for the indian woman I saw her at some distance behind a large cocoa-nut tree:—I walked towards her, but dare not keep my eyes steadily upon her lest she should run from me as she did before.—I called to her in English; and she answered in her own tongue, which I could not understand. I then called to her in the Malays, which I understood a little of:—she answered me in a kind of surprize, and asked me in the name of Oerum Footee (the name of their god) from whence I came, and where I was going:—I answered her as well as I could in the Malais, that I was from Fort-Marlborough, and going to Croy—that I was making my escape from the English, by whom I had been taken in war.—She told me that she had been taken by the Malays some years before—for that the two nations were always at war; and that she had been kept as a slave among them three years, and was then retaken by her countrymen. Whilst we were talking together she appeared to be very shy, and I durst not go nearer than a rod to her, lest she should run from me. She said that Croy, the place I was bound to, was about three miles distance—that if I would follow her she would conduct me to her countrymen who were but a small distance off.—I begged her to plead with her countrymen to spare my life,—she said she would, and assured me that if I behaved well I should not be hurt. She then conducted me to a small village, consisting of huts or wigwams. When we arrived at the village, the children that saw me were frightened and run away from me—and the women expressed a great deal of fear, and kept at a distance—but my guide called to them and told them not to be afraid, for that I was not come to hurt them—and then informed them from whence I came, and that I was going to Croy.

I told my guide that I was very hungry—and she sent the children for something for me to eat;—they came and brought me little round balls of boiled rice; and they not daring to come nigh, threw them to me—these I picked up and eat; afterwards a woman brought some rice and goats milk in a copper bason, and setting it on the ground, made signs for me to take it up and eat it, which I did, and then put the bason down again; they then poked away the bason with a stick, battered it with stones; and making a hole in the ground buried it. After that they conducted me to a small hut, and told me to tarry there till the morning, when they would conduct me to the harbour. I had but little sleep that night, and was up several times to look out, and saw two or three indians at a little distance from the hut, who I suppose were placed there to watch me. Early in the morning numbers came round the hut, and the female who was my guide, asked me where my country was?—I could not make her understand, only that it was a great distance. She then asked me if my countrymen eat men. I told her no—and seeing some goats, pointed at them and told her we eat such as them.—She then asked me what made me white, and if it was not the white rain that come upon us when we were small? (How they came by this notion I know not, but suppose that while she was over with the Malays she had heard something of snow from them, as they carry some trade with the English at Fort Marlboro and Bencoolen.) And as I wished to please and satisfy them, I told them that I supposed it was—for it was only in certain seasons of the year that it fell, and in hot weather when it did not fall the people grew darker till it returned, and then the people all grew white again—this seemed to please them very much.

My protectoress now brought a young man to me who, she said, was her brother, and who would shew me the way to the harbour;—she then cut a stick about eight feet long, and he took hold of one end and gave me the other— she told me that she had instructed her brother what to say at the harbour. He then led off and I followed. During our walk I put out my hand to him several times, and made signs of friendship—but he seemed to be afraid of me, and would look upwards and then fall flat on the ground and kiss it—this he repeated as often as I made any sign or token of friendship to him.—When we had got near the harbour he made a sign for me to sit down upon a rock, which I did; he then left me and went, as I supposed, to talk with the people at the water concerning me; but I had not sit long before I saw a vessel coming round a point into the harbour.—They soon came on shore in the boat.—I went down to them and made my case known, and when the boat returned on board they took me with them. It was a Dutch snow bound from China to Batavia;—after they had wooded and watered they set sail for Batavia:—being out about three weeks we arrived there:—I tarried on board her about three weeks longer, and then got on board a Spanish ship which was from Rio de la Plate bound to Spain, but by stress of weather was forced to put into this port. After the vessel had repaired we sailed for Spain. When we made the Cape of Good-Hope we fell in with two British cruizers of 20 guns each, who engaged us and did the vessel considerable damage, but at length we beat them off, and then run for the coast of Brazils, where we arrived safe and began to work at repairing our ship, but upon examination she was found to be not fit to proceed on her voyage, she was therefore condemned. I then left her and got on board a Portuguese snow, bound up to St. Helena, and we arrived safe at that place. I then went on shore and quitted her, and engaged in the garrison there to do duty as a soldier for my provisions, till some ship should arrive there bound to England. After serving here a month, I entered on board a ship called the Stormont—but orders were soon after received that no indiaman should sail without convoy; and we lay here six months, during which time our captain (Montgomery) died.

While I was at St. Helena, the vessel which I came out from England in arrived here, homeward bound; she being on the return from her second voyage since I came from England:—and now I made known my case to Captain Kerr, who readily took me on board the Princess-Royal, and used me kindly—and those of my old shipmates on board were glad to see me again. Captain Kerr at first seeing me, asked me if I was not afraid to let him know who I was? and endeavoured to frighten me; yet his conduct towards me was humane and kind.—It had been very sickly on board the Princess-Royal, and the greater part of the hands which came out of England in her had died, and she was now manned chiefly with lascars, (country born people): among those who had died was the boatswain and boatswain's made, and Captain Kerr made me boatswain of the ship—in which office I continued until we arrived in London—and it protected me from being impressed at our arrival in England.

We sailed from St. Helena about the first of November, 1781, under convoy of the Experiment of 50 guns, commanded by Captain Henry, and the Shark sloop of war of 18 guns—and we arrived in London about the first of March, 1782—it having been about two years and a half from the time I had left it.

In about a fortnight after our arrival in London, I entered on board the King-

George, store-ship bound to Antigua, and after four weeks passage arrived there—the second after we came to anchor in Antigua, I took the ship's boat and made my escape in her to Montserrat, which place had but just before been taken by the French.—Here I did not meet with the treatment which I expected; for on my arrival at Montserrat I was immediately taken up and put in prison, where I continued 24 hours, and my boat taken from me;—I was then sent to Guadaloupe, and examined by the governor.—I made known my case to him, by acquainting him with the misfortunes I had gone through in my captivity and in making my escape—he seemed to commiserate me—gave me ten dollars for the boat that I escaped in, and provided a passage for me on board a French brigantine that was bound from Guadaloupe to Philadelphia:—the vessel sailed in a few days—and now my prospects were favourable—but my misfortunes were not to end here; for after being out 21 days, we fell in with the Amphitrite and Amphene, two British cruizers, off the Capes of Delaware, by whom we were taken, carried into New-York, and put on board the Jersey prison-ship—after being on board about a week, a cartel was fitted out for France, and I was sent on board as a French prisoner:—The cartel was ordered for St. Malo's, and after a passage of 32 days we arrived safe at that place. [2]

Finding no American vessel at St. Malo's, I went to the commandant and procured a pass to go by land to Port L'Orient; on my arrival there I found three American privateers belonging to Beverley, in the Massachusetts. I was much elated at seeing so many of my country, some of whom I was well acquainted with. I immediately entered on board the Bucaneer, Captain Phierson:—We sailed on a cruize, and after being out 18 days, we returned to L'Orient with six prizes.—Three days after our arrival in port we heard the joyful news of peace;—on which the privateer was dismantled, the people discharged, and Capt. Phierson sailed on a merchant voyage to Norway.

I then entered on board a brig bound to Lisbon, (Capt. Ellenwood of Beverly), and arrived at Lisbon in eight days—we took in a cargo of salt, and sailed for Beverly, where we arrived the 9th of May, 1783,—being now only 15 miles from home.—I immediately set out for Cape-Ann, went to my father's house, and had an agreeable meeting with my friends, after an absence of almost six years.

New-London, May 10, 1788.
JOHN BLATCHFORD.

[N.B. *Those who are acquainted with the narrator will not scruple to give full credit to the foregoing account—and others may satisfy themselves by conversing with him. The scars he carries are proof of a part of his narrative—and a gentleman belonging to New-London, who was several months with him, was acquainted with part of his sufferings, tho' it was out of his power to relieve him—He is a poor man, with a wife and two children—His employment fishing and coasting.*]

Notes

1. Bushnell has verified that the *Hancock* was taken by the *Rainbow* and *Flora*. For further verification of Blatchford's ships and voyages, see Bushnell's introduction and extended notes.

2. The *Jersey* was the most notorious of all English prison ships, and it is estimated that as many as ten thousand American prisoners died while in captivity on the *Jersey*. Historical readers would have undoubtedly recognized the name and associated it with British cruelty. For a contemporary account of the *Jersey*, see Thomas Dring's *Recollections of the Jersey Prison-ship* (1829).

A Narrative of the
Captivity and Sufferings
of
Mr. Ebenezer Fletcher,
of Newipswich,
Who Was ... Taken Prisoner
by the British

Ebenezer Fletcher's account (1798) of his captivity as a wounded prisoner of war in the hands of the British and his death-defying escape, even before his wound had sufficiently healed, has gone through multiple printings over nearly 175 years. The first edition, printed by Samuel Preston in Amherst, Massachusetts, appeared some twenty-one years after the battle of Hubbardton (Vermont), where Fletcher received his wound. The second edition of the narrative, printed by Charles Kendall in Windsor, Vermont, appeared in 1813. Subsequent editions, printed by S. Wilder, appeared in 1927 and 1928, and a reprint of the Wilder edition was published by W. Abbatt in Tarrytown, New York, in 1929. The Fletcher narrative was published again in 1970 under the title *The Narrative of Ebenezer Fletcher: A Soldier of the Revolution*, and it was released again in 1976 for the bicentennial in the Eyewitness Accounts of the Revolution series. Fletcher's story has become emblematic of the life of the common Revolutionary soldier, and it has endured as an engaging account of one man's curious—if somewhat reluctant—participation in the Revolutionary struggle for liberty.

Fletcher was born in New Ipswich, New Hampshire, in 1761; in 1777 he enlisted in a New Hampshire battalion commanded by Nathan Hale. He is described as being "short in stature, being but five feet three inches tall, and proportionally slim, but remarkably active in his movements." Fletcher went through great physical pain and ran terrible risks in order to escape the British, despite admitting that "[s]ome of the enemy were very kind," and revealing that he considered at least two of his captors to be friends. He simultaneously reports, however, that "others were very spiteful and malicious." This complicated attitude toward the British in many ways serves as a reflection of the attitudes existing in the countryside to which Fletcher escapes; it is strewn with both pro- and anti-British households, making it imperative for Fletcher, an escaping wounded soldier in the Continental Army, to appeal to the proper household for assistance.

The main danger for Fletcher and the primary threat to his freedom existed in the form of the many "Tories" he found all around him. Several of the people he ran into were anxious to return him to the British, but he was able to win the support of a few, and he convinced a few others, not so sympathetic to his cause, at least not to betray him to the British Army. At one point, unsure of the allegiances of his host but exhausted and weak from his still unhealed wound, he threw himself on the mercy of a stranger and confessed: "I sat and viewed him for some minutes, and at last resolved to tell him from whence I came and where I wished to go, let the event be what it would." This ploy worked as the man held pro-American sentiments, but this scene also demonstrates the danger of recapture for Fletcher and the ever-present threat to freedom—existing for all Americans in the early days of the Revolution—that could be brought on simply by speaking to the wrong people.

In an interesting addition to the 1813 edition, a brief account of what happened to Fletcher after his escape is given: "Not long afterwards, an officer from the army hearing of my return ordered me to be arrested and returned to the main body of the American army, although my wound was scarcely healed." Remarkably, after the pains he took to escape, the army took away his liberty once more. The exclusion of this fact in the 1798 edition and its inclusion fifteen years later is interesting. In the rest of the 1813 addition to the narrative, Fletcher tells of his passing time uneventfully until his term of enlistment expired. He once more found himself a captive, but understandably he did not complain with the same vigor, nor did he apparently attempt another daring escape. The edition released in the 1970s ends with further new material, including a brief account of Fletcher's acquaintance with both General Lafayette and General Washington. Ebenezer Fletcher died on May 8, 1831, at the age of seventy-one.

RJ

NARRATIVE

OF THE

CAPTIVITY and SUFFERINGS

OF

Mr. EBENEZER FLETCHER,

OF NEWIPSWICH,

Who was wounded at Hubbarston, in the year 1777, and taken prisoner by the British, and, after recovering a little from his wounds, made his escape from them, and returned back to Newipswich.

WRITTEN BY HIMSELF.

Printed by SAMUEL PRESTON, AMHERST.
1798.

Title page of *A Narrative of the Captivity and Sufferings of Mr. Ebenezer Fletcher* (1798 edition; Rare Books Division, the New York Public Library, Astor, Lenox and Tilden Foundations)

I, Ebenezer Flectcher, listed into the Continental Army, in Capt. Carr's Company, in Colonel Nathan Hale's Regiment, as a fifer, and joined the Army at Ticonderoga[1] under the command of General Saint Clair, in the Spring of 1777, at which place I was stationed till the retreat of the Army which was the 6th of July following.

Early on the morning of the same day, orders came to strike our tents and swing our packs. It was generally conjectured that we were going to battle; but orders came immediately to march. We marched some distance before light. By sunrise the enemy had landed from their boats, and pursued us so closely as to fire on our rear.[2] A large body of the enemy followed us all day but kept far behind as not to be wholly discovered. Their aim was to attack us suddenly the next morning, as they did.

Having just recovered from the measles, and not being able to march with the main body, I fell in the rear. The morning after our retreat, orders came very early for the troops to refresh and be ready for marching. Some were eating, some were cooking, and all in a very unfit posture for battle. Just as the sun rose, there was a cry *"the enemy are upon us."*—Looking round, I saw the enemy in line of battle.[3] Orders came to lay down our packs and be ready for action. The fire instantly began. We were but few in number compared to the enemy. At the commencement of the battle, many of our party retreated back into the woods. Capt. Carr came up and says, "My lads, advance, we shall beat them yet." A few of us followed him in view of the enemy. Every man was trying to secure himself behind girdled trees, which were standing on the place of action. I made shelter for myself and discharged my piece. Having loaded again and taken aim, my piece missed fire. I brought the same a second time to my face; but before I had time to discharge it, I received a musket ball in the small of my back and fell with my gun cocked. My uncle Daniel Foster standing but little distance from me, I make out to crawl to him and spoke to him. He and another man lifted me and carried me back some distance and laid me down behind a large tree, where was another man crying out most bitterly with a grievous wound. By this time I had bled so freely, I was very weak and faint. I observed the enemy were likely to gain the ground. Our men began to retreat and the enemy to advance. Having no friend to afford me any relief, every one taking care of himself, all things looked very shocking to me; to remain where I was and fall into the hands of the enemy, especially in the condition I was in, expecting to receive no mercy. It came into my mind to conceal myself from them if possible. I made use of my hands and knees, as well as I could, and crawled about two rods among some small brush and got under a log. Here I lay concealed from the enemy, who came instantly to the place I lay wounded at. What became of my distressed partner I know not. The enemy pursued our men in great haste. Some of them came over the log where I lay. Some came so near I could almost touch them. I was not discovered by the enemy till the battle was over. When they were picking up the dead and wounded among the brush and logs, I heard them coming towards me. I began to be much terrified, least I should be found. I flattered myself that our men would come back after the battle was over and take me off; but to my great surprise, two of the enemy came so nigh, I heard one of them say, "Here is one of the rebels." I lay flat on my face across my hands, rolled in my blood. I dared not stir, being afraid they meant me by saying, "Here is one of the rebels." They soon came to me and pulled off my shoes, supposing me to be dead. I looked up and spoke, telling them I was their prisoner, and begged to be used well. "Damn you, says one, you deserve to be used well, don't you? What's such a young rebel as you fighting for?" One of these men was an officer, who appeared to be a pretty sort of a man. He spoke to the soldier, who had taken my shoes, and says, "Give back the shoes and help the man into camp." My shoes were given back by the soldier according to order. The soldier then raised me on to my feet and conducted to the British camp. Here I found a number of my brother soldiers in the same situation of myself. I was laid on the ground and remained in this posture till the afternoon, before my wound was dressed. Two doctors came to my assistance. They raised me up and examined my back. One of them says, "My lad, you stood a narrow chance; had the ball gone in or out half its bigness, you must have been killed instantly." I asked him if he thought there was any prospect of my getting well again. He answered, "There is some prospect." I concluded by his reply, he considered my case hazardous. The Doctors appeared to be very kind and faithful. They pulled several pieces of my clothes from my wound, which were forced in by the ball I received.

Some of the enemy were very kind; while others were very spiteful and malicious. One of them came and took my silver shoe buckles and left me an old pair of brass ones, and said, *exchange was no robbery;* but I thought it robbery at a high rate. Another came and took off my neck handkerchief. An old negro came and took my fife, which I considered as the greatest insult I had received while with the enemy. The Indians often came and abused us with their language; calling us Yankees and rebels; but they were not allowed to injure us. I was stripped of every thing valuable about me.

The enemy soon marched back to Ticonderoga, and left only a few to take care of the wounded. I was treated as well as I could expect. Doctor Haze was the head Doctor, and he took true care that the prisoners were well treated. Doctor Blocksom, an under surgeon, appeared to be very kind indeed: he was the one, who had the care of me: he never gave me any insulting or abusive language: he sometimes would say, "Well, my lad, think you'll be willing to list in the King's service, if you should get well?" My answer was always *no*. The officers would flatter me to list in their service; telling me they were very sure to conquer the country, since they had got our strongest post. I told them I should not list.

But among all the troubles I met with, I received particular favors from two of the British. This conduct appeared to me very remarkable; why or wherefore it should be, I knew not; but he, who hath the hearts of all men in his hands, gave me favor in their sight. They would often visit me, and ask me if I wanted any thing to eat or drink. If I did, I had it. The first time one of these friends came to me, was soon after I was brought to camp. As I lay on the ground, he asked me if I did not want a bed to lie on: I told him I did: he goes and gets a large hemlock bark, and finding many old coats and overalls, taken from the dead and wounded, and putting them in the bark, made me a bed, and laid me into it. He built a shelter over me with barks, to keep the rain from me, which was a great kindness as it rained exceedingly hard the next night. He went to a spring and brought me water as often as I wanted, which was very often, being very dry; my loss of blood occasioning much thirst. He asked me, also, if I wanted to eat. I answered yes; for having eat very little that day, I was very faint and hungry. He told me, he did not know as it was in his power to procure any thing for me, but would go and try. After an absence of considerable time (certainly the time seemed long) he returned with a piece of boiled pork and broiled liver, telling me this was all the food he could get. I thanked him and told him it was very good.

The next day he came and told me he had orders to march and must therefore leave me; was very sorry he could stay no longer with me; but hoped somebody would take good care of me; taking me by the hand he wished me well and left me.

The loss of so good a friend grieved me extremely; but I soon heard that my other friend was ordered to stay behind to help take care of the wounded. My spirits, which before were very much depressed, when I heard of this, were much exhilarated; and once more I felt tolerably happy. The difference in mankind never struck me more sensibly than while a prisoner. Some would do every thing in their power to make me comfortable and cheerful; while others abused me with the vilest of language; telling me that the prisoners would all be hanged; that they would drive all the damned rebels into the sea, and that their next winter quarters would be in Boston. They certainly wintered in Boston; but to their great disappointment and chagrin, as prisoners of war.

But to return. My wound being now a little better, I began to think of making my escape from the enemy. Two of my fellow prisoners agreed to accompany me; one of them being well acquainted with the way to Ottercreek. This plan, however, failed; for, before we had an opportunity for making our escape, Doctor Haze called upon my companions to be ready to march for Ticonderoga; telling them that the next morning they must leave this place. Thus I found, that as soon as the prisoners were able to ride, they were ordered to Ticonderoga. Being thus disappointed I begged of the Doctor to let me go with them. Says he, "You are very dangerously wounded, and it is improper for you to ride so far yet; but as soon as you are able you shall go." Being thus defeated I again resolved to run away, even if I went alone, and it was not long before I had an opportunity. As all the prisoners were sent off except us, who were badly wounded, they thought it unnecessary to guard us very closely. I soon was able to go to the spring, which was at a little distance from camp. Thither I often went for water for myself and the Hessians, who, by the way, appeared to be pleased with me, for I often waited upon them; brought them water, made their beds, &c. and I found I fared the better for it. I often walked out into the woods where we had the battle; went to the tree where I was shot down; observed the trees that were very much marked with the balls. One day as I was looking around, I found a few leaves of a bible; these I carried into the camp and diverted myself by reading them; for I felt much more contented when I had something to read. My friend, whom I have before mentioned, one day brought me a very good book; which he told me to keep as a present from him. This I heartily thanked him for, and whenever I was tired by walking, would lay down and read.

On the 22d of July, a number of men came down from Ticonderoga, with horses and litters sufficient to carry off the remainder of the wounded. Doctor Haze came to us and told us, that tomorrow we should all be carried where we should have better care taken of us. Says he, "I will send the orderly sergeant, who will see that your bloody clothes are well washed." This, he thought, would be very agreeable news to us. I pretended to be very much pleased, though I was determined never to go. I told the person, who lay next to me, that I intended to run away; desired him to make them believe I had taken the north road, if they inclined to pursue me, for I should take the south. Says he, "I will do all in my power to assist you, and wish it was possible for me to go with you."

I made it my business that day to procure provision sufficient for my journey. I had spared a little bread from my daily allowance, and although dry and mouldy, yet it was the best to be had. I had left, a large jack-knife the enemy had not robbed me of; I sold this for a pint of wine, thinking it would do me more good on my march than the knife, as I found afterwards it did. The wine I put in a bottle and carefully stowed it in my pocket. I was hard put to it to get my shirt washed and dried before evening. However, agreeing with some to make their beds if they would dry my shirt, it was ready to put on by dark. I then went to my tent, took of my coat and jacket, and put on my clean shirt over my dirty one, and having filled my pockets with the little provision I had saved, I began my march homeward shoeless; reflecting what I should do for so material part of my cloathing. It came into my mind that one Jonathan Lambart a day or two before had died of his wounds and left a good pair of shoes. Supposing my right to them equal to any other person, I took them and put them on, hereby reversing the old proverb, *He that waits for dead men's shoes will go barefoot.*[4]

It being dark I went out undiscovered and steered into the woods. After going a little way, I turned into the road and made a halt. Now was the trying scene! The night being very dark, every thing before me appeared gloomy and discouraging; my wound was far from being healed; my strength much reduced by the loss of blood, pain, and poor living: thus situated to travel alone, I knew not where, having no knowledge of the way, I thought it would be highly presumptuous. How far I should have to travel before I could reach any inhabitants, I could not tell: Indians, I supposed, were lurking about, and probably I might be beset by them and murdered or carried back; and if I avoid them, perhaps perish in the wilderness. Reflecting upon these things, my resolution began to flag, and I thought it most prudent to return and take my fate. I turned about and went back a few rods, when the following words struck me as if whispered in my ear: *Put not your hand to the plough and look back.*[5] I immediately turned about again, fully resolved to pursue my journey through the woods; but before morning, had I been possessed of millions of gold, I would freely have given the whole to have been once more with the enemy. The road in which I had to travel, was one newly opened, leading from Hubbartston to Ottercreek. The night being dark and the road very crooked, I found it very difficult to keep it; often running against trees and rocks, before I knew I was out of it; and then it was with much trouble that I found it again, which sometimes I was obliged to do upon my hands and knees and often up to my knees in mire.

About 12 o'clock I heard something coming towards me, what it could be I knew not. I, however, halted and looked back; it was so dark, I was at a loss to determine what it was; but thought it looked like a dog. That a dog should be so far from inhabitants, I thought very strange. I at once concluded that he belonged to the Indians, and that they were not far off. I however ventured to speak to him, and he immediately came to me; I stroked him and gave him a piece of my mouldy bread, which he eat and soon appeared to be fond of me. At first I was afraid he would betray me to the Indians; but soon found him of much service to me; for, after he came to me, I had not gone far, before I heard the noise of some wild beast. What is was, I could not tell. I had just set down to rest me, with my back against a tree, my wound being very painful. As the beast came towards me, my dog appeared very much frightened; lay close down by me and trembled as if he expected to be torn in pieces. I now began to be much terrified; I however set very still, knowing it would do no good to run. He came within two rods of me, and stopped. I was unable to determine what it was, but supposed it was a wolf. I soon found I was not mistaken. After looking at me sometime, he turned about and went off; but before long returned with a large reinforcement. In his absence I exerted myself to the utmost to get forward, fearing he would be after me again. After travelling about half an hour, I was alarmed with a most horrid howling, which I supposed to be near the tree which I rested by. Judge what my feelings were, when I found these beasts of prey were pursuing me, and expecting every minute to be devoured by them. But in the midst of this trouble, to my infinite joy, I discovered fires but a little way before me, which, from several circumstances, I was sure were not built by Indians; I therefore at once concluded they were the fires of some scouting party of Americans, and I made great haste to get to them, lest I should be overtaken by the wolves, which were now but a little behind. I approached so near the fires as to hear men talk, when I immediately discovered them to be enemies. Thus disappointed, I knew not what course to take: If I continued in the woods, I should be devoured by wild beasts; for having eat of the bodies which were left on the field of battle, they continued lurking for more. If I gave myself up to the enemy, I should certainly be carried back to Ticonderoga, and from there to Canada, and probably fare none the better for attempting to run away. Which way to escape I knew not; I turned a little out of the path and lay down on the ground to hear what was said by the enemy, expecting every minute they would discover me; the darkness of the night however, prevented. These howling beasts approached as near the fires as they dared, when they halted and continued their horrid yell for some time, being afraid to come so nigh as I was. After the howling had ceased, I began to think of getting round the enemy's camp; being pretty certain, that as yet, I was not discovered. I arose from the ground and took a course, which I thought would carry me round the enemy. After travelling a little way, I came to the foot of a high mountain; to go round it I thought would carry me too much out of my course; I resolved therefore to ascend it; with much difficulty I arrived at the top, then took a tack to the right; travelling that course sometime, I found I was bewildered and lost, and which way to go to find the road again I knew not, having neither moon nor stars to direct me; so I wandered abut in this wilderness till almost day, when I became so fatigued and worried, that I was obliged to lay down again: Judge what a persons feelings must be in such a situation.

I now repented of my ever leaving the enemy. Here I was lost in the woods with but a very little provision, my wounds extremely painful, and, to sum all, little or no prospect of ever seeing human beings again. Thus I lay and reflected, my dog walking round me like a faithful sentinel, till at length I fell asleep; but was soon alarmed with the noise of cannon, which I concluded by the direction must be at Ticonderoga. Never was sound more grateful to my ears than this cannon. I thought I might possibly live to reach the place, and though an enemy's camp, I would have given any thing to be with them again.

Soon after the morning gun was fired, I heard the drums beat in the camp which I had visited in the night; this noise was still more grateful, for I was now sure they were not at a great distance. With much difficulty I got on to my legs again, with a determination to go to their camp. I found however I could scarcely stand, for having laid down when I was very sweaty, I had taken cold, and was so stiff and sore, could hardly move. I now had recourse to my little bottle of wine, which relieved me very much, and then began to march towards the drums, which still continued beating.

After travelling a little way, I heard a cock crow, which appeared to be near the drums. I thought it of little consequence which object to pursue, both being nearly in the same direction. But the noise of the drums pretty soon ceased, and I stared for the other object, which soon brought me into open land and in sight of a house. I got to the door just as the man arose from his bed, who met me. After the usual compliments, I asked him how far it was to the British encampment? He answered about fifty rods. "Do you want to go to them?" says he. I never was more at a stand what reply to make. As none of the enemy were about the house, I thought if I could persuade this man to befriend me, I possibly might still avoid them; but if he should prove to be a tory, and know from whence I came, he would certainly betray me. I stood perhaps a minute without saying a word. He seeing my confusion spoke again to me; "Come, says he, come into the house." I went in and sat down. I will tell you, says I, what I want, if you promise not to hurt me. He replied, "I will not injure you, if you do no injury to us." This answer did not satisfy me, for as yet I could not tell whether he would be a friend or foe. I sat and viewed him for some minutes, and at last resolved to tell him from whence I came and where I wished to go, let the event be what it would. I was a soldier, said I, in the continental army, was dangerously wounded and taken prisoner, had made my escape from the enemy, and, after much fatigue and peril, had got through the woods, being directed to this house by the crowing of a cock. He smiled and said, "You have been rightly directed, for had you gone to either of my neighbors, you undoubtedly would have been carried to the enemy again; you have now found a friend who will if possible protect you. It is true they have forced me to take the oath of allegiance to the king; but I sincerely hope the Americans will finally prevail, for I believe their cause to be just and equitable; should they know of my harboring rebels, as they call us, I certainly should suffer for it. Any thing I can do for you without exposing my own life, I will do." I thanked him for his kindness, and desired him not to expose himself on my account.

After giving me something to eat and drink, he concealed me in a chamber, where, he said I might stay till the dew was off, and then must go out into some secret place in the bushes, there to continue till night; this he said was necessary as the enemy were often plundering about his house, and if I continued in it, would probably be discovered, which would ruin him. A little boy was set as a sentinel at the door, who was to give notice if any of the enemy came near. I had not been in the house half an hour, before a number of them came in, but with no other design than to buy some rum and milk, and to borrow a pot for cooking.

As soon as they were gone, the woman came into the chamber to dress my wound. She washed it with rum, applied dressings, and bound it up as well as she could. She showed every mark of kindness to me; but her husband, whose name was Moulton, in a day or two after I got to his house, was pressed by the enemy to bring stores from Skeensborough[6] with his team, and I never saw the good old man any more. His wife was in much trouble, least the enemy should find me in the house and be so enraged as to kill all the family. She permitted her little boy to guide me to the bushes, where I might secrete myself; she gave me a blanket to lie on. The boy went with me to my lurking place, that I might be easily found, so as to receive refreshment. When night came on, I was called by the boy to the house again, and took my old stand in the chamber; the woman fearing I should receive injury by lodging out of doors. She informed me that a man would lodge there that night, who was a tory, and brother-in-law to her husband; one who had actually taken arms against his country. I told her, I apprehended danger from tarrying in the house; she said there would not be any; I then lay snug in my straw.

In a short time the tory came for some drink; the indiscreet woman told him she had an American in her chamber, who had been taken prisoner by the British and had escaped. He asked her what kind of man I was: She told him I was a young fellow and wanted much to get home, and begged that I might not be taken back to the enemy or betrayed. His answer was very rough, and I began to think I was gone for it. I expected to be forced back; but the woman interceding so hard for me, softened the ferocity of my tory enemy. Knowing I was discovered, I crawled from my hiding place and began a conversation with the man. He asked me if I belonged to the rebel service? I told him I belonged to the continental service. "What is that, says he, but the rebel service." He addressed me in very insolent language, and said he was very sorry to have me leave the king's troops in the manner I had done, and he would have me to know I was in his hands. I was patient and mild in my situation, telling him I was at his disposal. My good mistress often put in a word on my behalf.

After some time spent in this way, the man asked me if he should chance to be taken, and in my power as I was in his, whether I would let him escape? I told him I should. "Then, says he, if you will promise this, I will not detain you; also, that if you are retaken before you reach home, you will not inform, that you have seen me, or been at my brothers." I gave him my promise. His advice to me was immediately to set out, for if I should stay long I might be picked up by some body or other; "And, says he, I advise you to travel in the night and hide in the day, for many volunteers are reconnoitering up and down the county." I concluded to travel; but my feeling landlady thought it best to stay a few days longer. My friend tory said it was best for me to travel as soon as possible. "If you are determined to go to night, said the woman, I will dress your wound and give you food for your journey." I told her I would go as soon as possible. She then dressed my wound for the last time, and filled my pockets with good provision.

After thanking her for her kindness, it being all the compensation I could make, and I believe all that she desired, I left her.

But before I proceed on my journey, I must just tell you, that my dog, who had accompanied me through many dangers, I was obliged to drive from me; when in the chamber he would commonly lay at the foot of the stairs. Mrs. Moulton often told me, she was afraid he would betray me, for as the enemy were often in, should they see the dog, might suspect that somebody was in the chamber. I told her, with much regret, to drive him away; she with her little boy tried all in their power to get rid of him, but in vain; the dog would stay about the house; at length she called me to drive him away; I came down, and after much difficulty effected it.

But to return. After being told the course I must take, I began my journey in the night, which was dark and cloudy, through the woods. I had not travelled more than two hours, before I got lost. I concluded I had missed the road, and having reached the end of the one I was then in, I began to think of going back. My wound began to be very painful, and I was so sore. I could scarcely go. While I was seeking for the road again, there came up a thunder shower, and rained extremely fast. I crawled into an old forsaken hovel, which was near, and lay till the shower was over; then went back about half a mile and found the road once more. The road being newly opened through the woods was very bad, and it was with much difficulty I could get along, often tumbling over roots and stones, and sometimes up to my knees in mire. I once fell and was obliged to lay several minutes, before I could recover myself.

About twelve o'clock at night, as I was walking in this wilderness, I was surprised by two large wild animals, which lay close by the road, and started up as soon as they saw me, run a few rods and turned about towards me; whether they were bears or wolves, I could not tell; I was however exceedingly terrified, and would have given any thing for my dog again. One of them followed me for a long time; sometimes would come close to me, and at others, kept at a considerable distance. At last, he got discouraged and left me, and certainly I did not regret his absence.

At day light, I came into open land, and discovered a house belonging to Col. Meads. I was not a little rejoiced to see his house, as I knew he would be a friend to me; but my joy was of short continuance, for as soon as I looked into the door, I saw marks of the enemy; every thing belonging to the house being carried off or destroyed. I thought it not prudent to go into the house lest some of the enemy might be within; so I passed on as fast as possible; it now began to grow light, and what to do with myself I could not tell. My friends had advised me to lay concealed in the day time and travel in the night.

When I viewed the depredations the enemy had made on the inhabitants, and finding many of them fled; not knowing how far I must travel to find friends, and my wound being very troublesome, I reflected long, whether to tarry and be made prisoner, or push forward through a dreary wilderness; death seemed to threaten me on all sides; however, I collected resolution sufficient to make to the east; I conceived myself exposed by my uniform and bloody clothes; to prevent a discovery by any who should be an enemy, I took off my shirt and put it over my coat, by which my uniform was covered; in this line I marched: it being the orders of the British for all tories, who came to join them, to appear in this dress, I considered myself protected. I travelled till the middle of the day before I saw any person; I then met a man driving cattle, as I supposed to the enemy. He examined me closely, and enquired if I was furnished with a pass? I gave him plausible answers to all his questions, and so far satisfied him as to proceed unmolested. I enquired of him, if he knew one Joshua Priest; he told me he did, and very readily directed me to the place where he lived. Leaving this man, I had not travelled far, before I met a number more, armed; being within about fifty rods of them, I thought to hide myself, but found I could not: I then made towards them, without any apparent fear. Coming up to them, I expected a strict examination; but they only asked me how far is was to such a town: I informed them as well as I could, and pushed on my way.

Being within a mile and a half of said Priest's, I saw two men making towards me: They came to a fence and stopped: I heard them say, "Let's examine this fellow, and know what his business is." One of them asked me where I was going: I told him to Joshua Priest's: he asked me my business there: I answered him, upon no bad errand: He says, "You are a spy:" I told him I was no spy; I did not like the fellow's looks, therefore dropped the conversation with him, believing he was one of the enemy. I resolved not to converse with any one, till I had arrived at Priest's unless compelled to. Being almost overcome with fatigue, I wished for rest; however, these men seemed determined to stop me or do me some mischief, for when I walked on, they followed me upon the run, and in great rage told me, I should go no farther, until I had made known to them who and what I was: saying, they had asked me a civil question, and they required a civil answer. I told them if they would go to Priest's, I would tell them all the truth, and satisfy them entirely; repeating to them I was no spy. They said they did not mean to leave me till they were satisfied respecting me. I then, in short, told them what had befel in the whole, and added, that I was well acquainted with Priest, and intended to tarry with him some time.

We all arrived at Priest's, who at first did not recollect me. After some pause, he told me he was surprised to see me, as my father had informed him I was slain at Hubbardton. I told him, I was yet alive; but had received a bad wound. His family soon dressed my wound and made me comfortable. I then in the presence and hearing of my tory followers, told Priest the story of my captivity and escape; also repeated the insolent language used by the tories towards our people, when prisoners with the enemy; finding Priest my friend, I said many severe things against the tories, and fixed my countenance sternly on those fellows, who had pretended to lord it over me and stop me on my way. They bore all without saying a word; but looked as *surly as bulls*.

I soon found these tory gentry had premeditated carrying me back, and were seeking help to prosecute their design. My friend Priest loaded his gun, and said he would give them a grist, if they dared come after me; but failing of getting any persons to join them, I was not molested.

I could often hear of my tory followers threatenings against me, to take me back, saying, I should be able to fight again, and do injury to the enemy. I feared these tories would do hurt; but my fears were quieted by finding the neighbors were my friends, and would afford me their protection. But I will write no more of tory plans.

After being at Priest's about ten days, there came, one morning, a number of persons to see me, and appeared very friendly and much concerned, lest I should be taken by the enemy. They informed me a man had arrived from Burgoyne's army, and said a party of Indians was to be sent forward to guard the town where I was, and protect the tories and their property: our people coming twice while I was at Priest's to take tory property. These people told me an honest story, and advised me to travel immediately. Being desirous to get home, I told my friend Priest I would not stay any longer. He says, "Don't be feared, I apprehend no danger from the Indians; tarry yet awhile for your wound is not healed; your are not able to travel through the woods: but do as you think best." These men cried out, "Escape, escape, for your life; the Indians will be upon you before tomorrow night."

Having resolved to go on, my friends furnished me with provision sufficient for my journey. Without doubts and fears I went on my way, and, after travelling all day, I arrived at a place called Ludlow. From this town the people all fled and left their habitations: Great was my disappointment! I spent the night in a melancholy manner; having neither fire nor bed to comfort my shivering and impaired body.

About day, I set out from the dreary house, which had sheltered me in the night. By travelling, I found I had taken cold, and that my wound was very painful. Desponding, I thought it best to go back about seven miles to some inhabitants, rather than to proceed homeward. Just before night, I arrived at the place of the inhabitants, seven miles back, who received me kindly, and took special care of my wound.

Just before sunset of the third day after my departure, I came to my old friend Priest's again, who appeared very glad to see me. Now it was not any friendship in my tory visitors, who advised me to escape, but for fear I should betray them; their reports afterwards proving all false.

At my old friends I stayed six weeks; in the mean time my wound almost healed. I was hospitably entertained by him.

Having heard that one Mr. Atwell, who belonged to New Marlborough, was in the neighborhood with a team to move a family, I agreed with him for a horse to ride. After a journey of a few days I safely arrived at New-Ipswich and once more participated the pleasure of seeing and enjoying my friends and acquaintance, and *no enemy to make me afraid.*

Signature

The End

Signature

Signature

[*The following three paragraphs are added to the end of the narrative in the 1813 edition.*]

Not long afterwards, an officer from the army hearing of my return ordered me to be arrested and returned to the main body of the American army, although my wound was scarcely healed. In a few weeks, I joined my corps, then stationed in Pennsylvania; having yet two years to serve my country in the tented field.

We afterwards went on an expedition against the Indians, to the Genesco country, where we burnt the huts and destroyed the corn of the hostile Savages—but found them little disposed to meet us in the open field. Finding few enemies in that quarter to contend with, we received, and gladly obeyed orders to return to New-England, where we remained the ensuing autumn. Nothing more of importance, to me or the reader, occurred, until the *three long years* rolled away, and I obtained my discharge.

And now, kind reader, wishing that you may forever remain ignorant of the real sufferings of the veteran soldier, from hunger and cold, from sickness and captivity, I bid you a cordial adieu.

EBENEZER FLETCHER.
New-Ipswich, Jan. 1813.

Notes

1. Fort originally built by the French in 1755 on Lake Champlain.
2. The British Army under General Burgoyne.
3. The battle in which Fletcher participated took place in Hubbardton, Vermont, on July 7, 1777.

4. Often attributed as a Danish proverb. In the first edition "proverb" is spelled "proverd." This error is corrected in subsequent editions.

5. A paraphrase of Luke 9:62, which reads in the King James Version of the New Testament: "No man, having put his hand to the plough, and looking back, is fit for the kingdom of God."

6. Skeensborough is a town at the head of Lake Champlain, since renamed Whitehall.

A Narrative of the Life and Adventures of Venture, a Native of Africa: But a Resident above Sixty Years in the United States of America

Although not widely read today, the story of the life of Venture Smith (1798) is one of the most significant early slave narratives in American print culture. Anthologized as recently as 1996 in *Unchained Voices*, edited by Vincent Carretta, and again in 1997 in *American Voices, American Lives*, edited by Wayne Franklin (and currently available in part or whole on numerous Internet sites of varying degrees of academic credibility), the narrative of Venture Smith has enjoyed a long print life. First published in 1798, after the illiterate Smith apparently recited his story to Elisha Niles, a former schoolteacher from East Haddam, Connecticut, *A Narrative of the Life and Adventures of Venture, a Native of Africa: But a resident above sixty years in the United States of America* is the story of a man, brought in chains from Africa, who toils and buys his freedom—and that of his family—quite literally by the sweat of his own brow.

The narrative is also one of the most interesting formulations of the myth of the self-made man in American print culture, a myth that has become central to the cultural narrative of American freedom and American exceptionalism. Venture boasts of his immense capacity for grueling physical labor and credits it as the means by which his own liberty, as well as the liberty of his family and other African Americans, is secured. It is somewhat troubling, however, that he also seems to perceive his own familial and personal relationships primarily in the same economic terms he uses to haggle with his various masters over compensation for his labor; at times his narrative voice sounds similar to those same men who owned him as a chattel slave.

Another interesting feature of the narrative arises from the fact that, although his life in America coincides with the colonies' fight for independence from Britain, he refers neither to war nor politics in his narrative. According to Wayne Franklin, "Venture Smith's narrative stretches back well before the Revolution, in which Venture's son Cuff fought, but the war is never mentioned by Venture himself, who had bought his own freedom during the Stamp Act crisis and that of his daughter Hannah in 1776" (294). In his preface to the original narrative, Niles attempts to establish this link between Venture and the Revolutionary era by describing him as "a Franklin and a Washington, in a state of nature, or rather in a state of slavery." Wayne Franklin concludes that "as the hero of his own account, Venture Smith was a strange legatee of the war he never mentioned" (295).

The transcribed version of Venture's story saw three printings during 1835, each containing the description "published by a descendant of Venture," raising the possibility that Venture's life—even after his death—once again can be viewed as a bartered commodity, helping to provide the financial means necessary to support his family. The version included in this volume is the first edition published in 1798.

What makes Venture Smith's story so intriguing as a slave narrative is the fact that he relates a good deal of information on his own African history, including his formative years and his abduction into bondage. The audience is offered a glimpse into the tribal culture of Guinea, Africa, a society far removed from the early American way of life—or so it would seem. Venture recounts his childhood and states that he is of noble birth. He then describes his homeland and the government of his father's kingdom in egalitarian terms, similar to those being purported by the founders of the new American republic: "[His father] was a man of remarkable strength and resolution, affable, kind and gentle, ruling with equity and moderation." This African king can be viewed as a model for early democratic leaders. Venture goes on to describe his father's response to an invading army's attempt to capture his people by suggesting that "[m]y father told the messenger he would comply rather than that his subjects should be deprived of their rights and privileges." Venture describes his father and his kingdom as if both came straight out of the Enlightenment and the age of liberal democratic revolution.

Venture's obsession with money and profit after he is freed stands out as a major theme in the narrative. Using his capacity for labor and his unique position in an emerging northern colonial economy, an economy slowly ridding itself of slavery and other unproductive financial influences, Venture finds great success, and as a result he inevitably associates the very concept of freedom with money and capital. He amasses a small fortune and suggests that this is the best way for all African Americans to secure their liberty and equality. He explains at the close of his narrative, "My freedom is a privilege which nothing else can equal," despite the fact that, for him, his freedom was always commensurate with a cash equivalent.

RJ

Preface

The following account of the life of VENTURE, is a relation of simple facts, in which nothing is added in substance to what he related himself. Many other interesting and curious passages of his life might have been inserted; but on account of the bulk to which they must necessarily have swelled this narrative, they were omitted. If any should suspect the truth of what is here related, they are referred to people now living who are acquainted with most of the facts mentioned in the narrative.

The reader is here presented with an account, not of a renowned politician or warrior, but of an untutored African slave, brought into this Christian country at eight years of age, wholly destitute of all education but what he received in common with other domesticated animals, enjoying no advantages that could lead him to suppose himself superior to the beasts, his fellow servants. And if he shall derive no other advantage from perusing this narrative, he may experience those sensations of shame and indignation, that will prove him to be not wholly destitute of every noble and generous feeling.

The subject of the following pages, had he received only a common education, might have been a man of high respectability and usefulness; and had his education been suited to his genius, he might have been an ornament and an honor to human nature. It may perhaps, not be unpleasing to see the efforts of a great mind wholly uncultivated, enfeebled and depressed by slavery, and struggling under every disadvantage.—The reader may here see a Franklin and a Washington, in a state of nature, or rather in a state of slavery. Destitute as he is of all education, and broken by hardships and infirmities of age, he still exhibits striking traces of native ingenuity and good sense.

This narrative exhibits a pattern of honesty, prudence and industry, to people of his own colour; and perhaps some white people would not find themselves degraded by imitating such an example.

The following account is published in compliance with the earnest desire of the subject of it, and likewise a number of respectable persons who are acquainted with him.

A

NARRATIVE

OF THE

LIFE AND ADVENTURES

OF

VENTURE,

A NATIVE OF AFRICA:

*But resident above sixty years in the United States of
America.*

RELATED BY HIMSELF.

New-London :
PRINTED BY C. HOLT, AT THE BEE-OFFICE.
1798.

Title page of *A Narrative of the Life and Adventures of Venture,
a Native of Africa* (1798 edition; courtesy of the American
Antiquarian Society)

A Narrative of the Life, &c

Chapter I.

Containing an Account of His Life, from His Birth to the Time of His Leaving His Native Country.

I was born at Dukandarra,[1] in Guinea, about the year 1729. My father's name was Saungm Furro, Prince of the Tribe of Dukandarra. My father had three wives. Polygamy was not uncommon in that country, especially among the rich, as every man was allowed to keep as many wives as he could maintain. By his first wife he had three children. The eldest of them was myself, named by my father, Broteer. The other two were named Cundazo and Soozaduka. My father had two children by his second wife, and one by his third. I descended from a very large, tall and stout race of beings, much larger than the generality of people in other parts of the globe, being commonly considerable above six feet in height, and every way well proportioned.

The first thing worthy of notice which I remember was, a contention between my father and mother, on account of my father's marrying his third wife without the consent of his first and eldest, which was contrary to the custom generally observed among my countrymen. In consequence of this rupture, my mother left her husband and country, and travelled away with her three children to the eastward. I was then five years old. She took not the least sustenance along with her, to support either herself or children. I was able to travel along by her side; the other two of her offspring she carried one on her back, and the other being a sucking child, in her arms. When we became hungry, my mother used to set us down on the ground, and gather some of the fruits which grew spontaneously in that climate. These served us for food on the way. At night we all lay down together in the most secure place we could find, and reposed ourselves until morning. Though there were many noxious animals there; yet so kind was our Almighty protector, that none of them were ever permitted to hurt or molest us. Thus we went on our journey until the second day after our departure from Dukandarra, when we came to the entrance of a great desert. During our travel in that we were often affrighted with the doleful howlings and yellings of wolves, lions, and other animals. After five days travel we came to the end of this desert, and immediately entered into a beautiful and extensive interval country. Here my mother was pleased to stop and seek a refuge for me. She left me at the house of a very rich farmer. I was then, as I should judge, not less than one hundred and forty miles from my native place, separated from all my relations and acquaintance. At this place my mother took her farewell of me, and set out for her own country. My new guardian, as I shall call the man with whom I was left, put me into the business of tending sheep, immediately after I was left with him. The flock which I kept with the assistance of a boy, consisted of about forty. We drove them every morning between two and three miles to pasture, into the wide and delightful plains. When night drew on, we drove them home and secured them in the cote.[2] In this round I continued during my stay there. One incident which befel me when I was driving my flock from pasture, was so dreadful to me in that age, and is to this time so fresh in my memory, that I cannot help noticing it in this place. Two large dogs sallied out of a certain house and set upon me. One of them took me by the arm, and the other by the thigh, and before their master could come and relieve me, they lacerated my flesh to such a degree, that the scars are very visible to the present day. My master was immediately sent for. He came and hurried me home, as I was unable to go myself on account of my wounds. Nothing remarkable happened afterwards until my father sent for me to return home.

Before I dismiss this country, I must just inform my reader what I remember concerning this place. A large river runs through this country in a westerly course. The land for a great way on each side is flat and level, hedged in by a considerable rise of the country at a great distance from it. It scarce ever rains there, yet the land is fertile; great dews fall in the night which refresh the soil. About the latter end of June or first of July, the river begins to rise, and gradually increases until it has inundated the country for a great distance, to the height of seven or eight feet. This brings on a slime which enriches the land surprisingly. When the river had subsided, the natives begin to sow and plant, and the vegetation is exceeding rapid. Near this rich river my guardian's land lay. He possessed, I cannot exactly tell how much, yet this I am certain of respecting it, that he owned an immense tract. He possessed likewise a great many cattle and goats. During my stay with him I was kindly used, and with as much tenderness, for what I saw, as his only son, although I was an entire stranger to him, remote from friends and relations. The principal occupations of the inhabitants there, were the cultivation of the soil and the care of their flocks. They were a people pretty similar in every respect to that of mine, except in their persons, which were not so tall and stout. They appeared to be very kind and friendly. I will now return to my departure from that place.

My father sent a man and a horse after me. After settling with my guardian for keeping me, he took me away and went for home. It was then about one year since my mother brought me here. Nothing remarkable occured to us on our journey until we arrived safe home.

I found then that the difference between my parents had been made up previous to their sending for me. On my return, I was received both by my father and mother with great joy and affection, and was once more restored to my parental dwelling in peace and happiness. I was then about six years old.

Not more than six weeks had passed after my return, before a message was brought by an inhabitant of the place where I lived the preceding year to my father, that that place had been invaded by a numerous army, from a nation not far distant, furnished with musical instruments, and all kinds of arms then in use; that they were instigated by some white nation who equipped and sent them to subdue and possess the country; that his nation had made no preparation for war, having been for a long time in profound peace that they could not defend themselves against such a formidable train of invaders, and must therefore necessarily evacuate their lands to the fierce enemy, and fly to the protection of some chief; and that if he would permit them they should come under his rule and protection when they had to retreat from their own possessions. He was a kind and merciful prince, and therefore consented to these proposals.

He had scarcely returned to his nation with the message, before the whole of his people were obliged to retreat from their country, and come to my father's dominions.

He gave them every privilege and all the protection his government could afford. But they had not been there longer than four days before news came to them that the invaders had laid waste their country, and were coming speedily to destroy them in my father's territories. This affrighted them, and therefore they immediately pushed off to the southward, into the unknown countries there, and were never more heard of.

Two days after their retreat, the report turned out to be but too true. A detachment from the enemy came to my father and informed him, that the whole army was encamped not far out of his dominions, and would invade the territory and deprive his people of their liberties and rights, if he did not comply with the following terms. These were to pay them a large sum of money, three hundred fat cattle, and a great number of goats, sheep, asses, &c.

My father told the messenger he would comply rather than that his subjects should be deprived of their rights and privileges, which he was not then in circumstances to defend from so sudden an invasion. Upon turning out those articles, the enemy pledged their faith and honor that they would not attack him. On these he relied and therefore thought it unnecessary to be on his guard against the enemy. But their pledges of faith and honor proved no better than those of other unprincipled hostile nations; for a few days after a certain relation of the king came and informed him, that the enemy who sent terms of accommodation to him and received tribute to their satisfaction, yet meditated an attack upon his subjects by surprise, and that probably they would commence their attack in less than one day, and concluded with advising him, as he was not prepared for war, to order a speedy retreat of his family and subjects. He complied with this advice.

The same night which was fixed upon to retreat, my father and his family set off about break of day. The king and his two younger wives went in one company, and my mother and her children in another. We left our dwellings in succession, and my father's company went on first. We directed our course for a large shrub plain, some distance off, where we intended to conceal ourselves from the approaching enemy, until we could refresh and rest ourselves a little. But we presently found that our retreat was not secure. For having struck up a little fire for the purpose of cooking victuals, the enemy who happened to be encamped a little distance off, had sent out a scouting party who discovered us by the smoke of the fire, just as we were extinguishing it, and about to eat. As soon as we had finished eating, my father discovered the party, and immediately began to discharge arrows at them. This was what I first saw, and it alarmed both me and the women, who being unable to make any resistance, immediately betook ourselves to the tall thick reeds not far off, and left the old king to fight alone. For some time I beheld him from the reeds defending himself with great courage and firmness, till at last he was obliged to surrender himself into their hands.

They then came to us in the reeds, and the very first salute I had from them was a violent blow on the head with the fore part of a gun, and at the same time a grasp round the neck. I then had a rope put about my neck, as had all the women in the thicket with me, and were immediately led to my father, who was likewise pinioned and haltered for leading. In this condition we were all led to camp. The women and myself being pretty submissive, had tolerable treatment from the enemy, while my father was closely interrogated respecting his money which they knew he must have. But as he gave them no account of it, he was instantly cut and pounded on his body with great inhumanity, that he might be induced by the torture he suffered to make the discovery. All this availed not in the least to make him give up his money, but he despised all the tortures which they inflicted, until the continued exercise and increase of torment, obliged him to sink and expire. He thus died without informing his enemies of the place where his money lay. I saw him while he was thus tortured to death. The shocking scene is to this day fresh in my mind, and I have often been overcome while thinking on it. He was a man of remarkable stature. I should judge as much as six feet and six or seven inches high, two feet across his shoulders, and every way well proportioned. He was a man of remarkable strength and resolution, affable, kind and gentle, ruling with equity and moderation.

The army of the enemy was large, I should suppose consisting of about six thousand men. Their leader was called Baukurre. After destroying the old prince, they decamped and immediately marched towards the sea, lying to the west, taking with them myself and the women prisoners. In the march a scouting party was detached from the main army. To the leader of this party I was made waiter, having to carry his gun, &c.—As we were a scouting we came across a herd of fat cattle, consisting of about thirty in number. These we set upon, and immediately wrested from their keepers, and afterwards converted them into food for the army. The enemy had remarkable success in destroying the country wherever they went. For as far as they had penetrated, they laid the habitations waste and captured the people. The distance they had now brought me was about four hundred miles. All the march I had very hard tasks imposed on me, which I must perform on pain of punishment. I was obliged to carry on my head a large flat stone used for grinding our corn, weighing as I should suppose, as much as 25 pounds; besides victuals, mat and cooking utensils. Though I was pretty large and stout of my age, yet these burthens were very grievous to me, being only about six years and an half old.

We were then come to a place called Malagasco.—When we entered the place we could not see the least appearance of either houses or inhabitants, but upon stricter search found, that instead of houses above ground they had dens in the sides of hillocks, contiguous to ponds and streams of water. In these we perceived they had all hid themselves, as I suppose they usually did upon such occasions. In order to compel them to surrender, the enemy contrived to smoke them out with faggots. These they put to the entrance of the caves and set them on fire. While they were engaged in this business, to their great surprise some of them were desperately wounded with arrows which fell from above on them. This mystery they soon found out. They perceived that the enemy discharged these arrows through holes on the top of the dens directly into the air. Their weight brought them back, point downwards on their enemies heads, whilst they were smoking the inhabitants out. The points of their arrows were poisoned, but their enemy had an antidote for it, which they instantly applied to the wounded part. The smoke at last obliged the people to give themselves up. They came out of their caves, first spatting the palms of their hands together, and immediately after extended their arms, crossed at their wrists, ready to be bound and pinioned. I should judge that the dens above mentioned were extended about eight feet horizontally into the earth, six feet in height and as many wide. They were arched over head and lined with earth, which was of the clay kind, and made the surface of their walls firm and smooth.

The invaders then pinioned the prisoners of all ages and sexes indiscriminately, took their flocks and all their effects, and moved on their way towards the sea. On the march the prisoners were treated with clemency, on account of their being submissive and humble. Having come to the next tribe, the enemy laid siege and immediately took men, women, children, flocks, and all their valuable effects. They then went on to the next district which was contiguous to the sea, called in Africa, Anamaboo.[3] The enemies provisions were then almost spent, as well as their strength. The inhabitants knowing what conduct they had pursued, and what were their present intentions, improved the favorable opportunity, attacked them, and took enemy, prisoners, flocks and all their effects. I was then taken a second time. All of us were then put into the castle, and kept for market. On a certain time I and other prisoners were put on board a canoe, under our master, and rowed away to a vessel belonging to Rhode-Island, commanded by capt. Collingwood, and the mate Thomas Mumford. While we were going to the vessel, our master told us all to appear to the best possible advantage for sale. I was bought on board by one Robertson Mumford, steward of said vessel, for four gallons of rum, and a piece of calico, and called VENTURE, on account of his having purchased me with his own private venture. Thus I came by my name. All the slaves that were bought for that vessel's cargo, were two hundred and sixty.

Chapter II.

Containing an Account of His Life, from the Time of His Leaving Africa, to That of His Becoming Free.

After all the business was ended on the coast of Africa, the ship sailed from thence to Barbadoes. After an ordinary passage, except great mortality by the small pox, which broke out on board, we arrived at the island of Barbadoes: but when we reached it, there were found out of the two hundred and sixty that sailed from Africa, not more than two hundred alive. These were all sold, except myself and three more, to the planters there.

The vessel then sailed for Rhode-Island, and arrived there after a comfortable passage. Here my master sent me to live with one of his sisters, until he could carry me to Fisher's Island, the place of his residence. I had then completed my eighth year. After staying with his sister some time I was taken to my master's place to live.

When we arrived at Narraganset, my master went ashore in order to return a part of the way by land, and gave me charge of the keys of his trunks on board the vessel, and charged me not to deliver them up to any body, not even his father without his orders. To his directions I promised faithfully to conform. When I arrived with my master's articles at his house, my master's father asked me for his son's keys, as he wanted to see what the trunks contained. I told him that my master intrusted me with the care of them until he should return, and that I had given him my word to be faithful to the trust, and could not therefore give him or any other person the keys without my master's directions. He insisted that I should deliver to him the keys, threatening to punish me if I did not. But I let him know that he should not have them let him say what he would. He then laid aside trying to get them. But notwithstanding he appeared to give up trying to obtain them from me, yet I mistrusted that he would take some time when I was off my guard, either in the day time or at night to get them, therefore I slung them round my neck, and in the day time concealed them in my bosom, and at night I always lay with them under me, that no person might take them from me without being apprized of it. Thus I kept the keys from every body until my master came home. When he returned he asked where VENTURE was. As I was then within hearing, I came, and said, here sir, at your service. He asked me for his keys, and I immediately took them off my neck and reached them out to him. He took them, stroked my hair, and commended me, saying in presence of his father that his young VENTURE was so faithful that he never would have been able to have taken the keys from him but by violence; that he should not fear to trust him with his whole fortune, for that he had been in his native place so habituated to keeping his word, that he would sacrifice even his life to maintain it.

The first of the time of living at my master's own place, I was pretty much employed in the house at carding wool and other houshold business. In this situation I continued for some years, after which my master put me to work out of doors. After many proofs of my faithfulness and honesty, my master began to put great confidence in me. My behavior to him had as yet been submissive and obedient. I then began to have hard tasks imposed on me. Some of these were to pound four bushels of ears of corn every night in a barrel for the poultry, or be rigorously punished. At other seasons of the year I had to card wool until a very late hour. These tasks I had to perform when I was about nine years old. Some time after I had another difficulty and oppression which was greater than any I had ever experienced since I came into this country. This was to serve two masters. James Mumford, my master's son, when his father had gone from home in the morning, and given me a stint to perform that day, would order me to do *this* and *that* business different from what my master directed me. One day in particular, the authority which my master's son had set up, had like to have produced melancholy effects. For my master having set me off my business to perform that day and then left me to perform it, his son came up to me in the course of the day, big with authority, and commanded me very arrogantly to quit my present business and go directly about what he should order me. I replied to him that my master had given me so much to perform that day, and that I must therefore faithfully complete it in that time. He then broke out into a great rage, snatched a pitchfork and went to lay me over the head therewith; but I as soon got another and defended myself with it, or otherwise he might have murdered me in his outrage. He immediately called some people who were within hearing at work for him, and ordered them to take his hair rope and come and bind me with it. They all tried to bind me but in vain, tho' there were three assistants in number. My upstart master then desisted, put his pocket handkerchief before his eyes and went home with a design to tell his mother of the struggle with young VENTURE. He told her that their young VENTURE had become so stubborn that

he could not controul him, and asked her what he should do with him. In the
mean time I recovered my temper, voluntarily caused myself to be bound by the
same men who tried in vain before, and carried before my young master, that he
might do what he pleased with me. He took me to a gallows made for the purpose
of hanging cattle on, and suspended me on it. Afterwards he ordered one of the
hands to go to the peach orchard and cut him three dozen of whips to punish
me with. These were brought to him, and that was all that was done with them,
as I was released and went to work after hanging on the gallows about an hour.

After I had lived with my master thirteen years, being then about twenty two
years old, I married Meg, a slave of his who was about my age. My master owned
a certain Irishman, named Heddy, who about that time formed a plan of secretly
leaving his master. After he had long had this plan in meditation he suggested it
to me. At first I cast a deaf ear to it, and rebuked Heddy for harboring in his mind
such a rash undertaking. But after he had persuaded and much enchanted me
with the prospect of gaining my freedom by such a method, I at length agreed to
accompany him. Heddy next inveigled two of his fellow servants to accompany
us. The place to which we designed to go was the Mississippi. Our next business
was to lay a sufficient store of provisions for our voyage. We privately collected
out of our master's store, six great old cheeses, two firkins of butter, and one
whole batch of new bread. When we had gathered all our own clothes and some
more, we took them all about midnight, and went to the water side. We stole our
master's boat, embarked, and then directed our course for the Mississippi river.

We mutually confederated not to betray or desert one another on pain of death.
We first steered our course for Montauk point, the east end of Long-Island. After
our arrival there we landed, and Heddy and I made an incursion into the island
after fresh water, while our two comrades were left at a little distance from the
boat, employed at cooking. When Heddy and I had sought some time for water,
he returned to our companions, and I continued on looking for my object. When
Heddy had performed his business with our companions who were engaged in
cooking, he went directly to the boat, stole all the clothes in it, and then travelled
away for East-Hampton, as I was informed. I returned to my fellows not long after.
They informed me that our clothes were stolen, but could not determine who was
the thief, yet they suspected Heddy as he was missing. After reproving my two
comrades for not taking care of our things which were in the boat, I advertised
Heddy and sent two men in search of him. They pursued and overtook him
at Southampton and returned him to the boat. I then thought if might afford
some chance for my freedom, or at least a palliation for my running away, to
return Heddy immediately to his master, and inform him that I was induced to
go away by Heddy's address. Accordingly I set off with him and the rest of my
companions for our master's, and arrived there without any difficulty. I informed
my master that Heddy was the ringleader of our revolt, and that he had used us

ill. He immediately put Heddy into custody, and myself and companions were well received and went to work as usual.

Not a long time passed after that, before Heddy was sent by my master to New-London gaol. At the close of that year I was sold to a Thomas Stanton, and had to be separated from my wife and one daughter, who was about one month old. He resided at Stonington-point. To this place I brought with me from my late master's, two johannes,[4] three old Spanish dollars, and two thousand of coppers, besides five pounds of my wife's money. This money I got by cleaning gentlemen's shoes and drawing boots, by catching musk-rats and minks, raising potatoes and carrots, &c. and by fishing in the night, and at odd spells.

All this money amounting to near twenty-one pounds York currency, my master's brother, Robert Stanton, hired me, for which he gave me his note. About one year and a half after that time, my master purchased my wife and her child, for seven hundred pounds old tenor. One time my master sent me two miles after a barrel of molasses, and ordered me to carry it on my shoulders. I made out to carry it all the way to my master's house. When I lived with Captain George Mumford, only to try my strength, I took up on my knees a tierce of salt containing seven bushels, and carried it two or three rods.[5] Of this fact there are several eye witnesses now living.

Towards the close of the time that I resided with this master, I had a falling out with my mistress. This happened one time when my master was gone to Long-Island a gunning. At first the quarrel began between my wife and her mistress. I was then at work in the barn, and hearing a racket in the house, induced me to run there and see what had broken out. When I entered the house, I found my mistress in a violent passion with my wife, for what she informed me was a mere trifle; such a small affair that I forbear to put my mistress to the shame of having it known. I earnestly requested my wife to beg pardon of her mistress for the sake of peace, even if she had given no just occasion for offence. But whilst I was thus saying my mistress turned the blows which she was repeating on my wife to me. She took down her horse-whip, and while she was glutting her fury with it, I reached out my great black hand, raised it up and received the blows of the whip on it which were designed for my head. Then I immediately committed the whip to the devouring fire.

When my master returned from the island, his wife told him of the affair, but for the present he seemed to take no notice of it, and mentioned not a word about it to me. Some days after his return, in the morning as I was putting on a log in the fire-place, not suspecting harm from any one, I received a most violent stroke on the crown of my head with a club two feet long and as large round as a chair-post. This blow very badly wounded my head, and the scar of it remains to this day. The first blow made me have my wits about me you may suppose, for as soon as he went to renew it, I snatched the club out of his hands and dragged him out of the door. He then sent for his brother to come and assist him, but I presently left my master, took the club he wounded me with, carried it to a neighboring Justice of the Peace, and complained of my master. He finally advised me to return to my master, and live contented with him till he abused me again, and then complain. I consented to do accordingly. But before I set out for my master's, up he come and his brother Robert after me. The Justice improved this convenient opportunity to caution my master. He asked him for what he treated his slave thus hastily and unjustly, and told him what would be the consequence if he continued the same treatment towards me. After the Justice had ended his discourse with my master, he and his brother set out with me for home, one before and the other behind me. When they had come to a bye place, they both dismounted their respective horses, and fell to beating me with great violence. I became enraged at this and immediately turned them both under me, laid one of them across the other, and stamped both with my feet what I would.

This occasioned my master's brother to advise him to put me off. A short time after this I was taken by a constable and two men. They carried me to a blacksmith's shop and had me hand-cuffed. When I returned home my mistress enquired much of her waiters, whether VENTURE was hand-cuffed. When she was informed that I was, she appeared to be very contented and was much transported with the news. In the midst of this content and joy, I presented myself before my mistress, shewed her my hand-cuffs, and gave her thanks for my gold rings. For this my master commanded a negro of his to fetch him a large ox chain. This my master locked on my legs with two padlocks. I continued to wear the chain peaceably for two or three days, when my master asked me with contemptuous hard names whether I had not better be freed from my chains and go to work. I answered him, No. Well then, said me, I will send you to the West-Indies or banish you, for I am resolved not to keep you. I answered him I crossed the waters to come here, and I am willing to cross them to return.

For a day or two after this not any one said much to me, until one Hempsted Miner, of Stonington, asked me if I would live with him. I answered that I would. He then requested me to make myself discontented and to appear as unreconciled to my master as I could before that he bargained with him for me; and that in return he would give me a good chance to gain my freedom when I came to live with him. I did as he requested me. Not long after Hempsted Miner purchased me of my master for fifty-six pounds lawful. He took the chain and padlocks from off me immediately after.

It may here be remembered, that I related a few pages back, that I hired out a sum of money to Mr. Robert Stanton, and took his note for it. In the fray between my master Stanton and myself, he broke open my chest containing his brother's note to me, and destroyed it. Immediately after my present master bought me, he determined to sell me at Hartford. As soon as I became apprized of it, I bethought myself that I would secure a certain sum of money which lay by me, safer than to hire it out to a Stanton. Accordingly I buried it in the earth, a little distance from Thomas Stanton's, in the road over which he passed daily. A short time after my master carried me to Hartford, and first proposed to sell me to one William Hooker of that place. Hooker asked whether I would go to the German Flats with him. I answered, No. He said I should, if not by fair means I should by foul. If you will go by no other measures, I will tie you down in my sleigh. I replied to him, that if he carried me in that manner, no person would purchase me, for it would be thought that he had a murderer for sale. After this he tried no more, and said he would not have me as a gift.

My master next offered me to Daniel Edwards, Esq. of Hartford, for sale. But not purchasing me, my master pawned me to him for ten pounds, and returned to Stonington. After some trial of my honesty, Mr. Edwards placed considerable trust and confidence in me. He put me to serve as his cup-bearer and waiter. When there was company at his house, he would send me into his cellar and other parts of his house to fetch wine and other articles occasionally for them. When I had been with him some time, he asked me why my master wished to part with such an honest negro, and why he did not keep me himself. I replied that I could not give him the reason, unless it was to convert me into cash, and speculate with me as with other commodities. I hope that he can never justly say it was on account of my ill conduct that he did not keep me himself. Mr. Edwards told me that he should be very willing to keep me himself, and that he would never let me go from him to live, if it was not unreasonable and inconvenient for me to be parted from my wife and children; therefore he would furnish me with a horse to return to Stonington, if I had a mind for it. As Miner did not appear to redeem me I went, and called at my old master Stanton's first to see my wife, who was then owned by him. As my old master appeared much ruffled at my being there, I left my wife before I had spent any considerable time with her, and went to Colonel O. Smith's. Miner had not as yet wholly settled with Stanton for me, and had before my return from Hartford given Col. Smith a bill of sale of me. These men once met to determine which of them should hold me, and upon my expressing a desire to be owned by Col. Smith, and upon my master's settling the remainder of the money which was due to Stanton for me, it was agreed that I should live with Col. Smith. This was the third time of my being sold, and I was then thirty-one years old. As I never had an opportunity of redeeming myself whilst I was owned by Miner, though he promised to give me a chance, I was then very ambitious of obtaining it. I asked my master one time if he would consent to have me purchase my freedom. He replied that he would. I was then very happy, knowing that I was at that time able to pay part of the purchase money, by means of the money which I some time since had buried. This I took out of the earth and tendered to my master, having previously engaged a free negro man to take his security for it, as I was property of my master, and therefore could not safely take his obligation myself. What was wanting in redeeming myself, my master agreed to wait on me for, until I could procure it for him. I still continued to work for Col. Smith. There was continually some interest accruing on my master's note to my friend the free negro man above named, which I received, and with some besides which I got by fishing, I laid out in land adjoining my old master Stanton's. By cultivating this land with the greatest diligence and economy, at times when my master did not require my labor, in two years I laid up ten pounds. This my friend tendered my master for myself, and received his note for it.

Being encouraged by the success which I had met in redeeming myself, I again solicited my master for a further chance of completing it. The chance for which I solicited him was that of going out to work for the ensuing winter. He agreed to this on condition that I would give him one quarter of my earnings. On these terms I worked the following winter, and earned four pounds sixteen shillings, one quarter of which went to my master for the privilege, and the rest was paid him on my own account. This added to the other payments made up forty four pounds, eight shillings, which I had paid on my own account. I was then about thirty five years old.

The next summer I again desired he would give me a chance of going out to work. But he refused and answered that he must have my labor this summer, as he did not have it the past winter. I replied that I considered it as hard that I could not have a chance to work out when the season became advantageous, and that I must only be permitted to hire myself out in the poorest season of the year. He asked me after this what I would give him for the privilege per month. I replied that I would leave it wholly with his own generosity to determine what I should return him a month. Well then, said he, if so two pounds a month. I answered him that if that was the least he would take I would be contented.

Accordingly I hired myself out at Fisher's Island, and earned twenty pounds; thirteen pounds six shillings of which my master drew for the privilege, and the remainder I paid him for my freedom. This made fifty-one pounds two shillings which I paid him. In October following I went and wrought six months at Long Island. In that six month's time I cut and corded four hundred cords of wood, besides threshing out seventy-five bushels of grain, and received of my wages down only twenty pounds, which left remaining a larger sum. Whilst I was out that time, I took up on my wages only one pair of shoes. At night I lay on the hearth, with one coverlet over and another under me. I returned to my master and gave him what I received of my six months labor. This left only thirteen pounds eighteen shillings to make up the full sum for my redemption. My master liberated me, saying that I might pay what was behind if I could ever make it convenient, otherwise it would be well. The amount of the money which I had paid my master towards redeeming my time, was seventy-one pounds two shillings. The reason of my master for asking such an unreasonable price, was he said, to secure himself in case I should ever come to want. Being thirty-six years old, I left Col. Smith once for all. I had already been sold three different times, made considerable money with seemingly nothing to derive it from, been cheated out of a large sum of money, lost much by misfortunes, and paid an enormous sum for my freedom.

Chapter III.

Containing an Account of His Life, from the Time of His Purchasing His Freedom to the Present Day.

My wife and children were yet in bondage to Mr. Thomas Stanton. About this time I lost a chest, containing besides clothing, about thirty-eight pounds in paper money. It was burnt by accident. A short time after I sold all my possessions at Stonington, consisting of a pretty piece of land and one dwelling house thereon, and went to reside at Long-Island. For the first four years of my residence there, I spent my time in working for various people on that and the neighboring islands. In the space of six months I cut and corded upwards of four hundred cords of wood. Many other singular and wonderful labors I performed in cutting wood there, which would not be inferior to those just recited, but for brevity sake I must omit them. In the aforementioned four years what wood I cut at Long-Island amounted to several thousand cords, and the money which I earned thereby amounted to two hundred and seven pounds ten shillings. This money I laid up carefully by me. Perhaps some may enquire what maintained me all the time I was laying up money. I would inform them that I bought nothing which I did not absolutely want. All fine clothes I despised in comparison with my interest, and never kept but just what clothes were comfortable for common days, and perhaps I would have a garment or two which I did not have on at all times, but as for superfluous finery I never thought it to be compared with a decent homespun dress, a good supply of money and prudence. Expensive gatherings of my mates I commonly shunned, and all kinds of luxuries I was perfectly a stranger to; and during the time I was employed in cutting the aforementioned quantity of wood, I never was at the expence of six-pence worth of spirits. Being after this labour forty years of age, I worked at various places, and in particular on Ram-Island, where I purchased Solomon and Cuff, two sons of mine, for two hundred dollars each.

It will here be remembered how much money I earned by cutting wood in four years. Besides this I had considerable money, amounting in all to near three hundred pounds. When I had purchased my two sons, I had then left more than one hundred pounds. After this I purchased a negro man, for no other reason than to oblige him, and gave him sixty pounds. But in a short time after he run away from me, and I thereby lost all that I gave for him, except twenty pounds which he paid me previous to his absconding. The rest of my money I laid out in land, in addition to a farm which I owned before, and a dwelling house thereon. Forty four years had then completed their revolution since my entrance into this existence of servitude and misfortune. Solomon my eldest son, being then in his seventeenth year, and all my hope and dependence for help, I hired him out to one Charles Church, of Rhode-Island, for one year, on consideration of his giving him twelve pounds and an opportunity of acquiring some learning. In the course of the year, Church fitted out a vessel for a whaling voyage, and being in want of hands to man her, he induced my son to go, with the promise of giving him on his return, a pair of silver buckles, besides his wages. As soon as I heard of his going to sea, I immediately set out to go and prevent it if possible.—But on my arrival at Church's, to my great grief, I could only see the vessel my son was in almost out of sight going to sea. My son died of scurvy in this voyage, and Church has never yet paid me the least of his wages. In my son, besides the loss of his life, I lost equal to seventy-five pounds.

My other son being but a youth, still lived with me. About this time I chartered a sloop of about thirty tons burthen,[6] and hired men to assist me in navigating her. I employed her mostly in the wood trade of Rhode-Island, and made clear of all expences about one hundred dollars with her in better than one year. I had then become something forehanded, and being in my forty-fourth year, I purchased my wife Meg, and thereby prevented having another child to buy, as she was then pregnant. I gave forty pounds for her.

During my residence at Long-Island, I raised one year with another, ten cart loads of water-melons, and lost a great many every year besides by the thievishness of the sailors. What I made by the water-melons I sold there, amounted to nearly five hundred dollars. Various other methods I pursued in order to enable me to redeem my family. In the night time I fished with set-nets and pots for eels and lobsters, and shortly after went [on] a whaling voyage in the service of Col. Smith.—After being out seven months, the vessel returned, laden with four hundred barrels of oil. About this time, I become possessed of another dwelling-house, and my temporal affairs were in a pretty prosperous condition. This and my industry was what alone saved me from being expelled [from] that part of the island in which I resided, as an act was passed by the select-men of the place, that all negroes residing there should be expelled.

Next after my wife, I purchased a negro man for four hundred dollars. But he having an inclination to return to his old master, I therefore let him go. Shortly after I purchased another negro man for twenty-five pounds, whom I parted with shortly after.

Being about forty-six years old, I bought my oldest child Hannah, of Ray Mumford, for forty-four pounds, and she still resided with him. I had already redeemed from slavery, myself, my wife and three children, besides three negro men.

About the forty-seventh year of my life, I disposed of all my property at Long-Island, and came from thence into East-Haddam. I hired myself out at first to Timothy Chapman, for five weeks, the earnings of which time I put up carefully by me. After this I wrought for Abel Bingham about six weeks. I then put my money together and purchased of said Bingham ten acres of land, lying at Haddam neck, where I now reside.—On this land I labored with great diligence for two years, and shortly after purchased six acres more of land contiguous to my other. One year from that time I purchased seventy acres more of the same man, and paid for it mostly with the produce of my other land. Soon after I bought this last lot of land, I set up a comfortable dwelling house on my farm, and built it from the produce thereof. Shortly after I had much trouble and expence with my daughter Hannah, whose name has before been mentioned in this account. She was married soon after I redeemed her, to one Isaac, a free negro, and shortly after her marriage fell sick of a mortal disease; her husband a dissolute and abandoned wretch, paid but little attention to her in her illness. I therefore thought it best to bring her to my house and nurse her there. I procured her all the aid mortals could afford, but notwithstanding this she fell a prey to her disease, after a lingering and painful endurance of it.

The physician's bills for attending her during her illness amounted to forty pounds. Having reached my fifty-fourth year, a hired two negro men, one named William Jacklin, and the other Mingo. Mingo lived with me one year, and having received his wages, run in debt to me eight dollars, for which he gave me his note. Presently after he tried to run away from me without troubling himself to pay up his note. I procured a warrant, took him, and requested him to go to Justice Throop's of his own accord, but he refusing, I took him on my shoulders, and carried him there, distant about two miles. The justice asking me if I had my prisoner's note with me, and replying that I had not, he told me that I must return with him and get it. Accordingly I carried Mingo back on my shoulders, but before we arrived at my dwelling, he complained of being hurt, and asked me if this was not a hard way of treating our fellow creatures. I answered him that it would be hard thus to treat our honest fellow creatures. He then told me that if I would let him off my shoulders, he had a pair of silver shoe-buckles, one shirt and a pocket handkerchief, which he would turn out to me. I agreed, and let him return home with me on foot; but the very following night, he slipped from me, stole my horse and has never paid me even his note. The other negro man, Jacklin, being a comb-maker by trade, he requested me to set him up, and promised to reward me well with his labor. Accordingly I bought him a set of tools for making combs, and procured him stock. He worked at my house about one year, and then run away from me with all his combs, and owed me for all his board.

Since my residence at Haddam neck, I have owned of boats, canoes and sail vessels, not less than twenty. These I mostly employed in the fishing and trafficking business, and in these occupations I have been cheated out of considerable money by people whom I traded with taking advantage of my ignorance of numbers.

About twelve years ago, I hired a whale-boat and four black men, and proceeded to Long-Island after a load of round clams. Having arrived there, I first purchased of James Webb, son of Orange Webb, six hundred and sixty clams, and afterwards, with the help of my men, finished loading my boat. The same evening, however, this Webb stole my boat, and went in her to Connecticut river, and sold her cargo for his own benefit. I thereupon pursued him, and at length, after an additional expence of nine crowns, recovered the boat; but for the proceeds of her cargo I never could obtain any compensation.

Four years after, I met with another loss, far superior to this in value, and I think by no less wicked means. Being going to New-London with a grand-child, I took passage in an Indian's boat, and went there with him. On our return, the Indian took on board two hogsheads of molasses, one of which belonged to Capt. Elisha Hart, of Saybrook, to be delivered on his wharf. When we arrived there, and while I was gone, at the request of the Indian, to inform Captain Hart of his arrival, and receive the freight of him, one hogshead of the molasses had been lost overboard by the people in attempting to land it on the wharf. Although I was absent at the time, and had no concern whatever in the business, as was known to a number of respectable witnesses, I was nevertheless prosecuted by this conscientious gentleman, (the Indian not being able to pay for it) and obliged to pay upwards of ten pounds lawful money, with all the costs of court. I applied to several gentlemen for counsel in this affair, and they advised me, as my adversary was rich, and threatened to carry the matter from court to court till it would cost me more than the first damages would be, to pay the sum and submit to the injury; which I accordingly did, and he has often since insultingly taunted me with my unmerited misfortune. Such a proceeding as this, committed on a defenceless stranger, almost worn out in the hard service of the world, without any foundation in reason or justice, whatever it may be called in a christian land, would in my native country have been branded as a crime equal to highway robbery. But Captain Hart was a *white gentleman*, and I a *poor African*, therefore it was *all right, and good enough for the black dog*.

I am now sixty nine years old. Though once strait and tall, measuring without shoes six feet one inch and an half, and every way well proportioned, I am now bowed down with age and hardship. My strength which was once equal if not superior to any man whom I have ever seen, is now enfeebled so that life is a burden, and it is with fatigue that I can walk a couple of miles, stooping over my staff. Other griefs are still behind; on account of which some aged people, at least, will pity me. My eye-sight has gradually failed, till I am almost blind, and whenever I go abroad one of my grand-children must direct my way; besides for many years I have been much pained and troubled with an ulcer on one of my legs. But amidst all my griefs and pains, I have many consolations; Meg, the wife of my youth, whom I married for love, and bought with my money, is still alive. My freedom is a privilege which nothing else can equal. Notwithstanding all the losses I have suffered by fire, by the injustice of knaves, by the cruelty and oppression of false hearted friends, and the perfidy of my own countrymen whom I have assisted and redeemed from bondage, I am now possessed of more than one hundred acres of land, and three habitable dwelling houses. It gives me joy to think that I *have* and that I *deserve* so good a character, especially for *truth* and *integrity*. While I am now looking to the grave as my home, my joy for this world would be full—IF my children, Cuff for whom I paid two hundred dollars when a boy, and Solomon who was born soon after I purchased his mother—If Cuff and Solomon—O! that they had walked in the way of their father. But a father's lips are closed in silence and in grief!—Vanity of vanities, all is vanity!

Finis.

Certificate.

Stonington, November 3, 1798.

These certify, that VENTURE, a free negro man, aged about 69 years, and was, as we have ever understood, a native of Africa, and formerly a slave to Mr. James Mumford, of Fisher's-Island, in the state of New-York; who sold him to Mr. Thomas Stanton, 2d, of Stonington, in the state of Connecticut, and said Stanton sold said VENTURE to Col. Oliver Smith, of the aforesaid place. That said VENTURE hath sustained the character of a faithful servant, and that of a temperate, honest and industrious man, and being ever intent on obtaining his freedom, he was indulged by his masters after the ordinary labour on the days of his servitude, to improve the nights in fishing and other employments to his own emolument, in which time he procured so much money as to purchase his freedom from his late master Col. Smith; after which he took upon himself the name of VENTURE SMITH, and has since his freedom purchased a negro woman, called Meg, to whom he was previously married, and also his children who were slaves, and said VENTURE had since removed himself and family to the town of East-Haddam, in this state, where he hath purchased lands on which he hath built a house, and there taken up his abode.

> NATHANIEL MINOR, Esq.
> ELIJAH PALMER, Esq.
> Capt. AMOS PALMER,
> ACORS SHEFFIELD,
> EDWARD SMITH.

Notes

1. Dukandarra is located in what is now the West African country of Burkina Faso.

2. A cote is a sheepfold.

3. Anamaboo is located on the coast of present-day Ghana.

4. Johannes are Portuguese gold coins with a value of about eight dollars, named from the figure of King John which it bears; often contracted into "joe," as a joe or half joe.

5. A tierce is a large cask. Two or three rods is between eleven and about seventeen yards.

6. The sloop was capable of carrying thirty tons.

History of the
Captivity and Sufferings
of
Mrs. Maria Martin,
Who Was Six Years a Slave
in Algiers

The fictional narrative of Maria Martin's captivity was one of the most popular Barbary texts published in the early Republic. Between 1806 and 1818 thirteen separate editions were printed in the United States. Interestingly, these editions do not all tell the same story. The first American edition was printed by William Crary, a Boston printer, in 1806, but a year later Crary published an entirely different text under the same title. Of the eleven subsequent editions, ten were reprints of Crary's 1807 text, while only one reprinted his original 1806 text. Because of its popularity and distribution, the 1807 narrative has been used as the copy text.

The differences between the 1806 and 1807 texts reveal Crary's attempt to make the Martin narrative more marketable. This attempt is also quite evident in the printer's construction of the narrative, which he (or a hired hack) first fashioned out of an earlier narrative. In 1804 Crary reprinted an earlier English text, *An Affecting History of the Captivity and Sufferings of Mrs. Mary Velnet, an Italian Lady*. According to the extended title, Velnet spent "SEVEN YEARS [as] A SLAVE IN TRIPOLI," where for three years "SHE WAS CONFINED IN A DUNGEON, LOADED WITH IRONS, AND FOUR TIMES PUT TO THE MOST CRUEL TORTURES EVER INVENTED BY MAN." To help market his sensational text, Crary included a lurid engraving of a bare-breasted woman chained up in a dungeon. Two years later Crary adapted the Velnet text for American readers by blurring the narrator's nationality, altering the action, and relocating the setting to Algiers. The same lurid engraving, however, was reused in the 1806 Martin text.

Both Velnet and Martin are helpless women loaded with chains and left to die in North African dungeons. Both use fervid, melodramatic rhetoric to describe their sufferings; both narrators, in fact, use the same rhetoric. In fashioning the Martin text, Crary inserted long passages from the earlier Velnet text into the new narrative. Yet there are important differences between the two. The Velnet text is an atrocity narrative of endless cruelty and torment. As the extended title advertised, Velnet endured "THE MOST CRUEL TORTURES EVER INVENTED BY MAN" that left her disfigured physically and emotionally. In the 1806 Martin text there are no extended scenes of innocent females suffering devilish torment. This first Martin narrative is much briefer than the Velnet text (fifteen pages compared to ninety-six) and is actually used as a supplement to dramatize a longer ethnographic work Crary labeled "A History of Algiers," which he adapted from Matthew Carey's *A Short Account of Algiers* (1794).

Crary must have been dissatisfied with the rough, uneven 1806 text, since a year later he published a much changed and expanded Martin text. Although still used as a supplement for the pirated Carey text, the 1807 narrative is twice as long as the first Martin narrative, and it provides a much greater richness of detail concerning four sensational subject areas: North African ethnography, slavery, cruelty, and sexuality. This second Martin text also borrows further passages from the original Velnet text and includes scenes of torment and torture. Here the "Algerines" are depicted as being not only barbarous, cruel, and tyrannical but also sexually profligate. The biggest difference between the 1806 Martin and the 1807 Martin is that the latter is forced to preserve her virtue from her master's lustful passion. While the first Martin is loaded with chains and placed in a dungeon after an unsuccessful escape attempt, the second Martin undergoes the same fate for her refusal to submit to her master's carnal desires.

Although the second Martin is clearly identified as being English—and returns to England after suffering her long imprisonment—she is clearly fashioned to appeal to American readers of the early Republic, being both freedom loving and virtuous. This latter narrative is much more of an indictment against slavery than Crary's first Martin text, and it is shaped to stir up the popular American passion for liberty while titillating readers with the sordid passions of North African slave owners. The combination was obviously marketable, as ten other printers reprinted the 1807 text, four of which added new engravings of the martyred Martin imprisoned in her dungeon. Significantly, this narrative did much to fashion early American attitudes toward both slavery and North African Muslims.

DW

HISTORY

OF THE

Captivity and Sufferings

OF MRS.

MARIA MARTIN,

WHO WAS SIX YEARS A SLAVE IN

ALGIERS:

TWO OF WHICH SHE WAS CONFINED IN A DARK
AND DISMAL DUNGEON, LOADED WITH IRONS,
FOR REFUSING TO COMPLY WITH THE BRU-
TAL REQUEST OF A TURKISH OFFICER.

WRITTEN BY HERSELF.

TO WHICH IS ANNEXED,

HISTORY

OF

ALGIERS,

*A Description of the COUNTRY, the Manners and Customs
of the NATIVES—their treatment to their SLAVES—
their LAWS and RELIGION—&c. &c.*

BOSTON—Printed for W. Crary.
1807.

Title page of *History of the Captivity and Sufferings of
Mrs. Maria Martin* (1807 edition; courtesy of the
American Antiquarian Society)

Illustration from *History of the Captivity and Sufferings of Mrs. Maria Martin*, "Maria Martin" (1807 Crary edition; courtesy of the American Antiquarian Society)

Illustration from *History of the Captivity and Sufferings of
Maria Martin* (1809 Rakestraw edition; courtesy of the
American Antiquarian Society)

Illustration from *History of the Captivity and Sufferings
of Mrs. Maria Martin*, "Maria Martin" (1811 Oram edition;
courtesy of the Rare Books and Manuscripts
Library of the Ohio State University Libraries)

Illustration from *History of the Captivity and Sufferings of Mrs. Maria Martin*, "Maria Martin" (1815 Berry edition, Western Reserve Historical Society)

Illustration from *An Historical Account of the Kingdom of Algiers . . .
to Which Is Annexed a History of the Captivity and Sufferings of
Mrs. Maria Martin*, "Maria Martin" (1815 Fay and Davidson
edition; courtesy of the American Antiquarian Society)

Illustration from *The Captivity and Sufferings of Mrs. Mary Velnet*, "Mary Velnet" (1828 Abbot edition; courtesy of the American Antiquarian Society)

I am a native of England, and was born in the year 1779 of respectable and wealthy parents. In the year 1797, I was married to capt. HENRY MARTIN, who was commander of one of the East India Company's ships. Being ever desirous of visiting some distant part of the world, I solicited and obtained consent of my husband to accompany him on a voyage to Minorca. Accordingly, on the 20th of June 1800, we set sail in the ship Unicorn, on board of which there were 100 souls, 12 of whom were passengers. We enjoyed for several weeks a pleasant wind and nothing occurred to obstruct our passage until the 27th July, when, at the very moment that the soft breeze fanned every soul to sleep, when every fear of danger was banished, all care forgotten, and the wearied lulled in the arms of Morpheus, to sweet repose, then, in an instant, we were all roused, by the striking of the ship on a rock! Our amazement and horror cannot be described—in order to do it, the reader must realize my feelings at that moment. We were soon overwhelmed by the tempest of the sea. The crew were in utmost confusion—some swearing, and others praying.

At day light next morning, we found ourselves in a deplorable situation, the ship on her beam ends with four feet of water in her hold, and a heavy sea continually breaking over us. In order to lighten the vessel, the foremast was cut away, and the guns thrown overboard, this plan had its desired effect, for in a few minutes we found ourselves afloat in deep water, and, saw astern of us, the rock that had caused us so much trouble and anxiety of mind. All hands being immediately set to work in repairing and clearing the ship of water, we had the pleasure of seeing ourselves the proceeding day in a situation to proceed on our voyage.

Nothing from this moment transpired, worthy of record, until the 14th of August, when we met a far more fatal disaster—about sun-set, we were alarmed at the sight of a vessel we discovered, which capt. Martin imagined to be a French frigate, and in order to avoid her, he altered the ship's course—the wind at this moment began to blow unusually strong, and with the night increased to a hurricane. The night was extremely dark, and the sea running high and breaking over us, rendered it impossible to keep a light in the binnacle—we were therefore obliged to lash the helm and trust to the mercy of the waves. At day light the storm began in some measure to abate—at 9 A. M. it entirely subsided.

At 2 P. M. as we were taking some refreshment in the cabin, the boatswain came and told my husband that the colour of the water had changed; upon which he reprimanded him, and told him that he had lost his senses, for it was impossible to be near any shore. When the sea changes its colour, it is an evident token that land is not far off, we continued our course under a foresail; but our terror and surprize was not to be exprest, when in the morning watch, my husband being on deck, discovered land right a-head, he came down immediately into the cabin, and with tears in his eyes, desired I would arise. By his countenance I judged that something extraordinary was the matter—I instantly arose and went on deck and plainly saw the land but a short distance a head! The land had the appearance of sand banks, and the ship's crew did all they could to weather them, but the ship having a round head, she would not obey the helm, therefore it was agreed to make in for the land, hoping, as it had the appearance of a bold shore, that we might, through Providence, land safe. It however proving ebb tide, the ship struck upon one of the banks, but by lightening the ship, and cutting away her masts by the board, got clear of that; but keeping still in for the shore, we soon after struck upon another sand bank, but not very violently, so we threw out our ship's anchors in hopes as we might ride out the tide; but the wind increasing, we dragged them, and were violently thrown upon another sand bank, where the ship stuck, and the waves dashed over us. There were several children on board, the dismal cries of whom at this awful moment, could not fail to pierce the hardest heart. Capt. Martin ordered the boat out to see if we could gain the shore that way, a number jumped into her, but ere they could leave the ship, she was staved to pieces.

There were on board two blacks, that were excellent divers (for the surge was so violent no one could stem the billows but by diving) who offered to get with a rope on shore, and fasten it from the ship to the rocks. The negroes accordingly plunged into the sea, and in a few moments we had the satisfaction to see them land and make fast the rope, by the assistance of which they again returned to the ship. My husband, the mate and myself ventured into the water first upon the awning of the ship, and got safe on shore. The captain's clerk, the boatswain, and two sailors next came on shore, but no sooner were they landed, than the rope broke, and as the two negroes had left us, all hopes of saving any more from the ship was at an end; alas! my ears are even pierced at this moment with their cries, which was more terrible than the storm.

Soon after our arrival on shore my husband, the mate and the boatswain, went in search of inhabitants, but in a few hours returned, and informed me that they could not discover any; our grief was now renewed, for we were apparently in as much danger of starving now, as we had been of drowning a few hours before.

While we were lamenting our condition we heard somebody hollow, up in the woods, which revived our drooping senses: but running to see who it was, we, much to our grief, found it to be one of the sailor's that escaped, who was hallowing to his companion.

When we were together, my husband proposed that we should walk to the southward, to see if it were possible to find any inhabitants; but in less than an hour, our journey was obstructed by an impenatrable wood, and we were compelled to return. We then steered our course northward, but were interrupted by large swamps. Thus marooned as we were, we went back again and could perceive the poor wretches in the vessel lifting up their hands to us for succour, Capt. Martin made signs to them to let them know that our condition was as bad as theirs. It growing near night, some of the poor creatures ventured into the water, but were soon drowned. In short, every object we beheld increased our horror. None of us had eat or drank for two days. My poor husband though quite cast down himself, endeavoured to cheer his fellow-sufferers; and that we might be sheltered from the inclemency of the night (which, to add to our wretched condition, proved a rainy one) the men by joint consent and labour while the day lasted, collected a great number of Palmetoe leaves, and with the fragments of trees built a hut, and sheltered it from the weather as well as they could. It was indeed a melancholy reflection to think of our condition, nothing to lie upon but the bare wet ground, and our cloaths that covered us with those upon our backs, dropping with rain and salt-water; no food nor hopes of getting any, and almost expiring with thirst. In the miserable hut we spent a wretched night; in the morning, by my request, we addressed ourselves to the all seeing power for succour. After our extempore orisons were over, we rose up and resolved to go into the woods, to gather if possible something to kill our hunger. We did not travel far before the mate, who was a little way a head, came running toward us, and told us that he discovered a few rods distant, a number of men of a very tawny complexion, armed with long spears; we did not hesitate a moment to meet them whether friends or foes, for we felt ourselves unable any longer to live without food. As soon as they discovered us they advanced towards us in full speed; when within hail, they accosted us in a language which we did not understand; my husband addressed them in English and then in French, but they did not appear to understand what he said, the mate then addressed them in Spanish, but with no better success—one of the sailors who had been a prisoner among the Moors, next addressed them in the Moresco language, and by one or two of them appeared to be understood, who, in reply, declared us "their prisoners."— By the request of my husband, the sailor, who had now become our interpreter, enquired the name of the country in which we were—the reply was, "you are in Barbary, 30 miles from Tenis, and 90 from the city of Algiers."[1]

We were at this instant surrounded by the Barbarians, who brandishing their spears, commanded us to follow them. The sailor told them that we were British subjects, with whom the Bey of Algiers was at peace; to this, however, they paid but little or no attention, but compelled us to accompany them. About sunset, we arrived at Mostaga, a village 27 miles from Tenis where we tarried that night, and the next morning proceeded for Oran. The news of our arrival was soon made known, and the inhabitants collected in great numbers to view us.— By our interpreter we discovered that those by whom we were captured, were representing us as natives of Portugal, that we were part of a crew of a privateer of that nation, which had been ship wrecked on their coast. As the Portuguese were then at war with no nation but the Algerines, the wicked lie of these unprincipled barbarians had its desired effect, and so enraged the multitudes that they could hardly be restrained from laying violent hands on us.

It appeared to be the policy of our captors to represent us as an enemy, as they well knew that we should be disposed of as such, and that they, agreeable to a law of their country, would be entitled to half of the purchase money—but, to the contrary, had it been known that we were British subjects the English consul at Algiers would have demanded us as such.

My husband's greatest concern, was, that we should be disposed of to different persons, and separated, never perhaps to see each other again,—and too soon were his expectations verified, for the day after our arrival, we were drove up like so many cattle which are exposed for sale, to the public market, where were gathered a great number of bidders; among them I recognized many of my own sex, which gave me fresh hopes of protection, but, alas! this fond hope was of but short duration, for so far from exhibiting any pity for me, they seemed rather to exult in my miseries! One of the ruffians who claimed me as their property, conducted me to the Cadi, or principal governor of the place, who was a little, ugly, old looking man, besmeared with dirt, barefoot and barelegged, to him I was recommended as a valuable in-door slave—he was very critical in his examination of my person, my limbs, teeth, eyes, &c. were very closely inspected. After undergoing a thorough examination by more than one hundred different persons, I was struck off to a Turk. I was then led out of the market-place, and committed to the care of his son, who was seated on a log a few rods therefrom awaiting the departure of his father.

Here for the first time I had a melancholly view of my unhappy fellow slaves, whose countenances, as they stole a pitying glance toward me, bespoke more than the tongue could express! They were employed in their daily occupation, which was to load large carts with rocks and huge stones blown from the ledges near the shore, and convey them to a valley about one mile distant; those employed to load the carts, had large collars about their necks, made much after the form of those worn by the West-India slaves; those allotted to draw the carts, were chained thereto. To witness the distress, and to hear the dispairing groans of those poor creatures, could not fail to draw a tear from the eye of any one but a merciless barbarian! Under the heavy weight of the lash, they were compelled to perform the severest tasks; half naked, their scorched and lacerated bodies exhibited a frightful proof of the brutality exercised toward them by the Barbarians.

A very great portion of the inhabitants of Tenis are Moors, a description of the manners and customs of which, may be entertaining to my readers.—They are of a tawny complexion, of a lazy, idle disposition, and cursed with all the vices of mankind; mistrustful to the last degree, false, jealous, and the very picture of ignorance. They style themselves musselmen, or true believers, yet their word is not to be relied on. They abominate the christians, for the very word in their language signifies *dog;* and are continually seeking means to destroy them. Mahomet has taught them in his Alcoran, that all who die fighting against christians, immediately enter into paradise, in triumph; nay, even their houses, if they die in battle are immediately translated into heaven.

Though Poligamy is allowed, yet they must marry but four wives, and must settle a dowry upon them; they are strictly forbidden marrying or having intercourse with a christian woman, those who break this law are immediately punished with death.

At their burials they hire professed mourners to grieve and cry at the graves of relations, and howl over them, asking them why they would die when they were provided with every thing that is necessary in this world. Their time is spent in eating, drinking, sleeping, dallying with their horses, &c.

They have usually a string of beads in their hands, like the roman catholicks, and to every bead they have a short prayer which as they repeat, they drop through their fingers. The prayer consists only in the different attributes of God, as—God is great, God is good, God is infinite, God is merciful.

The Cadi or (Governor) of Tenis only differs from his subjects in the larger propensity to their ill qualities, with the addition of a degree of cruelty and avarice.

I was one day a spectator to his wanton cruelty, having been sent on some errand by my Turkish master, I perceived him giving directions to some of his workmen; there were several carts drove by his slaves, with materials for his house, and as they passed him he bastinadoed some for going too fast, while others, thinking to mend that fault, were drubbed by him for going too slow; one poor creature, trembling for fear of what would follow, went bowing before his cart, but the Cadi, wounding his horse in the flank, he gave a spring, tumbled the wretch down and drove over him. Another following him, ran to assist his fellow creature, but the Cadi threw his dart and struck him in the shoulder; the slave drew it out, and upon his knees presented it to him again, which the Cadi (when the man had got a little distance from him) darted the second time into his body! the poor creature drew it out once more, and, covered with blood, gave it to him back again, but as he was stooping, he fell down with loss of blood at the barbarian's feet, who did him the favor to pin him to the earth through his back.

The Cadi is said to possess a great deal of wit and courage, is very active and expert in riding and hurling the dart. He drinks no wine because his religion forbids it, but when he taks opium, or drinks a certain mixture that he makes himself, compound with brandy, cinnamon, anniseed, cloves and nutmeg, woe to him that comes in his way. He's much addicted to women, having no less than four hundred concubines.

The Moors shave their heads close except one lock upon the crown of their heads, which they never cut off, they being taught that by that lock Mahomet is to draw them up to their imaginary paradise.

I could not forbear smiling to see the policy practiced by the Moors in one instance—walking one day about a mile from Tenis, after my release from captivity, it began to rain violently, I got under a tree to shelter myself from the tempest, but I observed several of the Moors to undress themselves with a great deal of precipitancy, make up their cloathes in a bundle, and sit on them stark naked; this was to prevent their being wet, while their naked bodies were exposed to the fury of the storm. When it ceased to rain, they walked a little way till their bodies were dry, and then dressed themselves.

The dress of the Moors chiefly consists of a robe or caftan of serge, woollen stuff, or blue and white cotton, and sometimes, but very seldom, of silk. They are also cloathed in a shirt, which is tied around the neck, and is so wide as to fold two or three times about the body; this is bound round the waist by a sash, in which is stuck a long knife like a bayonet, and sometimes two. The dress of both the men and women consists of such a large shirt, generally of black linen, and a cloth with which the women cover their head and shoulders; the men sometimes rolling it about their heads, in imitation of a turban, and sometimes around the middle. Some of the women wear their hair tied up in a knot, and others let it hang down; but the men are in general very negligent of it. They wear sandals, or rather socks, of Morocco leather, which raise to the small of the leg; and their heads are covered with a red bonnet, or cap, bordered with cotton. The long loose robe of white or striped cotton, or wollen stuff, above described, which they frequently wear over their capacious shirt, they call haik, and is extremely becoming. This robe has a long pointed hood that falls down behind, to the extremity of which hangs a tassel by a long string. However, the poor are cloathed after the manner of the negroes.

The women, as I before mentioned, wear a long cotton shift; this has long and wide sleeves; they have likewise large drawers, and a piece of calico, or linen, that covers them from head to foot, and flows in an easy manner behind. They are all adorned with ear-rings and pendants, which are valuable in proportion to the wearer's station and quality.

When a considerable number of tents or cabins are placed together, and form a kind of town or village, they call it Adouar. These villages are usually of a circular form, the tents standing very thick, and in the centre is an empty space in which they keep their cattle. They have centinels on every side of this encampment to guard against surprises from robbers, and from wild beasts. On the least appearance of danger, the alarm is given by the centinels, and soon spread over the camp; upon which every man able to bear arms stands on his defence. As these people never encumber themselves with much household furniture, these villages are easily transported from place to place. Indeed all the domestic implements belonging to a family are contained in a bag, or sack, which is easily conveyed tent and all, on the back of a camel to any distance. Their usual drink is milk or whey, and their bread, cakes made of millet. No inducements can engage them to continue a whole season in one place; for however useless and unnecessary their excursions may be, they would consider such an instance of inactivity as highly culpable.

When they happen to have a stock of wheat or barley, they deposit it in deep pits hewn out of the rock; these they contrive with abundance of art, in order to cause a constant draught of fresh air through the whole cavern, which is narrow at the entrance, and gradually enlarges itself in proportion to its length, which is sometimes above thirty feet.

In some parts of the country the people it is said have portable mills, with which they grind their corn as they want it. Their manner of eating resembles that of the Asiatics. At their meals they sit cross-legged round a covering of leather, or a mat of palm leaves, spread upon the ground, upon which their dishes or plates of copper or ivory are laid; and they never drink till they rise in order to wash, a ceremony that cannot be omitted without the greatest indecency. They never allow themselves more than two meals a day, one in the morning and the other at night, and the women are never allowed to eat with the men: Their repasts are short and silent, not a syllable being uttered till they have washed and returned to their pipe and coffee, and then conversations begins.

From this temperance in their meals arises that strong health which renders them strangers to medicine, the study of which was so much cultivated by their predecessors. The only distempers to which they are subject are dysenteries and pleurisies, both of which they are said to cure by the internal and external application of simples. The inhabitants are said to live to a great age, without experiencing what sickness is, seldom dying before the animal powers are wasted by years. With them a man at sixty is said to be in the prime of his life.

They believe the less they are connected with foreigners, and the more strictly they adhere to their primitive manners, the fewer are their maladies and diseases, and the greater their happiness.

The mothers have a passionate fondness for their children, and take the utmost care to prevent their being injured by any accident. The boys are permitted to marry as soon as they can purchase a wife, which is done by presents to the parents, of camels, horses, and horned cattle. They estimate the affection of the husband from his liberality, and the young lady is never delivered to him till by his presents he has made her parents sensible of his merits. If upon her being brought home he is disappointed in his expectations of her beauty or chastity, he may send her back; but in this case he forfeits the presents he had made.

A man has no sooner breathed his last, than one of his women, or some relation, puts her head in at the door of the tent, and bursts into a terrible cry; upon which all the women within the village set up a lamentable shriek and dismal screams, which alarm the whole camp or village.

With respect to the learning of the Moors it is so extremely limited, that few of them are able to read or write; yet some of them have a tolerable notion of astronomy, and talk with precision upon the stars, their number, situation, and division into constellations. The clear and serene sky in which they live has greatly assisted their observations, which advantage they have improved by a warm imagination and a happy memory: their system of astronomy is, however, so replete with fable and absurdity, that it is in general difficult to comprehend their meaning: yet with all their ignorance, they seem formed by nature for liberal sentiments, and with a taste for the polite arts, as their essays in poetry and music, which are far from being contemptible, seem to indicate.

From the softness and effeminacy of their music, it might be inferred, that these people are not very warlike; but if we may judge from some of their maxims, they are far from being pusillanimous. "Can any thing," they say, "be more dastardly, than to kill a man before you approach near enough to be distinguished?" Hence they never attack an enemy till they come within the length of their lances, and then, retiring to a proper distance, throw them or shoot their arrows with surprising dexterity. They fight chiefly on horseback with short stirrups, and by raising themselves high in the saddle, strike with great force. They never draw up their cavalry in long lines and extended wings, but in small detached squadrons, by which means they are less liable to be broke or thrown into confusion; and when such accident happens, are more easily formed.

The cruel oppressions which the Moors of Tenis suffer under the tyrannical government of Algiers, have greatly contributed to their degeneracy; and a more abject condition than theirs can scarcely be conceived.

Can we imagine a situation more adapted to depress the human mind, or render man completely miserable? But it is far from producing these effects: from their unparalleled patience under these various kinds of what others would esteem the greatest wretchedness, they enjoy a tolerable share of happiness.

On seeing a number of these Moors sitting at the doors of their wretched cots, half naked, some smoking, and telling merry tales, others singing or dancing, one would conclude them to be a happy, though a lazy people.

There are but few Turks in Tenis, they are a wretched crew of indigent, ragged, thevish fellows. These wretches being furnished with a gun, a sword, and other arms, are incorporated into some regiment, and soon obtain a vote and share in the government; and from that situation are raised from one post to another, till they obtain those of admiral, vizier, and even bey. The Turks treat their slaves very barbarously, at night they confine them in dungeons and in the day time compel them to toil in chains, and frequently allowing them only a little bread and water.

Having in the preceding pages minutely described the manners and customs of the Moors, who are the principal inhabitants of Tenis, I shall now proceed to give a more particular account of my own sufferings while among them.

My Turkish master having completed his business, after a few moments conversation with his son, by whom I was guarded, commanded me to arise and follow him. I was conducted through several filthy lanes and alleys, which led to the habitation of my new master—the house was large and commodious but not elegant—he was the possessor of between 40 and 50 christian slaves, all of whom, except ten, were Portuguese, nine of the latter were Napoleans, and one a native of England. I was extremely sorry to find one of my own countrymen in as deplorable condition as myself, yet in him I found a real and valuable friend, and without the aid and assistance of whom, I should in all probability at this moment have been still held in bitter captivity.

My unfortunate friend (whose name was Malcome, and who had been five years in captivity) informed me that our master was grand Vizier of the City, and a great favorite of the then reigning Bey of Algiers—that he was a blood-thirsty, cruel and inhuman monster, who, to his knowledge had put several of his slaves to death for no greater fault than that of complaining of indisposition, and an inability to perform their daily tasks.

He mentioned several instances wherein he had been most unmercifully tortured for attempting to communicate information of his captivity, to the English Consul, at Algiers—his nails had been torn from his fingers and toes, and his whole body lacerated in a manner not to be described. I could not discover one among the whole number of slaves claimed by the tyrant, but what wore some indelible mark of his severity. Some had lost a limb, some an eye, and others nails of their fingers and toes!—To me, this was indeed a shocking spectacle!—it gave me to understand what kind of treatment I should myself receive if so unfortunate as to incur the displeasure of the wretch.

Soon after my arrival I was divested of my cloathing and presented with a suit like those worn by the other captives; I was then conducted into an adjoining out house, which proved to be the cookery house, where the victuals for the slaves was daily prepared. On my first entrance I was much pleased to witness a number of my own sex employed, and who I judged by their dress and appearance were captives; I could not but flatter myself with the fond hope that I should find some one among them with whom I should be enabled to converse, but this fond hope was of short duration, for I soon found that, although slaves, they were all natives of Portugal, and wholly unacquainted with the English language.

As soon as I entered I was ordered to proceed immediately to business—we had placed over us as overseer, a woman, who if possible, surpassed her employer in acts of barbarity! She was a native of Morocco, and seemed to glory in having it in her power to torture and torment us by every means and in every way that her inventive faculties could give birth to.—The wretch would not unfrequently compel us for the least offence to strip ourselves naked, and then stand for a given number of minutes within a few feet of a blazing fire!—at other times she would throw hot embers and coals of fire into our bosoms, and shocking as it may appear, she in my presence deprived of life a poor unfortunate girl by strewing her naked body with hot rice!—Under the controul of such a governess, my readers will acknowledge that my situation must have been truly wretched—but, alas! we were slaves! and to a barbarous and unprincipled monster, deprived of our liberties, and compelled like beasts of burden to toil from morn to night!— our sighs and tears availed nothing, they were only productive of stripes!—there were but few among our number but would rather have chosen death than life.[2]

Confined and employed with the other slaves, in cooking, &c. as before mentioned, nothing worthy of record took place until about 13 months from the time of my capture, when the thundering cannon announced the approach of an event of no little magnitude. About 3 o'clock, P. M. orders were received from the grand Vizier (our master) for us to repair as soon as possible to a fortification at the harbour's mouth, on arriving at which, we discovered the cause of the alarm— the Napoleons with a well manned fleet of gun-boats, &c. had commenced a tremendous cannonade on the city, and we were ordered here for the purpose of conveying ammunition to the besieged, from the magazine, a business always allotted to female captives in time of action. At half past 7 A. M. the cannonade became terrible, while all was bustle and confusion among the besieged; they discharged some few cannon against their assailants, but without doing apparent injury.—At 2 P. M. the firing ceased but at 4 it again commenced, when red hot balls were thrown into the city, and with so good effect, that in a few moments the castle together with most of the public buildings were set on fire, and the greatest part of the city reduced to ashes; the slain and wounded were immense. I was at this moment employed as I had been during the whole siege in furnishing the Algerines with powder, yet I could have a fair view of what was going on, and was not a little pleased to see many of that barbarous nation made to bite the dust!

The Napoleons having expended all their powder, and probably feeling sat- isfied with the injury they had done their enemies, sailed out of the harbour in triumph at sun-rise the succeeding morning; orders were immediately thereupon issued for the prisoners (who had been employed in defence of the city) to assem- ble and assist in removing the rubbish and in burying the dead.—Heavens! what a scene presented to view! the streets were strewed with the dead and dying! On whatever side I turned my eyes, my attention was attracted by mangled bodies and detached limbs, bleeding afresh.—Among a number of captives employed in burying the dead, I thought I recognized my unfortunate husband, but dare not approach him, as my master kept a watchful eye on me.

The business allotted to the female captives, was to strip the dead, after which they were thrown into waggons and drawn off by the male captives, to what place I could never learn. The wounded were carried on the shoulders of captives to the hospitals, where they were visited by the Cadi, and presented with six dollars each.

After the bustle and confusion had a little subsided, we were again ordered to our place of confinement and labour, from whence we had been taken, we had not however been long here before we were again aroused by the discharge of cannon, and beating of the raritoo, a customary signal for slaves to assemble. It was at this moment that I could plainly perceive a sudden change in the countenance in my fellow captives, those in an especial manner who had been long in captivity. Our governess hurried us off as quickly as possible to the castle, at the door of which were assembled (as I judged) nearly 1000 people, and the captives were then continually flocking in—about 3 P. M. orders were given by the grand Vizier (my master) for the forming a procession, and it was at this moment that I learned the cause of our assembling—it appeared that during the late action a captive belonging to the Cadi, had made an attempt to escape, by swimming to one of the enemy's boats, but was observed, pursued, and retaken. The affair so exaiperating the Cadi, that he gave orders for his immediate execution. For the information of the reader, it may be well to mention, that on all such like occasions, it is ever customary for the captives to attend, generally, that they may be eye witnesses to those scenes of savage torture, inflicted by the barbarians on such as attempt an escape, in order to deter them from making a like attempt—this is customary throughout all Barbary.

About 4 P. M. a procession was formed, which moved to the place of execution in the following order, viz—the grand Vizier in front, mounted on a Buffaloe, on his right and left six Marabouts preceded by his Mamalukes, the latter attend him on such like occasions to guard his person, while the former ever accompany him to protect him from the powers of infernal spirits, for so credulous is he, that he doubts not but they are vested with power to do anything—next in succession followed a body of Turks, about 150 in number, armed with spears, scymeters and darts, and next followed the unhappy captive, pinioned and mounted on a Jack Ass, with his back towards the animal's head; the spectators and prisoners brought up the rear. At half past 5 we arrived at the fatal spot where the poor unfortunate captive was to suffer, we were ordered to form a semi-circle around the machine of torture, which bore the resemblance of a slitting mill, and when in motion, was so constructed as to cut the wretched victim into as small pieces as one's little finger.

The grand Vizier dismounted and ascended a lofty stage, a station always prepared for him on such occasions, and from which he gave orders for his executioners (three barbarous looking Turks) to bring forward the unhappy victim, at the same time commanding silence. The poor fellow was instantly dismounted and led up to the accursed machine; he was next stripped and his body washed by the Marabouts with a liquid as black as ink, this they do to prevent christians gaining admission among the saints of Mahomet, as they persuade their master that with the body, the soul is also coloured! The executioners were now ordered to perform their duty! one of them approaching the prisoner, threw him upon his back, and then pinioned him hand and foot; a cord about the bigness of a person's thumb was next made fast to his left leg, a little above the ancle bone, with which means of a windless, he was drawn to the fatal shears, which at the very moment were set in motion, slicing his left foot and leg in pieces of less than half an ounce weight!—Gracious God! a scene like this, was too much for human eyes to witness! a view of which, I was enabled thank heaven to prevent, by closing my eyes; but, alas! I could not close my ears against the shrieks and heart piercing cries of the unhappy sufferer!—thank heavens, the pains of death, of torment, were of but short indurance, for shocking to relate, in less than six minutes, there was not a piece of the unhappy sufferer to be found of the bigness of a dollar, there appeared nothing left of him but a mass of goared flesh cut into a thousand pieces.[3]

When these savage monsters had sufficiently glutted themselves with the blood of their victim, orders were given for the reforming of the procession, which was immediately done, we returning in the same manner as we came, my master riding in front brandishing his scymeter, the point of which, the callous hearted wretch had taken pains to stain with the blood of the murdered captive, as a token of triumph!

I was on my return again committed to the charge of my unprincipled governess, and by whom I was immediately reconducted to the house of confinement and labour from which I had been taken. In this dreary abode I much expected to spend the remainder of my days, yet *hope*, the soothing balm of life, would sometimes revive my drooping spirits—the pleasing anticipation of once more gaining my liberty, would sometimes afford moments of imaginary pleasure.

After a close confinement of nearly three years, I was one evening visited by my master, who was accompanied by my friend Malcome; the latter had been nearly eight years in captivity, and had learned to speak the language of the country extremely well, and many times proved serviceable to his master as an interpreter. Happily for me, this man was my friend—he could converse with me in presence of his master upon any subject with safety, as the Vizier understood not a word of English.—He informed me that his master pretended to harbour an unusual degree of love for me, and through fear of being betrayed and punished agreeable to the laws of the country, should he attempt by forcible means to gratify a lustful passion, he had commanded him to solicit my compliance, and to inform me that if I would willingly consent to indulge him in what he should request, he would extend to me the same liberty which his wives (or concubines) enjoyed!— but, continued my friend Malcome, fear not, do not be terrified at his threats; he will no doubt do every thing in his power to compel you to comply with his request, but should he attempt any such thing against your will, he will lose his head. This conversation was held in presence of my ruffian master, to whom my friend was to interpret my answer, which he informed me he did in the following words—viz:—that I would never consent to gratify him in his unlawful request, as it would be in direct violation of the laws of my God and my country.

The villain, after brow-beating me for this unexpected reply, desired Malcome to inform me that he would give me a day to consider on it, but if I should then refuse, he would adopt such a plan as should soon make me repent of my folly— saying this, he left me, thank heaven indued with that fortitude, that I had resolved sooner to die than to submit to his cursed proposals.

Early the succeeding morning I was again called upon by my master, accompanied by my friend Malcome, through whom enquiry was made whether I had concluded to comply with his Proposal; my answer, as interpreted by my friend, was—"no! I will sooner suffer death!" This was an answer as displeasing as it was unexpected to the tyrant—he became now like a mad-man, drawing his dirk, he threatened me with instant death, unless I would immediately comply with his request; but finding that I still persisted in my determination, he left me, swearing that my obstinacy should yet cost me my life! all this was interpreted to me by my friend, who, as he retired, told me that he would do all within his power to protect me from the violence of the wretch.

The plan next pursued by my master to accomplish his wishes, was, to represent me to his friend, the Bey, as a person sent into the country to conspire against the government! This plan, in part, had its desired effect, for no sooner was the Bey informed of this, than he ordered me to be conveyed immediately to Serfel (situated within a few miles of the city of Algiers) there to be confined (in irons) in an apartment of an old castle.

The room in which I was confined was built of rough stone, and the walls were about 8 feet in depth, it contained but one small window, with large iron gratings and which afforded so little light that I could hardly discern an object six feet from me. My furniture consisted of a three legged stool and a gallon stone jug, which was occasionally filled with stinking water.

On the second day of my confinement, a smith entered my apartment with a hammer and chains in abundance, which, alas, I too soon found were to be attached to my body!—an enormous collar was put round my neck, and another still larger round my waist, to both of which was attached a large iron chain, the end of which was secured by a ring in the wall. This ring was five feet from the ground, and only allowed me to sit down on the stool before mentioned.

In this situation they left me, helpless and wretched, preyed on by all the torture of thought, that continually suggested the most gloomy, the most dreadful images. My fortitude after some time, began to revive; I glowed with the desire of convincing the world I was capable of suffering what man had never suffered before. Often did I reflect how much happier I was in innocence, than the malefactor doomed to suffer the pangs of death, the ignominy of men, and the horrors of internal guilt.

The enormous iron around my neck pained me, and prevented motion. The chains that descended from the neck-collar were obliged to be supported first with one hand, and then with the other, for, if thrown behind, they would have strangled me, and, if hanging forwards, occasioned most excessive headachs. The little sleep I could have in such a situation may easily be supposed, and at length body and mind sunk under this accumulation of miserable suffering, and I fell ill of a burning fever. Reason, fortitude, heroism, all the noble qualities of mind, decay when the corporal faculties are diseased, and the remembrance of my sufferings, at this dreadful moment, still agitates, still inflames my blood, so as almost to prevent an attempt to describe what they were. Yet hope had not totally forsaken me. Deliverance seemed possible, especially should the Consul learn of my situation.

I continued ill about two months, and was so reduced at last, that I had scarcely strength to lift the water jug to my mouth. What must the sufferings of a female be who is confined in a dungeon so damp, so dark, so horrible, without bed or straw, her limbs loaded as mine were, with no refreshment but dry mouldy bread, without so much as a drop of broth, without a consoling friend, and who under all these afflictions, trust for her recovery to the efforts of nature alone!

Sickness itself is sufficient to humble the mightest mind; what then is sickness with such additions of torment? The burning fever, the violent headachs, my neck, swelled and enflamed with the irons, enraged me almost to madness. The fever and the fetters together flead my body so that it appeared like one continued wound.—Yet can it be supposed? there came a day! a day of horror, when these mortal pangs were increased!—I sat scorched with this intolerable fever, in which nature and death were contending, and when attempting to quench my burning entrails with cold water, the jug dropped from my enfeebled hands and broke! I had four and twenty hours to remain without water.

On my attendants visiting me the next day, they supposed me dead, as I lay motionless with my tongue out of my mouth. They poured water down my throat, and found life.

Gracious God! How pure, how delicious, how exquisite, was this water! My insatiable thirst soon emptied the jug: they filled it anew, bade me farewell, hoped death would soon relieve my mortal sufferings, and departed.

Three days had passed before I could again eat a morsel of bread. The irons every where round my body, and their weight was insupportable; nor could I imagine it was possible I should habituate myself to them, or endure them long enough to expect deliverance. A thousand reasons convinced me it was necessary to end my sufferings. I shall not enter into theological disputes: let those who blame me imagine themselves in my situation; or rather first let them actually endure my miseries, and then let them reason.

What strange thing is that called happiness! How shall I express my extreme joy, when after eleven months intolerable hunger, I was indulged with a sweet loaf of bread free from mould? The fond lover never rushed more eagerly to the arms of his bride; the famished tiger more ravenously on his prey than I upon this loaf; I eat, rested, surveyed the precious morsel, eat again, and absolutely shed tears of pleasure.

Oh Nature! what delight has thou combined with the gratification of thy wants! remember this ye who rack invention to excite appetite, and which yet you cannot procure; remember how simple are the means that will give a crust of mouldy bread a flavour more exquisite than all the spices of the east, or all the profusion of land or sea; remember this, grow hungry, and indulge your sensuality.

Alas! my enjoyment was of short duration. I soon found that excess is followed by pain and repentance. My fasting had weakened digestion, and rendered it inactive. My body swelled, my water jug was emptied, cramps, cholics, and, at length, inordinate thirst racked me all night. I began to pour curses on those who seemed to refine on torture, and, after starving me for so long to invite me to gluttony. Could I not have seated myself on my bench, and inclined my back against the wall of the dungeon, I should indeed have been driven to desperation: yet even this was but a partial relief. When my attendants opened my dungeon, they found me in a truly pitiful situation, wondered at my appetite, brought me another loaf; I refused to accept it, believing I should never more have occasion for bread; they however left it with me, gave me water, shrugged up their shoulders, and left me.

God of omnipotence! what was I at this moment! Was there, God of mercies!—was there ever creature of thine more justified than I in despair!—The moon shone clear, I cast a wild distracted look up to heaven, fell on my knees, and, in the agony of my soul, sought comfort but no comfort could be found, nor religion nor philosophy had any to give.—I cursed not Providence, I feared not annihilation, I dared not Almighty vengeance: God the Creator was the disposer of my fate; and if he heaped afflictions upon me he had not given me strength to support, his justice would not therefore punish me.

Early one morning I heard the doors of my dungeon unbarring—the doors of my dungeon for the last time resounded!—a gentleman clad in a christian habit accompanied by the keeper, entered—joy beamed upon his countenance—it was the English Consul—"I have come madam (said he) to liberate you from unjust and cruel bondage!"—Heavens, what joy did I feel on the occasion—it was a long time before I could be convinced of the truth of what he told me, nor could I believe it until a smith was sent for to knock off my irons.

I was now re-conducted out of the dark and dismal dungeon, in which I had been closely confined for three years. It appeared that my friend Malcome, in absence of his master, had been favoured with an opportunity to escape, which he improved and arrived in safety at Algiers; here he found the English Consul, and to him related the particulars of his captivity, and informed him of my wretched situation, and the principal cause of my unjust imprisonment. The Consul, accompanied by the informant, immediately waited upon the Bey, and made a demand of me as one of his Brittanic Majesty's subjects, unjustly and unlawfully held in captivity. The Bey at first discredited the story of Malcome, and seemed confirmed in the belief that I had been sent into the country for some treasonable purpose, but on being assured by the Consul that he would leave the country within twenty-four hours if I was not immediately released, the Bey consented to deliver me up.

The Consul conducted himself with a great deal of humanity towards me, he procured for me a suit of clothes of which I was very much in want, and promised to procure me a passage to England as soon as possible—I acquainted him with the misfortunes of my husband and those who were saved from the ship, but was unable to inform him what had become of them since I parted with them at the market house—he informed me that he would do all in his power to learn their fate, and if still living, he would procure their release immediately, but, added he, as it is not at the present moment convenient for me to go in search of them, and your health being much impaired by long confinement, you had I think embrace the first opportunity to return to your friends—I thanked him for his friendly advice as well as for the many services he had rendered me and told him that I would do whatever he should think best. Accordingly, on the sixth day of my liberation, I once more embarked to visit my native country, with a view of which, after a tedious passage of 45 days, my eyes were once more regaled.

As soon as I landed a carriage was procured for me at the expence of the captain, to convey me to the dwelling of my parents.—About sun-set I arrived, my aged father met me at the door—my sudden and unexpected arrival was too much for him, he fainted! Here it may be necessary to inform the reader, that as my friends had never received any news of the vessel or crew, they had concluded that we had all long since been buried in the deep.

Although providentially restored to my friends, misfortune and disappointment seemed yet to mark me for their own!—I had been flattering myself with the fond hope that on my arrival, I should be so fortunate as to meet with my husband, whom I flattered myself might have possibly escaped, but no news of him had been received since his departure. But, with what pleasure do I close this melancholly relation of my sufferings, by adding, that six months after my arrival, my husband arrived, and apparently, in a good state of health, having obtained his liberty through the influence of the British Consul.

Notes

1. In *The Crescent Obscured*, Robert J. Allison identifies "Tenis" as the city of Tenes. The narrator also mentions that she was taken to the city of Oran, which today is one of the largest cities in Algeria. In the original Velnet text, Mary Velnet was held as a slave in Tripoli, but in the revisions that became the Martin text, Algiers was used. This change was made to enhance reader recognition. Instigated by the English, Algiers had declared war on the United States in 1785 (and again in 1814), and both British and American newspapers reported erroneous stories of hundreds of American ships and captives taken by Algerian corsairs, including one story that Benjamin Franklin had been made a slave. Anxiety was great enough that Patrick Henry, then governor of Virginia, thought that an "Algerine" invasion was imminent. According to Allison, Algiers was a "symbol" for "lawlessness, for piracy, for plunder. It was the most vivid example of Muslim tyranny" (184).

2. This impassioned passage is taken word for word from the Velnet text.

3. Although various forms of Barbary torture and execution were insidious, there is no historical basis for the "slitting mill." This passage of atrocity is taken almost word for word from the original Velnet text, which describes the machine as a device "made in imitation of a Genoese Shaving-Mill" (44).

THE TRIAL OF
AMOS BROAD AND HIS WIFE
. . . FOR ASSAULTING
AND BEATING
BETTY, A SLAVE, AND
HER LITTLE FEMALE CHILD
SARAH

The Trial of Amos Broad and his wife on three several Indictments for Assaulting and Beating Betty, a slave, and her little female child Sarah (1809) is a departure from the other narratives included in this anthology. First, it never directly discusses liberty and captivity, although concern for these issues obviously prompted the New York Manumission Society to urge legal action against Amos and Demis Broad. Second, as a trial record, it includes a multitude of voices, most of them in third person. During the trial, Mr. and Mrs. Broad never speak in their own defense, and first-hand information from Betty is never offered to the court. Instead, the crimes against Betty and Sarah are revealed from the perspectives of nine witnesses for the people, two prosecutors, seven witnesses for the defendant, and one counselor for the defendant.

The only place where readers hear a first-person voice is toward the latter part of the record, after the Broads have been found guilty. Before the court sentence was read, Amos Broad, convinced he would hang for his crimes, uttered what the text calls a "dying speech." In this speech, Broad forgives his enemies, acknowledges the grimness of the charges against him, and likens himself to Jesus on the cross. He never apologizes for his crimes, which include torturing his slaves Betty and Sarah with exposure, starvation, and other perversions too singular to classify. Contrary to his expectations, Broad was not condemned to die. Instead, he was sentenced to 120 days in jail and a fine of $1,000, with another $1,000 retainer for his good behavior for one year. His wife, Demis, was fined $250.

Readers familiar with New York's slavery laws may be surprised to see Betty, Sarah, and the Broads' third servant, Hannah, referred to as slaves in the trial record. In New York the struggle for American independence inspired literature, political treatises, and newspaper features with a new rhetoric of liberty that, in turn, helped create sympathy for the plight of slaves. The New York Manumission Society, composed mainly of Quakers, was organized in 1785 with the aims of bringing forth legislation to end slavery in New York and enforcing compliance with laws relating to slavery. Its efforts were not in vain. In 1799 the New York legislature passed "An Act for the Gradual Abolition of Slavery." This law stipulated that any child born to a slave within the state after July 4, 1799, "shall be deemed and adjudged to be born free." These children were rather to be classified as indentured servants "of the legal proprietor of his or her mother, until such servant if a male shall arrive at the age of 28 years, and if a female at the age of 25." Unfortunately, for slaves such as Betty and Sarah, little distinction was made between indentured servants and slaves, socially or politically. However, in 1817, because of the prominence of cases such as the Broad trial, the New York legislature passed a second law that ended slavery, which took effect ten years later, on July 4, 1827.

The Trial of Amos Broad and His Wife, reprinted here with its original advertisement, was originally published in New York City by Henry C. Southwick in 1809. It was later included in the Lost Cause Press microfiche collection in the 1980s, and it was recently added to the Historical American Memory Collection.

In its advertisement notice, Southwick writes that the Broad trial is "deserving of universal notice." He goes on to claim, "None ever offered to humanity a more generous triumph—to unfeeling pride, a more impressive lesson—or whispered in the ear of the oppressed, more balmy consolation." Of all New Yorkers, Southwick would know this to be so. In addition to the printer, he was one of the twelve men who sat on the jury, sworn to weigh the indictment against Amos and Demis Broad.

Nor was Southwick the only jury member outraged by the Broads' behavior. The jury also included Nehemiah Allen, a member of the industrious and persistent New York Manumission Society, who helped bring the charges against the Broads. Readers are informed that Wilkins, the Broads' defense attorney, questioned the fairness of Allen sitting on the jury. But the three men presiding over the case, Peter Mesier, James Drake, and Pierre Cortlandt Van Wyck, overruled the challenge.

Despite what may seem a light sentence, Van Wyck claims to lay "a heavy hand" upon the Broads and notes: "This sentence gave, as might be expected, the most universal satisfaction." The greatest punishment the Broads' received, however, stemmed not from the cruelty of their actions but resulted from their disturbing the peace. The laws governing servitude were meant to ensure that masters, as well as servants, upheld their social obligations and roles. The Broads' crimes disrupted the peace by disrupting the social order. Fortunately for the innocents involved, Broad manumitted his slaves in the middle of the trial, although Van Wyck notes he was obliged to consider it "rather as the effect of fear, than as a mark of tenderness or contrition." In areas such as this, where the text lacks the objectivity contemporary readers expect from court records, the trial record offers some wonderful insight into how people of the early Republic thought about freedom, social obligation, crime, and the nature of justice.

CRB

District of New-York,

Be it remembered, That on the fourth day of March, in the thirty-third Year of the Independence of the United States of America, Henry C. Southwick of the (L.S.) said District, has deposited in this Office, the Title of a Book, the right whereof he claims as Proprietor, in the words and figured following: To wit,

The Trial of Amos Broad and his Wife, on three several Indictments for Assaulting and Beating Betty, a Slave, and her Little Female child Sarah, aged three years. Had at the Court Of Special Sessions of the Peace, held in and for the City and Country of New-York, at City-Hall, of the said City, on Tuesday, the 28th day of February, 1809. Present, the hon. Pierre C. Van Wyck, Recorder, Peter Mesier and James Drake, Esquires, Aldermen. To which is added, the Motion of Counsel in Mr. Broad's behalf, to mitigate the imprisonment of His person, and impose a fine—and the reply of Mr. Sampson. Also, the Prayer or Invocation of Mr. Broad, to the Court, for *Mercy*—and the Address of his Honor, the Recorder, on passing Sentence on the Defendants.

In conformity to the Act of Congress of the United States, entitled, "An Act for the Encouragement of Learning, by securing the Copies of Maps, Charts, and Books, to the Authors and Proprietors of such Copies, during the times therein mentioned.—And also to an Act entitled, "An Act, Supplementary to an Act, entitled, an Act for the Encouragement of Learning, by securing the Copies of Maps, Charts, and Books, to the Authors and Proprietors of such Copies during the times therein mentioned, and extending the benefits thereof to the arts of Designing, engraving, and Etching Historical and other Prints."

CHARLES CLINTON.

Clerk of the District of New-York.

THE

TRIAL

OF

AMOS BROAD AND HIS WIFE,

On three several Indictments for Assaulting and Beating

BETTY, A SLAVE,

AND HER LITTLE

FEMALE CHILD SARAH,

AGED THREE YEARS.

Had at the Court of Special Sessions of the Peace, held in and
for the City and County of New-York, at the City-Hall, of the
said City, on Tuesday, the 28th day of February, 1809.

PRESENT,

The Hon. Pierre C. Van Wyck, Recorder.
Peter Mesier and James Drake, Esquires, Aldermen.

To which is added, the Motion of Counsel in Mr. Broad's behalf,
to mitigate the imprisonment of his person, and impose a
fine—and the reply of Mr. Sampson. Also, the Prayer or Invocation of Mr. Broad, to the Court, for Mercy—and the Address
of his Honor, the Recorder, on passing Sentence on the Defendants.

New-York :

PRINTED BY HENRY C. SOUTHWICK,
NO. 2, WALL-STREET.

1809.

Title page of *The Trial of Amos Broad and His Wife . . .
for Assaulting and Beating Betty* (1809 edition; courtesy
of the American Antiquarian Society)

Advertisement.

The evidence contained in the following pages, is too interesting to humanity and good morals, to be sunk in silence or oblivion.—Since the object of municipal law is not so much vengeance on an offender, as by the example of its punishment to deter others from crimes—publicity is essential to its ends. That the pains shall light on few, and the example benefit many, is the sentiment of enlightened jurisprudence. If this be true, there never was a case more deserving of universal notice; never one more characteristic of a nation's justice; none ever offered to humanity a more generous triumph—to unfeeling pride, a more impressive lesson—or whispered in the ear of the oppressed, more balmy consolation.

The Report.

At a Court of Special Sessions of the Peace, held in and for the City and County of New-York, at the City-Hall, of the said City, on Tuesday, the 28th day of February, 1809.

PRESENT,

THE HON. PIERRE C. VAN WYCK, *Recorder.*

PETER MESIER,
AND
JAMES DRAKE.
} *Esquires, Aldermen.* } *Justice of the Sp. Sessions.*

The People of the State
of New-York,
vs.
Amos Broad:
} An Indictment for Assaulting and Beating Sarah, his Slave. [1]

The same
vs.
The same.
} For an Assault and Beating of Betty, his Slave.

The same.
vs.
Demis, the Wife
of Amos Broad.
} For Assaulting and Beating Sarah, A Female Child of the said Betty, aged three years

On each of which indictments the defendants were severally and respectively convicted.

One of the jurors, Mr. *Nehemiah Allen*, was challenged by the traversers Counsel, as being a member of the Manumission Society, under whose auspicious the prosecution had been instituted. The Court, without hearing any argument, over-ruled the challenge, and the following gentlemen were the Jurors sworn to try the several indictments:

Joshua Waddington,	*Alexander C. Wiley,*
Evander Childs,	*Amos Belding,*
Henry Overing,	*Nehemiah Allen,*
William Betts,	*Henry C. Southwick,*
James McConnel	*Conrad Brooks,*
Simon Stebbins,	*Edward Mooney.*

Witness for the People.	Witness for the Defendant.
Margaret Faupell,	*Elizabeth Valentine,*
Mary Shaffle,	*Sarah Willis,*
Henry Baird,	*John Minshull,*
Maria Tillick,	*Rebecca Swain,*
Lavina Van Wyck,	*Jane Griffith,*
David Felder,	*Mary Hutchinson,*
Charles Marsh,	*Philip Wiley.*
William S. Burling,	
Robert Gourlay.	

Counsel for the prosecution, RIKER, District Attorney, and SAMPSON. For the Defendant, WILKINS.

Trial, &c.

The ATTORNEY GENERAL in a grave and impressive manner suited to the nature of the subject, opened the case on behalf of the People. He made few observations, but stated the testimony correctly and substantially as it came afterwards from the mouths of the witnesses. To avoid repetition therefore, it is published as it was taken down by one of the counsel concerned in the cause.

1st. Witness for the People:

Miss Margaret Faupell, worked at Mr. Broad's nearly a year, she had seen much cruelty on the part of Mr. and Mrs. Broad towards their servants, had seen Mr. Broad strip the slave Betty naked in the coldest weather, when the snow was on the ground. She had seen him whip her in the kitchen, and afterwards turn her out into the yard, and keep her there half an hour; the slave begged for her cloathes, which after much entreaty he permitted her to have, ordering her at same time to beg his pardon. The witness said to answer in a question put to her, that she was not an eye witness of the whipping, at the time she now alluded to, but that she saw the bunch of rods which the Defendant took to whip her with, and heard her cries. She saw the Defendant throw three or four bowls of water upon her. She stated further, that this unfortunate slave Betty had been sometimes locked up and kept without food, and among other instances of more refined cruelty, she stated one particularly, which the Defendant himself had avowed in her hearing; that he had obliged Betty to swallow glauber salts out of a bowl at a time when she was in good health, *as a punishment.*[2] Several questions were put to the witness, as well by the Jury as the Counsel, touching the conduct and character of the slave; to see by what acts of hers such treatment could have been provoked. The witness answered that the faults imputed to her were mere trifles; that she was a very willing servant; and witness believed, with a good master would have been a very good one; but from the witnesses expressions it appeared that she was rather stupified by terror than guilty of any wilful fault—It was asked if she had ever heard that the slave had run away, the witness answered that she had not, and that Mr. Broad never suffered her to go out of the house.

With respect to the child of this unfortunate mother, an infant of 3 years of age, on whom Mr. Broad practised many cruelties; she related, that on one occasion she had seen him rub its face so violently upon the carpet as to hurt it very severely and occasion much blood to flow. She had seen him kick this baby, and once throw it upon a bank of snow. She had seen him knock it down repeatedly.

The witness was next desired to state what she knew of Mrs. Broad's treatment of the infant. She began by saying, that she had seen her both beat the child and whip the mother. The counsel for the defendant was about to object to any evidence of an assault upon the mother by Mrs. Broad, inasmuch as she was only indicted for assaulting and beating the child; when the attorney general recalled the question he had put to the witness, and desired her to say nothing of any cruelties of Mrs. Broad towards the mother, and to confine her testimony to the beating or ill treatment of the child. Some questions were then put by way of cross-examination to the witness, and being asked whether she had not, before going to the Grand Jury, declared that she knew nothing of all this; she replied with earnestness that she never had said so; but as soon as she found that enquiry was to be made, and that she might be called upon to state the truth, knowing that the truth could not be agreeable to Mr. Broad, she left his house about a fortnight ago, and had not spoken to him from that time til now. She being further questioned, added that Betty was sometimes kept so hungry, that she had out of compassion given her part of the dinner she had carried to Mr. Broad's for herself.

2d Witness for the People, Miss Mary Shaffle, The principal fact to which this witness testified, was her having gone one morning early into Mr. Broad's house, and there saw Betty with her hands tied up over her head, and the defendant Broad setting before her in a chair with a cowskin in his hand. She had seen Broad kick the child, because when he had ordered it to walk it would not go fast enough to please him. She never had heard it even said that the wench had attempted to run away.

3d Witness for the People. Henry Baird, had seen Betty tied up by the hands to a line in an upper room, which appeared from the witnesses testimony to have been a ware room where beds were kept for sale.

4th Witness for the People. *Maria Tillick,* had worked two years at Mr. Broad's and left it about three months ago. She had not seen the defendant Broad actually whip Betty, but she had seen him force her to carry a bundle of sticks with which he was going to whip her, and had seen her return afterwards crying.

With respect to her infant, Broad used to make her stand by the door in the coldest weather, and would not suffer her to sit down, and when the baby got tired and sat down he would kick her. The witness had seen him nip the infants ear, and sometimes lift her up by it, and once saw him carry her across the floor by the hold of her ear; with one kick she had seen him send her across the store. He used to make her stand by the hour in the cold, till the child's ancles became swelled, and she became crippled by kicking and bad treatment, and had the appearance of being frost bitten. The witness was proceeding to relate how Mrs. Broad horse-whipped Betty, when the objection was made that the *lady* was not indicted for the offence, and that part of the case was therefore suppressed. It appeared however, that both master and mistress acted so cruelly towards the slaves, that the witness was shocked, and often went out of the way to avoid the painful sensation which their screeches occasioned her. She once saw the little girl's head cut open, and stated that Doctor Gamage was sent for, and came to dress the wound. Being questioned as to the pecuniary circumstances of Mr. Broad: she had often heard him say he was worth a great deal of money. He kept one store as an Upholsterer, and his wife another as a Milliner. Witness never had any personal disagreement with Mr. or Mrs. Broad, but left them in order to go to housekeeping

5th Witness to the People. *Levina Van Wyck.* Had worked nearly two years at Mr. Broads, had often seen him horsewhip Betty, after stripping her first he took her to the kitchen and whipped her; sometimes he would whip her with a horsewhip and sometimes with rods: and after she was whipped would turn her naked into the yard, or into the cellar and keep her there in the severest frost for half an hour at a time; and after he suffered her to come in, he forbad her to come near the fire. Witness had heard Mrs. Broad enquire where Betty was, and had heard her husband answer that he had her away—that she was tied up.

The slave was kept so the whole day. The witness had also given her a share of the provisions she had carried for herself, finding that she was kept without food and was hungry. Witness had seen both Mr. and Mrs. Broad throw water upon her; had seen Mr. Broad kick the infant in the breast till it gasped for breath. She had seen Mrs. Broad strike her other female slave Hannah, and was proceeding to state some particulars of cruelty towards her, when she was stopped upon the technical ground before mentioned, namely, that it was a substantive indictable offence, distinct from that of which Mrs. Broad now stood indicted, and that it could not be legally given in evidence on the present trial. She then affirmed that Mr. Broad had not only thrown water upon Betty, but after doing so, had turned her out in the cold, and kept her there till the water froze into ice upon her. She saw Mrs. Broad whip and kick the child, and throw a case knife at her head, which cut so large a gash, and made her bleed so excessively, that Doctor Gamage was sent for to sew it up, and went up stairs with Mr. Broad. The child at the time the knife was thrown at her, was standing beside the sofa. Mrs. Broad told the Doctor that the child had fallen against the sofa, and cut herself, but the witness positively saw her throw the knife, and saw it strike the child.

6th Witness for the People. *David Fielder*, Had worked with Broad some time, he had not seen defendant strike his slave Betty, but he had seen her with her hands tied and stripped nearly naked. Witness said Mr. and Mrs. Broad used to send for him and his old woman (his wife) to take care of their children; upon which one of the counsel for the prosecution asked emphatically if they had children; and the question seemed to vibrate upon every heart. Witness answered that they had five young children: had seen Broad with his shirt sleeves tucked up, standing over Betty with rods in his hand, whilst she lay on the kitchen floor naked as she was born.

Here the case of the prosecution rested.

1st *Witness for the Defendant, Sarah Willis*, Said she had lived three years with Mr. and Mrs. Broad—that she had always seen the servants have plenty to eat, and never saw them struck. Upon further examination, said she had not lived there—had been there frequently—daily—the last time she worked there, was a few days, about three months ago—acknowledged she had seen the other witnesses give some of their meat to Betty. A question was put to her on behalf of the Defendant, whether Betty had not been in the habit of washing herself in the yard with soap-suds, which produced a visible effect, different from what the Defendant expected from it.

2d. Witness for the Defendant. *Elizabeth Valentine*, said she had been frequently at the defendant's house, and that the slaves were well fed and clothed.

3d. Witness for the Defendant. *Mr. John Minshull*, he knew Mr. Broad merely as a neighbour, was not acquainted with his family, but would relate merely what the servants had said in his hearing. He was passing by the defendant's door, and entered into conversation about the cause that was coming on. Witness cautioned him to be clear in the evidence he should produce, as one story was good till the other was heard. Defendant called the servants, and he the witness questioned them. The child said she had fallen against the sofa and cut herself, they said they had no complaint to make of bad treatment, either of Mr. or Mrs. Broad. They looked as if they were well kept, well treated, and well clad. Mr. and Mrs. Broad were very industrious as the witness understood, very attentive to their customers, and lived harmoniously with all their work-people, and paid attention to their business. It appeared upon nearer examination, that the conversation the witness related, took place the evening before the trial.

Miss Faupell was again called; and stated in addition to the evidence that she had before given, that she had seen Broad the very day that he had forced Betty to drink the glauber salts out of the bowl, order her to scrub the cistern, and that Mrs. Broad objected, that it might kill her; that Mr. Broad then desisted, but that on the next day he made her go in almost naked, with a petticoat in slits and without shoes or stockings. She saw him also when Betty brought a teapot, because he said she had put too much water in it, order her to hold out her hand, and pour boiling water upon it; using at the same time this expression—"Am not I a good doctor to doctor negroes?"

4th. Witness for the Defendant. *Rebecca Swain*, said she had lived backwards and forwards working for Mr. Broad eight years—her occupation was washing in the kitchen—never saw any thing improper—saw the servants well clothed and getting of food—witness being asked is she was there when the child's head was cut, answered she was not.

5th. Witness for the Defendant. *Jane Griffith*. This witness was an elderly woman and deaf: said she was in the kitchen when the child was hurt, did not see the child, but was told she fell against the sofa, and heard them cry that its head was *cut*. The question was then put to the witness, whether Miss Van Wyck had not told her that the child fell against the sofa, and she answered that she had not. This witness also asserted that she never saw Mr. Broad beat the servants.

The defendant next produced his daughter, *Eliza Broad*, an infant, to judge from her appearance, of nine or at most ten years of age. It was objected by the attorney general, that a child of such tender years ought not to be admitted; particularly in a case where no necessity called for it. A sufficient number of witnesses had already been called by the defendant, provided the jury gave them any credit, or believed what they said of importance enough to counterbalance the testimony of so many unimpeached and disinterested witnesses, who had positively deposed to the facts in proof of the charge. And least of all in a case where parental authority might be supposed to have entire sway, and when her father was sitting close by her. Some questions were put to the child by the court, as to her knowledge of the nature of an oath. At first she said she was not acquainted with it, and it being observed that she ought not to be prompted in the answer she was to give. She was asked by Sampson of counsel for the prosecution, how she knew her own age. She answered that her mama had told her not long ago. When desired to say why her mother had told her so, she said because she asked her; she could not say why she happened to ask her particularly; she was questioned as to the occasion of asking so lately, what she had never asked before. To this the child gave no answer, and the attorney general proposed that the family bible should be sent for, where probably the age of the children was inscribed: but it appearing that there was no such thing, the court put an end to the discussion by rejecting the witness.

6th Witness sworn on the part of the Defendant. *Mary Hutchinson.*—A question had been put by the defendant, to his counsel, on the examination of Miss Van Wyck, and in the hearing of the jury, whether she had not, prior to her giving in her testimony, declared that she knew nothing of the matter. This witness was examined as to what she knew of the fact, and she testified that, instead of saying she knew nothing of the matter, Miss Van Wyck had asserted to the prisoner's face, in this witness's hearing, that he had whipped the servants and turned them out naked. She had only said that she did not know who informed, but not that she knew nothing of the matter. Her words were, that though she did not know who first informed, yes she would certainly state the truth, when called upon to do so. She was asked by the defendant's counsel, whether the black woman, Betty, had not been in the habit of washing herself in the yard with soap suds, and answered that she had not. The question was put with a view of giving to the affair of the cistern, the colour of the voluntary act of the slave; but it produced a quite different impression. The witness said she had heard Mr. Broad say something of that kind, a few days ago, but never heard it from any body else.

7th Witness for the Defendant. *Philip Wiley*, said he had lived with the defendant since November, except three weeks. This witness spoke of the humanity of Mr. and Mrs. Broad, towards their slaves, and of their being well fed and well cloathed—said he had heard defendant desire Betty to go and wash herself, because she was dirty; that this was since the complaint was instituted. Witness still lives with Broad. Upon cross examination, said he never knew her to wash naked; never understood that it was her general custom to wash herself naked in the yard with soap suds; never knew that she did so. Witness further stated that Mr. Broad had sent him lately to invite Miss Van Wyck and Miss Faupell, to come to him and receive the wages that he owed them; and the answer was, that he owed them nothing.

Miss *Faupell* re-examined—stated that Mrs. Broad had, on Christmas day, taken away Betty's clothes, and forced her, entirely naked, to go about the house, and make three fires. Heard Mrs. Broad herself talk of it, and avow it. Witness repeated that her reason for leaving Mr. Broad's, was nothing else than that she had determined to tell the truth, and did not think it proper to stay there longer.

With respect to the testimony of Mrs. Griffith, this witness contradicted her in a most material point, for she affirmed, that Mrs. Griffith, who here on oath, had denied ever having seen any whipping of Betty in the kitchen—had frequently told her that she had seen Mr. Broad whip Betty.

This contradiction being so manifest, and irreconcilable, it became necessary for the jury to decide to which party credit should be given. Accordingly, Mrs. Griffith was called up, and the witnesses were confronted. Mrs. Faupell, a young person of a very interesting appearance, asked the other with earnestness, if she had never told her she had seen Betty whipped in the kitchen; and Mrs. Griffith admitted, after some hesitation, that she had once had; and the witness stated an additional fact—that Mr. Broad had said to her, that though she did come to court, she need not tell the whole of what she knew.

7th. Witness for the People.—*Charles Marsh*, said he, with two or three of his friends, had entered into conversation with Broad, and, among other things, asked him why he had sent his wench naked into the yard in such cold weather? The defendant's answer was, that she was dirty, and he ordered her out naked to wash herself. Mr. Marsh was also asked if any thing had been said of soap suds, and answered also in the negative: but to questions put to him on the subject of Broad's general treatment to his servants, he answered, that it was generally understood to be very base.

8th. Witness for the People.—*W.S. Burling.*—His testimony went to corroborate that of the young ladies; having heard their statement in the beginning, and the evidence they now gave upon the trial: he declared that they were perfectly consistent; and that both the young girls told him, their reason for quitting their service was, that they had determined to tell the truth, and therefore did not think it safe to stay longer at Mr. Broad's.

9th Witness for the People.—*Robert Gourley*—Lives a few doors from the defendant. Seeing the little child trembling and looking sick, was induced to ask what ailed it. Broad answered that it was a dirty child, and accused it in coarse terms of that which is equally imputable to every infant; adding, that he wished it was dead. It appeared to the witness as if it was ricketty. There was a doctor present who recommended a vomit, but defendant answered, that he would be troubled with no such thing.

Charles Marsh. This witness was again called to state the character which the defendant bore as to the treatment of his servants. This was objected to by his counsel, and the objection shortly answered on the ground of reciprocity, by Sampson, on the part of the prosecution, who urged that the defendant had put his character, in this respect, in issue, by offering testimony himself on that point, and making it part of his defence; and the court permitted the witness to proceed, who testified that the reputation that Broad bore for cruelty to his servants, was bad: that a female apprentice had once been taken from him by the authority of a court of justice, because of his ill treatment to her. His character in Albany had been the same, where he had kept the whole city in disquietude: and all his neighbours now could testify the same thing of him in New-York.

Cross-examined: asked if he could name any neighbours that would say so. Witness named several; for instance, Mr. White, Mrs. Gerard, Mr. Roberts; and Mr. Spencer, now in court, and no doubt ready to answer, if the court thought proper.

The evidence closed here: and Wilkins declined summing up to the jury; but made a proposal; that the defendant should voluntarily and instantly manumit the mother and her child, and also, the third slave named Hannah, whose case was not involved in the present indictment. Deeds of manumission were immediately prepared, and the court ordered that the defendant should be permitted to go home in custody of an officer, which he did in company with several members of the manumission society, into whose benevolent charge the astonished victims were delivered. This proposal of liberating the slaves was made after a conference with several members of that society, who were attending the trial.—They readily listened to a condition so congenial to the principles of their association: but the jury by Mr. Waddington their foreman, after pronouncing the verdict of guilty, expressed openly their opinions, that the forfeiture of the slaves was by no means an adequate punishment. Their concern on this head was however quieted by a remark of the court, that it certainly should not be so considered. The prisoner having been brought back in custody, was recommitted to Bridewell.

Friday, March 3, 1809.

This day Mr. Wilkins moved in mitigation of the sentence, on behalf of the defendants. He proposed to lay before the court an affidavit of Doctor Gamage, touching the pregnancy of Mrs. Broad, and the danger which might accrue to her health, from so great a shock as the imprisonment of her husband must necessarily give her. The affidavit was not read, but the doctor, Mr. Wilkins said, was expected instantly, and would depose to that effect. The court indulged him with a considerable delay, and the attorney general, desirous that the proceedings should bear every mark of candor, and the conviction and sentence be stamped with the seal of justice, admitted the fact of pregnancy, as if it had been sworn to.

Mr. Wilkins began by disclaiming every thing bearing to the colour of justification of the conduct of his client, nor did he attempt to justify the conduct of his wife. He did not attempt to interpose between them and the sentence of the offended law; but stated in eloquent terms, the wounds which a woman's sensibility must endure, in a situation so critical, from the ignominious imprisonment of her husband. He stated her to be already almost frantic with agitation and grief. He prayed that the punishment might be so modified as to fall upon the guilty alone, and not be extended to little children, in whom there could be no crime. The object of the law can never be intended to be the punishment of the innocent. Punishment is cruelty, when the guiltless suffer by it. Punishment is meant to deter the guilty, and so to prevent guilt in others. The punishment of the unoffending cannot effect that purpose. It is more an angry sentence than a wise and humane one, that visits the sins of the fathers upon the children. If the defendant is a sordid man, punish him by his avarice, and that will make him feel. Let him suffer in his property, by the loss of the servants he has ill treated. Add to that such a fine as may make him feel still more, and so without disgracing his children, or depriving them of the care or protection of a father, let that father, who is the only offender, satisfy the very rigour of the law. But even if excessive humiliation be necessary, think how great a portion of it he must endure in the general indignation that is raised against him. Already I am informed that this trial is in the press. Is that no punishment? That his name shall be sent abroad to the four quarters of the world, branded with shame; that he becomes an object for scorn to point her slow unmoving finger at. Public justice, public opinion, it is said, demands it; popular opinion is ever vehement and violent; but it should never influence the decision of a tribunal of law. With public opinion a court of justice has nothing to do: but mercy is ever becoming to the judgement seat. Let the punishment then be such as that law and mercy may walk hand in hand, and every end of justice will be answered, except its vengeance.

Sampson, on the part of the prosecution, rose to answer the observations and arguments of the opposite counsel. To which Mr. Wilkins made some opposition, observing that counsel should not be heard in aggravation of punishment: that it was contrary to the tenderness and humanity of the law. Besides, added he, the attorney general is the proper and official prosecutor, and it belongs to him, and to him only, to call for punishment, and to enforce it.

Sampson, in answer to this objection, observed, that it would be a strange privilege accorded to a man, whose crime his ingenious advocate had thought proper to say was beyond measure or example, that he should be favoured, after conviction, with a hearing, upon affidavits, and that hearing be without reply. In misdemeanors where the punishment was only to be measured by the discretion of the court, it was doubtless right that the court should have what could be urged on either side, to enlighten and inform its judgement, because the facts that serve to prove or disprove the issue, do not always go to shew the degree nor quality of the offence; from thence has arisen the practice of laying affidavits before the court, after conviction, and of hearing counsel as well in aggravation as in mitigation of the sentence. Upon conviction, the province of the jury ceases; they are *functi officio*. It is there that the court find themselves called upon to see what judgement should follow; and the words by which their judgement is recorded, shew it; for, after the entry of the conviction, follow these words—"whereupon it is considered." The court is bound to consider and to deliberate; and nothing that can enlighten their judgement is, or ought to be, excluded. In civil actions which sound in damages, the jury assess the damages, which then become certain; and the court have only to consider whether the record will warrant their judgement, and then to award execution according to law.—In actions where the thing demanded is certain, the jury have nothing to find but the fact in issue, and the court have only to adjudge its accuracy in due form. In criminal cases, whether there is, or is not, a certain punishment, either by common or statute law, the jury have nothing to do with the measure of the punishment: where it is fixed, the court have nothing to do but to award it: but when the law has fixed no punishment, it rests in the discretion of the courts: and never is an earthly tribunal invested with so high a trust, or held to a more high responsibility, than in the exercise of that discretion; and therefore whatever can aid it in the due administration of so great a trust, is fitting to be heard.

When this nation in the full exercise of sovereign power thought proper to adopt the English code, it adopted of necessity that practice which is its incident. And on what principle then can it be said that in a matter of so high importance, one party shall be heard and not the other; on one hand stand the public right; on the other, those of a convicted individual; let the law be sensible and tender of the accused, least he fall before an unjust persecution, but let not justice be denied to the community, and the convicted offender be set above the law, and entitled to an *ex parte* hearing. Let justice in this, as in every other case, hold the balance with an even hand. Let there be reciprocity, which is true justice.

With respect to the attorney general. He is certainly the official prosecutor, but does it then follow that he is so exclusively. Why then is it that in England, he seldom appears but when the offence immediately affects the execution itself. Why is it that when he does appear, he seldom or ever acts alone, but is seconded sometimes by other public officers skilled in the law, or by select and chosen counsellors, associated with him. I have myself been almost as often for the prosecution as for the prosecuted, even in my own country, and in troubled times; and when the prosecution was not in the sense of the execution, the complaining party has desired that I should be associated with the public prosecutor, and it has never been refused to me. That the same principle has been adopted here, is proved from this; that we have often seen the learned counsel who makes this objection, associated with the same attorney-general whose associate I now have the honour to be, and if he thought it was a wrong indulgence, he would not surely have claimed it on behalf of our client. The attorney general is certainly qualified, eminently, for the duties he has to fulfil; so much so that the self possession and recollection he evinces of the multitude of facts and cases as he has to attend to, has often astonished me; as well as the patience, kindness, and diligence, with which he attends to everyone: but when the whole is calculated, he has scarcely one minute to bestow upon each case, and if he chuses to accept of any assistance, he certainly is entitled to it.

The court intimating to Mr. Sampson that it was disposed to hear him, he proceeded:

May it please the Court—There may be moments, when justice, seated on the throne of grace, may deck herself in smiles and courtsies. There are occasions when she will connive at little crimes, and rather piously countenance small errors, than suffer too heavy pains to fall on venial sins; or knit her angry brow for slight offences. But there are times when sterner looks become her; when she must wield her sceptre, and come forth arrayed in majesty. Such is the attitude in which we now invoke her; such the form wherein you, her earthly ministers, are now to view her. Read her commands in words of awful import, and give them efficacy. Where mercy has been shewn, let mercy be. Where guilt is wiped away by long contrition, let forgiveness follow. Shew mercy to the humble and the meek. But let not that fair thing be prostituted at a ruffian's beckon. Let that rich treasure which belongs to justice, be better husbanded. Let it not be idly squandered to the undeserving, for so the meritorious may be robbed. If man's offences call for punishment, and law requires examples—if some must suffer, that justice may be vindicated, let it be those whose guilt admits of no alloy; and whose example may carry with it the strongest test of rectitude. What then are this man's crimes? Wherein are they compatible with mercy? Where was mercy when he scourged the naked slave, and turned her out to smart, exposed to the keen frost? Who talked of pity then, when she lay naked, prostrated at his feet, when he stood over her, his sleeves tucked up, his scourges in his hand, a ruthless, barbarous, brutal executioner? Where was compassion, when he kept the shuddering wretch beneath the biting blast of searching winds; and fearing that her sufferings were too gentle, drenched her first with water, and then kept her till the piercing breath of winter had crusted her shivering limbs with icicles? Where was that seraph pity, when he forced this unoffending, unresisting being to hold out her own hand until he poured upon it boiling water? There was a Roman tyrant whose atrocious acts, the page of history, has handed down to endless infamy. He made his slaves hold out their hands till, for his sport, he shot arrows in between their fingers. He was a villain, but yet his pride was, not to hurt the slave; he used address to save him from the wound. But here, was dull malignity and sullen cruelty. His very jest were felonies. "Am not I a good doctor, he asks, to doctor negroes?" Were these givings merciful, will they now entitle him to mercy? Or, was it merciful, to force the miserable being, whom fortune had submitted to his atrocious will, to swallow large draughts of drugs and sickening inducements? No, but his counsel, whose nature is too pure to be the advocate of inhumanity, has disclaimed all mercy as to him, and chosen a different ground which I shall now examine:—

He has a wife! the mother of five children! and he, their father! Gracious heaven! How does this thought recoil upon his head? Where were the tender feelings of a father, when he could kick and buffet a poor baby, that had, under heaven, no protector, to use his giant force to knock it down? To kick it till it gasped for breath; to keep it fixed, trembling in the chilling frost, until its poor limbs were gangrened; to drag and lift it by its little ears; to wish it dead, and make its dawn of life, the age of innocence and playful gambol, a scene of misery, decrepitude and anguish. How could that child offend? If he was a man, how could the little helpless thing provoke him? Was he a father, and could he do such deeds; and having done them, dare he talk of mercy!

But it is said, that, for his wife's sake, you should be pitiful. It is true, that nothing pleads so strong for sympathy, as woman's tender accents. And often have the lamentations of a wife, the sorrows of a mother, disarmed the hand of justice. But there is a great difference between melting grief of virtuous woman, and the hysterical stomaching of rage, and the suffocations of wounded pride. There is a charm in woman's prayers, which man can scarce resist. There is more power in female gentleness than in a giant's strength. But since it is her gentleness that constitutes her empire; that once abandoned, the lovely charm is fled; the sacred spell is dissipated; her syren voice is like the unseemly owl. Where were the virtues of a female heart, when this woman, whose sensibility is so strongly urged, far from restraining her brutal, barbarous husband; joined with him, heart to heart, and hand to hand, to practice such disgraceful outrages. Where was the delicacy of her gentle sex, when she exposed to the yet innocent eyes of her own offspring, the spectacle of female nakedness? Where were her sex's feelings, when, like a fury, she brandished the bloody scourge? Where were the mother's sympathies when, to the acute sufferings of a wretched mother, were added to those pangs, more poignant, and more cutting to a mother's soul, than her own corporal sufferings? When all the fiend-like torments were exhausted upon the person of a wretched mother, there still remained for her, another self, through which she could be tortured. One source of sensibility remained, and that exhaustless, a mother's love. That tender tie that all creation owns; that strong affection that exceeds the love of life, or love of self. That tie that holds through life, and is the last that nature severs. This was not overlooked: and well the wretched mother's heart was wrung. 'Tis true, no cries could pierce her, for tears and groans, and cries were silences by the hand of terror. But let her who is a mother speak, and say, were the child whom she had borne with pangs and throes, been in her sight so maimed—so bruised—so blighted, what would be her feelings? I therefore say, in terms—her sex disowns her—and he who pleads for lovely woman, pleads against her.

The next ground urged by the counsel for the defendants, is their children.

For their sakes it is said, the punishment, whatever it may be, should be modified: and imprisonment be commuted for a pecuniary fine. If the children were of an age to feel and partake of the shame of their father, which they are not, still it would be no ground to move the court; because among the convicts who will this evening or to-morrow croud that dock (pointing to the dock) in order to receive the sentence which their crimes have brought upon them, many will have both wives and children; children as innocent as those of the defendants, and wives much more so: wives who stand unconvicted and unaccused. If to have wives and children were to attone for every crime, impunity would be too general.

It is said besides, that these children will be deprived of the care and tutelage of a father, at an age when they stand most in need of it. But I think the lessons he has been used to give them, of indecency and cruelty, can be no loss. But on the contrary, his separation from them may be a lasting benefit to them: perhaps to him. Humiliation may soften him: seclusion may reform him. By suffering he may learn what pity means. Silence and meditation may amend him. If that should happen, he will return a better father and a better man, and his children may bless the day when he was taught to feel. But upon what principle is it proposed to the court, to accept of pecuniary satisfaction to the public. Is it a ransom that is offered? Captives in battle may be ransomed: Men who fall into the hands of Arabs, Moors, or Tartars, may offer ransom:—but will the idea be endured, that because a man has money, his person shall be privileged: might not every culprit say, I have money, I can buy impunity, and pay my debt to justice with my purse.

As to the voluntary manumission of his slaves, there are two ways of viewing it. If it were from contrition, and as an offering of penitence, it should not then be set forward as a bargain with the court. This court will doubtless pronounce such sentence as the offence may seem to deserve. That sentence cannot affect life or limb, and beyond this court there is another power which may still be appealed to, if any future facts or circumstances should merit favor. The manumission of the slaves is certainly one consideration. And if it be a punishment, and not a spontaneous expiation, it is a punishment bearing strong characteristic marks of justice, inasmuch as the very objects which have been the instruments of crime, are become the instruments of punishment. How far it may go in the judgement of the court, to shorten the period of imprisonment, is a matter for its wisdom to determine: but as a ransom or a bargain, it can surely avail nothing.

The nature of the defence was ill-calculated to conciliate lenity. The crafty and deliberate plan to falsify the truth, and create artificial proofs—the story of the soap suds—the sending for the two young persons to receive wages when none was due to them—the mock trial held before that Mr Minshull, on the eve of the trial here in court, where the wretches were under the atrocious influence of tyranny and terror, made to bear false witness against themselves: all this persisted in till the moment the jury were about to give their verdict, shews that there was no contrition. It was like a death bed repentance under the influence of fear. It would be cruelty, then, in the court, to mar, in its very inception, a new-born sentiment of virtue. Give it time, if it be sincere, to strike root and become permanent. Let the motive which produced it continue till the reform is complete.

It is seldom, too seldom, that acts of oppression, such as this, are brought to light. The master's authority—the silence which fate, for I will not call it law, imposes on the slave, who cannot be a witness to tell his own complaint; gagged; and reduced to the state of the dumb brute, that must suffer and be silent—the want of sympathy among those who are more apt to construe murmurs to crimes, than to hear them with compassion—all these are weighty obstacles to justice.

How long had these beings suffered under the lash of a cruel master, and a more pitiless mistress, before it pleased Providence to send them deliverers in the hour of their deepest despondency? But for those compassionate young women who marked their cries with feeling, and relieved their hunger with their bread, justice had still slept. But for the generous interposition of those whom the reproaches of the unthinking, the difficulties of the law, unpaid labour and contention, cannot weary in their humane pursuits, how could their cries have reached this merciful tribunal? How could truth have pierced the clouds that hung upon her? How many stripes would, by this time, have been added to the countless numbers which they have received, and of which the laws and rules of evidence, during these trials, have shut out from notice? Perhaps the last stroke of affliction might have reached that wretched mother, and some wound of knife or club might have left her to mourn, in silence, over the death of her infant, which she dared not otherwise record than in the tablets of her bleeding heart.

If the court should, after this, and after so many difficulties surmounted, and a case so fairly proved, pronounce their sentence with a faultering or unsteady voice; or diminish any thing of the awe which should belong to it; it were as good to proclaim, with sound of trumpet, a general impunity for all such cruelties.

One topic remains. It is said that this trial is already in the press. If it be, it is surely so much the better. The justice of this land is public justice; as administration is public; its ends are public. When the law punishes, it is not for revenge. It is not to torment the individual for the sake of his torment, but to make such an example as may deter all others. How can this be done if his sentence be not known? Who can be deterred by an example which he has never heard of? And here again I am the advocate of mercy, when I say, that we should leave secret punishments for the seraglio, the inquisition, or the Divan. There the bow string, or the rack, may do their silent office. But I wish this trial, with the just sentence which shall follow it, may be mounted on the wings of the air, and spread where winds can blow, or ships can sail; because wherever it goes, it will be an example to the guilty, and a trophy to humanity. It will be a magnificent testimonial of a nation's justice; to show that though unfortunately slavery has been entailed upon its institutions, and interwoven with them almost past the power of exterpation; yet that the bitter draft is tempered and qualified with the balm of mercy, and that there is for the wretched, a superintending spirit, which, in the moment of their deep despair, can raise them up to liberty and light. I feel, therefore, that in calling for punishment, I am contending for mercy. Did I think other wise, the world has not wherewith to bribe me to join in any persecution. But I feel the conviction of my conscience, that what I do is right; and I trust that no argument used will shake the solemn determination of the court, to pronounce a sentence suited to its object.

Mr. Wilkins rose to reply, and proceeded without any objection on the part of the attorney general. He began by saying, that whatever satisfaction it might give him, on this, as on other occasions, to hear his friend address a court and jury, it seemed almost a presumption in any man to attempt to colour the facts, or heighten the effect of the evidence disclosed upon the trial. Certainly the cruelties proved were extreme, and fit to rival with the deeds of Warren Hasings, or whoever had been more cruel. But that was no answer to the motion he now made. This was an appeal for mercy to the court; not on behalf of the offender himself: but the supplication of five little innocent children, who had done no wrong. Their tender voices were crying for mercy; and unless there be some motive of imperative necessity, why should it be withheld from them? If the court be persuaded that one sentence must involve them in great and lasting distress, without effecting any purpose of justice, but what a different sentence might as well accomplish; will they not adopt that sort of punishment which will exempt the innocent, and fall entirely on the guilty. There is none but the Deity, who can visit the sins of the fathers upon the children. The reason why a prisoner, who is brought to the bar and tried, and convicted of the worst of felonies is sentenced, capitally, is not so much that the offender shall be sacrificed to appease an angry power, or to the names of the dead, as that his example should terrify other offenders from the commission of such crimes; and there is not meant for vengeance, but for prevention. Prevention, therefore, is the only end; and the means are always good enough, if they be subservient to the end. In felonies where there is no discretion in the court, there can be no appeal to that discretion; but where the court has that discretion, and it is appealed to, it is certainly the duty of the court so to modify it, as that the most good, and the least hardship may result from the exercise of it. In other crimes, the judges are forced to read the sentence of the law, without being allowed even where they might wish it most, to ward off its heavy hand; there, if greater punishment would fall upon the innocent than on the guilty, they may say it is hard, but it is written in the law.

The counsel then read from the amendments to the Constitution of the United

States, the following article: *"Excessive bail shall not be required, nor excessive fines imposed, nor cruel and unusual punishments inflicted."* Article 6th. And also the 7th and 8th sections of *"an Act concerning the rights of citizens of this state."* Laws of New-York, p. 48. *"That no citizen of this state shall be fined or amerced without reasonable cause, and such fine or amercement shall be always according to the quantity of his or her trespass or offence, &c."*

That excessive bail ought not to be required, nor excessive fines imposed, nor cruel and unusual punishments inflicted."

He also read a passage from *"Pailey on crimes and punishments,"* to show that punishment was not founded upon the *"lex talionis;"* that is to say, so much pain for so much guilt; but so much as will serve to prevent future crimes. And that it should not stretch beyond the necessity which called for the example. If beyond the measure of the crime, it was unconstitutional; if beyond the necessity of example, it was inhuman. In this case, if the imprisonment of the father should inflict too severe a pain upon the children, it would be a violation of the constitution; of the laws of the state; of the rights of the citizens; and of the great and universal law of humanity.

See then whether this prisoner has not already been brought to the stool of repentance? Is there not enough for example sake; where he shall have every day to work and toil, to regain the sum in which he shall be fined? Will not every day and every transaction remind him, that he is making retribution for past crimes, and warn him against further transgressions? If so, the punishment will be adequate to the offence. It will be what the law requires, and I ask no more.

Saturday, March 4.

The prisoner was brought to the bar, in custody of the keeper of the City-Prison; and it being demanded of him by the Clerk, if he had any thing to say, why the court should not pronounce judgement against him according to law; he requested leave to wait till his wife should arrive, when he should have something to offer. In this he was readily indulged; and the spectators who crouded the court, waited in silent and anxious expectation. After a few moments Mrs. Broad arrived, but without expressing, by her countenance or demeanor, any of those marks of deep sensibility which her eloquent counsel had so pathetically announced. Mr. Broad then proceeded in the following words:—

"I hope the court and the assembly will be merciful to me—I freely forgive all my enemies who have persecuted me.—All who have families, tender and feeling, as I have—all who are fathers of families—I hope my case will serve as a warning and example to them all. I have nothing to say, but that I have been convicted of great and enormous offences—I stand here for crimes that are very great— I forgive all my enemies. I pray the blessed redeemer, who ascended into the regions of glory—whose prayer was, when on the cross, 'Father, forgive them, for they know not what they do.' I pray God to have mercy on all. I pray for my enemies, and those who have given evidence against me. All who are fathers of families, that are placed as *sentries* over them—who look to them as we look to our heavenly father.

"This life is constantly passing away; one generation coming in and another going out. I pray that we may live as if it were eternal; and look to him who reigns over all, to keep us out of temptation—and enjoy the crown which Christ has prepared for those that believe in him.

"We are liable to faults and errors, and insufficient in ourselves to direct the least of out actions, without the assistance of an all-seeing God. May the court and the assembly take notice of my situation. I forgive the malice of my enemies, who have persecuted me, and that their sins may be pardoned; and that they may, at the last hour, be prepared for death. I pray for my enemies, that they may be forgiven."

It was imagined, by many of the bye-standers, that the prisoner, smote by his conscience, was seized with the idea that he was to be sentenced to be hanged; and the strong affinity which his discourse bore to what are usually termed dying speeches, was calculated to inspire that belief.

The recorder, in a very solemn and impressive manner, delivered the sentence of the court. After stating the indictments, and the convictions thereon, he said the circumstances which had come out in evidence, had filled the court with astonishment, that cruelties so enormous should have been perpetrated within this city, and with impunity for so long a time.

He then went through the various acts of cruelty, and made upon each, some impressive and strong remark. He dwelt upon the refinement of terror by which the slaves were brought to deny their master's cruelty, and to excuse him to enquirers—on the aggravated wretchedness and profligacy of making a naked woman, in the most inclement season, go through his house, and before the eyes of his family, on Christmas day—a day set apart for the observance of religious duties. If you had belief in that religion, which seem rather in your mouth than in your heart, you could never have done this. After such transactions, it is to be feared that your religious expressions are but canting hypocrisy, and they cannot certainly alter the determination of the court.

It appeared, added the judge, that on one occasion, so submissive was that slave, and so broken-hearted was her condition, that she was obliged to stand till you poured boiling water on her hand, and dared not utter a single complaint, for fear of a repetition of your cruelty. He stated, in strong terms, the atrocities committed on a child, now but three years old, and at the time of the most shocking of those barbarities, only two years old.—The kicking of it till the breath forsook it—carrying it by the ears, and then adverted to the acts of Mrs. Broad, so disgraceful to her sex; and mentioned the throwing the knife at its head, and the wound inflicted upon it; with the crafty denial of it, in a way that recalled to every hearer the horrors of the scene.

Had not you, at length, become so callous and lost to shame, as to practise these things without reserve or disguise, they would not have been known even to the young persons who have testified them, and by whose evidence you are now brought to justice.

From what has appeared, we have reason to presume, that much more cruelty remains behind, of which no evidence has transpired. It is fully proven by these witnesses, by whom you sought to defend yourself, that not only terror prevented the complaints of the slave, but that they were forced to deny the very violences of which their bodies bore testimony.

The feeling which the public appear to have testified, is an honorable sentiment; but it is not upon that the court ground their sentence; but upon the just principle that the punishment should be a terror to others, and prevent future transgressions against humanity.

Such crimes may be often committed, and yet seldom reach the ears of a tribunal of justice; seeing that the unhappy condition of slaves precludes them from making their complaint on oath, so that any judicial enquiry can be founded upon it. It is, therefore, on the same principle, that punishments are in other cases, proportioned as well to the enormity of the offence, as to the difficulty of counteracting it, and the necessity of example, that it was determined, in this case, to lay upon you a heavy hand.

The court have taken into consideration your manumission of the slaves, which they are obliged, however, to consider rather as the effect of fear, than as a mark of tenderness or contrition. They have, nevertheless, weighed that circumstance, and considered it to its full amount in the mitigation of the term of imprisonment, which you are to undergo; as they have, also, the amount of the fine they mean to impose.

The Sentence.

The sentence of the court, therefore is, that on the first indictment for the assault and battery upon your slave Betty, whereof you stand convicted, you be imprisoned, in the City Prison of the City of New-York, for the term of Sixty Days, and pay as a fine, the sum of *Five Hundred Dollars.*

That on the second indictment for the assault and battery upon Sarah, her child, you imprisoned within said City Prison, for the further term of *Sixty Days,* and pay an additional sum of *Five Hundred Dollars*. And the court having evidence that you are a disturber of the peace in your neighbourhood, further order that you enter into a recognizance, at the expiration of your imprisonment, as aforesaid; yourself in the sum of *One Thousand Dollars*, conditioned for the good behavior of yourself and your wife, for the term of one year; and that you stand committed until this sentence shall be fully complied with.

And with respect to your wife, the Court considering her situation, impose a fine of *Two Hundred and Fifty Dollars*.

This sentence gave, as might be expected, the most universal satisfaction.

The End.

Notes

1. In 1788 New York State adopted a law that allowed owners to free a slave if that individual could become self-supporting. However, it was largely ignored, hence Betty's description as a "slave." A 1799 gradual-emancipation law stipulated that females born after 1799 would be free at the age of twenty-five and males born after 1799 would become free at age twenty-eight. This law, too, was not implemented. Finally, in 1817, New York State completed plans for emancipation in the state with a law that would manumit those born before 4 July 1799, effective 4 July 1827. African Americans celebrated the latter date as New York's Emancipation Day.

2. Glauber's salts are sulphate of sodium, a purgative. They are named after John Rudolf Glauber (1604–68), a German chemist who first made them.

The Narrative of
John Thomson,
One of the Persons
Intended
to Be Massacred

The days leading to the War of 1812 were tumultuous ones for Americans. The war was controversial and had many detractors, especially as the war hawks had no solid plan to manage the struggle and thus no way to convince the nation that is was necessary. In Massachusetts, Congressman Josiah Quincy defiantly proclaimed he "could not be kicked" into waging war. He was not alone in his resolution. Many considered the impending conflict dishonorable, fruitless, and perhaps unconstitutional. On the eastern seaboard, people with maritime interests worried that a state of war would threaten their investments, a concern that overruled their anger over the large number of American men being impressed into British service.

In Baltimore, Maryland, however, the vast majority supported the War of 1812. Baltimore was a prospering Republican city, composed mainly of French, German, and Irish refugees, many of whom hated Great Britain. Still, the city was not without Federalist supporters. Some people, including Alexander Contee Hanson and Jacob Wagner, editors of the *Federal Republican* newspaper, thought that war against Great Britain would be an unnecessarily dangerous risk for the young country. On June 20, two days after the declaration of war, they wrote that the war was "inexpedient" and claimed it bore the marks of "undisguised foreign influence." Public outrage at the *Federal Republican*'s declaration was prompt and violent.

On July 27, 1812, Hanson received warning that his home would be attacked. Fifteen to twenty friends gathered there to defend Hanson and his property. While Hanson and his supporters were able to hold off the mob for a time, violence prevailed. John Thomson, one of the men holed up in Hanson's home on the twenty-seventh, experienced the horrors of mob rule. After the ordeal, he wrote *A Narrative of John Thomson*, which provided a detailed account of the torture the men endured. Many were beaten mercilessly, and one survivor, Ortho Sprigg, wrote: "There is not a solitary ray of compassion, or even of common humanity, to illuminate the gloom of the diabolical atrocity that shrouds the behaviour of those ruffians."

John Thomson was, himself, beaten with clubs, tarred and feathered, and set afire while alive. His life was spared only because he shamed the mob, daringly comparing them to "savages." As a condition for his life, however, Thomson had to agree to give up the names of every man in the house and everything he knew of their politics.

The text that follows recounts the events of that horrific incident. It was recorded on August 6, 1812, under the title *Narrative of John Thomson, one of the persons intended to be massacred with Gen. Lingan and others, in the Gaol of Baltimore, on Tuesday, July 28th 1812* and published in Boston by Nathaniel Coverly. It had been previously published in the *Federal Republican* and the *Maryland Gazette*. A provacative and sensational text, Thomson's *Narrative* was widely reprinted in newspapers throughout August, reaching as many as eighteen printings. The next separate edition was published under the same title in Salem, although the publisher is not indicated, perhaps out of fear of anti-Federalist sentiment. The last record of John Thomson's narrative comes in a larger collection, entitled *An Exact and Authentic Narrative, of the events which took place in Baltimore, on the 27th and 28th of July Last*. It is a collection of eyewitness accounts of the incident, to which Thomson's narrative is attached. The *Exact and Authentic Narrative* ends with a notice entitled "Public Feeling: Town Meeting," which records a meeting of the citizens of Georgetown, who expressed their dismay and outrage that mob rule could override free speech and the rule of law. They resolved to have the minutes of their meeting published in three newspapers, the *Federal Republican*, the *National Intelligencer*, and the *Maryland Gazette*. Their resolutions voice concern that if citizens could not agree on national activities in a unified manner, the country was in grave danger.

Fortunately, the issues that temporarily divided Americans were resolved by the end of the war. The war's conclusion renewed the economy, and Americans began to prosper. And although the end of the war marked the beginning of the end of the Federalist party, citizens managed to resolve public debates more peacefully (at least for the next few decades). Unfortunately, however, there was no final satisfaction for John Thomson and his comrades. Although a clear record of the torturous event in Baltimore existed, and a grand jury indicted Lewis, Wilson, and Mumma for charges associated with the incident, ultimately, none of the accused men in the mob were ever convicted.

CRB

THE

NARRATIVE OF

JOHN THOMSON,

ONE OF THE PERSONS INTENDED
TO BE MASSACRED WITH GEN.
LINGAN AND OTHERS, IN
THE GAOL OF BALTI-
MORE, ON TUESDAY,
JULY 28*th*, 1812.

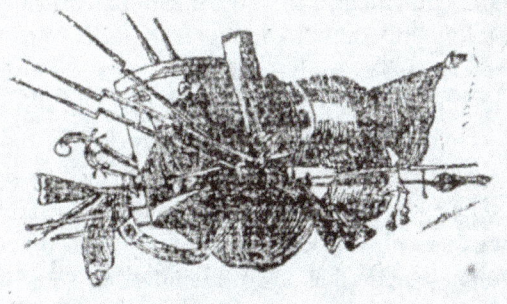

BOSTON:
& PRINTED BY NATHANIEL COVERLY, JUN'R,
CORNER OF THEATRE ALLEY.

Title page of *The Narrative of John Thomson*
(1812 edition; courtesy of the American Antiquarian Society)

On Monday the 27th July last, I was invited by Mr Hanson to his House; and in the evening about twilight, I went there and found from 15 to 20 gentlemen in his house, most of them known to him.[1] I was told that an attack upon the house was threatened that night, which they had made preparations to resist and defeat. I saw some muskets, pistols and swords in the house, for the purposes of defence. After being there sometime, I understood an arrangement had been made that in case of an attack, the direction of the defence was appointed to Gen. Lee. About 8 o'clock, a number of persons were collecting at the front of the house, who were very noisy and began to throw stones at the windows, and they broke several of them. The house was in front completely closed, the door and inside window shutters being shut; till the stones broke the glass and burst open the shutters. Mr. Hanson spoke from the second story to the mob, and told them if they did not desist they would fire upon them, and he warned the spectators to go away. Gen. Lee in the house, told them not to fire unless it should be absolutely necessary, and the doors were forced. The mob continued to encrease and to throw stones more violently, which broke the windows of the first and second stories, Gen. Lee directed a volley to be fired from the upper story over the heads of the people in the street to frighten them away without injuring them. This was executed and nobody was hurt. The mob huzzaed, were still more violent, and broke open the lower door: they were then fired upon, and a man fell at the door upon the inside thereof, who was immediately taken up and removed by some of the mob. This must have happened about 10 o'clock, or after, Judge Scott made his appearance and came into the house, the door having remained open after it was broken, and requested us to leave the house, he was told we should do no such thing, that we could not be secure unless the civil authority interfered, that we were lawfully employed with Mr. Hanson in protecting him and his house against violence, and whenever the mob would disperse or the civil authority interfere, we would retire to our homes and not before. During the night, we continued to defend ourselves, and never fired but after some new and violent attack. I believe it probable several were wounded. The mob during the night retired and gathered again, and attempted some fresh damage. Just about, or before daylight, the mob brought a fieldpiece,[2] which was planted near the house, and in front of it, but was prevented from being discharged by the arrival of capt. Barney's troop of horse, some of whom were stationed round the house, and six of them having dismounted, took possession of the front room on the first floor, and of the back yard. Hanson and his friends occupied the same places which they had done during the night, so things remained, until Edward Johnson, the Mayor, Gen Stricker, John Montgomery, the Attorney-General, James Calhoun, Lemuel

Taylor, and several others arrived and proposed that we should leave the house. We answered we had no objections to leave the house, provided the mob would retire, or we could get home with safety. The mayor said the mob could not be dispersed, nor would they be satisfied without we went to the gaol, and that we should be protected from them in going to gaol, and while in it.

To this proposal, most of us expressly objected. Gen. Lee principally carried on the conversation on our part with the Mayor and Gen. Stricker. The Mayor, Gen. Stricker and Attorney-General severally declared and assured us, that we should be protected as well in going to the gaol as in it, and the mayor pledged his life and his honour that we should be safe, and that he would die with us if we should be hurt. Gen. Stricker expressed himself in similar terms. Also Montgomery, Taylor, Calhoun and their companions gave us assurance of safety if we went to gaol: after those assurances and finding the civil authority would not make any exertion to disperse the mob, we consented with the advice of Gen Lee to deliver ourselves up to the civil authority. The Mayor declared his opinion that we would not be safe in the gaol without a guard, and he and gen. Stricker promised there should be one. About 8 or 9 o'clock on Tuesday forenoon, we left the house and went under the care and custody of the mayor who preceded us, and we were placed between two lines of infantry, consisting as it appeared of about 50 of the militia; about 20 dragoons mounted, advanced before us to the gaol: general Stricker marched on foot with the infantry, and an immense concourse of people were in the streets, some of whom went along, and we were abused in the most opprobrious language; some stones were thrown with violence at us, one struck Mr. Kilgore and cut him badly in the forehead, and another struck Mr. Bigelow, and nearly knocked him down. The distance from Hanson's house to the gaol was about one mile.

At our arrival at the gaol door and as we entered it several of us were struck by some of the mob whom we found there. Being delivered into the custody of John H. Bentley, the gaoler, sometime in the forenoon, we were put in a room in the common criminal department, where we remained the rest of the day. The dragoons and infantry left the gaol soon after we were placed in it, and they did not return, nor was there any military guard afterwards. In the afternoon the mayor came to us in the gaol, and assured us that there should be a guard, and that preparations were making to send one. He told us he would lose his own life before we should be hurt. Gen. Stricker was also at the gaol, outside of it. The mayor having been with us about 20 minutes, went away leaving us in the belief that there would be a guard of armed militia sent to protect us in the gaol; during the afternoon we were told several times by persons admitted to see us that the militia were called out and assembling. Late in the afternoon two butchers one named Mumma and the other Maxwell, came into our room, the former having a key in his hand, Mumma asked the names of several of the prisoners: I told

him. Mr. Hoffman said he wondered Mr. Bentley should suffer so many men
to come into their room who had no business there. Mumma answered that he
come there on Mr. Bentley's business. They were personally known to me and
some of my fellow-prisoners, we suspected their intentions were not good, and
I inquired of Mr. Bentley if Mumma was a friend of his, Bentley answered he
pretends to be so. I replied you ought to know him well before you trust the key
of our room in his hands, and I proposed he should lock the door and give me
the key through the grate. On the inside the door cannot be unlocked, and there
was the outer door locked. Bentley refused, saying I cannot do so as you are a
prisoner under my care. The door was immediately locked by somebody, and
the mob very soon began to assemble from various quarters, but no troops were
arriving. This excited much alarm in our room, it being after sunset, and we
apprehended we were to be sacrificed. About dark the back door of the gaol was
beset by the mob who entered it without breaking it by force. By whom it was
opened I do not know but by hearsay. They began to break down the wood and
iron gratings in the passage leading to our room, which took them at least three
quarters of an hour. They had the light of torches. The grating of our room was
opened instantly without any exertion, which makes me believe it was opened
by some one having the key, and I believe either by Mumma or Maxwell. The
first person I recognized at the grating was Henry Keating, who keeps a Printing
Office, and him I should have killed with my pistols, but for Gen. Lee, who laid
hold of my arms and begged me not to fire, and also prevented Mr. Murray from
firing. It had been agreed that Mr. Murray and myself, being the strongest men,
should rush out and make the best of our way, and every person was to escape
as he could. Some of the mob rushed into the room, and Mr. Murray and myself
rushed out, both of us armed, I had a pistol in each hand and he a dirk and a
pistol. We made our way through the passage and hall without injury till I was at
the front outer door, when I was struck on the back of my head with a heavy club
by some man I had passed, which threw me forward from the head of the steps,
and I fell headlong down about 12 feet. There I saw a gang of Ruffians armed
with clubs, ready to destroy whomsoever should pass down the steps, and six
or seven of them instantly assaulted me while down, and beat me about the head
until I was unable to rise. Some then dragged me twenty or thirty yards while
others were beating me with clubs, they then tried to make me stand on my feet,
and looking round I perceived Lemuel Taylor, and I called upon him to prevent
those men from taking my life. He told the men to desist and said they had beat
me enough and begged them not to take my life; they said they would kill me;
he again repeated that I was beat enough, and desired that I should be let alone,
and he would be security for my forthcoming in the morning. They disregarded
what he had said, they dragged me along and it was proposed to tar and feather
me, and as I went along they continued to strike me with sticks and clubs, one

fellow struck at me with an axe who missed me, when they had dragged me a considerable distance and into old town, they met with a cart and put me into it, and dragged it along themselves to a place where they got tar. I had left my coat in the gaol, and they tore my shirt and other cloathing and put the tar on my bare body, upon which they put feathers.

They drew me along in the cart in this condition; and calling me traitor and tory and other scandalous names, they did not cease to beat me with clubs, and cut me with old rusty swords. I received upon my head, arms, sides, thighs and back, upwards of 18 cuts of the sword. On my head one cut was very deep, beside which my head was broken in more than twelve places by other instruments, such as sticks and clubs, I received a few blows in my face and very many severe bruises on different parts of my body; my eyes were attempted to be gouged, and preserved by means of the tar and feathers. About the same time, as I was lying in the cart, a fellow struck both of my legs with a bar of iron swearing damn my eyes, I will break your legs. I drew my legs up, and he was led to think, and to say he had broke them. Soon after I received a blow with a club across my eyes, upon which I lay as if dead, supposing it would stop their further beating me; remaining so for some time, I was struck upon my thighs, which I bore as if dead; a villain said he would soon see if I was dead, and he stuck a pin into my body twice, at which I did not flinch, but I still remained senseless as if dead. Another said he would show if I was dead, he pulled a handful of tar and feathers and set fire to it, and stuck it on my back, which put into a blaze what was on my back. I turned over suddenly, and rolled apon the flame which put it out before it reached too great a height, but I was burnt in several parts. I then raised upon my knees and addressed them, "for God sake be not worse than savages, if you want my life take it by shooting or stabbing." Often I begged them to put an end to it. Upon this one said don't burn him, another said we will hang him, one in the shafts of the cart turned round and said to me "if you will tell the names of all in the house and all you know about it, we will save your life." Believing all the damage was done which could be done by them, I did not hesitate to say I would. They took me out of the cart upon the causeway at Fell's Point, and carried me to the Bulls Head Tavern, there I gave them the names of all the persons in the house which they took in writing, and the reason of our being in the house, which was to defend Mr. Hanson and his house against violence with which he had been threatened. They detained me about an hour at this tavern, and offered me some whiskey, of which I took several glasses, being extremely thirsty and weak from the loss of blood. They then made we walk, with several persons on each side upholding me, towards the watch house, where they said I should be kept till the morning, and that I should swear to what I had said before a magistrate by nine o'clock, or if I did not they would hang me. On my way I was unable to proceed, and stopped twice for rest. When I first stopped, some of them said they had got all they could of me, and they would now hang me. I rose and went on, and some who were against hanging me followed, and I was obliged by weakness to stop again, when it was proposed again to hang me, and one person said they would cut off my head and stick it on a pole. The vote was taken and carried for hanging me; but some said they should not hang me, that my life had been promised upon condition of disclosing what I knew, and that the information I might give them would be of use to them. I was then moved to the watch house, and delivered to the captain of the watch about two o'clock in the morning who was told they held him responsible for my body at nine o'clock. I laid myself on the floor, a doctor was sent for by the captain of the watch, who came and having removed the tar and feathers, sewed up the wounds on my head, and dressed them. Between nine and ten o'clock the mob was gathered at the watch house, and some were for hanging me, saying that I had not sworn to what I had told them before a magistrate before nine o'clock, as had been stipulated, and one of them said the rope was ready. I observed it was not my fault that I was not able to go to a magistrate, and that I was ready to swear to it if they would bring one. They then brought a magistrate of the name of Galt, who took my affidavit, in which was stated the names of the persons in the house, the causes of their meeting and the name of the person under whom they were acting in the house. It was read aloud, and at this period the Mayor, Mr. Taylor and some others arrived, who said they would take me to the hospital out of the hands of these men. Mr. Taylor said he had no idea of seeing me alive. The doctor had lent me a shirt, and I was now provided with a pair of trowsers. The Mayor sent for a carriage, but the mob said I should not ride in it, that a cart was good enough for me, and a cart was brought, into which I was placed, stretched out in the cart and exposed to a hot sun. About 11 o'clock, I was carried to the hospital, the distance of a mile, the Mayor accompanying me amid, the noise of a great concourse of people. There I heard the groans of Gen. Lee, in a room adjoining, who had been said to be dead.

After the crowd had dispersed, some of my friends who did not think me safe, sent me a carriage into which I was put, without losing a minute, and Gen. Lee was put into the same carriage. We were hurried away into the country, in our wounded, bruised and mangled condition; we arrived at Yorktown, Pennsylvania, on Saturday evening, the first of August, where we received the humane and friendly sympathies and attentions of the inhabitants, and the medical aid of two gentlemen of the faculty. Possessed of a strong constitution and in the prime of life, I cherish the hope, that I shall survive all the bruises and wounds, which have been so cruelly and maliciously inflicted by a wicked and lawless mob, and that I shall be again restored to the full use and enjoyment of my bodily powers. Given under my hand this 6th August, 1812.

JOHN THOMSON.

Notes

1. Alexander Hanson was editor of the *Federal Republican* newspaper. When he wrote an editorial opposing the war, a mob of four hundred watched and cheered as his newspaper office was destroyed.

2. A fieldpiece is a cannon mounted on wheels, for use by a marching army.

Seventeen Years' History, of the Life and Sufferings of James M'Lean, an Impressed American Citizen and Seaman

The narrative of James M'Lean gives an account of his seventeen years of impressment in the British Royal Navy, "[e]mbracing but a summary of what he endured while in the British service, during that long and eventful period." The work was printed "for the author" in 1814, in Hartford by B. & J. Russell. Three entries are recorded in the *National Union Catalog*, all from the same year with nearly identical physical descriptions, suggesting that several runs of the same edition were made. The fourth entry in the *Catalog* is also from 1814 and is listed as a second edition; all printings are similarly marked "for the author."

The length of the captivity described in this autobiographical account is staggering. Beset with misfortune almost immediately after putting out to sea in 1796 and captured by a British ship not long thereafter, M'Lean spends much of his time trying to convince his various captors that he is an American (he records being born and residing in Windsor, Hartford County, Connecticut) and not a Scottish, Irish, or English seaman fleeing from his ship and his duty. M'Lean hopes the document he calls his "protection" will establish his nation of origin and literally protect him from being pressed into service. However, when he shows this piece of paper to his captors, the British officers curtly disregard it: "I replied, [I was] an American and shewed him my protection. He answered 'you may be, but we cannot trust protections.' " Through repeated attempts to prove his nationality in a like manner, M'Lean earns the nickname of "Scotch Yankee" from several of the officers under whom he is forced to serve.

Such a response by M'Lean—trying to avoid impressment by showing written documentation, coupled with the description given of him in the title of the narrative ("an impressed American *citizen* and seaman")—suggests both the outrage of Americans over the British practice of impressment and the government's inability to protect its citizens. However, without a large naval force to guard its merchant ships, methods such as issuing documentation (protections) were ineffective. Eventually, M'Lean loses his printed protection outright and is left with no recourse for freeing himself other than escape.

M'Lean persists throughout the narrative, however, in attempting to use legal means to free himself, all the while looking for opportunities to flee. He repeatedly appeals to the American consul in London, writing to this man himself and encouraging his parents to do the same. In a letter dated December 22, 1805, he pleads with his parents that they "not neglect to write to the Consul immediately," hoping the American diplomat will intercede on his behalf. M'Lean also lobbies to be sent to England for trial, where he will be able to prove his citizenship and country of origin decisively—his day in court, if you will. The hoped-for trial never comes, and eight more years pass before M'Lean is able to reach home through his own stratagems. The 1805 letter in which he makes the appeal to his parents was printed as an appendix to the narrative.

The continual resistance to impressment in this narrative is unique and indicates how dearly Americans regarded their personal liberty. The text also indicates, if not indicts, the U.S. government's inability to prevent such abductions from taking place on a regular basis. M'Lean is forced to escape the British on his own, and he achieves his highly sought-after freedom only after repeated escape attempts and untold cruelty. His captivity is long and painful and perhaps as tragic as any account given in this genre, simply due to the number of years he remained a prisoner.

RJ

I was born in Windsor, in the County of Hartford, in Connecticut, where my parents are still living, with other relatives:—to add *acquaintance*, except what may be the offspring of the few months that have elapsed since my return, is of course denied to me by a long absence from my native country.

At the age of ten years I first went to sea, and performed several voyages to the West-Indies in the merchants service with tolerable success. In the year 1796, I undertook a voyage to the West Indies in the brig *Michael*, of Hartford—Arnold, master, belonging to Middletown. We sailed from New-London on the 27th of August, and had a fair wind and pleasant weather; nothing particular happened until the third of September, when in L. 29, 32, N. we fell in with a severe gale of wind from the N. W. It blew excessive hard, and having cattle on deck, Capt. Arnold concluded that it was not safe to heave the vessel to;[1] we then hove all our hay overboard to clear our decks as much as possible; we sent down our

SEVENTEEN YEARS'

HISTORY,

OF THE

LIFE AND SUFFERINGS

OF

JAMES M'LEAN.

AN IMPRESSED

AMERICAN CITIZEN & SEAMAN.

EMBRACING BUT A SUMMARY

OF WHAT HE ENDURED,

WHILE DETAINED

In the British Service,

DURING THAT

LONG AND PAINFUL PERIOD.

———

WRITTEN
BY HIMSELF.

———

HARTFORD :
PRINTED FOR THE AUTHOR,
BY B. & J. RUSSELL.
1814.

Title page of *History, of the Life and Sufferings of James M'Lean*
(1814 edition; courtesy of the American Antiquarian Society)

top gallant-yards, and took all our canvass in, except our close reefed foretop sail; our Capt. thought it prudent to scud, so we kept away before the wind and sea, as it blew a perfect hurricane, and continued until about seven o'clock the same evening, when Capt. Arnold went to relieve Mr. Jepson, at the helm (as Mr. Jepson, being our chief mate had been there four hours) and the Capt. knew he must want some refreshment; but he had not been five minutes at the helm, before a very heavy sea struck us upon our larboard quarter, by which our ship went over with her tops in the water, and the sea breaking in upon us on all quarters. The Capt. says "jump and cut the lanyards of the rigging, that the masts may go away." We shiped a very heavy sea, which cleared the deck. The Capt. says "jump aft, and lash yourselves." Our ship was at this time lying on her beam ends, and every sea was breaking over us. We continued in this situation until day light of the 4th; by this time one of our pumps was drawn out; the other broken off; and at the same time our ship was filling with water. The gale still continued, and we could not move, as we were all lashed upon the taffel,[2] and the sea constantly washing over us. All this time our clothes were mostly washed off us, and we expecting every minute our ship to sink. We continued in this situation until the 6th, when the wind abated and the sea became more calm; but we dare not stir from our situation. We were suffering much for want of water, being obliged to drink salt water, and our own. On the 8th it became quite calm, and the sea smooth; at this time our ship was lying with about two feet of water on her main deck: with the assistance of an iron bar, we made a hole through her main deck, and got at part of a cask of water; we lashed it to our night-heads, and after we had quenched our thirst, then we began to want food. By this time our hatches were all washed off and the water had a free passage through the hole. We had a number of barrels of Indian meal stowed in the hole; and one man undertook to dive after it, which he did and by the third attempt with the help of a rope, he succeeded in working a cask out, which we secured by lashing it in the weather-crotch. We lived upon Indian meal, and water until the 10th in the morning; when we saw a large shark playing around us; upon which we made a running bowling knot, and hung it over the taffel, as our ship had sunk so low, that our feet were continually in the water. The shark making for our feet, run into this bowling knot whereby we caught him; we cut him into thin slices, and laid them in the sun on those parts of the ship that were out of water, by which they became some roasted. We remained in this state, subsisting upon our meal, water, and shark, until the morning of the 16th, when we discovered a sail to windward, steering in a direct course towards us. About 4 o'clock P.M. she came to our assistance and took us on board: we were so weak and low, that we was unable to walk. The sloop that took us off the wreck, proved to be Capt. Bowman, from Alexandria, bound to Cape Nicolia-Mole. He delayed no time, as nothing could be saved from the wreck. He treated us with all that humanity that his circumstances would permit, and our condition require.

We were now nine in number, vis. the master, mate, and seven seamen. We concluded, when we left the wreck, that she could not keep any part above water more than four or five days. Nothing remarkable occurred until the 24th, when we arrived at Turks Island.[3] We gradually gained strength until our arrival at said Island. On the 25th, I, together with two more of the hands saved from the wreck, embarked on board a brig bound to New York, of which one Brown was master. The Captain, mate, and remaining seamen went on board another brig bound for New-York, and on their passage were cast away on Cape Hatteras shoals, and every one perished. Nothing in particular happened to me until I arrived at New-York; which was about the middle of October, in a most naked and destitute situation. The day after my arrival, I went on shore, without money or clothing. In this unfortunate condition, when I knew of none in that city to whom I could apply, He, who commands the wind and storm, and to whom the elements are in perfect obedience, gave me immediate relief, by the arrival of a brother that day in a ship from London. As soon as he recognized my countenance, he procured me relief, and clothed, and fed me at his own expence, for three weeks.

I remained in New-York until about the 10th or 12th of November, when I had so far recovered my health and strength, that with the advice and assistance of my aforesaid brother, I undertook another voyage to the West Indies, on board the brig Juno,—Shaler, Master, bound to Cape Francois. Nothing remarkable happened during the voyage; but made a prosperous one, and returned to New York in March, 1797. I remained at New-York till April when I shipped on board the Glory-Ann, of Philadelphia, then lying in New York, bound to Liverpool; after experiencing many severe storms, during our passage, in which our vessel sprung a leak, we arrived at Liverpool on the first of June, where we docked our ship, refitted, and in July we sailed for the Coast of Africa. After good passage, we arrived at a place called Malemoo, near the mouth of the Congo River, some miles to the East, about the 20th of November. Here we remained until January, 1798. After completing our cargo, we sailed, and nothing remarkable happened during our passage. On the 10th of March, we arrived at Grenada. I must begin a second part of my misfortunes, which, if I were to detail them at full length, would fill a large volume; but I shall study brevity, and only narrate some of the more prominent features of all my sufferings, leaving it for an after time, to relate the same, with more prolixity. We had no sooner let go our anchor, than an English Man of War's boat came on board and pressed me and two more of the Seamen, and carried us on board the Madrass, 50 gun Ship. commanded by John Dilks, who immediately asked me for my protection.[4] I immediately shewed him one from a Notary Public in New York, by the name of Keyes; he replied, "I could get one, if I was in America, for half a crown, as good as that." He further said, "it is of no use for you to pretend that you are an American, for you was born in Scotland." The first Lieutenant, then stepped up and said "yes, that he was, for I knew his friends in Greenock." The Capt. then made answer, "he shall then do his duty in the main-top." I then went off the quarter deck, down below. The day following I went to the Capt and told him I hoped he would send me aboard of my own ship, as I was an American citizen; to which he replied, "*You Scotch Rascal*, if you do not go to your duty, I'll punish you." I then went to my station. Several days after, while we were letting a reef out of the main top sail, the sail go tore; he immediately said it was my fault "for I was a sulky rascal." He ordered me to be seized, and the boatswain's mate to punish me; which he did by giving me twelve lashes on my bare back with cat o nine tails; he then ordered me to be cast off and sent to my duty. Soon after, this ship was ordered to England, and I was removed to the Vengeance, of 74 guns, and ordered for Gibraltar, to join Lord Nelson's fleet. We then sailed up the Mediterranean, in pursuit of the French Fleet. On our passage we touched at Malta, and got intelligence that they were seen steering a direct course for Alexandria. We made all sail possible in pursuit, and on the 1st of August made Alexandria, and saw the French fleet lying at anchor in Aboukir Bay. Lord Nelson immediately made signal to clear for action. The same afternoon the action commenced, and by twelve o'clock at night, the L'Orient, one of the largest French ships, blew up. We ceased firing for near two hours whilst employed in saving the men belonging to the wreck. Then we renewed the action, and by 10 o'clock the next day the whole of the French fleet were in our possession, except the Guillaume Tell, Genereaux, and two frigates, who made their escape in the night. We then took all the prisoners out of the French ships, and rigged them with jury masts. I was then sent on board the L'Tonnant, of 84 guns, and ordered for Lisbon on the 24th of December. We lay at Lisbon until the 20th of July, 1799; then was ordered for Plymouth and having fair winds and pleasant, we arrived there about the 12th of August. The day after our arrival I was sent on board the Cambridge, guard ship, where I remained until the 1st of September, when I was drafted on board the Windsor Castle, of 98 guns, and ordered for Torbay, to join the channel fleet. I was frequently threatened, and received much abusive treatment, but without any actual punishment. In the latter part of November, I went on shore with a watering party; before we set out, I put on two shirts, and two pairs of trowsers, and had about seven pounds sterling in money. I now resolved to make my escape as follows. I first enquired of a Fisherman the right road to Plymouth, which he directed me. I then made a bargain with the Master of a fishing boat, and agreed if he would take me safely to Plymouth, I would give him three pounds; which he received, and carried me safely there. I enquired if there were any American ships there, and found there was none. I then went on board an English merchant ship, and went to Shields in the north of England; from thence I worked my passage to London. I then shipped myself in the Eliza, an American ship, belonging to Boston. We left London and came to Falmouth, in the west of England, where we purchased a load of fish, and sailed for Leghorn. Nothing remarkable happened until our arrival; here we sold our fish, and took in load for Messina, in Sicily. From there we sailed for the Gulph of Venice. Here we loaded with a cargo of oil, and sailed for London, where we arrived about the middle of August, 1800. I there received about forty pounds sterling for my voyage. I now went on board an American schooner, belonging to Boston, expecting once more to see my native country; but judge of the sad reverse:—while my bosom heaved with joy, and I fondly anticipated the pleasure of visiting my aged parents, and fraternal friends, a sudden storm arose and baffled every effort, to keep our course, and we were driven back, and obliged to put into Portsmouth.

Here we lay until the 24th of December, when we sailed with a fair wind, and pleasant weather, until we came off the Lands End;[5] here we fell in with a gale of wind, which obliged us to put into Falmouth. While we lay here, I went on shore for water; while watering, an officer came down to the boat, with a guard of soldiers, and asked me "what countryman I was." I answered, an American. He said "that I must go with him;" upon which he put me into the guard house, and ordered the guard to take good care of me, as he presumed I was a deserter from the navy; here I remained all night: the next morning he sent me on board the Pique Frigate. I went to the Captain and showed him my protection; he replied that "he had plenty, like me on board, and that he did not believe I was ever in any part of the U. States; you are either Scotch or Irish;" with that, I pointed out to him the vessel I belonged to, and begged him to let me go on board to get my clothes. He said, "you shan't go, for I'll cloathe you!" and ordered a boatswain to see that I did my duty. He then ordered me off the quarter-deck, and with that I went below, where I remained until the following day, which was January 18th, 1801, when all hands were called to up anchor. When they had all got on deck, (except myself) an officer came to me and asked, "why I was not at work, to help get the ship under way?" with that he took hold of me and pushed me along. The Capt. calls out, "who is that?" to which the officer replied, "it is the man that came on board yesterday." He replied, "send him aft here." I then went aft. He said "Me noble Scotch Yankee, if you don't go to work, I'll find means to make ye." He then ordered me forward on the fore castle, and ordered the boatswain to see that I did my duty. We now made sail for Gibraltar; and nothing particular happened until we arrived. I was often threatened but never punished. We received orders to sail immediately for Malta. Here we watered our ship, and proceeded up the Mediterranean to join Lord Keith, and fell in with him off Alexandria. The Capt. asked me "if I would join; if not he would send me on board the Toudryant, Lord Keith's flag ship;" which he did on the 6th of March. When I came on board, the Admiral asked me "What countryman I was."

I replied, an American, and shewed him my protection. He answered, "you may be, but we cannot trust to protections." He then ordered me to do my duty on the forecastle, which I did. On the 9th of March we came to anchor in Aboukir Bay, and landed 27,000 men. The French came down from the heights, to prevent their landing, but it was effected with the loss of 3000 of the British. The same day, the French were driven back twelve miles, when the British halted. On the 22d the British again attacked them, and drove them into Alexandria, with great loss on both sides: on this day General Abercrombie, the British commander, was mortally wounded, and was brought on board of the Admiral's ship, where he died. Nothing remarkable happened on board the fleet, until about the middle of May, when we went in pursuit of five French ships, which we heard were on the coast. Our ship, and four more got under weigh, and went in pursuit: had a cruise of five days, without being able to find them; we again returned into port. We remained here until the latter end of September. The history of the different battles that were fought, and success, or defeat attending them, I shall commit to the pen of some more able historian, to transmit to posterity; suffice it, for me to relate some of the most prominent features of my sufferings for the term of years before related, and shall study brevity. I will not attempt to embellish my narrative, in order to excite commiseration, for my misfortunes; but proceed to relate the same with all the accuracy possible.

During the time we lay at anchor in the Bay, I was frequently sent on shore; but had no opportunity to make my escape. We left Aboukir Bay at the time last mentioned, and sailed for Malta in company with five sail of the line, and arrived safe, the first of November; where we stripped our ship, and fitted for sea; which was completed by December. About this time I heard the news of Peace between England and France. I now had some prospect that Peace would enable me again to return home. Liberty was granted to all the ship's company to go on shore, except myself and a few more Americans, impressed as I was. In January, 1802, one night, whilst hoisting our boats up, a midshipman came to me, and said that "I did not pull:" I told him he could not show me how. He told me "I was an insolent rascal," and went aft and reported me to the commanding officer; and I was immediately put in irons. The following day the Capt. came on board, and called me aft, and asked me "how I became so insolent to the midshipman." I answered I did not know that I was. He said "I'll make you know:" with that, all hands were called, and I was ordered to strip; they seized me up, and gave me twenty four lashes with a cat o-nine-tails, on my bare back and told me "if I ever committed the like fault again, he would double the punishment." I then returned to my duty and tarried there until August, when we sailed for Gibralter and arrived on the 1st of October. Here I found the American frigate Essex, by which I sent a letter to my parents; and this was the first communication I had made to them, after I went [on] my last voyage from home.

We continued as a guard ship at that place until January, 1803, when we sailed for England, and after a good passage we arrived at Portsmouth in February. Lord Keith went on shore, and we were ordered round to Plymouth, where we expected to be paid off. While we were stripping the ship, I went to the dock yard with some part of the rigging, and left the working party and was going out of the dock yard; the lieutenant caught me and brought me on board as a prisoner; and reported me to the Capt. who ordered me to be stripped and take twelve lashes, as usual, which was inflicted. On the first of March, I was turned over to the Raisonable of 64 guns, when we were ordered on the Downs station, where we continued until March, 1804; then we were ordered to Chatham, to refit. We refitted, and were ordered in to the North Sea, off the Texel; where we cruised until August; we then received orders to sail for Portsmouth, where I received twenty pounds sterling. We were next ordered to cruise off the west of Ireland, and continued there until February we were ordered to Plymouth, to fit out as fast as possible, to join the expedition going against the Cape of Good Hope. At this time I wrote several letters to Mr. Erving, the American Consul at the port of London; but received no answer. I likewise sent him a copy of my protection; but still received none.

Having received indifferent treatment, and being often threatened with punishment, I felt reluctant in going such a voyage, and so far distant from my native country. I now once more formed a resolution of quitting the ship and regaining my lawful liberty. At this time we were lying in Bantry bay, in the west of Ireland; I then belonging to the Gunner's crew: while getting under weigh, I was busy hauling in a buoy rope; the lieutenant came to me and said "D———m you, don't haul," and struck me with the speaking trumpet; knocked out two of my teeth, and cut my face shockingly, and caused much effusion of blood, saying at the same time "you are one of the Scoth yankees;" to which I replied, no I am a true born American; with that, he said, "no reply, you rascal! go to your duty." We were now lying in Corsen bay, about five miles from Plymouth dock yard; when we received orders to prepare for sea as soon as possible. On the 10th of April, 1805, the boatswain came to me and told me, "that I must go on shore to get the spare sails off." Now I thought this a good opportunity to make my escape; accordingly I put on what clothes I could without being discovered by the officers. We then went to work, and got the sails all down to the boats: the boats were then all ordered off on board the ship. I then went and stowed myself away, among some planks, waiting until the boats were gone off. At this time the officer missed me, and sent a party of men in search. They came so near me that I could see them, but at night they went to their boats and went on board. I thought it a good opportunity to quit my hiding place, when I saw the boats at the distance of one mile and a half from the shore: about this time the labourors in the yard went out, and I joined in their number, which was about 300, and went out at the gate with them. I immediately took coach, and went to Cat water; a place where merchantmen usually lay. On the following day I made enquiry for American merchantmen, but found there were none. I then fell in with a Capt. of an English merchantman, and found he was bound to Lisbon: I told him I was an American, and wanted passage there. He told me he would given me a passage if I would lend a hand to work the ship; to which I agreed, and went on board, and we got the ship ready for sea as soon as possible. In the meantime I got into conversation with him, and was satisfied that he could be trusted with my secrets. I informed him that I had run away from an English man of war; he said he was glad I had told him, and he would carry me safe. On the 14th we got under way, with a fair wind; we had then to pass through the men of war. The captain told me that he had procured me a place below, in case any of the men of war sent their boats on board; but we were not boarded by any. We then made all sail possible to Portsmouth, to join the convoy, where we arrived on the 16th. During the time we lay there, we were boarded by a boat from a man of war: I went into the stow hole, the captain had made for me, and they left the ship without making any discovery. On the 22d we weighed and sailed for Lisbon, where we arrived at the 12th of May. The captain treated me with the greatest hospitality during the voyage, and when we arrived at Lisbon, he made me a present of Fifty Dollars. The day following I went on board an American schooner, bound to France. We left Lisbon the 1st of June, and after a pleasant passage of five days, we arrived at Brest, where the schooner was sold. I then took my land jackets on board, and shaped my course for Rochefort, where I arrived about the 14th. I now went on board a French brig bound to Cayenne, in the West Indies. I thought if I could get there, I might find some way to get home. Before we sailed, I received about Sixty Dollars for the work I had done on board. The 12th of August we weighed, and made sail for the Island of Teneriffe, where we arrived about the middle of September, when we watered our ship, and took twelve 6 pounders on board, and fitted out as a letter of marque. We left Teneriffe the last of September, with a fair wind shaping our course for Cayenne. Five days after we left Teneriffe, we fell in with, and captured a large English merchantman, from Liverpool. Bound for the coast of Africa. We then put back to Teneriffe, where our prize was sold. We now once more got under way for Cayenne, and on our passage fell in with an English frigate; she fired six 24 pounders into us, and killed the man that was steering the ship; with that we hove too; they immediately sent their boats and took us all on board. In the confusion, I lost every thing, and especially my protection. They would not allow me to take an individual article that I had. When we came on board we were put into the *galley*, a place where they keep their pigs. Here we were kept through the night. The next morning we were all mustered on the quarter deck. The Captain examined us, and asked me "what countryman I was." I replied, "that I was an American." He immediately said, "that I was an Englishman," and ordered me into irons. I was stripped of every thing, except a shirt, two pair of trowsers, and a jacket. I was put into irons on the lower deck, with nothing to lie upon by the hard planks. My allowance was half a pound of bread, and same quantity of meat, and a scanty pittance of water. In this situation I remained until we arrived at St. Helena. I was frequently called up, and pointing to the fore yard, the captain would say, *that was the place he meant to hang me*. On our arrival at St. Helena, I was sent to the main guard house on shore, with a pair of irons on my legs, weighing fifty pounds, and a guard set over me. I continued in this situation about fourteen days, during which time I became extremely lowzy, and my legs were so swelled that I was unable to move. A week afterwards I applied to the governor, when he sent one of his aid de camps to examine my legs. He reported my situation, and my irons were ordered to be taken off.

When they were taken off, I was unable to walk. I then wrote several letters to my parents, by American ships, then lying in the road, acquainting them with my situation and desiring them to write to the American Consul in London; as I expected to be sent to England for trial. My subsistence here was scarcely sufficient to keep me alive. On the 5th of January, 1806, I was sent on board the Medusa frigate of 36 guns, capt. J. Gore. When I got on board, he told me that I was here as an Englishman, that had been fighting against my king and country. I told him that I was an American, and that I had had the misfortune to lose my protection. He told me he should not put me in irons, that I might consider myself a prisoner, and have the liberty of walking about the decks. On the 6th of January, we left St. Helena for Portsmouth, where we arrived the 27th of February. During our passage the captain behaved exceedingly well to me, and gave me the same allowance as the ships company, and also some cloathing. The day after our arrival I was put into irons. I then wrote to Mr. Erving, the American Consul in London, who returned me an unsatisfactory answer. During our time of lying here, a new captain joined the ship, and I continued in irons until the 7th of May, when the capt. called me up, and said, *"I might think myself well off that I was not hanged;"* and that he was going to send me on board the Chiffane frigate of 36 guns, P. Campbell, commander. When I went on board, he ordered me to do my duty on the fore castle. (Before this, I had exerted my utmost to get clear, as an American; but all to no purpose) I now went to my duty on the fore castle. On the 20th of May, a new capt joined the ship, named John Wincewright, who proved to be a worthy man. We lay here until June 16th, when we received orders to sail for Gibraltar, and from thence we went to Malta; where we watered and refitted our ship: here we received orders to go to Messina, and take Gen. Fraser on board, and bring him to Gibralter. Here we landed him, provisioned and watered our ship, and were ordered to cruise off Minorca. Here we continued six weeks. One night we saw a Spanish packet lying at anchor under the west side of Minorca; we manned our boats, pulled in and boarded her, with the loss of two killed, and five wounded. We now came down to Gibralter and sold our prize, my share of which was $17. We refitted our ship, and were ordered by the Admiral to cruise off Cardagena, on the coast of Spain, where we continued three months without falling in with any thing. We then came back to Gibralter, and were from thence ordered to join Admiral Pervis, off Cadiz. We joined him in Feb. 1807, where we continued cruising until the latter part of May. We then returned to Gibralter, where we refitted and took in water, and on the 1st July received orders to cruise off Cape St. Vincents, where we continued until the latter end of November, when we sailed for Gibralter, took Gen. Moore on board, and brought him to Lisbon. We then returned and joined the Admiral off Cadiz; he ordered us to Gibraltar to take a convoy of merchantmen for England. We sailed from Gibralter, in Feb. 1809, with about sixty sail of merchantmen, and arrived at Portsmouth, in March. Here all the ships company were put into a hulk, and the ship went into dock, where she continued until May. We then refitted, took in provisions and water, and received orders to sail for the East-Indies; on the 4th of June I received twenty four pounds sterling. The 10th of June we got under way: touched at Madeira and took in wine and water, and continued our voyage. Fourteen days after we passed Madeira, we fell in with and captured a Spanish packet from Corunna, bound to Mont Video. After taking out her men, we burnt the packet, and continued on our voyage, and arrived at Bengal Sept. 22d, and took on board a pilot, to proceed up the river, and came to anchor in Dimond harbour. Here we stripped our ship and refitted. Now our ship's company began to be sickly, and our captain thought best to get out of the river. We then took Gen. Malcom on board, and proceeded towards Bombay; the sickness increasing among us so fast that three or four died daily. We arrived at Bombay in November, when we received orders from Admiral Drury, to go to Buzro, in the Persian Gulph; on our passage, we touched at Muscat and proceeded up to Buzro; took in the packet and returned to Bombay, where we arrived in May, 1809. I now went on shore for the first time since I left St. Helena, in 1806. The next day I went on board, when we refitted our ship, and proceeded on an expedition up the Gulph of Persia, against the Pirates. We arrived at Muscat the latter end of September, in company with the Caroline frigate and five Transports; having on board one regiment of European soldiers, and one regiment of Seapoys. We now proceeded up the gulph to attack Russeleimer, a place of resort for Pirates, where we came to anchor, and landed the soldiers. They attacked and destroyed the town with 30 vessels lying in the harbor, carrying one gun each. We then embarked our troops, and went higher up the gulph, to attack Lufft, where we landed our soldiers and seamen, took and burnt the place, with the loss of a number killed and wounded. We again embarked our troops, and proceeded down the gulph, to a place called Shiness.

This being a strong place, we landed and built a battery, which mounted two 24-pounders, one 18, one 9, two 6's, and one 7 inch mortar, which were manned by the seamen belonging to the two frigates. In the morning we opened our fire by which we made such a breach in the walls, that at 4 o'clock, P M. the soldiers entered and put every soul to death. Their number was calculated to be at least 1400, who lay promiscuously scattered on the ground, men, women, and children. Such an indiscriminate slaughter, although among barbarians, must naturally fill a feeling mind with the keenest sensibility—but such was our orders.

We now embarked our troops, and proceeded down to Muscat. Here the Caroline left us, and proceeded with the transports to Bombay. Here we was visited by the Grand Seignior of Muscat. We now completed our supply of water, and proceeded up to Buzro; took the packet, and proceeded down to Bombay, where we arrived the latter end of March, 1810. We now stripped and refitted our ship, and received orders from Admiral Drury, to take a convoy to China. We left Bombay on the 1st day of May, with eighteen sail under our convoy. Nothing important happened until going through the straits of Malacca, when we were obliged to let go our anchor several times. After we passed the straits of Malacca and Salampere, we came into the Chinese sea, where we had remarkable fine weather, and arrived at Macoa, and proceeded up the river as far as Champee; here we let go our anchor, and the merchant ships went up to Wampoo. We lay here several days, and completed our watering, when we sailed for Meneia, where we arrived the latter end of November. We here took in upwards of $100,000 in specie, and then went back to Wampoo, and landed the money. We now got under way, and went out back of China, with an intention of going to Japan. After beating several days, we bore up, and came to an anchor at Champee, and lay here until the merchant's ships had taken in their cargoes, and dropped down the river. We then got under way, and came down to Macoa; where we lay until the following day, Dec. 10th. We then made signal for the convoy to weigh; when we proceeded towards Bombay, with a fair wind and pleasant weather. Nothing particular happened until we came into the straits of Malacca, when we fell in with the wreck of a ship; we immediately sent a boat, and found the master and one seaman lashed to the ship, which we soon relieved and brought on board. The master informed us, that in coming through the straits they struck on a sand bank, bilged, and filled with water. They immediately took the boat, and went on shore. He went to the wreck, hoping to save some property; but it began to blow, and stove the boat, and they must have perished, if we had not taken them off. We now proceeded on our way, and off the island of Salone, fell in with the Caroline frigate, who informed us, that they had a letter from Admiral Drury for the Capt. on which we sent a boat and got the letter; as soon as he read it, he told us that we had orders to proceed immediately for England. We then made all possible sail for Bombay, where we arrived in Jan. 1811. We then completed our store of water and provisions, and proceeded to sea; shaping our course for Point a Gall, where we arrived the first of March. We then took five sail of large Indiamen under convoy, and sailed on the 16th of March. Nothing happened until we came off the Cape of Good Hope, where we experienced a heavy gale of wind. Our ship proved very leaky, and we expected she would have gone down. The gale continued for three days; when it abated, we found we had lost all our convoy; we made the best of our way to St. Helena, where we arrived about the middle of June. Here we completed out water, and got ready for sea. During our stay here we buried three of our men. We now got under way in company with the Beleace, 64, and the Menelaus frigate, with twenty sail of large Indiamen under convoy, bound for Portsmouth. After a fine passage we arrived there on the 12th of August. Our ship was then laid up, and all hands sent on board the guard ship. I got liberty to go on shore, which I did and returned again in two days on board, where I remained until the 12th of Nov. when I went on board the Harmony, transport, as boatswain. We sailed from thence to Deptford, where we took in a load of provisions, and came round to Portsmouth. Here I received fifty pounds sterling. We next shaped our course for Gibraltar, where we arrived on the 4th of Jan. 1812. I left Gibralter on the 6th and arrived at Minorca on the 20th. Here we lay until the 28th of March, when we discharged our provisions, and sailed for Malta, where we arrived the 12th of April. We then took in a cargo of bread and wine, and returned to Minorca; discharged, took in ballast, and went to Palermo; from thence we came to Minorca, and from thence to Alicant in Spain. There we assisted in landing 12,000 English soldiers. We then sailed for Minorca; from thence we went to Malta, and from there to Gibralter. We lay here until the 2d of Jan. 1813; we then got under way for England, and arrived at Portsmouth on the 20th, having performed seven days quarantaine at the Northern Bank. We then proceeded to Hull, in Yorkshire. Here I was frequently on shore, and at one time went eighteen miles from thence. We lay here until the 24th of March when we steered for Gottenburg, in Sweden, and from thence to Memel, in Prussia; there we took in plank and returned to Gottenburg, and from thence to Hull; here we discharged our plank, and from thence came to Portsmouth. We now took in provisions for Lord Wellington's army, and left Portsmouth on the last of September, and sailed for Corunna, where we arrived on the 8th of October. I now thought an opportunity presented itself for me to make my escape, which I effected in the following manner. I went ashore in a boat, and made an agreement with the master of a Spanish schooner, to take me round to Port au Port in Portugal, where I procured a passport from the American Consul and went on board a Portuguese schooner bound for Lisbon, for which passage I paid ten dollars. I immediately went to the American Consul at that place, and made my case known, and asked him if there were any ships bound directly for America. He told me there was; he likewise told me to go to the tavern and get what I wanted to eat and drink, and come to him the next morning; which I did. He told me there was a brig bound to Charlestown, that I might go on board and see the Capt. I accordingly went and staid four days; then I came on shore, and fell in with the Capt. of the Zodiac, who informed me that he should sail the next morning, and if I would go with him to the Consul's, he would accompany me, which I did. I immediately took my *dunage* and went on board.

The following day, Oct. 18th, I sailed, and after a pleasant voyage of thirty days, we arrived at Newport, in Rhode Island. The next day I got on to the American shore, after an absence of more than seventeen years. Within three days I reached my father's house, and I leave it to you to judge of my feelings and their's, on this interview. The sympathetic tear could not be suppressed; parental and filial affection, were mutually interchanged, and every sentiment congenial to friends, was endeavored to be reciprocated.

I cannot close this short narrative, of more than seventeen years of my life, without acknowledging a SUPERINTENDING PROVIDENCE, who guides the fates of men. To that GOD, who has secured me from so many dangers; protected me from the watry element; covered my head in the day of battle; given me health and strength equal to my day; preserved me from any corruption, to which I was exposed; and finally has returned me to my friends in health; To HIM, let grateful homage be paid.

The following letter was written to, and received, by my father, after my having been captured in the French brig of war. *(See page 16.)* [6]—On receipt of it my father made application to the late Chief Justice Ellsworth, who resided in Windsor, and who, being personally acquainted with me, wrote to the American Consul in London, that I was an American born citizen.

Several other Gentlemen, of Hartford, wrote at the same time; to each, and all of whom, though not so fortunate as to owe my freedom to their representation, I am, nevertheless, at this time, happy to acknowledge my obligation.

I am told by my Father, that he saw and conversed with Mr. Lyman, (the Consul to whom these communications were made,) after his return to America, and that he acknowledged the receipt of them, and stated that my discharge was procured, and sent down to the ship. For myself, I was never so lucky as to hear of it till my return home. Probably, there was not wanting some one to make a *Discharge*, of as little consequence as a *Protection*.

J.M'LEAN.
"ST. HELENA, December 22, 1805.

DEAR FATHER AND MOTHER"
"I hope these lines will find you in a good state of health, as they leave me, at present.

"I have met with a great misfortune.—I was on my passage home, in a French Brig, and falling in with an English frigate was taken and brought into this port, where I now am held as a prisoner of war. At the time the English boats were boarding us, I happened to lose my Protection, and on my coming on board the English frigate, their Captain immediately said, "I was an English subject," which I denied strongly. I was sent on shore here, along with the rest of the prisoners, and in a short time are to be sent to England, where I expect I shall have a further overhaul.

"Now, Dear Parents, if you will be so good when you receive this letter, as to write to the American Consul in London, and send a Certificate, of my Age, place of Birth, &c. signed by some of the head merchants in Hartford, you will, perhaps, save my life, as the English Captain seems very inveterate against me. By the time my trial comes on in England, your answer will be with the Consul, where, on my arrival, I shall immediately apply.

"Now I hope, Dear Parents, that you will not neglect to write the Consul immediately.—I am very sorry that I have neglected writing to you so long, but I intended to be at home with you by this time, and should, most likely, if I had not met with this accident. Give my best love and respects to my Brothers, Sisters, and all enquiring friends; so having no more to say, I remain your loving and dutiful son,

"JAMES M'LEAN.

"P.S.—Do not neglect writing on any account whatever, for I expect to be in England, in a very short time."

Error.

Page 8, line 5, instead of the *Ganges*, in which the writer is stated to have joined the fleet at Gibralter, it should be the *Vengeance*.

Notes

1. "Heave to" is a nautical term meaning to bring a ship to a standstill with its head to the wind.

2. The taffel is the rail around the stern of a ship.

3. Turks Island lies in the North Atlantic, southeast of the Bahamas and north of Haiti.

4. This is a reference to M'Lean's proof of American citizenship.

5. M'Lean is referring to the town of Lands End in extreme southwest England.

6. The captivity M'Lean refers to on page 16 of the original narrative is on page 173 of the present text.

A Narrative

of the

Captivity and Sufferings

of

John Turner

...among the Ladrones

Rumblings of piracy on the South China coast in 1790 grew to storms of considerable proportions by 1805, when as many as fifty thousand to seventy thousand Chinese pirates joined into a loose confederation and seized control of coastal trade and fishing operations, forcing local governments to react. The seven-point pirate contract focused on conduct at sea, distribution of property, business transactions with outsiders, and the standardization and regulation of internal procedures. For these pirates, or Ladrones as they came to be called, piracy was not only their business but a way of life.

For John Turner, capture by the Ladrones resulted in a six-month captivity,[1] which led to the 1814 publication of his narrative in New York. According to the text Turner was the first officer on the *John Jay* out of Bombay, a trading vessel owned by the Baring Company, when he was taken by the pirates in December 1806. Having left the *John Jay* in a jolly boat to pick up a pilot at Macao before proceeding to Canton, Turner and six lascars were captured after one man was stabbed and the others had jumped into the water. In order to save the *John Jay*, Turner lied to his captors, telling them that his ship was heavily armed with twenty guns when in truth she carried but two. The Chinese junk on which Turner was taken carried eight guns and more than one hundred men and could have easily captured the *John Jay*. Turner was to remain a captive on this and other pirate ships until late May 1807.

Since ransoming captives was a significant source of income, the Ladrones urged Turner to write letters to his captain and employers in an effort to raise the necessary funds. The ransom started at $3,000 and rapidly grew as high as $30,000 within three weeks. Captain Gray of the *John Jay* offered $500, and negotiations proceeded until Turner was eventually released for an amount ranging from $3,000 to $4,000 on May 22, 1807. Throughout his captivity he declared that he was constantly threatened with "cruel death" but provided little detail in the narrative concerning the Ladrones' use of torture and the execution of captives. There was one incident described, however, when a "Mandarin" sailor taken off a government ship sent to suppress the pirates was nailed to the deck and beaten with rattan canes until he expired. One might conclude that his shipmates were similarly treated. Compared to the discipline on board a British naval vessel, however, the pirates were not all that cruel toward their captives. Although Turner claims that he was beaten, he generally received decent treatment, since he was far more valuable to his captors for ransom than the lascars captured with him. He states that he was able to "enjoy perfect health" and that his captivity was far more of an inconvenience than a hardship. With the economic incentives provided by sizable ransoms, the Ladrones—or "sea bandits," as they were sometimes called—were nowhere near as ruthless as the pirates of the Caribbean.

The John Turner of the American narrative is actually based on a historical British figure. The narrative was originally a British imprint, published in the *Naval Chronicle*, a monthly periodical, in 1808 (volume 20, pages 456–72). Begun in 1799 and published until 1819, the periodical offered British maritime news, action reports, naval intelligence, and superb information on high-ranking officers of the British navy. Almost immediately after its serialization, the text was offered for sale by the London printer Thomas Tegg, in 1809, as *Sufferings of John Turner, chief mate of the country ship, Tay, bound for China, under the command of William Grieg including the seizure of him and six Lascars in the cutter, and their captivity and danger amongst the Ladrones, with a description of the strength, discipline, manner, &c. of these pirates, their depredations and conduct towards their prisoners; also, A curious account of Peter Serrano, who having escaped from shipwreck, lived seven years on a sandy island, on the coast of Peru*. Tegg captured the London reprint and remainder trade as the Ladrones had captured Turner, boasting that he was "the broom that swept the booksellers' warehouses." He prided himself on cheap publishing, and his business records bear this out. Between 1800 and 1840 he printed four hundred titles, about two a week. Among his specialties were vivid tales of shipwrecks and captivity narratives—he published twenty-two such texts between 1800 and 1820. The Turner text was neither his first nor his last, as Tegg obviously served a broad market of readers hungry for protogothic tales of extraordinary experience. Among his better-known and better-selling titles was a shipwreck narrative, *Correct statement of the loss of the Earl of Abergavenny, East Indiaman, John Wordsworth, Commander*, an often republished twenty-eight-page text that bibliographers have yet to date accurately.

The Turner text was also included in Alexander Dalrymple's *Further Statement of the Ladrones on the Coast of China Intended as a Contribution of the Accounts published by Mr. Dalrymple*, reportedly published in London in 1812. The next appearance of the Turner text was the New York narrative printed by Largin and Thompson for the publishers and booksellers George and Robert Waite. Between 1809 and 1819 George Largin and Thomas Thompson published a handful of books, among them the Turner text. In an effort to Americanize the narrative, the Waites, or their ghostwriters, made several changes. Turner was aboard the *John Jay*, not the *Tay* as in the British editions. The captain was Gray, not Greig. In an advertisement included in the New York edition, Turner was identified as Captain Turner, and the facts of the narrative were attested to by Captain William S. Clark, commander of the United States Gun Boat no. 42, stationed in New York. According to records contained in "Naval Affairs" (*American State Papers*, vol. 19), there was no one by the name of Clark listed as a captain, master commandant, lieutenant, or midshipman for either of the years 1814 or 1815. Also, gunboats of this period were placed under the command of lieutenants, not captains. Ironically, what was offered in 1814 to authenticate the text was itself inauthentic. A final change that should be noted is that the Americanized text is forty-four pages in length, not the twenty-eight pages of the Tegg edition. The New York edition apparently enjoyed decent albeit not spectacular sales, as did Tegg's.

The Turner text is not nearly so bloody as the pirate accounts that sold so well to a reading public with a voracious appetite for captivity narratives. Still, what the text does deliver is a detailed, reliable record of Chinese pirates—the businessmen of the pirate world—and not so much the romanticized pirates depicted in the gripping sea stories of the day. The Ladrones are portrayed to be calculating pirates motivated by an economy of capture and ransom—pirates with an eye toward the bottom line and thus pirates somewhat out of character with what the Western world has come to know in print and later in film.

DW & BC

DISTRICT OF NEW-YORK,
Be it remembered, that on the twenty-first day of December in the thirty-eighth year of the Independence of the United States of America, G. & R. Waite, of the said District, have deposited in this office the title of a book, the right whereof they claim as proprietors in the words following, to with "A narrative of the captivity and sufferings of John Turner, first officer of the ship John Jay of Bombay, among the Ladrones or Pirates on the coast of China. Showing the manners and customs of the names—Their mode of warfare.—Treatment of prisoners, and discipline,

A

NARRATIVE

OF THE

CAPTIVITY AND SUFFERINGS

OF

JOHN TURNER,

FIRST OFFICER OF THE SHIP JOHN JAY
OF BOMBAY,

AMONG THE

LADRONES OR PIRATES,

ON THE

COAST OF CHINA,

SHOWING THE MANNERS AND CUSTOMS OF THE
NATIVES.—THEIR MODE OF WARFARE.
TREATMENT OF PRISONERS,
AND DISCIPLINE.

WITH THE DIFFERENCE BETWEEN THE

PIRATE AND THE CHINESE,

IN THE YEAR 1807.

WRITTEN BY HIMSELF.

NEW-YORK:
PUBLISHED BY G. & R. WAITE, BOOKSELLERS, NO. 64 &
38 MAIDEN-LANE.
Largin & Thompson, Printers, No. 5 Burling-slip.
1814.

Title page of *A Narrative of the Captivity and Sufferings of
John Turner* (1814 edition; New York State Library)

with the difference between the Pirate and Chinese, in the year 1807. Written by himself."

In conformity to the Act of the Congress of the United States, entitled "An Act for the encouragement of Learning, by securing the copies of Maps, Charts, and Books to the authors and proprietors of such copies, during the time therein mentioned." And also to an Act, entitled "An Act, supplementary to an Act, entitled an Act for the encouragement of Learning, by securing the copies of Maps, Charts, and Books to the authors and proprietors of such copies, during the times therein mentioned, and extending the benefits thereof to the arts of designing, engraving and etching historical and other prints."

THERON RUDD.
Clerk of New-York District

Advertisement.

The publishers of the following interesting narrative, are authorised to say, that the facts therein stated are known to be strictly correct, by Captain William S. Clark, now commander of the U. S. Gun Boat, No. 42, of the New-York station, who has been intimately acquainted with Capt. John Turner, the author of the Narrative, for several years: they have therefore no hesitation in recommending it as worthy the attention of the public.

I sailed in the John Jay from Bombay, bound to China, as first officer.—After a pleasant passage of 35 days I arrived at Maccoa Roads, where we came to anchor in order to get a pilot to proceed up Canton river. Accordingly I took with me six hands, or Lascars, in the jolly boat, and made the best of my way to Maccoa for a pilot. I had not proceeded far when I saw boats standing towards me which I took to be fishermen, though I found afterwards they were Ladrones. One junk in particular seemed to be coming from Maccoa, she then being some distance to the northward of Cabareta Point. Having stept the masts and weighed, we pulled and sailed towards Maccoa, being about two thirds of the way between Kow-Kow and Cabareta Point. The junk before mentioned standing towards us as near to the wind as she could, observed a boat put off from along side of her, pulling towards us, and which I imagined to be a Compradoce's boat.[2] On her coming closer observed she was full of people, and as I was loading a musket they fired a gun at us from their bow, and as we were pulling towards each other we closed almost immediately, when they boarded us, stabbing one of the men in the back, and one of them striking at one of the Ladrones with his sword. I jumped overboard to avoid the blow, that was returned; they shortly after took me up, and the tide having in the mean time set the boats along side the junks, they ordered us to go on board of her. She mounted eight carriage guns, six pounders.

I was immediately plundered of all I had about me, and by the information of one of them who spoke a little English, I understood we were prisoners to the Ladrones. They questioned me closely respecting the force of the ship, of which I informed them that she mounted twenty guns, larger than theirs were, and had one hundred and fifty men. I cautioned the Lascars, if questioned separately, to say the same; but had the junk attacked her, she would inevitably have carried her; the Jay having no other arms belonging to her than the two guns afore mentioned, and six musquets, two of which were by the boat with me; and as to ammunition for the guns, she had but eleven cartridges, which with a quantity of musquet cartridges, was all the powder we had in the ship.

They immediately bore up and stood down to the Typa, two other Ladrone junks having now joined them. In about three hours after came to an anchor at Lumpa-Cow, where there were several others.

On the 8th it blew a heavy gale and was remarkably cold, I desired the man, who spoke a little English, to inform the captain of the junk that I suffered much from the cold, and would thank him to order the person who had taken my greatcoat to return it, which he did, and it was restored to me stript of its buttons.

On the 9th I was sent on board the junk in which the chief of the flag resided, while the Lascars were on board the vessel that captured us. The chief junk mounted ten guns, of which two were long eighteen pounders, and the others sixes and nines.

On the 10th, by the interpretation of a Maylay (one of those taken in the boat with me) who understood a little Chinese, I learnt that the Ladrones demanded 3,000 dollars for our ransom. I immediately wrote two letters for Canton, one to Messrs. Baring & Co. who were agents for our ship, and the other to Captain Grey, informing them of my unfortunate situation, and of the sum demanded for our ransom. I have every reason to believe that the fishermen to whom they were entrusted destroyed them.

On the 11th a Chinese came on board who understood English, and informed me that the Ladrones demanded 10,000 dollars for our ransom, which if not given they would annihilate us. He offered, if I would write Captain Grey, to pay ten dollars to carry letters to Whampo. I accordingly wrote again to Mr. Baring requesting his assistance.

On the 14th an Armenian was brought on board who spoke Moors. He had been captured by them about seventeen months before, in a Portuguese brig from Manilla to Maccoa, in which he was a passenger. He partly relieved me for the present of my apprehensions of being murdered, and he remained on board until the 24th, when he was sent to look at some wounded men in another junk, as he had before assisted in one or two cures. On the 15th we weighed and made sail in company with about 70 Ladrone vessels, and stood to the north east, between the islands. On the 18th we anchored at Wong-chong-chow, when we attacked two places defended by forts, neither of which they carried. I did not see the attack, as the flag junk seldom or never fights unless first attacked.

Jan. 11th 1807. Three Ladrone junks came from Maccoa, by the man who had captured us to bring me to him, saying that the Mandarines would pay the ransom, they having now raised it to 30,000 dollars, which at first I could scarcely give credit to. On the 13th I repaired on board another junk, where I was more certainly informed that 30,000 dollars were insisted on. They also alleged that it was not the English who were to pay this sum, but the Mandarines by the Vice Roy of Canton's order. And they informed me, that four men belonging to the Mandarines of Maccoa, had been with them to say, that the Mandarines would pay our ransom; enquired how much they wanted, and where I was; they were told that the above mentioned sum was requisite, and that I was on board a junk to the eastward. These men desired I might be sent for, and promised to bring the sum required. The truth of these circumstances was confirmed to me by the Armenian. The Ladrone captain then ordered, that I should write to the Mandarines, and tell them, that if the ransom did not come in three days, he would certainly murder us all.

Not knowing how to address them, I wrote to Mr. Drummond at Maccoa, informing him of the above particulars, requesting that if what I heard to be true, he would be good enough to use his influence with the Mandarines to hasten our relief; should his influence have no effect, I had no hopes unless the honourable Company took pity on my unfortunate situation; at the same time stating, that I was continually threatened with death. Mr. Drummond could not have received this letter, having left China previous to its being written; and I know not whether it fell into the hands of any other gentleman.

Among the captures made daily, there was taken, on the 18th, a small Mandarine boat, with four men in her; one of whom was brought on board the junk I was on board of. Their cruelty to him, as also to another, which I shall mention hereafter, has made an indellible impression on my mind. He was nailed to the deck through his feet, with large nails; then beat with four rattans, till he vomited blood. And after remaining sometime, in this horrid state, he was taken on shore and cut to pieces. The others, I believe, were treated in a similar manner.

On the 19th, I received a letter from Capt. Grey, dated Dec. 28, informing me that 500 dollars were offered for our ransom, and that if the Ladrones should refuse to deliver us up, vengeance would be taken on them. Capt. Grey's letter was accompanied by one addressed to J.W. Roberts, Esq. desiring him to pay the money. On our being brought to Maccoa, I informed the Ladrones of what was offered by my commander; who had sailed by this time, and I had no money of my own. But they still continued to think, that the Mandarines would release us; for my own part, I much doubted it; and wrote by the bearer of the foregoing, to Mr. Roberts, desiring he would be good enough to answer my letter and inform me of the truth of what I had heard, concerning the Mandarines, and requesting, should it not be true, that he would inform Mr. Drummond, that the threat used against them, was productive of no other effect, than their threatening to murder us, should such vengeance be attempted. As this was the case, I begged that no force might be sent, but that I might be left to my wretched fate, until I could either effect my escape, or procure assistance from England, and I requested that a few clothes might be sent to me, as I suffered much from cold. Shortly after there came another man from the Mandarines, offering, as I was told, the sum of 5,000 dollars for our ransom, which they refused; insisting on 25,000, beside other things.

The next day there was taken a Canton chop boat, in which there was taken twenty-two passengers going to Maccoa. Several of them spoke English. One of them named Afoo, an intelligent man; I soon formed a friendship, which afforded me no small degree of consolation, during the rest of my captivity. Sometimes we would bewail together our hard fate, which had thrown us in the hands of cruel pirates; at others, encouraging each other, with the hopes of one day obtaining our release.

The Ladrones now passed over to Wong-chong-chow, in order to keep their new year. The Armenian now begged to be sent to the junk he was before on board of, which they complied with, as he had cured those who were either slightly wounded or had sores, for which services, he not only received no recompense, but was even worse treated than before.

On the 7th or 8th of Feb. I wrote at the desire of Afoo, a letter to Mr. Beale, requesting him to lend Afoo the sum of 200 dollars to complete the amount demanded for his ransom. At the same time, informing him of my own distressed situation, beseeching him to make it known, and receive whatever they might think proper to contribute for my relief; in doing which, he would lay me under infinite obligations.

After passing a few days of the New-year in Wong-chong-chow, [we] left it to go near Maccoa. Nothing particular took place for some time, otherwise than the Ladrones often wished me to write to the British gentlemen at Maccoa and at Canton, requesting their assistance. I always asserted that I was unacquainted with any of them, as never being at China before. They threatened that if I did not get released shortly they would put me to a cruel death, unless I assisted in working their guns. Of this I constantly told them I knew nothing of, as I belong to a merchantman and not a ship of war; they persisted however in insisting that this could not be the case. Here I must not neglect to mention the kind treatment that Afoo and myself experienced from the purser of the junk in which we were. This man had been taken by the Ladrones about three years before, and not having money to ransom himself, accepted of the situation he then held, in hopes on a future day to obtain an enlargement. He often invited us to come and set in his cabin, and one evening when we were all three together talking about our unfortunate situation, we mutually swore that the one who might get first released, should use every exertion in his power to procure the release of the others. Afoo was the fortunate man, having by the generous assistance of Mr. Beale, completed the sum required for his freedom, which he obtained on the 22d of February having been just a month in the hands of the Ladrones. He repeated his assurances of making every possible effort for our release; and I embraced this opportunity of writing to the British gentlemen at Canton and Maccoa, soliciting their assistance.

About this time the Ladrone captain who had taken me left the vessel; he was to take the command of a smaller junk, from the following circumstance: on board a small junk, two men had been forming a plan to run away, but being overheard and information given to the captain, they were flogged, and put in irons; they were then brought on board the chief of the squadron (who was the captain just alluded to) desiring that they might be put to death. This the chief would not allow, on which the captain and some of the people of the small junk armed themselves and insisted that their quest might be complied with. The chief still refusing, a quarrel took place, in which the captain and people were driven to their boats. One or two of them were wounded. On account of this misconduct, the captain was obliged to leave the Ladrones; and the chief on consulting their gods respecting a successor to him, found himself called upon, to give up his own vessel and to take command of the small one, which was done accordingly.

March 1st, received a letter from Afoo, with some clothes which was sent me by Mr. Beale, but before I had time to acknowledge the receipt of them, the Ladrones got under way and stood to the south west, passing at a short distance two or three hundred sail of Mandarine and salt boats coming from the westward, and in two or three days we came to stay where several other Ladrones were laying. Here they hauled their vessels on shore, and cleaned their bottoms. I was ashore at this place for about an hour, being the first time since I was taken prisoner.

At this place a man was put to death with circumstances of peculiar horrors, being fixed upright, his bowels were taken out and his heart likewise, which they afterwards soaked in spirits and ate. The dead body I saw myself. I am well assured that this shocking treatment is frequently practised to those, who having annoyed them in any particular manner, fall into their hands.

From this place we sailed to Tyho, when I was ordered on board the small junk commanded by the chief of the squadron; sailed from thence in company with five small junks, leaving several others lying there; three days after they joined us, and I was informed by the Lascars that they had fallen in with some Mandarine vessels, had engaged them and taken a small one which they burnt, having thrown every person overboard. We now kept beating to the north east, and the next day parted company.

One evening about sun set, saw two Ching-chow junks to which they gave chase. The force of the Ladrones being four large and three small vessels, they attacked the first one they came up with, and after some time finding she was too heavy for them took the guns out of one of the small vessels, and made a fire ship of her. They laid her along side the Ching-Chow junk to windward and set fire to her; in doing which one of the Ladrones was much burnt; she burnt very well, but there being little wind, and the junk's main sail the opposite side, there was nothing that could take fire except the hull; in about ten minutes they shoved her off from along side, which the Ladrones seeing, gave her a few more shot and then stood from her.

Two days after as we were laying between the island in company with three other Ladrone vessels, saw in the forenoon several Mandarine junks making all sail towards us, immediately got under way and run to the south west; the Mandarine junks pursuing us with a force consisting of twenty two large junks; in the evening, fell in with fourteen sail, large and small, of the Ladrones, and came to an anchor under the lee of an island. The next morning got under way and stood to the north east; at 8 o'clock in the forenoon saw the Mandarines at anchor in-shore of us, who shortly after got under way, and though much superior in force to the Ladrones, they never attempted to get near them. The Ladrones turning to windward about three leagues off and the Mandarines close in shore, the former neither appearing to seek, nor the latter to avoid an engagement; at four in the afternoon the Mandarines still outside.

Shortly after this, the purser afore mentioned, informed me that three or four thousand dollars would be accepted for my ransom. I wrote to Mr. Beale to that purport, from whom I had received two or three encouraging letters, during my confinement. The next day the purser left the Ladrones, having obtained his release by a plan concerted between him and Afoo.

On the 22d of April, Afoo came to the Ladrone junk, in which I was, and informed me that he had been with the chief of the Flag from whom he had a pass for three months, and that he had been endeavouring to induce him to lessen the sum demanded for our ransom; which I believe was of considerable advantage. After treating with the chief of the squadron sometime, (by whose boat I was taken) it was at length agreed on, that 2,500 dollars should be given. Afoo then left us to return to Maccoa, having first obtained a pass to secure the above sum, when bringing it, from being taken by any other Ladrones.

April 28th; in the morning when lying at Lumpa-cow, news was brought that several Mandarine vessels were coming. The Ladrones immediately got under way, when one of the captains hailed the junk I was on board of, saying, we are equal to them in force, and therefore we will not run. Immediately they hove about, and stood toward the Mandarines. The force of the former, eight large and ten small, of the latter, ten large and five small. The Mandarines showed no disposition to wait for them, but made all possible sail to get away. Fortunately for the Mandarines, when within musket shot of giving up the chase, the Ladrones saw the Portuguese frigate at an anchor, distant two miles.

The Ladrones now made sail to the eastward, and arrived at Wong-chong-chow in three days. On the 9th of May a Chinese who had been dispatched by Afoo, came to the Ladrones, telling them, there was an English ship lying off Sam-cock, which had money on board, and, that if they would carry us there and anchor in sight, the sum demanded for our ransom would be sent. We were then put on board another junk with two others to accompany her, and proceeded to Sam-cock. I was at this time informed that one of the Lascars had made his escape a few days before. On our arrival there, saw nothing of the ship; the Chinese who had come to the Ladrones went to Maccoa, thinking the ship might have been there, as it was dirty weather. Next morning the Ladrones stood towards Maccoa in order to discover the ship; but on observing twenty-five sail of Mandarine junks, made sail towards Wong-chong-chow, at which place they arrived next morning and we were welcomed on our returning with the promise of having our heads cut off.

On the 21st a letter was brought me from Capt. Ross informing me he had money on board for our ransom, and wished to know where we were to be had, and at what place we should stay. Of this I informed the Ladrone chief, who said he would send us the next morning, and allowed one of the Lascars to go with a letter to Captain Ross, telling him that one of the Ladrones would anchor in sight and fire a gun, when if he would send a boat with the money, they would let us go. At midnight myself and the remaining Lascars were sent away with five vessels in company, and the next forenoon arrived in sight of the honourable company's cruisers, Discovery and Antelope, when one of the Ladrone row boats went to make the signal; shortly after a fishing boat brought a letter from Capt. Ross, saying he perceived the signal, and would immediately dispatch the jolly boat with the money, of which I informed the Ladrones, desiring they would go nearer the ship; they then put us in a smaller vessel for that purpose, observed the Discovery had dispatched her boat; but as she was pulling towards us, another Ladrone that was out on a cruise passed between the vessel I was in and the Discovery's boat, at which she fired two shot and dispatched a row boat in chase of her. Upon this the Discovery's boat put about and pulled towards the ship, fearing some treachery; but another making a signal from the vessel I was in, they left off chasing and bore down to us. The fisherman who brought me the letter having overtaken the jolly boat, accompanied her to the Ladrones with the ransom, which after having taken out and counted, they let us go; one of their row boats was sent to accompany us part of the way to prevent our being molested by any other Ladrone vessels, and about three in the afternoon of the 22d of May, I arrived on board the Discovery where I was sincerely congratulated on my happy deliverance.

During my confinement or captivity, of five months and a half, I was fortunate enough to enjoy perfect health, notwithstanding the inconvenience to which I was subjected.

My fare was like that of a common Chinese, consisting for the most part of coarse red rice, with a little salt fish. In vessels so crowded as the Ladrone boats generally are, the accomodations may easily be conceived wretched, and this inconvenience I felt severely. At night the space allowed me to sleep in was eighteen inches wide and four feet long, and if at any time I happened to extend my contracted limbs beyond their limits, I was sure to be reminded of it by a blow or a kick.

For the first five days after being taken I was used kindly, but afterwards my treatment was very indifferent; several times I have been struck and kicked by the meanest Ladrone, while useless expostulations were all I could offer in my defence. Often was I threatened with cruel death, till at length their threats almost failed to intimidate me; though I was well aware, that I had no hopes of justice, or humanity from so unprincipled a set of robbers.

I cannot describe my feelings during my captivity, and it is impossible for any to conceive them, but those who have been placed in a similar unfortunate situation. Even when I expected daily to be ransomed, I was under the most dreadful apprehensions, that some treachery on the part of the Ladrones might render useless the effort of those who had interested themselves in my liberation, and perpetuate my confinement among those pirates. But I shall leave these painful reflections, to acknowledge the obligations I lie under to those gentlemen, by whose exertions my release was happily procured, and for which I shall ever feel most grateful.

[*Conclusion of his narrative respecting his confinement. He now proceeds to make a few remarks respecting force, discipline &c. of the Ladrones, as far as came within his knowledge during his confinement.*]

Numbers and Force.

The total number of vessels engaged in acts of piracy on the south coast of China, and which are known to Europeans by the name Ladrones, is as nearly as I can conjecture, between five and six hundred sail; these are of different sizes; the largest may be about two hundred tons burthen, the smallest does not exceed fifteen, but the majority are from 70 to 150 tons. Like other Chinese vessels, their draught of water is much less than the generality of Europeans of the same burthen, as they have not been built by the pirates themselves, but are vessels which from time to time have fallen into their hands. There is nothing in their construction, or their appearance, to distinguish them from the common Chinese trading vessels.

The largest mount 12 guns, from 6 to 12 pounders, and some of them have even a few eighteen pounders; the rest carry metal according to their size, with

long wall pounders, match locks, pikes with bamboo shafts from 14 to 18 feet
in length, which they throw at a distance like javelins, also, shorter ones with
shafts of solid wood; the pike part being similar to the blade of a dirk, and made
sharp on both edges, those they use when at close quarters, for which they also
use short swords, about eighteen inches in length. Like the guns of the Chinese
forts and junks, those of the Ladrones are mounted on carriages without trucks,
having neither breechings nor tackles, and always run out directly a beam, and
never pointed fore and aft; they are obliged (when making an attack) to wear off
in order to bring the guns to bear on the object, a man standing by to fire when
having good aim. The guns are previously elevated or depressed according to
the distance, having in this manner discharged their broadside they haul off to
reload.

The number of men in each junk is generally considerable for its size, the
largest have upwards of one hundred men, and the smallest seldom ever less
than thirty, I have averaged the whole at fifty men, and the number of junks at five
hundred, neither of which suppositions, exceeds the truth. The total number of
those pirates amount to twenty-five thousand men.

Independent of the force above-mentioned, several vessels have belonging to
them a row boat, mounting from six to ten wall pieces and swivels, also well
armed with boarding pikes and swords, and according to their size, carry from
eighteen to thirty-six men; these are rigged with one or two mast and sail like the
Chinese boats, and pull from fourteen to twenty oars, they are more particularly
employed in going close along shore at nights, plundering and desolating villages,
that does not pay them tribute and carrying off such of the inhabitants as fall
into their hands; they chiefly infest the mouths of the rivers, Maccoa, and such
places as have small trading vessels, they in general leave the large junks an hour
or two before sun-set and return about noon the following day; though they are
sometimes absent two or three days, lying at anchor during the day, so as not
to be seen by those on whom they intend making their depredations. At dusk
they sally forth and plunder whatever may fall in their way. Sometimes when
unsuccessful they go on the sides and tops of hills, and on perceiving any boat
or vessel, which they are able to capture, immediately give chase to it.

The Chinese Ladrones are abundantly supplied with shot from Maccoa and
Whampoo; stolen I presume, by the Chinese, from the forts and shipping at those
places, and brought by them for sale. I have seen such a quantity of eighteen pound
shot brought, that they were refused; and which I had every reason to believe was
brought from Whampoo. When at close quarter they frequently use nails, the
fragments of iron pots, &c. which supply the place of grape and cannister shot.
The powder is of Chinese manufacture, which they readily procure at different
places.

Their numbers are kept up and even considerably augmented, partly such of
their captives as are unable to ransom themselves; and by Chinese, who volunteer

their services daily from different parts of the coast. It will be scarcely credited how great the number of this latter description is. I have frequently seen from five to ten come at one time, and on one occasion upwards of thirty, some of these were, doubtless, vagabonds, induced by poverty and idleness to embrace this criminal mode of life, but many were men of decent appearance, and some of whom brought money with them. The only reason I heard them assign for their conduct, was that the Mandarines of their district, were unjust and they came there to avoid their oppression. These men are at liberty to leave the Ladrones when they think proper; as several went away after being only a month with them. At one time they used to come and go, in such quick succession, that the chief I was with, refused to allow any to join them, unless they agreed to remain eight or nine months, at the expiration of which time, they were at liberty to go or remain. But greater numbers of them remain four years, and it is on them that the command of their junks chiefly devolve.

Discipline and Division.

The whole body of Ladrone junks I have seen, who are under the command of five chiefs, all independent of each other; the vessel of each chief being distinguished by a particular flag at the foremast head. The division by which I was captured, had a red triangular flag with a white scolloped border. A second division has a black triangular flag without any border. A third has a square red flag without a border. A fourth has a red triangular flag with a plain yellow border. And a fifth is distinguished by a square flag blue, white and red, horizontally.

The division bearing the red flag with a white border, is much superior in force to any of the others.[3]

Each junk has a captain who directs in a general way, all the operations on board, and whose authority is sufficiently respected by the crews. The management of the sails and steerage of the vessel are entrusted to two experienced persons, whose orders in those points are attended to and executed by the others. Under them were three or four men similar to our boatswains mates, in point of duty.

During the time of action or chace, the captain assumes a more active part and directs all their movements. In every vessel there are a certain number of men of approved courage and fidelity, who have volunteered their services to the Ladrones, these work the guns and are the most forward in all hazardous enterprises, should the captain fall, one of these generally takes command. I never saw any of the crew flogged or beaten in a Ladrone boat, though I have seen them put in irons.

The captain is generally better dressed than the common Ladrones, he also fares better and the officers or assistants mentioned above, are partakers of his meals.

Each division is formed in several squadrons commanded by an inferior chief, by whom the captains are generally appointed, and from whom they receive their orders. He is responsible for his conduct to the chief of his division. Sometimes the whole of the squadrons join their forces, and frequently a few vessels sail in company, according to the force they expect to meet.

Nature of Their Depredations and Treatment of Prisoners.

All vessels that frequent the coast of China, are liable to be attacked by them, except such as by paying a tribute to one of the Ladrone chiefs, have obtained a pass, and which pass, is respected by all the other divisions. Numbers not only of fishing boats, but of the country merchant junks, have availed themselves of this protection.

The farms and villages upon the coast which have no forts in their neighbourhood, are equally subject to the depredations of the Ladrones, and their inhabitants are, for the most part, willing to compromise for their safety by paying a tribute.

This tribute is collected from the villages every six months, from the boats annually. And the sums obtained in this manner must be considerable. As a proof how far these passports are respected, I will mention one instance, the commander of a squadron having plundered and detained a fishing boat that had a pass, and on the circumstances being represented to the chief of the division, the commander was not only obliged to give the boat to its owner, but to pay five hundred dollars for the detention and losses sustained.

If a vessel they capture happens to have made resistance, they in general murder some of the crew and cruelly treat the residue, but if they suspect the crew of having destroyed or secreted any thing, though none are murdered, yet they are severely punished. In other cases they are satisfied with the plunder and detention of the crew.

The punishment alluded to above, is inflicted in the following cruel manner. The unhappy victim being first stripped of his clothes, has his hands tied behind him, a rope passing from the mast head, then made fast to his joined hands by which he is hoisted from the deck; and while thus suspended, repeated stripes are inflicted on every part of his body, with a rod formed of two or three rattans twisted together. Blood frequently follows the stripes, and in some cases the miserable sufferer is left suspended by his hands for upwards of an hour.

When any of the Mandarine boats fall in their hands, the persons are most cruelly treated, of which an instance is given in the narrative.

All the prisoners they take who are possessed of any funds, are expected to ransom themselves. The ransom demanded is generally as much as they think the person can raise, either from his own fortune or by the assistance of his friends. I know of no instance when on the ransom being brought, that the person was not given up. Should those who are supposed capable of paying for their ransom, refuse to do so, they expose themselves to the cruel treatment aforementioned.

Those who are unable to pay their ransom, are detained and obliged to assist in working the vessels and other duties, they are not even allowed to go on shore for water, without some of the voluntary Ladrones accompanying them armed. Notwithstanding these precautions, they sometimes effect their escape, but if retaken, are severely treated and put to death. I have understood that in five or six years, they obtained a release if they wished it, but the habits they have acquired or a dread of their being recognised as Ladrones, prevent the greater part from returning to their former occupations.

With respect to the women who fall into their hands, the handsomest are reserved by them for wives and concubines; the chiefs have frequently three or more, the others seldom more than one. And having once made choice of a wife, they are obliged to be constant to her. No promiscuous intercourse being allowed among them, but the greater part of the crew are satisfied without them. A few are ransomed and those that possess no beauty are turned on shore. Children taken, are generally brought up among them as servants &c.

When a vessel is taken and the owners do not ransom her (which is sometimes done) both vessel and cargo are destroyed, if not wanted by the captors, but in general the best vessels are made use of and armed as Ladrones, the cargo when of use to them is distributed to the ships of the squadron, and it is in this way they are partly supplied with necessaries.

Whatever monies is found in their prizes is brought to the commander of the squadron, as also the sums received for ransom of prisoners and goods.

Of this a trifle is given to the immediate captors, part of which is reserved to purchase provision and other necessaries, for the use of the squadron. And a certain proportion, I know not what, is paid to the chief of the division.

From this source and that of the tributes formerly mentioned, there is generally a large quantity of specie on board of their vessels. I have been told from fifty to one hundred thousand dollars. Out of this they supply such squadrons as have been unsuccessful in their cruizes.

The Ladrones find not the least difficulty in procurring provisions and all other necessaries on the coast, for which they pay honorably. The fishermen are generally the bearer of those supplies.

The Ladrones do not possess that desperate cholar, which is characteristic of other pirates, yet I conceive they are by no means devoid of courage, having frequently seen them stand well during an action. I was told by an Armenian and some Portuguese, who had seen more of them than I had, that they are apt to flinch when wounded, I have heard the Ladrones declare, they were not afraid of the Chinese or any other government, attacking them, and that nothing would give them greater pleasure than to meet the Mandarine junks, at a distance from Maccoa, on nearly equal terms. As an instance how well they will defend themselves when hard pushed, I may mention a circumstance of a Ladrone junk, falling in with four Mandarines, all larger than herself, which after an engagement of some time, she beat off, having one man killed and two wounded.

I have heard them also assert, that when an opportunity offered and no foreign ships at Whampoo, they would make an attack on Canton, and should the Portuguese cruisers oppose them, they would burn them. Whether this was bravado or not, I do not pretend to say, but certain it is, they cruise among the islands, in small bodies, and singly without fear or molestation.

In the foregoing accounts I am certain I touched upon some points, with which the gentlemen residents at Canton, are much better acquainted than I can possibly be, but I thought it better to run the risk of stating some facts which may be already known, than withholding any that is not.

Finis.

Notes

1. Originally a Spanish term (*ladrón*) for highwaymen, the word *ladrone* came to be generally applied to pirates of the South China Sea during the late eighteenth and early nineteenth centuries. For discussions of Chinese pirates, see Dian H. Murray's *Pirates of the South China Coast, 1790–1810* (1987) and her chapter, "Chinese Pirates," in David Cordingly's *Worldwide Illustrated History of Pirates* (1996). For a more colorful and historical account of Chinese pirates, see "History of the Ladrone Pirates" in Charles Ellms's *The Pirates Own Book* (1837). The word *lascars* was generally applied to all Asian seamen who worked on European ships.

2. *Compradoce* seems to be a misspelling for *compradore*, which refers to a native Asian agent employed by European businesses as an intermediary in commercial transactions.

3. The Red Flag Fleet was originally commanded by Cheng I, but after his death during a storm his wife, Cheng I Sao, also known as Mrs. Cheng, took command of the fleet. The largest of the confederated pirate fleets, the Red Flag Fleet is estimated to have had more than three hundred junks and from twenty to thirty thousand pirates (Murray, "Chinese Pirates" 223).

The Life and Adventures

of

Joshua Penny

... Who Was Impressed

into the

British Service

The Life and Adventures of Joshua Penny (1815) was one of a number of maritime impressment narratives made popular by American outrage over the British practice. Between 1803 and 1812 the British navy impressed between five thousand and six thousand American men and illegally stopped and searched 528 American flagships. Although the British only claimed the right to impress its citizens who were deserters from the Royal Navy, American seamen who had papers attesting to their citizenship were not safe from press-gangs. Indeed, this is the case with Joshua Penny, who relates: "I had frequently seen the papers of neutrals torn in pieces by the press-gang, and thrown into the fire—declaring their protections good for nothing." For Penny, the hardship of impressment was a double blow. It was an egregious repudiation of his liberty, since impressed men were treated as slaves, and it was also an economic hardship, since his most productive years as a worker were not compensated. In fact, Penny earned only four dollars during the eleven and a half years he was held in captivity.

The Life and Adventures of Joshua Penny, which Penny published himself, may have been a way for him to profit from his unfortunate experiences. Whatever his intentions, Penny's text was only printed once in America, by Alden Spooner in Brooklyn, New York, in 1815. The only reissue of Penny's work came in 1982 in Cape Town, South Africa, for the South African Library reprint series. The following copy is taken from the Spooner edition, which includes Penny's narrative, a collection of letters about his captivity, and a poem about kidnapped seamen. The footnotes included in the text are Penny's own.

Penny took to the sea in 1788, when he was fifteen years old, primarily as a way to earn a good living and to satisfy his curiosity about the world. He was first harassed by press-gangs in Liverpool in 1793. In order to escape them, he signed on to a slave ship and went to the Caribbean. Despite his efforts, he was forced into British service in Jamaica in 1794. The treatment he received as an impressed man was malicious and cruel, which Penny records in a bitter, matter-of-fact manner. In time he managed to get on board a French warship, *La Diable à Quatre*, headed to St. Domingo to put down an uprising, about which Penny wrote: "Such scenes of murder and rapine as were witnessed, are too shocking to relate, *Pandemonium* seemed let loose." Penny finally made it home to Long Island in 1805.

While Penny was away at sea, the United States under Thomas Jefferson's leadership had been going through a delicate balancing act to remain neutral during the Napoleonic wars. These efforts were strained in 1805 as the Royal Navy warships became more aggressive to Americans at sea, stopping and searching their ships, impounding their cargo, and impressing Americans into service. Jefferson, still not convinced that America needed a navy after the Tripolitan War, commissioned gunboats, shallow-water vessels designed to protect American ports and sea harbors, rather than heavy frigates or gunships of the line. This decision left American merchant ships unprotected and hampered safe trade with the West Indies and other lucrative markets. It also provided little incentive for the British to return the American seamen who were being held hostage. In an attempt to dissuade the English, the United States passed the Non-Importation Act in 1806, which prohibited the importation of British goods that could be obtained elsewhere or produced at home. As American merchants could not afford to decrease their sea trade during this time, the act was largely ineffective; exports of American goods rose from $20 million in 1792 to $138.5 million in 1807. Then the Embargo Act of 1807 prevented all land and seaborne trade with foreign nations. When the embargo was lifted in 1810, Americans were again subject to increased intimidation, seizure, and impressment. Thus, British impressment practices were still a source of public outrage when Penny's narrative was released.

Despite Penny's title, the narrative does not focus exclusively on his impressment. The last third of the text describes his involvement in the War of 1812 and his subsequent second captivity by the British. In 1813 Penny became involved in radical political and military activities on Long Island Sound, which were being led by America's foremost naval hero, Stephen Decatur. In March 1813 Congress passed the controversial "Torpedo Act," which pledged to pay anyone who burned, sank, or destroyed a British warship a bounty equal to half the ship's value. Penny was undoubtedly engaged in one, if not two, serious tactical schemes to sink the British ship *Ramilies*. This activity eventually led to Penny's capture by the Prince Regent's people and imprisonment on Melville Island for a period of nine months. Penny's assertions of unjust imprisonment are verified by a series of letters between Benjamin Case, the major commanding the troops in the United States at Sag Harbor, and Captain Sir Thomas M. Hardy of the Royal Navy, which are included in Penny's narrative. Another letter of some importance concerning Penny, which is not in his narrative, is from President James Madison to Secretary of the Navy William Jones, which claims, "putting him [Penny] in Irons for the cause alleged, should be instantly retaliated, and notice given to the British Commander, that the orders for that purpose will continue to be executed, until Penny shall be relieved."

Throughout Penny's narrative, his patriotism and bitter anti-British position echo the sentiments of a large segment of the American public. However, Penny's work does more than simply appeal to readers who had unfavorable experiences with the British naval forces. Readers cannot help but be moved by the author's solitary experience in captivity among people who were not his own, the violence perpetrated against him, and his fear of losing his American identity and autonomy.

CRB

Southern District of New-York, ss.
(L.S.) Be it remembered, that on the twenty-fourth day of January, in the thirty-ninth year of Independence of the United States of America, *Joshua Penny*, of said district, has deposited in this office the title of a Book, the right whereof he claims as author—in the words following, to wit:

"The Life and Adventures of Joshua Penny, a native of Southold, Long-Island, Suffolk county, New-York:—Who was impressed into the British service, and in one of his attempts to escape, was fourteen months on the Table Mountain, at the Cape of Good-Hope, and saw no human being during that time. In another instance he resided some time among the Hottentots: Interspersed with many curious incidents and hair breadth escapes. Also, an account of his being taken out of his bed, by Commodore Hardy, on the night of Aug. 21, 1813—and carried to Halifax: where he suffered nine months imprisonment.

"Never give it up for one bad job."

In conformity of the Act of the Congress of the United States, entitled "An Act for the encouragement of Learning, by securing the copies of Maps, Charts, and Books to the authors and proprietors of such copies, during the times therein mentioned." And also to an Act, entitled "an Act, supplementary to an Act, entitled to an act for the encouragement of Learning, by securing the copies of Maps, Charts, and Books to the authors and proprietors of such copies, during

THE

LIFE AND ADVENTURES

OF

JOSHUA PENNY,

A NATIVE OF SOUTHOLD, LONG-ISLAND, SUFFOLK COUNTY,

NEW-YORK:

Who was Impressed into the British Service, and in one of his at-
tempts to escape was fourteen months on the Table Mountain, at
the Cape of Good Hope, and saw no human being during that
time. In another instance he resided some time among the Hot-
tentots.

INTERSPERSED WITH MANY

CURIOUS INCIDENTS AND HAIR BREADTH ESCAPES.

ALSO,

AN ACCOUNT OF HIS BEING TAKEN OUT OF HIS BED BY COMMO-
DORE HARDY, ON THE NIGHT OF AUG. 21, 1813—
AND CARRIED TO HALIFAX;

WHERE HE SUFFERED

NINE MONTHS IMPRISONMENT.

———

" Never give it up for one bad job."

———

NEW-YORK:
PUBLISHED BY THE AUTHOR.
1815.

PRINTED BY ALDEN SPOONER, BROOKLYN.

Title page of *The Life and Adventures of Joshua Penny*
(1815 edition; Rare Books Division, the New York
Public Library, Astor, Lenox and Tilden Foundations)

the times therein mentioned, and extending the benefits thereof to the arts of designing, engraving and etching historical and other prints."

Theron Rudd,

Clerk of the Southern District of New-York.

———

The publication of this narrative has unavoidably been delayed. Poverty has hitherto prevented the narrator from discharging his duty to the public, and yielding to the repeated solicitations of his friends.

His country has waged war, principally for the security of commerce and the protection of her seamen; it therefore has become a duty to publish such facts, within his knowledge, as expose to the world the imperious and barbarous conduct of the common enemy, on the great highway of nations. The obligations imposed on this narrator, shall be faithfully discharged. The reader will perceive him to be without pretensions to scholarship, and that it was almost impossible for him to have kept a journal; yet he may rest assured, that nature has endowed him with a retentive memory, and that his memory has received impressions too deep to be effaced, until he ceases to exist.

The British *"maritime code"* is diametrically opposed to the rights and immunities of every other nation on the terraqaeous globe. Those who regard the rights of an American sailor as those of an American citizen, and who can sympathise in the sufferings of their fellow men, will listen to my story and overlook its necessary imperfections.

My father, Edward Penny, lived and is yet living at Southold, in the county of Suffolk, on Long-Island, where I was born on the 12th of September, 1773.—My parents had nine children, and like most others with a numerous progeny, they were very poor. My mother at an early period summoned her boys to attend her, for the purpose of determining their future pursuits for a livelihood. She examined us in rotation, and on asking me, "Well, Joshua, what will you do for a living in this world?" I answered, that I intended to go as far as sea and land would carry me.

At fourteen years of age, I was bound by indenture to Dr. John Gardiner, who lived in that place with the reputation of being an excellent physician, and was, certainly a good man. At the expiration of one year, I urged my father to cause my indenture to be cancelled, because I was anxious to try my fortune at sea. This was done, and I entered on board of a sloop under command of Capt. Webb, and sailed to Guadaloupe. On our return to New-York I visited my friends, who were rejoiced at my safe arrival, expecting to find me disgusted with a seafaring life. In vain they pressed me to remain quietly at home until I should be better educated. They were disappointed; my fondness for the sea was undiminished.

I solicited for and obtained leave to visit my brother, in Philadelphia, but on my arrival at New-York, went from one vessel to another inquiring if a cabin boy was wanted, without ever asking to what port they were bound; when at last I went on board the brig *Perseverance*, George Lippencott, master. Being very small for one of my age; he asked me whose child I was, and if I had my parents' liberty to go to sea? I told him that I had been once with their permission, and wished to do the same again. Upon this he shipped me at two and a half dollars per month, which I thought great wages, and must confess that for once I did feel proud. The brig sailed for Port Royal, Virginia, up the Rappahannock river.

On this passage I was maltreated by the mate, who happened to be a rough Irishman. I had complained to the captain of his ill usage, but the mate, after receiving a reprimand, grew worse, and threatened to throw me overboard, if I should enter any more complaints against him. In the evening when the brig was ready to pursue her voyage to Portugal, the captain and mate both went on shore, and gave me an opportunity to desert.

My chest, with a codfish and half a dozen biscuits in it, was put into the boat which took me on shore. I buried my chest in the sand, and travelled all that night in the woods. The next morning I was in the road and discovered two men on horseback: They hailed and asked me whither I was travelling? I answered, that "I knew not where I was going, and hardly knew from what place I had come." One of these men (laughing) said, "well then, my lad get on my horse and I will soon show you where you come from." He then inquired how far I had travelled since 9 o'clock the preceding night, and on my telling him, he demanded the reason for leaving captain Lippincott. He asked me if the captain was not a clever man? "Very clever and fatherly (said I) but the mate is an Irish bull-dog, he has beaten me almost to death." These men took me to the captain, who sent us all on board, and there demanded the cause for thus absconding. I told him the mate had treated me so ill that I was afraid to go with him. He next inquired for my chest; and I pointed out the place where it was buried.

The mate in my absence, had accused me of stealing some articles that were missing, and now jumped into the boat to go on shore; but the captain choosing to go without him, proceeded to the chest, which he found to contain no other plunder than the codfish and biscuits, as I had represented. He commended me for providing *as I had done* previous to the escape; and turning to the mate, charged him to prefer no more such accusations against me, on peril of being kicked overboard.

The brig was laden with corn, and sailed for Oporto,[1] but on her passage she encountered many severe gales of wind; in one of which she lost a deck load of oars and sweeps. This happened in the Gulf, but was not the only damage she sustained. Laden with corn, in bulk, it became necessary to scuttle her deck and throw over the swelling corn. We reached Figura in distress, and there discharging the residue of her cargo, loaded with salt. We reached the port of Norfolk after a long tedious passage, on an allowance of water. Here we remained only twenty-four hours, and sailed for New-York, where the captain paying me something more than the amount of my wages, discharged me.

From this time I went occasionally to the West-Indies, and coasted from New-York to Charlestown. In the last of these trips, two Irish gentlemen, passengers, prevailed on my captain to release me, as they had agreed conditionally with me, that if I would accompany them to their intended trading establishment, they would instruct me as far as they were able, to read, write, &c. Their names were Parsons Pau, and Anthony Carrol. With these gentlemen I went to a spot forty miles west of Augusta, in Georgia, where they pitched their tents and trafficked with both whites and Indians. A residence there of twelve months was long enough for one of my roving disposition.

The time had as yet passed agreeably enough with men like these, but my fortune was unmade. Nothing was neglected which wore the charm of novelty. I was often out on hunting parties, and one day while in pursuit of game, we had caught a large Opossum. Mr. Carrol being unused to the pranks of this animal, insisted on carrying it upon his shoulder. The Opossum, who had feigned death without any advantage to himself, fastened his teeth upon the Hibernian's neck. He was hugely terrified at this unexpected assault—threw himself on the ground, and rolling over in an anguish and affright, exclaimed, "I'm dead! I'm dead!" He was not relieved by his companions, until experience had taught him a severe lesson on hypocrisy. On leaving these men, I led to Augusta a young wolf, which they had purchased of an Indian, and gave me on my intended trip to Ireland. With this they assured me my fortune would be made in their native country. At Augusta I embarked for Savannah, with my wolf, a few clothes and a trifling sum in cash.

The brig Minerva, of Portsmouth, N.H. captain E. Schofield, was lying at Savannah, bound to Cork. In her I took passage and was within three days sail of our destined port, when the brig was boarded from a French privateer. The precious wolf, chained on deck, attracted the first notice of our Frenchman, the officer particularly amused himself by pricking it with his sword. They retired soon after to the cabin, where they examined the Minerva's papers, drank freely of porter, and returned carelessly on deck. The officer inadvertently approached too near the offended wolf, who revenged the affront received, by thrusting his teeth through the boot of his antagonist. The wound was inflicted near the officer's heel, from which blood started over his boot. This enraged him—he drew a pocket-pistol with which the wolf was instantly dispatched. Thus were my prospects of amassing wealth, blasted in a moment!

This was the first year of their revolutionary war (1793) with England. They had already manned so many prizes, as they informed us, that we were suffered to proceed without further molestation. In three days more we were in Cork, when the captain told me, that, "since my wolf was lost I could not do better than to tarry with him." But I wished to travel, and had a certificate given me by Messrs. Pau and Carrol, which was directed to their friends at Nenagh, in the county of Tipperary. The wolf skin was sold for three of their seven shillings. No sooner was I in readiness to commence the journey, than a press gang took me to a 74; the captain of this ship looked at my certificate, and humanely ordered me to be set again on shore. On the road I was often taken up on suspicion of being a deserter. Dressed in a rifle frock (hunting shirt) my appearance there was novel, and in passing the houses of the rich, was invited to enter. Here I was uniformly well treated—furnished with meat, bread and butter—a guinea or half guinea to defray expenses on the road. For about three weeks, however, I was among the poorer class, where the only food is milk and potatoes. They received me hospitably, and never insulted me with the opprobrious epithet of *yankee*.

I soon formed a very favorable opinion of the Irish character, which opinion to this day remains unchanged. The elder brothers of Messrs. Pau and Carrol were living in affluence at Nenagh. They received me kindly—told me I should be welcome to stay with them, and amuse myself as long as I thought proper. Six months' residence was sufficient for one whose fortune was yet to make: things around me were robbed of all their novelty, and a recruiting serjeant appeared at the nick of time. This man *stimulated* me too freely. I enlisted, and went to Dundagh where the regiment lay. There I immediately caught the itch, and was sick of a pleurisy. The doctor, when I had remained three weeks in the hospital, reported me well. I drew shirts, shoes and stockings—the taylor also had taken the measure for a red coat. With him I left the measure—and that night shipped on board a brig which sailed directly for Liverpool. The captain on our arrival, paid me to my satisfaction, and urged me to return with him; but I had fallen out with Ireland—and declined.

This affair should have remained unpublished, were it consistent with my design. It is however, some apology for a young man unskilled in the arts employed to entrap mankind, that the recruiting officer had first intoxicated his prey, and took advantage of his weakness. In my senses I should not have enlisted—but I must not conceal or misrepresent, however the naked truth may affect my character. Experience is a stern instructor, and I have profited from this quarter.

Among other things, I had discovered that an American in the dominions of his Britannic majesty, should be provided with a protection—even then his safety is not ensured. Proof being made of my citizenship, before James Murray, Esq. American Consul at that place, I ventured to continue in Liverpool for two weeks. Although lodged in the press-room as often as every other night, I never produced my protection until the regulating captain came to examine us in the morning, because I had frequently seen the papers of neutrals torn in pieces by the press gang, and thrown into the fire—declaring their protections good for nothing; that "they could buy them any where for a quarter of a dollar." How wretched is that government, which compels men to become murderers of their countrymen, and exerts her power to entrap and enslave those whom she professes to preserve free! A government of force, like that of England, is worse than the government of the American Indians.

Liberty is mocked by that nation which enslaves her subjects on pretence of rendering their condition more prosperous. Compel a man whom you stile free, to abandon his wife, his children, and every thing else he values in this world, to become your slave on ship-board! How dare you call that a land of freedom where this practice prevails, countenanced by its laws. "Where liberty dwells, there is my country."[2]

Those in America who chime in with this foe to the human race, are fit subjects for an English ship of war; they deserve to be under discipline in a floating purgatory, until they have learned to unite in support of the only government where liberty delights to dwell.—There they shall, with my petition be sent, until they have learned to commiserate the fate of an impressed sailor. My indignation must be suppressed.

Tired of being haunted by a press-gang, I engaged with captain Matthews of the ship Budd, bound to the African Slave coast. Our voyage to *Annamaboo* had been tedious, but we were not long detained there. We sailed with a cargo of 382 slaves for Jamaica. Nothing remarkable happened on the passage, except that we descried a sail at such a distance, that it was impossible to ascertain her colors. Our ship had 14 guns, which were fired at the strange sail as long as she could be seen: this courageous attack lasted about an hour; but our imaginary enemy did not appear to take the least notice of us. The captain, at Port-Royal, reported the affair; and according to his account, we had beaten off a French privateer of 18 guns. His report acquired him great credit there.

Soon after our entry in that port, the captain called the doctor, and said in presence of the ship's company,

> "See here are no less than eleven of those wenches pregnant by me, for which I shall get the more by fifty guineas per head. I have never had a less number on any voyage I ever made: yet I have one of the handsomest of women for a wife in Liverpool, who has never had a child,"[3]

Not many days had passed after our arrival, ere were again haunted by press-gangs, and our whole crew impressed. We were put into the Alligator frigate of 28 guns, under the command of captain Africk. Four of us were Americans; the others chiefly Danes and Swedes. A fever raged in this ship, and out of forty men, there were eleven corpses to be interred on the first morning.

No sooner was the captain on the deck in the morning, than we were ready with our American protections. He said, "men I will not look at your protections—my ship is in distress, and I will have men to carry me to England." He refused to hear a word on the subject of liberating any one of our number. The ship got under way, and the next morning went into Montego Bay, and anchored in the harbour at 8 o'clock in the evening: her boats were manned to board the merchants' ships lying there; and impressed from them without discrimination. This business of kidnapping continued until daybreak, when they got under way in season to prevent applications for relief. There were forty men impressed that night, some of whom were American mates and supercargoes—some had been taken out of their beds on shore, without liberty to dress themselves. We ran down to the fleet in the offing, of 114 sail merchantmen waiting for this ship to join the convoy of two ships of the line and the brig Jack Tar. The next day however, our ship was dispatched by order of the admiral, on a commission to Havanna; we lay twenty-four hours at the Moro-Castle then went to sea and rejoined the fleet.

The next day I was taken sick of a fever—was soon deprived of my sense, and when I first recollected myself, was out of my hammock and attempting to walk on deck; sudden blindness prostrated my feeble frame, when I heard a general shout "there goes another dead yankee." I was returned into my hammock; the doctor shortly after came along, and on finding a corpse next to me, he called his lob-lolly boy and chid him for not seeing that dead man's hammock cut down; adding, "that other man (meaning me) will be dead before 12 o'clock; and you ought to have the dead removed immediately, to make room for me." My fever was broken, so that the doctor's prophetic sentence was entirely harmless.

On our passage to England we fell in with an American schooner, laden with poultry, apples and cider. She was brought to, and her whole cargo purchased by the fleet. This yankee vessel was saved the trouble of going to the West-Indies—returning with casks of sea-water for ballast. One of our convoy, a king's transport of 14 guns, took fire suddenly in drawing spirits. Many persons, even ladies, jumped overboard; no lives were lost.

The sick had recovered after reaching the English Channel, and all the im-pressed seamen taken from Jamaica, were ordered on the quarter deck. The captain then addressing himself to us, said, "I want to know who of you im-pressed in Jamaica, are willing to take his majesty's bounty: it is customary to allow impressed men twenty-four hours to consider whether they will accept this privilege; if not, they are on arriving at Spithead, to be put on board some vessel bound to foreign parts, where they shall not have opportunities to write to the d——d consul." He called me singly and said, "You have been the sickest, and I have been a father to you: do you refuse the king's bounty?" I answered (pointing to an arm chest) if he would give me that chest full of guineas and a lieutenant's commission, he could not tempt me. He replied, "you had every day for two months, a dish from my own table, which no other man in this ship has had, and now you refuse to take the king's bounty! You are a d———d yankee rebellious rascal!" At Spithead we were called on deck with our baggage: What was next to be done with us we were left to conjecture. A part of our company expected to be set on shore—others had previously written letters to be sent to the consuls of their respective nations; but all were disappointed. A launch conveyed us along side of the Stately 64, captain Douglass. In two hours our squadron was ordered to sea. This squadron consisted of the America 64, commodore Blanket,[*] Ruby 64, Rattlesnake sloop of war, and two frigates, beside the *Stately* whose names I have forgotten. We had put our letters on board of a passage boat; and were sailing to some unknown part of the world. The officers, alike ignorant with the men, bet on our destination. Bets were laid on Batavia, Botany Bay, &c. but after being at sea ten weeks, we made the *Table Mountain;*[4] and every preparation was made for action. The next morning at day-break we were joined by admiral Elphinstone, with three 74's, three frigates, two sloops of war, and a gun brig. At 8 o'clock, the signal to clear away for action was hoisted on board the admiral's ship, and repeated by the commodore. We entered False Bay, where the Dutch had one fort of 8 guns, and another of four.[5] Fifty men, who composed the whole force there, spiked their cannon and retreated to Cape Town, leaving our fleet to take possession of every thing. A frigate and man of war brig lay in the harbour. We pillaged the East-India stores on shore—stove the casks of wine and spirits, which ran like rivulets to the sea. The liquor was said to be poisoned by the Dutch. English sailors would have drank the spirits, with permission, if they had really believed it to be poisoned; provided they could have got fairly drunk before they died. Our land forces were on shore the next day.

One evening, shortly after our arrival here, while hoisting in our boats, we were alarmed by the cry of fire! The surgeon's mate in a fit of intoxication let a candle fall into the surgeon's chest, which was open. The candlestick in its fall had broke some bottles, the contents of which instantly took fire. The flame rushed out, streaming from under the after hatchways to the quarter-deck. Orders were immediately given to hoist out all the boats. The order was executed with dispatch; but the boats no sooner struck the water, than they sunk with the crowd of men jumping into them. Few had the presence of mind to assist in extinguishing the fire.

I had jumped overboard and hoped to effect my escape, but when within gun shot of the shore was picked up by another ship's boat. All were taken and saved by the boats, except the captain's steward—he was a Guinea negro, who is as

---

[*] This Commodore had shot his purser on the quarter-deck and was tried for the murder. The court-martial sentenced him to death, but gave ninety-nine years and one day to repent in—confining him to never merit any higher station in his majesty's service, than that of commodore.

often steward of a ship, as a fool is employed in the palace of a British king. The fire was extinguished without any other loss.

Having often witnessed the *great* alarm at a *little* fire in a British ship, I am not at a loss to account for the horrors inspired by an American Torpedo.

Col. M'Kenzie's regiment marched from Simon's Town to attack a garrison at Muisenburgh, on the road to Cape Town. There our regiment was repulsed with the loss of sixty Highlanders. While we continued at Simon's Town 3,200 sailors were landed to reinforce the regular troops. They drilled us every day for five weeks; and general Craig with admiral Elphinstone and commodore Blanket, reviewed us once in every week.[*]

One day a serjeant undertook to drill our sailor corps, when we threw down our arms, refusing any longer to be under land officers. General Craig thereupon wrote to the admiral that the sailors were mutinous, and refused obedience to his officers. The admiral sent him word that the sailors were in the right, and they should be commanded by their own lieutenants, or if that would not do the captains should take charge of their own men. The lieutenants took command, but they had to go through the process of drilling before they were capable of instructing us.

Provisions became scarce, we were on an allowance of half a pound of salt meat and three-fourths of a pound of bread. The general's cow approaching too near a sailor sentinel, and not giving the countersign, was of course killed upon the spot. Pigs suffered death in the same way: thus we procured a seasonable supply of fresh meat. We were led by the guard to our ships, all in irons and fastened to a rope. The admiral instantly released us; and sent us ashore with a letter addressed to the general, informing him that "the sailors had as much right to eat fresh meat as himself." From that period there was a misunderstanding and coolness between those officers.

In the rear of this town there was a large green with a high spot where stood an hospital; this was our parade ground; and we were marching at a review around this hospital, the day previous to our contemplated march for Cape Town, when one of our ship's lieutenants, crowded at one corner of the building, in his haste to give the word of command, "left wheel!" cried, "luff you buggars and weather the hospital!"—The general laughed; and falling, rolled over in the dirt in his convulsions. We were pronounced fit for action, but must be exercised in shooting at a target. Accordingly a rock was fired at which was in the water. The

---

[*] The British account states, that—"The rocks of Muisenburgh were, by a few shot from a man of war, soon cleared. The British troops were led on by general sir James Craig, under the orders of sir Alured Clark. The Dutch *regular* troops retreated to Wynberg a tongue of land projecting from the east side of Table Mountain, 3 miles from Cape Town." Sir Alured Clark might have been there perhaps without my knowing it: but I do know that my account of the attack an Muisenburgh is correctly given. for I was in that unsuccessful battle.

admiral had given out that whenever an American should fire, the rock would smoke. About one of ten who fired, drew smoke from the rock; and on being asked by the general, "What countrymen are you?" His answer uniformly was, "I am an American."

The army (as I must call it) marched to make a new attack on the Dutch garrison at Muisenburgh, a distance of eight miles. Our main body proceeded by the shore, under cover of a sixty-four and a sloop of war, while a picket guard pushed their way over part of the mountain, to the camp which was at its foot. To make head against our main force, were ten of the Dutch artillery with two 24 pounders, 1 howitzer, and 2 smaller pieces. Their guns were on a platform, but exposed as they were, they threw ten shot into the Stately's hull, which killed ten of her men. One of their shot split an 18 pounder of the Stately. None of the Dutch were killed, but it was imprudent to oppose our "overwhelming force," and they retreated to Constantia plantation.*

The militia (for there were no regulars here) were either Dutch or civilized Hottentots, with whom we contended at Muisenburgh. We captured it without difficulty, and lay there or near it for three months, waiting for a reinforcement. We had frequent skirmishes on our foraging parties, in which I frequently volunteered; because vegetables were to be found in the deserted gardens; besides I was intent on the discovery of some convenient place for concealment, when ever I could make my escape from these man-stealers.

A party of eight under a sergeant, travelled to the top of a neighbouring mountain in the rain. One of our party mounted a rock and cried out "Dutchmen coming!" The serjeant flying, ordered us to follow him; but two of this party were Dutch, and we had discovered ourselves to the English enemy as we had preconcerted. The Dutch soldiers supposed us to be deserters and were marching towards us. When they were at gun shot distance from us, we laid down our arms and met them. They took us to their camp—treated us with Constantia wine and mutton tails of the best quality. In short they had nothing too good for us. They knew we had deserted, for this was not the first party; and asked us the cause of our desertion? We answered them truly, that we had been impressed and wished to return home. They sent us to Cape Town in a waggon without a guard; the inhabitants on the road where we halted, treated us very handsomely.

When we had arrived in town we were taken before the governor, who ordered us clothed and victualled at a boarding house. He told us we had our choice to go into the garrisons or amuse ourselves in town. We had as much wine as we could drink, and ran about the streets as we pleased, until the Cape should be surrendered. Here we had remained two months, when the governor called all who were deserters from the British (about 40) and told us that a

---

* The English call it Wynberg.

British reinforcements of 14,000 men had arrived, on their way to India; and had summoned the garrison to surrender: that it would be given up the next morning at 8 o'clock; and that we might retire into the country, where we would be well received by the inhabitants. Our knapsacks were loaded out of the Company's stores, with as much as we could carry away. We retired to the bushes on a hill about two miles from town, and drank Dutch wine that night. The next morning at 9 o'clock the British made their entry within the walls of that town, which was strongly fortified and said to have 500 cannon mounted for its defence. The Dutch governor betrayed the town; yet the English might have captured it with their 20,000 men.*

Our party travelled two days in company, to a Dutchman's house. This man could not speak English, but through our interpreters, he advised us to separate in squads of three each. After that time, whenever we came to a cross road a section filed off, until I was one of the last three. We had frequently called at the dwelling houses of the inhabitants, who always came to the door with wine and brandy, but dared not entertain us. They were kind enough to direct us on our way, and give us the distance to the next house.

Water was so rarely found, that we took that in calibashes. There was plenty of tropical and other fruits. Our trio, i.e. Jacob Cogswell, of Boston, one Vanderweit a Dutchman, and myself, continued its course about four days, when we arrived at the house of a farmer named Saerl Overalsten. This man informed us that this place was 100 miles from the Cape, that it was† at the head of the Klanvis Riviere, which emptied into the sea at 50 miles distance. We continued here ten days, hunting with his sons and otherwise amusing ourselves. The sons of our host went on their annual visit to this river's mouth, in quest of fish; on this occasion we joined their company. We had been two weeks at the river's mouth, living on fish and ostrich eggs, when this course of life became an old affair. The ostriches were always in sight, and in such numbers that at a distance they appeared like a drove of cattle. While fishing one day we discovered two men walking on the beach, which at first alarmed us. They approached us, and being interrogated, stated that they "had deserted from the whaling ship John, of London, which was then lying 40 miles from us—that captain Gardiner, formerly of Nantucket, commanded her—that he had killed one man and split the head of another with a broad-axe—that they had left the ship at anchor and were very hungry." They lodged with us that night; for if they were English, they had also suffered under

---

* This happened three months after the capture of Muisenburgh. We had been in Cape Town about two months before it was surrendered. This Dutch governor betrayed the garrison and retired to England, but did not long outlive his treachery. The British do not conquer such strong places—they buy them.
† In the division of the four-and-twenty rivers.

the tyranny exercised on board an English ship. They had been advised by a Hottentot of the capture of the Cape, and we confirmed the account which had been given: their tongues were in their element that night.

Cogswell and myself took it into our heads to visit this ship at anchor, whose crew was waging war with whales. We set off the next morning with fish and a calibash of water, reached the ship in twenty-four hours. A whale-boat at the mouth of the Groot Vis-Riviere, which belonged to the John, was watering. The crew confirmed the story which the two deserters related. They said it was a murdering ship, and they had calculated to leave her, but had heard of the surrender of the Cape to the English. With them we went on board, and satisfied the inquiries of the captain. He said he was much in want of men; for two of his d——d rascals had deserted from him. He said they had ten days more of whaling to be done before they sailed for St. Helena. We shipped; and a few days after she was discovered to be so leaky, that it was doubtful whether she would reach St. Helena.* The character of the captain was correctly given. One evening after killing two or three whales, I asked Cogswell whether he preferred to remain here or go among the Hottentots? He chose to stay. I went on shore to get fresh water and some vegetables; the latter were indeed wanted, since the scurvy had rendered the crew nearly incapable of duty. The best of my way was made for the fishing party, and on finding the waggons had left there, pursued the track until I reached them. I went with them to their home. Mr. Overalsten inquired what had become of *Yacoub*? I told him how it was, and that I would sooner continue with the Africans than go to sea with an Englishman. True, I had heard that captain Gardiner was a yankee, but who does not know that a renegado is a refined aristocrat. Jonas, said the good Dutchman, you have done right—you shall want nothing as long as you stay with me. He called me Jonas because my name here was Jonas Inglesberg; he had from the first learned that I was from Long-Island, and perhaps of Dutch extraction.

We lived with this honest Dutchman two or three months, and during this time were frequently visited by a neighbour whose name was Frederick Leemburgh. This man wished me to live with him. He owned 50 or 60 slaves, and told me I should have nothing to do at his plantation but oversee a little his negroes. He would give me victuals and clothes but nothing more.

With him I had been six months, when his waggons returning from the Cape, brought news papers containing a public notice that the English had possession of the district, and that if any inhabitant while under English laws, should entertain a deserter, he should be transported to Botany Bay for life. He then told Vanderweit and me, that he was in such dread of the British tyrannical laws, he dared not

---

* This ship was never afterwards seen. I examined both at St Helena and in London, years after this period.

entertain us any longer, but advised us to travel into the interior, as long as inhabitants were to be found.

The *Bosjesmen* were at that time making inroads on the frontiers, and our company was very acceptable to the Dutch party who were forming to act on the defensive, at Cold Bockveld. People at this place very willingly entertained us, and we joined them on their march to attack the enemy's camp. These Bosjesmen, or Boschmen[*] are savages. In that vicinity they had lately pierced a stake through the body of a woman—murdered all her children and drove off her flock. We marched in the tracks of wild beasts about three weeks; the Hottentots on bullocks, subsisting on flour conveyed in sacks, wild honey, and roots resembling American ground nuts. Our force was 40 men exclusive of 50 or 60 Hottentots; the latter were our scouts, and brought us intelligence in the night, that they had discovered our enemy dancing about their fires, and drinking a liquor made from honey. They piloted us within gun-shot of the encampment, where we laid in ambush until sunrise. The Bosjesmen had poisoned arrows, and our Hottentots were armed with arrows of reed, pointed with steel fastened into bone. Our foes slept in huts or tents, and the first one who showed himself was a boy stirring the coals. He was shot down. This brought them out of their tents like a swarm of bees. They threw showers of arrows at us while we lay among the rocks; but our fire dispersed them. Of our party one Dutchman was killed and two wounded. One Hottentot refusing to have the poison cut from his wound, also died. We found in the hostile camp twenty or thirty dead bodies, and a woman with nine children. The woman was shot, because no prisoner can be admitted into any settlement, over the age of eleven years. This was the same party that had impaled the woman above mentioned, and murdered her family.

These Bosjesmen are from four feet four inches to five feet high. They have no chief or political head, but rove in hordes much like the other inhabitants of the forest. We returned to Cold Bokeveld with the nine captive children in baskets, slung on the oxen by a girth which passed round the bodies five or six times, and drawn *taut* by two Hottentots. These oxen will carry four hundred weight, and in travelling five or six weeks will tire a horse carrying one hundred.

The poison used by the wild Hottentots is of two sorts; the one is the sap drawn from an incision made on the north side of a certain tree, into which the arrow's point is dipped. The other is taken from a snake. During my continuance here, a party returned from a tour to the country where they kill sea-cows.

The Caffrees sometimes come here to trade with the Christians, who described to me their persons and character. These Caffrees were much larger that the white, inhabitants with whom they trafficked. They are black as jet, dressing themselves with burnt roots, charcoal and stinking grease, like the Hottentots.

[*] Bushmen.

In hunting, the whole Kraal, armed with spears (not with bows and arrows like the Bosjesmen) inclose the wild beasts and drive them to the centre. They keep themselves at the distance of a rood between each person, and no one animal of all the various kinds must be suffered to pass on penalty of death. The person who flies is instantly massacred as a coward. Their spears are made of bamboo poles, with a feather to keep its course, and a harpoon or lance at the other end. They obtain their iron from the wrecks of ships. In the punishment they inflict they seem to imitate the lion. A Hottentot shepherd informed me, that "sitting on a mountain near a precipice, he had seen a lioness bring her prey toward her young, and when near their bed spring suddenly upon them; those young who sneaked off in fear, she killed for cowardice; but kindly fed the remaining." My informant was seventy years old, and worthy, as I believe, of implicit confidence.

I had been one year or longer absent from the Cape, and grew weary of the interior country; I had advanced a few days on my way back, when I met an inhabitant who said, he had a man on his plantation who deserted from Cape Town at the time of its surrender to the English. I found this man, who told me his name was John Johnston, of Bristol, in R. I. He joined me in hopes of reaching our beloved country.

At two or three days travel from the town we halted at the house of John Van Reinesbargh. Here we refreshed ourselves at the desire of our host, for three or four days, and then travelled toward the town till within three or four miles of it. On this road we fell in with another fellow-deserter; he could pass for a Dutch African, and we sent him on to reconnoitre. He came back next day and reported that the fleet we had left in the bay were all gone except the Stately, (the ship from which I had taken leave) and the Rattlesnake, sloop of war; but a number of other ships had arrived there in our absence. He further stated that seven men had been recently shot for desertion, and there had been a great naval mutiny in England. On the arrival of this news at the Cape, the sailors hoisted a sailor's jacket—three cheers on board each ship, and adopted the same regulations which had been adopted in England.

We went into the town at mid-day, dressed like the inhabitants of the country. The landlord at whose house we were, said there were some merchant ships in want of men, but it was impossible to avoid the English patrols who were searching every house for deserters. I asked the landlord if the captain of the Robert Morris was living? He answered me, that the captain was dead. That ship was cast away on the evening of my escape; and I thought to tell them, in case of being apprehended, that I belonged to that ship and had been in the country to procure a livelihood. That night the patrol came and demanded what countrymen we were. We all answered that we were American. Johnson and myself were lodged in jail that night. The next morning we were told by the Fiscal, that every such character in town, who could not give a *correct account* of himself, must be kept in jail until the trials of the sailors for mutiny were terminated. There were about twenty in confinement on suspicion of having deserted. Our bed was the naked stone floor; and our rations of provisions were nothing but bread and water and one spoon full of salt.

Admiral Clark ordered the prisoners to be examined by each guard-ship, until the whole had gone through, so as to ascertain whether there were any who had ever belonged to any ship with their knowledge. Every day three or four lieutenants made us stand up for examination. They asked our names and what countrymen we were? How we came there? &c. All of us had come there in ships; but none happened to be English. I told them of the Robert Morris, whose wreck was then in sight. The officers told each of us that they knew us; and we had belonged to the same ships, or certainly to the same squadron with themselves. They promised we should not be hurt *if they could help it*. We knew the consequences of detection as well as they could tell us; and if we prevaricated or concealed the truth, we acted as most others do who endeavour to *preserve their lives*.

It is the duty of every American to avoid imprisonment in a British ship of war. It ought to be the first article of the impressed seaman's creed, that a British vessel of war is a Pandora's box—a nefarious floating dungeon, freighting calamities to every part of this lower world.

One day, looking through the grates I espied an officer whom I knew to be a lieutenant of the Stately! Judge of my feelings, when I knew that if I was detected, I should be lashed to the cannon's mouth and blown in pieces, for having deserted in an enemy's port! I lost my courage at the sight of the officer; but before he entered the prison door fear forsook me, and I was perfectly at ease. The officer, tapping me on the shoulder, asked if I was an American? Yes, I answered. "Is not your name Joshua Penny?" My name is Jonas Inglesburg; I never deny my name nor country. He continued, "can you deny that I know you?" No sir, I replied angrily, every officer who has been here these three weeks has known me, and of course you *must* know me.

None except two Englishmen had confessed desertion; and the Fiscal was ordered by the admiral to ship the rest on board the first merchant ship which should arrive. We were then put on board of an Indiaman at this time lying in port, where we remained a few days making preparation to sail. The admiral told our captain that two men had deserted from his ship the preceding night; and he was correctly informed they were in our ship—he must have them delivered to him, else he would take the whole crew. This was a *finesse* of the admiral. Villainy often assumes the regular form of law and right, with these tyrants of the sea. Our captain could do no otherwise than tell the admiral "to search and welcome."

All of us who had been liberated from the jail, were now taken on board of the admiral's ship, TORMENTOR 74. I was transferred to the Sceptre 64, and after lying in Table Bay four or five months, was drafted to cruise in the Rattlesnake, off the Isle of France (Mauritius) under commodore Luzaco, of Guernsey, who commanded the Jupiter 54. The Rattlesnake, a few days after she sailed, parted from the fleet in a gale of wind, and did not rejoin it until eight days after the squadron had commenced the blockade of Port Louis, the only harbour and town of that island. Soon after this we captured a Danish cutter laden with silks and satins, and I was immediately put into the prize, which sailed for the Cape. This pleased me, for I hoped to have another opportunity to get from the fangs of these harpies. This was a tedious passage, and when we were four days sail from port we had only one junk bottle of water to a man. It was calm when the fleet hove in sight, but we hoisted signals of distress and boats came off which towed us in.

The prize was stripped, and we were returned on board the ships to which we had respectively belonged; and thus my hopes of escape were again blasted. I was drafted to the Sphinx, a ship of 20 guns, bound to cruise off St. Helena. An American whaling ship lay near us at St. Helena, and four of us who messed together, all Americans, agreed to escape to the whaler; and after bribing the sentinel, plunged into the water. The others succeeded; but not being a good swimmer, I rested on our buoy and got with difficulty into the ship's head by climbing on the cable.

One of the three who effected their escape was James Hall. He attempted to escape from on board of the Sceptre, before our draft from that ship, by swimming to an English Indiaman. He stowed himself away on board the Indiaman, but when the watch list was called the next morning, he was missed. The captain of the Sceptre, on receiving the report of Hall's absconding, ordered all boats out to search the ships in port. He was found in the first ship they searched, and was of course to be punished. All hands were called to see the culprit flogged; and stood as usual with their hats off. Hall was young, with thin skin; and on receiving three strokes of the *cat*, cried out "Oh captain! for God's sake forgive me!" The captain then suspending the punishment, asked the unfortunate young man "if he would now promise to attempt no more to runaway?" To which Hall answered, *"No, by G——d captain, I will never give it up for one bad job."* As often as this solemnity occurs, the surgeon stands by the captain, to give notice of the man's fainting. After three strokes more were given, the surgeon communicated the danger of the patient; upon which the cat was again arrested. Hall, scarcely able to articulate; addressing himself to the captain, said *"Captain, we Americans can't bear flogging like you Englishmen, we are not used to it."* The captain turned, and walking off, with difficulty refrained from laughing aloud; but the whole ship's company smiled, though they dared not laugh. Hall was released, because this captain did not happen to be a barbarian. I have always noticed, that when an American was whipped he fainted.

A few days after my unsuccessful attempt to reach the American ship, in St. Helena, all hands were called to get our ship underway, and on calling the fore-top-men, the three yankees were missing. The captain then called the purser's steward to ascertain the missing yankees' mess. I was then called upon to relate what I knew of their running off. I told the captain, as a number of men had been on shore watering the ship, I thought they had been there on duty. That was a falsehood, but *was not malicious*. He asked me if I could swim? No, I answered. He then took a book out of his pocket and said, "You are a yankee, sir, and have been seven years in the navy without ever being flogged, and *now I'll flog you if you are God Almighty's first lieutenant!!!*"

All hands were now called on deck to witness my punishment; and I was immediately seized up. My senses left me when I had received three strokes of the *cat*. I fell (so I was afterwards informed) hanging by the wrists, with my head on one shoulder, until the whole number of stripes had been applied. The surgeon informed the captain of my condition, when the captain said, *"he shall take his dozen, dead or alive!"* I was cut down, and at the first recollection of myself, they were washing my face with a tub of water.

We sailed for the Cape, but on the way fell in with a French privateer. The privateer brought us to action; we exchanged a few shots and run. The Frenchman had a less number of guns and was of inferior force—none of us were hurt! On our arrival at the Cape, captain Alexander was taken out of his ship and sent to England, to be tried for cowardice. Cowards are always cruel. I shall forbear to dwell on this wretch's character, in order to shun the censure of being revengeful.

I was drafted a second time from the Sceptre, and with fifty others put on board the Jupiter, after she returned from the Isle of France, with some other commander, whose name I do not remember. Information came to hand that a French frigate was cruising off the Cape, and as we were leaving the land in pursuit of her, she hove in sight, standing for us. Our drum beat to quarters and we prepared for action. A few broadsides were exchanged—seven of our men were killed and fourteen wounded; the first lieutenant's arm was shot off, and he died the day following. This was the same man who came out with me in the Stately, and who examined me in the prison at Cape Town. The captain on his return was tried by court-martial. He pleaded that the weather was so rough he could not work his lower deck guns: but his men proved his plea to be unfounded. The French frigate followed our ship to the port, and the admiral, hoisting his flag on another ship, ordered his ship to the Isle of France, since he knew the Frenchman belonged there. The admiral's ship had Port Louis blockaded three days before the French frigate appeared at the harbour's mouth. She was captured by the 74; and on arriving at the Cape, the admiral asked the French captain why he did not fight his 74? "Because," said the Frenchman, "I have manned so many of your Indiamen, that I had not men enough. Beside, my ship old, no good for much." Our two decker ship had 54 guns: yet, we ran from this French frigate of only 44 guns.

Commodore Luzac's squadron brought in 40 sail of prizes, in about five months from his departure for the Isle of France. The admiral ordered the smallest prize to be sold, and the money to be distributed among the sailors in that squadron. The prize money amounted to eight dollars per man. The first installment we received, and were to receive the other four dollars at some time after; but when the second payment became due, I was not to be found, and four dollars is all I have ever received for my services rendered his majesty.

A packet arrived from England with the important intelligence, that a British sloop of war, of 18 guns, had captured a Spanish 74! On the receipt of this news the yards of every ship were manned, and three cheers given. Our captain said, "Huzza! my boys! if this is the way our seamen fight, the wars will soon be over, and we shall be paid off!" A person who was present at that splendid affair, informed us, a little after, that this was the fact: A British 74, a frigate, and a sloop of war were in company, and the Spanish ship under the guns of them all; when the sloop of war was ordered to go along-side the Spaniard, and order him to strike his colors.

Not long after this the 4th of June came, when the seamen are allowed to get drunk, because this is their king's birth day; and when the 4th of July came, I applied to Lt. Pingally for liberty to get drunk. He said "go along forward, you yankee rascal." The captain then spoke to him, when he, as I suppose, informed him of my request. He called me to him, and asked—What do you mean, sir, by asking permission to do what you know is contrary to the regulations of this ship? I recollect sir, said I, that about a month ago you gave the English liberty to get drunk because it was their king's birth day; and now I want the liberty to rejoice on my nation's birth day. The captain laughing heartily, ordered that two gallons of wine and one of brandy be procured from the shore for me and my *yankee mess* to rejoice. We all liked this captain. The glass passed merrily round in our *yankee mess*, of thirty in number, and they began to sing *Hail Columbia, happy land!* A north countryman, who called himself the bully of the ship, came along for the purpose of fomenting a quarrel, and told us—"get out of the way, you d——d yankee buggers." This was, consequently, taken as an insult. I gave him an unceremonious box on the ear, and asked if that was what he meant. Yes, he answered, it is exactly what I want. A few blows were passed between us, when the officer between decks coming up, ordered *fair play*—he had observed that several others were aiding my antagonist by pelting me. A few more passes were made at each other; at last I struck him with the left hand, and in drawing back found two of the bully's teeth sticking in the joint of one of my fingers. My antagonist, on losing his front teeth, yielded immediately.

I was then put on the surgeon's list as unfit for duty. The finger is stiff to the present time. This appeared to me a good opportunity to improve for my deliverance, so that I resolved to counterfeit inability, if necessary to attain this end. I continued six months under the doctor's care, and he reported me *incurable;* but the captain said "the yankee feigns his sickness, so as to get at liberty—to run away from the hospital." This the surgeon told me; but soon after put me once more on the list of *incurables.* The captain then told the surgeon that I was not so sick as I represented.—The surgeon replied, he understood his own business, and I was immediately ordered into the boat with a sick company going to the hospital, under the care of the surgeon's mate, who was to attend us on shore. The hospital was situated at the foot of Table mountain, half a mile from the shore. I was put into a blanket, slung on an oar and carried by two men.

The doctor's mate, ordered the men to follow him through town in single rank, and I was in the rear of this procession. We had not proceeded far before we came to a wine-house, where I begged the sailors to set me down, as I was very *thirsty.* They very readily complied, knowing they should get some wine.—I called on the landlord, as we entered his house, for a bottle of Constantia wine and three tumblers. I took my glass, and paid the landlord while the sailors were drinking theirs. I proposed going immediately, judging however that they would never budge while any wine remained. As soon as they became engaged, I pretended an occasion of necessity to retire out of the back door, and helped myself by the chairs until fairly out, and it was safe to become as well as ever I was in my life. I went hastily through the back yard into another street, which enabled me to get through the town and reach the thicket of bushes at the skirts of Table mountain, which I had often looked to as a place of refuge. I had this in contemplation long before, because I had been acquainted with the mode of living in similar places, and had taken the precaution to provide myself with a belt to fasten around me, containing a knife, a small brass tinder-box, and eleven dollars.

Here, feeling myself secure from pursuit, I meditated leisurely, and at length determined to spend the residue of my days on this mountain, if the British ships should not leave the Cape. I resolved to become a breakfast for a lion, sooner than be taken to another floating dungeon.

I returned into the town in the dark, and laid in my supply of goods—this was two loaves of bread, a calabash of brandy and a flint. This was as much as I could take, although my money was not all spent, which had been saved out of my rations of grog for this purpose. My dress was composed of one shirt, one Guernsey frock, and one pair of duck trowsers, with a hospital cap.

Thus equipped I marched on my tour up the mountain, without waiting to hear what return the doctor's mate would make to our captain of the sick *Jonas Ingleberg*, for that was my name on board the ship. My destiny seemed providential; for the first news I had of the Sceptre, was that she sunk soon after I left her, in a gale of wind, without weighing her anchors, and every soul on board perished in her.

There are no trees on Table mountain, and I climbed the cragged rocks through the bushes, and ascended, or attempted to ascend, all night; yet frequently returned to the place last left. I was much fatigued, and sometimes found a spring of water, where my calabash was very useful. It was unsafe to make a fire that night on a mountain fronting the ships, yet I was in danger from the wild beasts, who were often near me, and seemed reluctant to get out of my way. I knew the wild beasts were numerous here, and of almost every species. The next morning, I perceived that the ships lay far below, and could not discover me.

This mountain is green in every season, and it seems, from the water, that a cat might be discovered upon it: but I found nothing else than gullies, cragged rocks piled on each other, and scrubby bushes in their crevices. Here I began to think of preparing for subsistence, and, on searching, soon found a hive of bees among the rocks. This wild honey is so plenty, that a man from Cape Town will return, home, loaded, the same day he leaves it. The Hottentots had taught me the process of obtaining this honey, and having a wooden pipe, I proceeded to the cavity of the rock, covered with wax, and introducing the stem of my pipe through the entrance of the bees, blew in the smoke, which caused the bees to retreat into the interior. The second night I could make a fire under the cover of a rock, and regale myself with brandy and honey.

When I had ascended four days from the mountain's foot, I lost sight of the fleet and the bay. My course now was over level rocky spots, of 30 or 40 feet in width, on which I saw innumerable herds of goats hosts of antelopes, wolves, tygers, and leopards. The three latter are the only animals considered dangerous here, except the venomous snakes. The baboons are here numerous and large. At first, they would apparently take no notice of me; but soon after would be seen on a precipice, 100 feet above, throwing stones at me.

At last I reached the summit, and selected a spot, in view of the Western Ocean, for my residence. I occupied a cavern which secured me from storms, near a spring of good water. My whole stock of provisions being nearly exhausted, I thought it time to recruit. Necessity invents the means in these cases. I sallied out with a stone in my hand, and had not advanced a great distance when I espied an antelope on the brow of a precipice. I threw the stone at the back of his head, and tumbled him to the bottom; where, by a circuitous route, I found my game, whose skin I drew over his head, and cutting the meat into strings, hung it on sticks put into the crevices of my habitation. This meat when dried, I broiled and eat with toad-sorrel for my sauce. Besides this I had honey and good water. It seemed rather hard at first, to live without bread, salt, and articles deemed necessary in former days; but at the end of two or three weeks I lived very contentedly. While among the Hottentots I had learned their method of making a very pleasant beverage resembling metheglin. I was fortunate enough to find an old hollow tree, which I cut off with my knife, and seized a green hide on one end for a bottom. Into this tub honey and water was put to stand twenty-four hours; then was added some pounded root to make it foment. This root, in use among the frontier Hottentots, does not resemble any of my acquaintance in America, but makes an excellent drink in this preparation. I had ground-nuts and a root with a stem one inch above the ground, with three leaves as small as those of the garden pink. This root, of the size of a junk bottle, is eatable; yet is not as good as the water-melon, which the Dutch call it. It is probable the *kameroo* from the description given me of its size and shape.

My clothes, by creeping through the rocks and bushes, were so tattered that I had become almost naked. In this extremity I made a needle from the bone of a beast; the eye of which being made with my sharp pointed knife, enabled me to sew with the sinews of my antelopes. With the skins I equipped myself completely from head to foot. The skins were dressed by rubbing sand on the flesh side with a stone; and furnished me with moccasins, *shin-fenders*, or leggings to the knee; a short petticoat fastened round my waist, and a hunting frock. The hair was worn inside when cold, and turned outside when warm. It is almost unnecessary to add that I wore a *superb cap*.

Thus accoutred, it is natural to suppose me somewhat elevated, although without a looking-glass. Pride must have a fall—I was soon afflicted with lice. By procuring an entire new suit, and changing my residence, these tenants of the skin abandoned me. It was not troublesome to change my quarters; and by often shifting my abode for a new tenement, I acquired by occupation dwellings enough to make my territory called a city. Thus I lived, unannoyed by wild beasts or press-gangs; until one day I crept out of some cragged rocks, and came inadvertently into a large concourse of wolves, in their season of making love. They soon surrounded me; some within 20 feet. I stood ready with my knife to defend myself; when at last, one turned off, another followed, till they all had sneaked off apparently ashamed of themselves and left me alone. I used to kill *darsies* or mountain rats, which eat grass, and are choice food.

At each full moon I cut a notch in the root, which hung to a silken cord about my neck; and this was the only account I kept of time.

Once I undertook to descend the western side of the mountain to the sea shore, where I could often see vessels in clear weather; but the mountain being very steep on that side, with so many rocks that I frequently let myself down by taking hold of bushes, until I seemed sliding into the sea without power to stop. In two days I returned, and gave up experiments in that direction. My practice was to eat twice in the day; and when cooking in the evening always heard the howling of wild beasts, and often saw the light of their eyes, when attracted about me by the smell of meat.

My residence was not on the summit, but in a convenient place for hunting; near some height, on which I could cramp my game. I often went over to the eastern front to view the ships; and continued to do so until twelve notches were made upon the calender fastened to my neck. I had become perfectly reconciled to my condition—had abundance of meat, sorrel, honey and water; and every night could sing my song with as much pleasure as at any period of my life. In fine, I never enjoyed life better than while I lived among the ferocious animals of Table Mountain; because I had secured myself against the more savage English. I now discovered some vessels at sea, on the western side of the mountain, but was unable to distinguish them as ships or other vessels, the clouds being so far below me.* However, I suspected the fleet had sailed from the Cape—mustered my provisions, and stowed them in a knapsack, made of a skin drawn over the head, after splitting it on the hind-legs. The skin of each hind-leg was tied to that of the fore-leg on the same side, and my arms passed through the loop, the neck hung at the bottom down my back.

I now left my numerous habitations for the last time. During my residence I had never been able to discover the vestige of a human being, except myself, having ever ventured here. I travelled one day and part of a night, without being able to discover any shipping, on account of intervening clouds. I often was compelled to travel five miles on the mountain, without gaining in descent one hundred rods. The second day in my descent, the air being clear, I saw the bay, and one vessel only. I concluded to pursue my course until I could ascertain her character. Continuing on the next day, I perceived that vessel to be a brig; and having no top-gallant-masts, took her for a merchantman.

Determined to push for her immediately, I descended to the foot of the mountain, and rested there till after day break. It was only half a mile to the shore. A British regiment I supposed to be stationed in the town; yet I thought no person would know me after so long an absence, especially in my mountain dress: But to avoid their notice of my uncouth habit, I turned the hair side inwards. I marched through the town unobserved by any one except two or three servants, who continued to gaze obliquely at me as long as I could see them. The boat was coming to the shore as I approached it, with two men and the captain, as I supposed.

I tried my power of speech to prepare myself. The captain landing advanced guardedly towards me, I stepped up to meet him and asked if he wanted to ship a man? He was surprised to hear me speak, and asked "What in the name of God are you! man or beast?" He at last stepped up to me and giving me his hand, said

---

*This mountain is 1330 feet high.

"this is no place to talk—jump into the boat and go on board." The boat was ordered to return for him in half an hour; into it I sprung, and was soon snug on board.

When the captain returned he sent for me in the cabin and ordered me two suits of clothes. I put them on, and took my beard off for the first time in fourteen months. He then heard a short story of myself, and said he supposed me to be a deserter; but that I had nothing to fear if I would go with him.

This brig was under Danish colors, but the captain and property were English, as he told me—and was bound to St. Helena, and thence to London. On learning that I had deserted the Sceptre, he informed me that she had been sunk fourteen months: he pointed to a monument on shore over the bodies of her crew which had been driven on shore and there interred. We were a few days making ready to sail for St. Helena, which place we reached without accident. The governor detained us here until the India fleet arrived to take us under convoy. Lying here four months, I found this captain to be a truly good, humane man. He let me have money to spend there, and although no agreement was made for any wages he had compassion on me. While we lay there the India ship called the Indian Chief, of Philadelphia, lay near us. I wished to return home in her; yet I could not without deserting—and who would be so ungrateful as to desert from such a captain. At sight of the American flag tears streamed from my eyes. I rushed on board, and every American I saw seemed nearer of kin than any brother I left at home. The conversation which ensued may be conjectured. Among other things I told them of the loss of my protection, and asked if they had lost a hand? A young man answered "yes, we have lost my brother John Porter, of your height and complexion." Taking his protection, I went to our brig and told the captain to put me down on the log-book, John Porter. He laughed and said it was very well thought of. The India fleet arrived and I was taken into the Admiral Hughes, an India built ship of 2200 tons, which took our captain's brig in tow to England. It was a very boisterous passage, and the brig often hoisted signals of distress. Her hands were nearly worn out at the pumps; but received only 20 dollars per month; while those of us who had been transferred at St. Helena, were paid 22 dollars and fared well. When I was taken out of the brig and along side of the Admiral Hughes—who should I behold but lieutenant Pingally, 1st. of the Sceptre, which had foundered when he was on shore. He was the first person who spoke to me. He stood on the gang-way; called me aside and said, "Inglesberg, don't you know me?" "Yes, your honour, perfectly." The first opportunity that offered so as not to expose me, he asked where I had been, &c. I hope said he it was nothing that I had done which made you desert. He then told me what had happened after I left the Sceptre. He said that the surgeon's mate was unable to give a satisfactory account of the dead Inglesberg. You and I said he, "seem to be born for some fortunate end. I went on board of that ship and had returned on shore not two hours, before it blew so hard that it was impossible for a boat to reach her. At 4 o'clock that (Sunday) afternoon she hoisted signals of distress; and fired distress guns until 8 o'clock in the evening, when we heard no more from her, and suppose she sunk immediately." That harbour, for six months in the year, is as unsafe to lie in as the Gulf of Mexico.

We arrived at the Downs, the boisterous weather notwithstanding. A French fishing row-galley had taken one of our India ships within the chops of the English Channel. This I had from the captain of the brig, after our arrival in London, who said letters from their friends in France stated their capture and arrival there.

The regulating captain at the Downs made us all pass in review before him and answer his interrogatories. He catechised me and received my answers, thus— "What countryman are you?" An American, sir. "Where is your protection?" Here it is, said I, (showing him the one obtained at St. Helena.) "How did you come here?" I told him I entered at St. Helena. Lieutenant Pingally stood all this while looking at me, over the interrogating captain's shoulder, and laughed. He, however, after seeing me clear of these fellows clutches, called me aside and told me that "he was appointed to the command of a 20 gun ship, and if I would go along with him, I should have as good an office as I could merit." I refused, and he said, "Well, I wish you safe home: If I can never man my ship without impressment I never wish her manned. I knew you to be an American, or perhaps I should not have suffered you to get off as you have." This was a good Englishman, and any one who was acquainted with him would gladly leave any other ship and run to him. The captain of our brig, at Deptford, was glad to see us once more. He paid us all off, with two dollars extra to those who had fared so well in the "Admiral Hughes," and then discharged us.

We went to London, with too much money not to loose a little. I had lived so long without the privilege of spending any thing, that I, too, was gentleman while my money lasted. Two ladies sitting by a window, said, "There goes two sailors, gentlemen for a week." "Yes," said one, "and there sits two strumpets for life." No man spends his money more to his own notion than a sailor.

At length I sought a birth in an American vessel; but there were so many Americans waiting to go home that I could get no chance to work my passage. Fortunately I found the ship Dauphin, of Boston, captain Wallace, bound to Charleston, South-Carolina. In her I had a pleasant passage to Charleston.

When I beheld my native country I was in an ecstacy of joy. Here I found Mr. Enoch Rider, of Sag-Harbor, on Long-Island, and who is now living there. With his assistance I procured me a better protection than the borrowed one at St. Helena. I had engaged to return to England in the Dauphin, because I was with my countrymen, was poor, and was ambitious to try my fortune once more. The captain had paid me fourteen dollars per month; and engaged to give me 48 dollars per month, if I would return with him. Captain Wallace, considering my situation, favored me with a month's advance pay, and liberty to spend my time on shore while the ship took in her cargo of cotton.

We experienced heavy gales of wind on this voyage. Our boats and anchors were lost in the English Channel, and we put into Dartmouth to repair our damages whence we proceeded to London. Here the cargo was disposed of and the vessel sold. Thus was I again set adrift; but soon after learned that it was a common practice with some merchants to make a *sham sale* of their vessels, and get a new crew to work their passage home. By this *yankee trick* they gained, in the whole voyage, notwithstanding the high wages in a southern port.

I expended all my money while waiting for an opportunity to return. At last I went to Wappingstairs, where I found an American schooner, which had come from France expressly to procure American seamen. Captain Charles Smith, of North-Carolina, who had commanded a French privateer, been taken three times by the English, and as often escaped from prison, now commanded this schooner. On this passage, an English frigate brought us to, and ordered us on board. The captain of this frigate had been once taken by captain Smith, and now observed to him, that he had left off privateering and became merchantman. "Yes," replied captain Smith, "but this does not afford me pocket-money, and I'll soon try it again." On this the Englishman threatened to flog him; but looking at his clearance, set him at liberty, telling him, "You are an insolent rascal."

In two hours more we were at Morlaix: from this we were conveyed thirty miles to Brest. The ship in which we were to enter was called La Diable a Quatre, (the devil on all fours.) She had been captured by the English and by them called the Danæ; converted into a sloop of war under the command of lord Proby, and sent to cruise off the coast of France. He was called the greatest tyrant in the British navy. Two men whom he punished with the *cat* jumped overboard the same day in consequence of his tyrannical conduct—the seamen in their rage rose upon him, and run the ship into Brest. There she was exposed to sale—purchased by the American consul and made an American ship. The sailors called her former commander Dog Toby. But we entered her under captain Edward—for Virginia.

The French suspecting us of intending to be captured by the English, would not suffer us to go to sea for a twelvemonth. She was known to be a remarkable fast sailing ship. While we lay thus, at this port, news reached us of the treaty of peace at Amiens. Brest and the fleet were brilliantly illuminated, and great rejoicings took place over this nest-egg of future wars.

An armament was fitted out for St. Domingo under general Le Clerk, the brother-in-law of Bonaparte. Our ship was freighted thither, and we had on board a Mr. Cooper with his family. One of his daughters died and was thrown overboard near Tenerife, and another of them ran off with a French officer at St. Dommingo. We sailed in the month of December 1801; and he entered the bay of Samana on the 28th of the same month; but we put into Cape Francois.

The general had 20,000 troops. As our squadron was entering, we received a few guns from the fort; but on returning a broadside the blacks blew up the fort; as we continued our course the negroes blew up another magazine, said to contain 1500 barrels of powder, and set the town on fire. The sailors were permitted to plunder on shore; and entering houses in flames, we forced open desks and bureaus with the chimney crane. Buckets of melted dollars were taken on board; but the officers seized the whole as we threw them on deck. Three of us had found a bag of plate; and when the officers took this from us to divide among themselves, we mutinied and were for some days kept in irons. After my discharge, at this port I lived on shore to speculate. Such scenes of murder and rapine as were witnessed, are too shocking to relate, *Pandemonium* seemed let loose. A city laid in ashes, was to be rebuilt and after this commenced boards were 100 dollars per 1000. The high prices of every thing, at first rendered it difficult to obtain subsistence on the land: but I lived there to see the mark is glutted. It was so unhealthy, that for some time there were hardly *well* enough to bury the *dead*.

I had been long waiting for an opportunity to return home, though my fortune had not been made; when the sloop HERO, of Stonington: capt. Nathan Fellows, arrived. In her I took my passage, much pleased with the captain's behaviour towards me. We had a very pleasant time until we made Montock—the east end of my native island; which I had not seen in so many years before. This was the most agreeable sight my eyes ever beheld, and in a paroxism of joy I wept: but my eyes dwelt on the green hill, crowned now by its lofty elegant light-house. Language is inadequate to the expression of my feelings, and would be lost on the cold heart that has worn out its action in one monotonous course at home.

We closed the voyage at Stonington in 21 days from St. Domingo. Here I waited two days for a conveyance to Long-Island—procured a passage in a lighter, captain Clark, of Rocky point. It was Sunday morning, in June 1808. A violent thunder storm drove us on shore at Oyster Pond Point, where the lighter, by a surge was suddenly thrown on me, and fastened me to the stones and sand. I cried murder, and captain Clark extricated me; but finding me much hurt, carried me on his back half a mile to a house, and then took me in a carriage to his own dwelling. My knee was fractured and much swelled, but captain Clark and his wife did every thing in their power for my relief, during my stay; and their kindness shall never be forgotten while I exist. How happy would be the condition of mortal man, if all were like captain Clark and his charitable companion. A carriage was dispatched to my father's house, only eight miles from me. I learned that my father yet lived; and I told the messenger to inform him that his lost son was living and that was all he could boast of—that if any of my young friends were living, also, they most come and see me. My youngest sister, whom I had left a child, came into the room where I was lying and walked the room without my knowing her. Mrs. Clark asked me if I knew that woman? I told her that I was too much distressed with pain to notice her; particularly as she was a woman. However the discovery was made, and my sister returned home with me.

I found my parents rejoiced to see me, as may be well imagined, when it is known that *I had been absent eleven years and six months.*

I had written to them from the Cape of Good Hope, from St. Helena and elsewhere, but they had received no letters from me in nine years, except one dated at Cape Francois, which they received shortly previous to my arrival. This letter they conjectured was a forgery, because it was not in my junior hand writing. In short, they had long since buried me. Two of my sisters and one brother had died in my absence.

Here I hobbled on crutches until my recovery, and spent the residue of the summer in visiting my friends. In December I was married. My employments were from this period, either coasting or going to the West Indies.

I was in my own coasting vessel at New-York, when WAR was declared against Great Britain! I immediately sold my vessel, and resolved to put myself in an attitude to annoy the enemy of my country, and the scourge of the terrestrial globe. I returned to my home at Three-Mile-Harbour, in the township of East Hampton, determined to avail myself of the first opportunity of doing mischief to those who had so long tortured me. [6]

The British landed frequently on Gardiner's Island, in sight of my house, on the opposite side of Gardiner's Bay. Commodore Decatur being blockaded in New-London, I crossed the Sound in my boat, and informed him there was an opportunity to apprehend some of those men. He ordered four boats to proceed under my direction as pilot, and crossed the Sound in the night of the 26th of July, 1813: It being very dark, we missed one boat on our arrival at Three Mile Harbour. The militia of East Hampton were alarmed at our approach and repaired to attack their invaders; but on finding that we were not British, they let us sleep that day: and when the night was nearly spent we crossed to Gardiner's Island, where we landed at daylight and concealed ourselves on shore. The Ramilies 74, sir Thomas Hardy, and the Orpheus frigate, captain Pigot, were lying in the bay. [7]

We perceived by our glasses that they were fitting out nine of their boats; viz. two launches, four cutters, two barges and a gig; which last contained captain Pigot, who commanded the squadron of boats. They had one 18 pounder on the bow of a launch belonging to the Ramilies; and a carriage gun in the frigate's launch. They were manned by 160 marines and sailors, whom we counted as they went down the ship's side. Lieutenant Gallagher, our commander, told me, that "if they do not attack us with more than twice our number, I am determined to meet them. The instant they attempt to land we will rush on them with charged bayonets." We had calculated to take them by surprise. They rowed to the opposite side of the island where lay our boats. We had every reason now to think they had been informed of our expedition, and instantly went to hurry off our boats from Great Pond to the Fire-Place, while the British aimed to cut us off. They fired on us for about half an hour, and threw shot in all directions about us, while we were rowing in our whaleboats. Their last 18 pound shot struck about six feet from the boat's stern, and threw water all over us, when the lieutenant ordered us to "avast oars and give the British three cheers for that shot." It was calm and we could hear captain Pigot give orders to "elevate that gun—the shot fell short." The next shot would strike half a mile beyond us. We felt ourselves safe and put into Three Mile Harbour. Our enemy returned to Gardiner's Island, to abuse Mr. Gardiner for suffering us to come there; as if he could help it. Our arrival, and this cannonade alarmed the town of East-Hampton once more—but the militia came too late to capture the enemy's boats, which had grounded but got off again.

Captain Pigot could securely insult Mr. Gardiner for permitting Yankees to come on his island, when every body knows that he could not have been apprised of it in season to prevent them, and wanted the power if he had known it. He is very critically situated—in the power of the British, and consequently censured by both parties.

We refreshed ourselves and found, the next day, the crew of the missing boat under the command of midshipman Ten Eyck, who joined us and related their proceeding. They found themselves at Gardiner's Island, and left the boat on the beach at sunrise. When they had retired into the woods, they observed a British boat to land—take possession of their boat and take her off; leaving behind them seven men and officers, whom they took prisoners without resistance.—One of the enemy attempted to run; when one of the men under Ten Eyck put a ball through his hat and brought him to the ground unhurt. The prisoners were the 1st and 2d lieutenants, the sailing-master and four men of the Ramilies, who submitted themselves to our midshipman and five or six men.

The lieutenant, on being told he had his choice to be paroled or go to the American squadron, at first hesitated; but being obliged to answer immediately, concluded to be paroled. They were paroled, and our men went from Mr. Gardiner's house to his whale-boat, which they necessarily took into possession, and crossed the bay to the Fire-Place. The next day we started for Sag-Harbour, and thence to New-London; after an absence of five days.

I returned home in my boat alone, as I went. Lieutenant Gallagher recommended me for my conduct in that affair; and besides my compensation for this service, the commodore approved of what I had done.

A short time after this, a stranger from New-York came to me and said, that he had been advised to make application for my assistance in a *torpedo*, to explode the craft which infested our bays and harbours. I agreed without hesitation to embark on the enterprize; and conducted him to places where we might unobserved, watch the motions of the enemy. Unsuitable weather for several days, prevented the execution of our designs. The ships shifted their anchorage every night, so that we found the object impracticable, and abandoned a project which might have succeeded any where but in a *blue-light* region. I again left New-London and returned to my house—open to the bay, and in sight of the British ships.

I expected a commission, and it became necessary for me to go properly recommended to commodore Decatur for the purpose of getting me into the service. A recommendation of me, as a suitable person to command a row-galley, was subscribed by some persons of respectability in East-Hampton, and the officers of the garrison at Sag-Harbour—backed by a certificate of the collector at that port. I left Sag-Harbour with the intention of crossing the Sound from my own house, as soon as I should have an opportunity.

The next morning, Sunday, August 20, 1813, a boat was discovered taking sounding near my house, in the creek. I hastened to my nearest neighbour, who lived at some distance, and both of us advanced to attack the boat. We were armed—the boat made off and went along side the Ramilies. I suspected their design, for I saw them viewing with a glass and pointing to my house. In consequence of discovering that boat, I concluded to desist from crossing the Sound until the next day, when I could remove my family to a safer place, and have a guard here that night. I had made application for a guard and expected it; but thought to take a short nap before it should arrive. I had been sleeping about half an hour, when the house was surrounded by people who had lain in ambush among my corn, growing near it. My wife, three little boys, old Robert Gray and a female Indian, composed, with myself, the family. The eldest of my children was nine years old; the youngest three, and were all in bed.

The first salutation was three spiteful raps with the fist, at the door. Being awaked I rose up in bed, and demanded, "Who's there?" "Decatur's people," was their answer—"Mr. Penny, we want you to get up immediately." I was satisfied, however, that they were the Prince Regent's people—sprang out of my bed, and in my shirt ran for my gun. I had to pass through two doors before I reached the kitchen, where my gun was hanging. They heard me, as they afterwards said, both when I went to bed, and when I left it. They saw me through the window as I opened the kitchen door, and I observed the heads were very thick there. My gun lay on hooks, so near the floor overhead, that in my hurry I was baulked in attempting to get it down. When they perceived me aiming for the gun, they burst in the door, and surrounded me. I was seized with one hand on the gun, and expected no quarters. They took me, with my arms extended by two men, who held them, to the door, where stood lieut. Lawrence, 1st of the Ramilies. He presented a pistol to my nose, and attempted to shoot me. I never saw more fire issue from a lock in my life—it flew into my eyes—it rolled on the floor; but as luck would have it, missed fire!

I then addressed him, not at that time knowing his name—"Officer," said I, "you are determined, I see, to murder me. I hope you will be gentleman enough to take me out of the sight of my wife and children first." He then, with a tremulous voice, said, "It is presumption in you, Mr. Penny, to make any resistance—I have 500 men around you." I told him "I did not make any resistance—was stark naked, and as many had hold of me as could touch me." He added, "It is Sir Thomas Hardy's orders to blow your brains out if you should make the smallest resistance." My wife followed us to the door and shrieked; upon which a sergeant of marines struck her with the breech of a gun, the point of which he thrust at her left breast, with so much violence, that she is unwell from that cause to the present time.

They led me about ten rods to their boat—one officer before and another behind me; and two others marched with their naked cutlasses on each of my shoulders. As soon as we had entered into the boat, the lieutenant threw on shore a bag of shavings; and ordered the only man on shore to "burn that d——d rascal's house." I spoke to the lieutenant—"Sir, you are not surely going to burn my wife and children!" The man who received the lieutenant's order, told him the "match was out; and he could not make fire." It appeared they had come prepared to burn the house, but were afraid of the militia; and thus hurried off.

The lieutenant said—"From the appearance of that woman, she is not in a situation to take off her children to the woods—we'll let it stand. Never mind the house men, let us go and burn his boat." My boat was about twenty rods from us, at anchor in the creek near a thicket: we proceeded about half way to it, when I laid down in the bottom of the boat. The lieutenant asked me why I did so? I answered that since his pistol had not killed me I did not wish to be killed by the militia of my own country, who might throw a shower of balls from the bushes. "Aye," said he, "is that the case?" Then stamping with his foot on the bottom of the boat, he cried "about with the boat! pull round men! pull round men!" He was much agitated and left my boat uninjured. They hurried the boat out of the creek, nearly half a mile, as fast as possible; and getting fairly out he ordered the men to lay on their oars: "Hurra!" said he, "we've got *Tom Pedro* safe enough now—let's drink some gin:"[8] The lieutenant handed some to me first, but I told him that "after him was manners." All drank, and a dialogue commenced which lasted 'till we reached the ship. He began—"Where are your documents which you obtained yesterday at Sag-Harbour, to carry to Decatur?" "They are in my pocket; and if you had been gentleman enough to have let me got my clothes, you could have had my papers." I knew he dared not go back; besides, I could not avoid this language after the usage I had received. The servant girl had gone out of the house with my coat, in a pocket of which these papers were; and on her exclaiming, "you are not going to take Mr. Penny without his coat or other clothes!" He said, "d——d the clothes, we've got him, that's enough." He continued—"Well, your papers will never do *you* any good, or any one else. You'll get disappointed in obtaining a commission in a row-galley. Your character has been given me by a fellow in that boat which you saw taking soundings, and a d——d good description of your house he gave us; with woods on one side and a corn-field on another. He told me there was nothing to be seen of your house until you come within three rods of it; and could then see three poplar trees." He perceiving my teeth to chatter with the cold, gave me a boat-cloak to put around me. "You have some d——d good friends" continued he, "who live close by you, or you would not have met with this misfortune. I have been informed by one of your own countrymen, that you deserted from a British ship of war; and are the most inveterate enemy of the British within five hundred miles of here. You have been assisting in Decatur's expeditions; and also concerned in conducting those d——d TORPEDOES!" I am a true-born American, sir, said I, that I will not deny. I have never been employed by my government, but am ever ready to engage in her service against her enemies; whenever and wherever called. He told me that I should undoubtedly suffer death; because I had been concerned in torpedoes, which was contrary to the law of nations.

I then asked him if it was not contrary to the law of nations to blow up a number of their men, in Canada, for the sake of destroying a greater number of our men? "Yes (he said) and if you Americans could have caught the one who communicated fire to the magazine, they would have hung him, as we shall you." I told him I was a prisoner, and they dared not hang me on the word of a *traitor*! He inquired if Decatur was concerned in torpedoes? I told him "such questions were very improper." Between 11 and 12 o'clock we reached the Ramilies, with her boats about her to guard against torpedoes.

I was conducted up the ship's side as naked as when they put me into the boat; and had to wait on the quarter-deck, until the officer had reported his expedition to Sir Thomas. All the other officers came up to gaze at me, while my shirt in tatters was hanging by the wristbands. They afterwards took me below and put me in irons, to lie without clothes on the bare deck, alongside of old Robert, whom they had also brought with them.

Early next morning the master of arms brought us a pot of cocoa and some bread, and told us he could get nothing else for us until after 12 o'clock. He then went off, but came running back before our cocoa had cooled so that we could drink a drop of it. He took off the pot, saying it is the order of Sir Thomas that "you have nothing but bread and water." And nothing else did I have until we arrived in Halifax; eighteen days after they had kidnapped me.

The second day, they crammed me into a hole which is in the after part of the ship. They let me through a narrow scuttle down to her stern-post, where I remained nine days, and found it difficult to breathe in this dark place. It was so cramped that I could neither lie strait nor stand up.*

Leaving me in this dungeon, let us hear what passed on shore relative to my case. I do not know that we can do better here, than to transcribe the following correspondence and introduction to it, from the Columbian—a news paper printed in New-York.

"Case of Joshua Penny.

"The seizure of Mr. Penny, (mentioned in our paper of yesterday) having excited considerable interest in the public mind, we have obtained copies of the correspondence which took place on the subject, between commodore Hardy and Major Case, commanding officer at Sag-Harbor, and present them to our readers. The grounds of the prisoner's seizure are made quite plausible by the commodore's statement, though the reason for his detention and refusal of exchange, supposing him to be a legal prisoner of war, is evidently bad; and we should be pleased to hear of two British officers being put in close confinement in retaliation. The commodore appears to be informed of the most private and confidential transactions in our ports and vessels—what dependance he has a right to place on his informants, and by what means he procures his intelligence, the public will judge."

(Copy.)

"Sir Thomas Hardy, Commander of H. B. M. Squadron off Gardiner's Island.

"Sir—The inhabitants of the town of East-Hampton have requested of me a flag, which I now authorize, for the purpose of demanding Joshua Penny, a native born citizen of the township of Southold, on this Island, and a resident of the town of East-Hampton.

"He is demanded as a non-combatant, being attached to no vessel as a mariner or corps military whatever, but was taken by force by your men from his own house unarmed.

"The bearer of this flag is lieut. Hedges, an officer under my command, in government service. You will have the goodness to deliver Mr. Penny to lieut. Hedges; as he cannot consistently be retained as a prisoner of war by any article in the cartel agreed on, ratified and confirmed by the agents of each of our governments for the exchange of prisoners.

---

* The British refused me a Bible, and I, according to my custom was singing Psalms, when a midshipman overhearing me, said "he is a d——d Psalm-singing Yankee."

"Given under my hand, at the garrison of Sag-Harbor, this 23d day of August, 1813.

"BENJ. CASE, *major commanding the troops in the U.S. service at Sag-Harbor.*"

(Copy.)

"His Britannic Majesty's Ship Ramilies, in Gardiner's Bay,
August 23d, 1813.

"Sir—I have the honor to acknowledge the receipt of your letter of this day's date, and as I do not wish to detain lieutenant Hedges, the bearer of your flag, I will do myself the honor of replying to your letter to-morrow by a flag of truce.

"I have the honor to be sir, your very humble servant.

"THOMAS M. HARDY, *captain.*

"To major Case, commanding the troops in the U. S. service at Sag-Harbor."

(Copy.)

"His Britannic Majesty's Ship Ramilies, Gardiner's Bay,
24th Aug. 1813.

"Sir—As it was late yesterday afternoon when I had the honor of receiving your letter of the 23d instant, requesting the release of Joshua Penny, I did not judge it proper to detain lieut. Hedges for my reply.

"I now beg leave to inform you, I had received certain information that this man conducted a detachment of boats sent from the United States squadron under the command of commodore Decatur, now lying in New-London, from that port to Gardiner's Island, on the 26TH of July last, for the express purpose of surprising and capturing the captain of his Britannic majesty's frigate Orpheus and myself, and having failed in that undertaking, but making prisoners of some officers and men belonging to the Orpheus, he went with the remaining boats to Three Mile Harbor. The next account I had of him was his being employed in a boat contrived for this purpose, under the command of Thomas Welling, prepared with a torpedo, to destroy this ship, and that he was in her at Napeug Beach, when this ship and the Orpheus were in Fort Pond Bay, last week. He has also had a certificate given him on the 18th of this month, by some of the respectable inhabitants of Easthampton, recommending him to commodore Decatur, as a fit person to be employed on a particular service by him, and that he has for some time been entered on the books of one of the frigates, at forty dollars per month;

add to which, this notorious character has been recognized by some of the officers and men of this ship, as having been on board here two or three times, with clams and fruit; of course, as a spy, to collect information of our movements. Having been made so well acquainted with the conduct of this man for the last six weeks, and the purpose for which he has been so actively employed in hostilities against his Britannic Majesty, I cannot avoid expressing my surprise that the inhabitants of Easthampton, should have attempted to enforce on you a statement so contrary to fact. I therefore cannot think of permitting such an avowed enemy to be out of my power, when I know so much of him as I do. He will therefore, be detained as a prisoner of war, until the pleasure of the commander in chief is known. Robert Gray, an inoffensive old man who was taken with Penny, I have landed; as it does not appear that he is one of his accomplices in the transactions I have alluded to.

"I think proper to enclose a copy of my letter to justice Terry, to warn the inhabitants of the coast against permitting the torpedoes to remain any where near them.

"I have the honor to be, sir, your most obedient humble servant.

THOMAS M. HARDY, *captain of H. B. M's ship Ramilies.*
Major Benj. Case, commanding the troops in the
U.S. service at Sag-Harbour."

(Copy.)

"His Majesty's Ship Ramilies, off New London, Aug. 23, 1813.

"Sir—Having received positive information that a whale boat, the property of Thomas Welling, and others, prepared with a torpedo, for the avowed purpose of destroying this ship, a mode of warfare practised by individuals from mercenary motives, and more *novel* than honorable, is kept in your neighborhood; and as from the *very good information I obtain from various sources* there is no doubt these persons will soon be in my power, I beg you to warn the inhabitants of the towns along the coast of Long-Island, that wherever I hear the boat or any other of her description, has been allowed to remain after this date, I will order every house near the shore to be destroyed.

"I have the honor to be, sir, your obedient servant.
"THOMAS M. HARDY, *capt.*
"—Terry, esq. justice of the peace, Southold, Long-Island."

This letter to esquire Terry is a proof that the writer was a bitter enemy to the torpedo; but, a paragraph in the editorial department of the Long-Island Star, will further illustrate this topic.

"Wednesday, September 8, 1813.

"By our attentive correspondent at Sag-Harbor, it appears that com. Hardy's persecution of Joshua Penny is principally on account of his having piloted a torpedo boat, commanded by Thomas Welden; which boat was discovered by the guard-boats, and made its escape only by frequent *diving*. The commodore threatens to lay waste the towns and show no mercy to the inhabitants that harbor torpedoes, which, as he informed lieutenant Hedges, had given him so much inquietude that it had taken almost all the hair from his head!"

Why there should be a complaint against this species of warfare as being dishonorable, I cannot understand; unless it proceeds from a man subject to the horrors. It is in our enemy's power to avoid American torpedoes, by keeping out of our harbours; and I cannot for my life, see any difference between killing your enemy with balls, bomb-shells, rockets, &c. and blowing them up by torpedoes. In both ways ships may sink, or some body get hurt; and it is no objection that it is a "novel" mode of warfare.

The objection never ought to come from those, who hire savages to destroy indiscriminately, the man in arms and the helpless innocent female with her infant in the cradle—or, what is too horrid to name—who can tamely listen to such an enemy, or to its partizans in this country, when he has heard of their Vandalism at Washington, and of the violation of female chastity on our coast! An American who would hesitate to blow up such infernal monsters as Cockburn and his myrmidons, deserves no country to own him; he is worse than savage, who deals out this hypocritical whining at the NOVEL mode of using torpedoes, to drive the invading Goths and Vandals from our sacred soil. I know I displeased Sir Thomas Hardy, by aiding in the attempt to blow him to the moon; but I am also out of humour, that I was prevented from teaching a useful lesson to the invaders. Had there been no treachery in my country, we should have succeeded: as it is, we have caused them uneasiness; and perhaps have kept them more from our harbours than otherwise could have happened.

I am now returned to my dungeon. We were on our passage, and shipped a sea which poured through the stern-port and filled my prison nearly full. The sentinel who stood over me sung out, "Tom Pedro is drowned! Tom Pedro is drowned!" Then I was taken out almost dead—put in irons and confined between two guns, on the hard deck, during the voyage. On our arrival I was sent to Melville prison,[9] under an escort of one serjeant, one corporal and nine men, to conduct me only! There were about thirty other prisoners in the Ramilies, taken out of coasters, &c. whom commodore Hardy detained until he sailed, as hostages to protect him against torpedoes, with which he was haunted on the station off New-London.

A few days after my imprisonment in the hole, lieut. Lawrence came to ask me questions which I did not think proper to answer. He said "it was by order of Sir Thomas." I told him that "if Sir Thomas wished to know, he might send for me, and ask his questions himself." He said, "Your character is so heinous to him that he cannot endure you in his presence." I told him "it was not in character for a friend to his country to answer his interrogatories; I should not."

Another time, the master-at-arms told me "it is Sir Thomas Hardy's opinion that you will be hung; but if not, you will be taken to England and detained until the close of the war; and be at last tried as the laws of nations direct. Should I have to hang you, I should be sorry to have you suspect an innocent person of having betrayed you. Whom do you suspect to be your betrayer?" I told him "I did not know. I had observed a number of boats were often trading with the ships in the day time, and it might be a trader. I thought it would come to light sooner or later."* He told me who had sold me; and added, "but no one in the ship, except Sir Thomas Hardy, knows how much he got, but I suppose he got a large sum. If you wish to be liberated, you can. Sir Thomas has ordered me to ask you if you will discover to him that torpedo? If you will, he says you shall be liberated, and have 3000 dollars." I felt too much insulted to answer him.

While I lay in Melville prison, 400 prisoners arrived from Bermuda; some of whom had been masters of vessels, mates, or supercargoes. They told me that on their passage they heard Sir Thomas talk of me and my betrayer. He said "he had seen in a yankee newspaper an account of his having given the man 1000 dollars for his services in apprehending me; but it was not so—he had only given him 200 dollars." Afterwards he said, "I gave him up his vessel, which, perhaps, *might make 1000 dollars.*"

While I remained here, a stranger in the habit of a citizen came to inspect my legs for scars, and examine me for the purpose of identifying me as the husband of a woman in town, who said she had lost a husband, and from the description given her, I must be the missing husband. I told this man that my wife was on Long-Island. Not long after, I was summoned to a house where this woman and my former examiner were sitting, with a table covered with decanters and glasses. This man, after having led me into the room, asked the woman if she could swear that I was her husband. She answered, that she "could not, but that I looked much like him." Then turning to me, asked "If that was my wife?" No, I answered, I would not give my wife for ten thousand of her. This created a laugh and ended in drinking.

I satisfied myself that this woman was a common prostitute, and my examiner

---

* I think, now, I know the man; but his name shall not disgrace this publication. Besides, I am too poor to litigate.

a justice of the peace. But they were unable to make a British subject of me, by this or any other stratagem. She requested the company to leave the room to herself and me; but I refused and retired with the others—one of whom laughing said, "I believe you don't like our English women very well."

While I was in prison I was visited by many people, and teazed with many questions relative to torpedoes, which I generally found means to evade. An officer of an Irish regiment called one day and wished to speak to me, and asked me, within hearing of a number of the prisoners, if I was the inventor of torpedoes? I was tired of being quizzed on this subject, and therefore told him I knew as little of torpedoes as one of his countrymen, who having put up at a tavern in America, was asked by the landlord, if he would have a *warming-pan* to take up to his bed. "Yes, by J——s" says he, *"and I'll eat a bit of it at any rate."* The Hibernian swelled, and retired amid the shouts of the prisoners.

I was taken sick of a fever and accounted dangerous. The attending physician said, "there were more inquiries after my health than there was about any other man's in prison; and when he told them I should not live till 10 o'clock that night, there was more lamentation than he had ever known in a prison." This was told me when I was recovered from danger.—I found the principal cause of this unusual interest they had taken, was, that I had been barbarously kidnapped. I was released in consequence of my having been taken contrary to the stipulations referred to in major Case's letter to the commodore, dated the 23d August, 1813.

I was landed at Salem from the cartel. The marshal of that place told me, that I should be provided with every thing necessary to make me comfortable. I was bare-foot and bare headed; but the inhabitants of that town supplied me with what I needed, and treated me with great kindness. I was enabled to go on in the stage to New-London. At Providence, a printer was kind enough to take his hat about the streets; and procured a handsome collection of money from the inhabitants, to defray my expenses on the way. In short, I was very kindly treated by my generous countrymen, and offer them my tribute of acknowledgment.

From New-London I crossed the Sound to my own house, where I had the satisfaction of finding my family in good health, after my absence of nine months and nine days. I had not been long at home before I was invited to engage in another torpedo enterprize; but this failed in consequence of bad weather—and I removed my family, as advised, to Sag-Harbour.

It was never my good fortune to command a torpedo; and perhaps I might then have been unsuccessful; but I should be pleased to have the privilege of terrifying John Bull, and avenging myself while I was engaged in the service of my beloved country. Like poor Hall, *"I shall not give this business up for one bad job."*

JOSHUA PENNY.
Sag-Harbour, Jan. 1815.

From the Public Advertiser.

The Kidnapped Seaman.

Sons of FREEDOM break your slumbers,
    Hear a brother's piercing cries,
From amid your foe's deep thunders,
    Hear his bitter griefs arise.

Seized by ruffians on the ocean,
    From his kindred borne away,
Forced to render his devotion
    To relentless tyrant's sway.

See! with ruthless hands they chain him,
    Iron fetters bind his arm;
Better that they first had slain him
    And reliev'd from future harm.

See his naked body streaming,
    Rills of blood beneath the lash;
See his eyes indignant beaming,
    Sparkling vengeance as they flash.

Though his body scarr'd with gashes
    Sinks beneath a brutal hand,
His soul still scorns the fiend-like lashes,
    And turns to view his native land.

"O my country," hear him calling,
    "When, O when, the happy hour,
"That the sailor saves from falling
    "In these demons lawless power?"

Shall we hear his sad petition
    Echoing o'er our hills and dales,
And turn unmov'd from his condition,
    While his miseries he bewails?

Sons of freedom, arm for battle,
    And avenge your brother's cause;
Let your thund'ring cannon rattle
    for our country and our laws.

Notes

1. Oporto, a major maritime port in Portugal, is located on the northern bank of the Douro River

2. The quotation is attributed to Benjamin Franklin and is derived from a letter he wrote to David Hartley on December 4, 1789.

3. Given the length of the journey, at least some of these women must have been noticeably pregnant by the time they reached the slave markets. As Captain Matthews notes, this increased their value to prospective buyers. So notable was a pregnant slave that they were listed in a separate category in many ships' logs.

4. Table Mountain is sculpted from sandstone and rises 3,550 feet above the bay. Penny writes that it is 1,330 feet high.

5. Penny befriends a Dutchman in South Africa. The Dutch and English conflict is alluded to in the next several pages. The Dutch, English, and French all saw the value of the Cape as a strategic outpost on the route to empires in the East. Only the Dutch set up a mainland base for their East India Company (VOC), in 1652, to provide passing ships with food, water, and hospitalization for sick sailors. The British took possession of the Cape during the French revolutionary wars and held it as part of a colony after 1795, save for the brief return of Dutch rule from 1803 to 1806.

6. The government's offer of financial award to those who could sink a British ship in the Torpedo Act of March 1813 led many people to try attacking the ships. The deadliest occurred on June 25 off New London.

7. The *Ramilies* is a famous British ship in the War of 1812. Captain Sir Thomas Masterman Hardy blockaded the eastern exit between Montauk Point and Block Point with *Ramilies* and the *Orpheus*. Decatur decided to venture his squadron through the narrow and treacherous Hurl (Hell's) Gate.

8. This allusion is ambiguous. "Tom" followed by another word denotes the character of the person to whom it is applied, forming a quasi-proper name or nickname. A pedro (or pedrero) is a piece of ordnance originally for discharging stones or broken shot and for firing salutes.

9. Located in a small cove on the mainland side near the head of the Northwest Arm, the British purchased the island in Melville Cove for £1,000 in 1804 to serve as the site of a military prison; it was named for Viscount Melville, who was lord of the admiralty at the time. The prison held French and American prisoners of war from the Napoleonic wars and the War of 1812, British military prisoners, and even German prisoners of war during the First World War. When prisoners died, they were buried on a nearby small peninsula of land that came to be known as Deadman's Island. When numbers swelled, prisoners were also kept on floating hulks just off Melville Island.

An Affecting Account
of the
Tragical Death of
Major Swan,
and of the Captivity of
Mrs. Swan and Infant Child,
by the Savages

In 1826 James Madison acknowledged that, "next to the case of the black race with in our bosom, that of the red on our borders is the problem most baffling to the policy of our country." Certainly the "Indian problem" was baffling, yet what made it so baffling was more the popular perception of Native Americans than the actual indigenous populations themselves. Significantly, sensational narratives such as the Swan text helped to shape popular perceptions of both Native Americans and the "Indian problem."

Narratives generated from Native American captivity had been, for well over a century, frequent publications in American print culture, and although the structural pattern remained consistent—moving from attack to captivity and then to redemption—the textual focus shifted from sacred to secular concerns. During the decades before and after the Revolution, Indian captivity narratives were less concerned with spiritual salvation than with more worldly forms of deliverance. Whereas early narratives could be read as an individual's spiritual crisis with larger societal implications, later narratives were far more political and polemical—as well as sensational. Throughout her ordeal, Swan, for instance, mentions God only once when, anticipating a decapitating tomahawk blow, she "seized upon the moment . . . to implore the forgiveness of that Being before whom [she] expected so shortly to appear!" Her only other religious reference comes after three months of captivity, when she bemoans the fact that she may never again enjoy the "society of a christian people."

The Swan text is typical of early-nineteenth-century captivity narratives in that it reflects the ideological primacy of white America's constitutional rights, natural rights, and human rights. In its stylization and embellishments, the narrative reinforced stereotypes, justified westward expansion, and encouraged Indian removal policies. Combining seemingly benevolent ethnographic impulses with lurid, sensationalized, anti-Indian propaganda, the Swan text helped to forge an American identity by its depiction of Indian savagery.

Thirty miles southwest of St. Louis, Eliza Swan and her infant son were captured after she and her husband, Major Swan, were ambushed. The Major Swan of this narrative is almost certainly the Major Caleb Swan known for his field journal and sketches in the Talladega area in what is now northern Alabama and for his report, "Position and State of Manners and Arts in the Creek, or Muscogee Nation in 1791," when he served as a deputy agent of the Creek Nation for the secretary of the War Department under Henry Knox. Swan's 1791 field report was published for the first time in 1847 in Henry Rowe Schoolcraft's *Information Respecting the History, Condition and Prospects of the Indian Tribes of the United States* under the direction of the Bureau of Indian Affairs established within the Department of the Interior. Swan was almost certainly involved in another scouting mission for the government when he, his wife, and young son were tricked into coming to shore by a frightened, lost man, who later turns out to be French and even later receives his own reward for such deceitful behavior at the hands of their brutal "Saux" captors. In response to a gentleman who is curious as to the "particulars of the tragical death" of her husband, Mrs. Swan vividly outlines her capture, tribulations, and eventual release.

The *National Union Catalog* lists three possible publications of this narrative, all twenty-four pages, and all by H. Trumbull of Boston. The first *NUC* listing is entitled *An Affecting Account of the Tragical Death of Major Swan, and of the Captivity of Mrs. Swan and Infant Child, by the Savages in April Last* as being "Issued with the reprint of the 1813 ed. of U.S. War Dept. Message from the President relative to murders committed by the Indians." This is the narrative used in volume 33 of the Garland Library of Narratives of North American Indian Captivities (1978). *NUC* lists a possible 1816 edition as including "A narrative of the life and death of Lieut. Joseph Morgan Wilson." The edition that follows was also printed by Trumbull, in Boston, in 1815 and is the only Early American Imprints edition listed.

This narrative is rich in terms of its perception of wilderness. While still desirous of returning to her "own country," Swan finds the frontier landscape no longer frightening. Here are woods replete "with wild beasts of every kind, and almost every tree with birds," where a "pure and most excellent" water pours from mountain crevices, and where even rattlesnakes will not bite unless provoked. It is a country where she joyfully accepts the "juice of a small weed" from her Indian rescuers for her cuts and bruises. During her final trip of "90 miles . . . through an almost pathless wilderness" to retrieve her child from a Spanish trader, Swan described her march as "more like performing a journey through a pleasant country in a coach, than traversing a wild desert."

Certainly the narrative reinforced unfortunate stereotypes and portrays Native Americans as drunks who cannot resist a plundered bottle of brandy and as cruel savages who revel in torture. There are two major torture scenes in Swan's narrative that draw interesting parallels. The first scene is after the attack, when the Sioux stop to avenge the loss of several tribe members. After choosing the Frenchman for this retaliation, "it was determined to roast the wretched captive alive! For this purpose they led him into a neighboring thicket, stripped him naked, bound him to a tree, and piled dry brush with other fuel, at a small distance in a circle round him." Following a night of horrific nightmares, Swan is soon rescued by the members of the "Akinsaw nation," a self-professed friendly tribe of Native Americans who probably would have been part of the band of Eastern Cherokee. With the permission of the Spanish governor, this particular band of Cherokee had moved west of the Mississippi prior to 1800, to a territory bound by the Arkansas and White rivers. While not cruel to their white "visitors," these Indians are portrayed as crueler than any hostile tribe, since when among them Swan witnesses "the whole village, men, women, and children, . . . torturing [their own captives] in whatever manner they pleased, each apparently striving to exceed the other in cruelty—they first tore off their scalps, and then cut off their fingers and toes, joint by joint; they next dug out their eyes and filled their sockets with hot embers; and next drew out their tongues by the roots!" Such inflated descriptions of atrocity encourage readers to perceive little difference among Native Americans, regardless of their alliances or attitudes.

Such scenes were not uncommon in post-Revolutionary narratives of Indian captivity, and Swan's readers would have expected such scenes of cruelty and savagery. Swan herself displays a familiarity with the genre when she notes that had she "now but possessed the courage of some of the heroines of my sex, whom history informs us, have distinguished themselves on similar occasions, I might have embraced this opportunity to revenge my husband's death, and to have made my escape." Although Swan at this point questions her courage, her readers would not have. By first presenting the striking engraving of Eliza Swan raising a protective hand to an armed Indian, as her husband lay prostrate and dying against a tree, and then by continually depicting her in contradistinction to her captors, the narrative clearly reinforced the antithetical conventions that separated Anglo-Americans and Native Americans. As a print commodity, the Swan text was produced to attract readers by exploiting the most common—and the most unfortunate—stereotypes.

SSB

AN AFFECTING ACCOUNT
OF THE
TRAGICAL DEATH
OF

MAJOR SWAN,

AND OF THE CAPTIVITY OF

Mrs. SWAN and infant Child,

BY THE

SAVAGES,

IN APRIL LAST—(1815.)

☞ This unfortunate Lady and her little Son
were taken prisoners by the INDIANS, at a
small village near St. Louis, and conveyed
near 700 miles through an uncivilized wilderness, where they were fortunately redeemed by a Spanish trader, in July
last.

In vain she intreats — in vain attempts to ward the
* * * * * * * * *fatal Blow!*

BOSTON,

Printed by H. TRUMBULL, and for Sale by him
and at A. Mayo's Book and Sationary Store,
High Street, by the gross, dozen & single.
(Copy Right Secured.)

Title page of *An Affecting Account of the Tragical Death of Major Swan* (1815 edition; courtesy of the American Antiquarian Society)

Illustration from *An Affecting Account of the Tragical Death
of Major Swan*, "Eliza Swan defending her husband"
(1815 edition; courtesy of the American Antiquarian Society)

DISTRICT OF MASSACHUSETTS, to wit:

Be it remembered, that on the twenty-sixth day of September, A. D. 1815, and in the fortieth year of the independence of the United States of America, Henry Trumbull of the said District has deposited in this office, the title of a book the right whereof he claims as proprietor, in the words following, to wit: "An Affecting account of the tragical death of Major Swan, and of the captivity of Mrs. Swan and infant child, by the savages, in April last—(1815.)"

☞ This unfortunate lady and her little son were taken prisoners by the Indians, at a small village near St. Louis, and conveyed near 700 miles thro' an uncivilized wilderness where they were fortunately redeemed by a Spanish trader, in July last.

In vain she intreats—in vain attempts to ward the
——Fatal Blow!

In Conformity to the Act of Congress of the United States, intitled "An Act for the Encouragement of Learning, by securing the Copies of Maps, Charts and Books, to the Authors and Proprietors of such Copies, during the times therein mentioned," and also in an Act, intitled, "An Act for the Encouragement of Learning, by securing the Copies of Maps, Charts, and Books to the Authors and Proprietors of such Copies, during the times therein mentioned; and extending the Benefits thereof to the Arts of Designing, Engraving and Etching Historical, and other prints.

Wm. S. SHAW, Clerk of the Districtof Massachusetts.

"DEAR SIR,

"As you expressed a wish in your favour of the 20th ult. To obtain the particulars of the tragical death of my unfortunate husband, and of the cruel captivity of myself and little son, by the Savages, I shall so far comply with your request as to attempt to detail such particulars relative thereto, as will enable you to form some idea of what must have been my unhappy situation, while in the hands of the vile barbarians.

On the 2d of April last, as my husband, myself and little son, with two boatmen, were descending a small river 30 miles south west of St. Louis, in a small open boat (my husband being employed on a public expedition) a white man was discovered on the western shore, who, with a plaintive voice hailed us and begged that we would come and take a poor prisoner on board, that was endeavoring to make his escape. This pre-concerted plan of the artful savages had its desired effect. My husband ordered the boat towards the shore, and did not discover his mistake until the Indians (ten or twelve in number) rose from their ambush, fired, shot one of the boatmen dead, and severely wounded the other. My husband at this instant, as the only remaining means to save himself, with sword in hand leaped on shore, calling upon his surviving companion to follow him!—the wounded boatman however in attempting to gain the shore, through loss of blood, was unable to effect it, and fell an easy prey in the water to the savages. My unfortunate husband having chosen a favourable position, unquestionably bravely defended himself, and kept the Indians at bay until fatally wounded by a musket ball in the breast, which brought him to the ground—in this situation I found him!—three savages lay dead at his feet—but, overpowered by numbers, one of the merciless miscreants with an uplifted tomahawk was about to dispatch him, when I, half distracted with a view of my bleeding husband, beging for mercy, rushed between him and this vile savage!—but in vane did I intreat, in vain attempt to ward the fatal blow!

The savages having compleated their bloody work, by scalping the mangled remains of my poor unfortunate husband, and those of his no less unfortunate companions, I was stripped of my gown, shawl, stockings and shoes; loaded with as many of the packs which the boat contained as could be piled upon me, and compelled in this manner to accompany the Indians through a pathless wilderness, for many a tedious mile—not priviledged to embrace or nurse my infant babe, which was but eleven months old, and which was carried in a fur sack, by one of their young squaws.

In three days I think we must have travelled nearly 100 miles—my feet became so much bruized and scratched that the blood dropped fast from them—the overflow of milk of my breasts gave me too intolerable pain, and I intreated my savage masters to permit me, for a few moments, to nurse my poor babe, but my intreaties were productive of nothing but abuse and severe blows! Exhausted with bearing a burden above my strength, and frantic with torments exquisite beyond endurance, I entreated of the Indian who first captured me, and who claimed me as his prisoner, to knock me on the head and take my scalp at once, or relieve me of some of the heavy burden which I was about to sink under— upon which, contrary to my expectations, he ordered some of the packs to be taken off, and gave me a pair of mocasons: and what was a far more pleasing indulgence, permitted me for a few moments to nurse my babe, which I did, seated upon a log—with what apparent extacy did my poor little infant view its mother, and receive its natural food, of which it had been deprived for the last four days—indeed, so great was its hunger, that it was with some difficulty that I prevented its biting me! and when my savage master ordered me to arise and deliver it in charge of its savage mistress, it is impossible for me to describe to you the manner in which it clung to its mother's bosom, and the deep and melancholly impression which its screeches made upon my half distracted mind! Alas! mothers, only are capable of judging! and they can have but a slight, very slight conception of what my feelings then were.

Having on the morning of the fifth day, from that of my captivity, arrived at the boarders of a river of considerable wedth, the Indians halted to prepare canoes to transport themselves and baggage by water.—While engaged in this business, a second party of their nation, who had been on an expedition against some of the white settlements, either by appointment or by accident, fell in with them— they were about twenty in number, frightfully painted, and were loaded with plunder of every kind, but had neither prisoners or scalps—that they had lost some of their party was probable from the apparent grief and emotions of sorrow, with which they related to their brethren the particulars of their expedition, in the mean time exhibiting some spare caps and blankets, pierced with shot and stained with blood, which probably belonged to their deceased friends—in confirmation of this opinion, there could be nothing greater than the horrid grimaces and angry gestures with which they occasionally eyed us, who were the unhappy prisoners of their less unfortunate comrades.

Here (although it is said that misery loves company) I am sorry to inform you, that I and my poor little babe, were not the only captives of these merciless barbarians—a white man, apparently about 40 years of age, and whom by his dialect I judged to be a Frenchman, was also an unhappy fellow prisoner—he was the same who by the savages had been made an unwilling instrument of in decoying my poor unfortunate husband on shore!

It was evident by the appearance of the Indians last mentioned, that they were demanding of our captors, one or both of us, to be sacrificed according to their savage custom, in retaliation for the loss which they had sustained—nor were my apprehensions altogether unfounded, for after a consultation among themselves of near an hour, it appeared by their determination to fall to the lot of my unhappy fellow prisoner to die! A scene of horror, infinitely greater than had ever met my eyes before, was now preparing. It was determined to roast the wretched captive alive! For this purpose they led him into a neighboring thicket, stripped him naked, bound him to a tree, and piled dry brush with other fuel, at a small distance in a circle round him. They accompanied their labors, as if for his funeral dirge, with screams and sounds inimitable but by savage voices. Then they set the piles on fire and the blaze ran fircely round the circle, which soon reached the wretched captive, whose screeches and dying groans were such as would pierce the heart of any but cannibals! This sight, at the very idea of which all but savages must shudder, afforded the highest diversion to his inhuman tormentors, who demonstrated the delirium of their joy by correspondent yells, dances and gesticulations. The savages continued their powwas and hellish orgies until the fire had nearly wholly consumed the body of their victim! when they withdrew to partake of the plunder which the last party had brought. There was no article with which they seemed so much pleased as with a bottle of brandy, which they found deposited in the pocket of a pair of old portmantua's—with this liquor they all (even their squaws and children) became intoxicated: insomuch, that but a few of them were long enabled to stand or sit up. Had I now but possessed the courage of some of the heroines of my sex, whom history informs us, have distinguished themselves on similar occasions, I might have embraced this opportunity to revenge my husband's death, and to have made my escape— but the fear of surprize, and the dreadful death that I should subject myself to in such a case, deterred me—I did not however let pass this opportunity once more to impart nourishment to my half famished babe!—perceiving the squaw who had it in charge, like the others, stretched upon the ground and overcome with the liquor, I cautiously approached her, and by prostrating myself beside her, was enabled again to nurse the poor little sufferer—as it was carried after the manner in which the Indians usually travel with their young children, with its body enclosed in a blanket, I could not with safety disengage it, but having its head at liberty, I was enabled to nurse it in the manner above described.

With reluctance I was once more compelled to leave my poor infant, which, turning its little head, with a pitiful moan, its eyes followed me until I had hid myself from its view by squatting down beside my savage master, the place usually allotted me while he slumbered. As I had been almost a stranger to sleep since the unfortunate moment of my capture, it was equally vain that I now attempted to gain the repose which nature required—with a mind filled with horror at the recollection of the tragic scene that I had so recently witnessed, and harrowed with the reflection that I should meet with a similar fate, with the thoughts of leaving behind me in the hands of barbarians my helpless infant, put far from me all thoughts of repose. If for a single moment I gave way to the pressing calls of nature, I was quick aroused by the frightful spectacles which my wild imagination was continually presenting to my view—sometimes I would imagine myself placed upon an awful precipice, from which the savages were about to precipitate me—at another I would conceive myself placed in a situation similar to that of my late unhappy fellow prisoner, bound to the fatal tree, and encompassed with burning faggots!—and at another instance I instance I perceived my poor husband lying wounded in the situation that I saw him when I first reached the shore, begging for mercy! Such were the dreadful spectacles that haunted my distracted mind!

Not until the sun had arisen to a considerable height, did the savages arouse from that state of stupidity and insensibility so peculiar to an intoxicated Indian;—about noon they entered their canoes, and steered (as I judged) a south west course. At ten at night a furious storm arose, the rain descended in torrents, attended with a tremendous wind, while violent claps of thunder and sheets of vivid lightning followed close one upon another, almost without interval—the water, agitated by the wind, dashed furiously over our slender barks, which the affrighted savages were obliged continually to bail to prevent their sinking!—for my own part, I lay at the bottom of one of their boats half immersed in water, and perfectly indifferent as to what the final issue might be of this tremendous hurricane—I rather preferred than dreaded a watery grave: as by thus ending my days, would, I was confident, put me out of the power of the barbarians, who I had no doubt intended me as a victim to feed their savage fires! For two hours I lay thus cramped and trampled upon by the savages, who were trembling for their own personal safety—I at one time became so exhausted, that I felt that I had but little longer to combat with the shafts of affliction! Nature appeared to be making her last effort, and a few moments longer would most probably have consigned me to a watery grave, had not the Indians at length succeeded in reaching the shore.

I was hauled from the boat by my heels, and lay upon the sand almost breathless and with scarce strength to support myself, until aroused by a severe blow on the neck with the butt end of a lance, which one of the Indians carried—an old bear skin was thrown over me, in which situation I was conducted to a kind of bush tent, which the savages had hastily thrown up to shelter them from the storm, which continued to rage with unabated fury.

Half famished with cold and hunger, I should probably this night have made my final exit, had it not been for the humanity of an aged squaw, who being left to guard me (while the others went in search of the remaining boats) permitted me to dry my cloathes by the fire which they had enkindled, and gave me a small piece of broiled bear's flesh and some parched corn to eat.

At day break, the party who had been out in search of their companions, returned with an unusual degree of melancholly depicted in their countenances—it appeared that they had discovered the two boats which contained the residue of their friends drifted on shore, and as their Indian whoops and yells were unanswered, they concluded they must have all perished.

No sooner did these savages make known their discovery of the boats &c. to a party of their brethren who had been in a different direction, than they, one and all, set up a dismal howl, and rent the air with their lementations: exhibiting marks of the most ungovernable anguish and despair!—but, when they discovered me bewailing the loss of my poor babe (which must inevitably have met the fate of their companions) they reproved me for my weakness, signifying to me that my tears would be a disgrace to an Indian! that they only lamented that they had not taken my young papoose's scalp, with which to decorate their cabins.

About 9 o'clock the succeeding morning, the storm having subsided, the few savages that remained continued their journey by land through thick wood and high grass; and soon after began to ascend a very steep mountain—they were now obliged to unload their baggage, the greater part of which they were compelled to leave behind, while with the residue, they succeeded with difficulty by slow degrees in crawling up the hill—what rendered the ascent the more difficult, was the frightful chasms which had been formed by the torrent of water that had fell the night preceding. The mountain grew steeper, the paths more obstructed by fallen trees, brush and briars, and the breaches more frequent as they ascended. As you must suppose, in my weak and emaciated state, it was with the greatest difficulty that I was now enabled to obey the commands of my savage masters!—if I complained of my inability to keep pace with them, I was either unmercifully beat or pulled headlong after them!—my hands and knees were cut to pieces by frequent falls, and my face torn by the multitude of thorny bushes!—about 9 in the evening the Indians reached the summit of this lofty mountain, probably the highest in the western world—here, as in our passage up we met immense droves of deer and buffaloes: the latter of which did not seem to regard us as enemies, but only removed to the right or left, or stood still, gazing upon us as we passed—bears were most sought after by the Indians, as they esteemed their flesh preferable to any—the woods appeared filled with wild beasts of every kind, and almost every tree with birds, variegated with an infinity of colours.

On the top of the mountain the Indians encamped for the night—but I found it here equally impossible to gain that repose which my savage masters appeared to enjoy, the many severe wounds which I had received upon my feet, hands, &c. from the thorns and briars, gave me intolerable pain—and having nothing but the bare ground to lie upon, I was continually tormented by the painful bites of large black ants, with which my lacerated body was almost covered during the night—their bites caused considerable inflammation, and the pain nearly as great as that which arises from the bite of a scorpion!—I was too under continual apprehension that I should be attacked by the rattle-snakes, with which the mountain seemed to abound, the savages having killed several the day preceding—I was confident that I heard frequently during the night a noise like that caused by the shaking of their rattles (which is similar to that occasioned by a rapid motion of your finger upon a piece of paper) nor can my apprehensions be said to be altogether without cause, for in the morning as I was surveying on every side of me, the multitude of my nocturnal tormentors (the ants) with which the ground appeared black, I espied one of these venimous serpents, lying coiled within two yards of my head!—he was of an unusual size, seven or eight feet (as I judged) in length, and had upwards of twenty rattles—his lying so near me during the night, without apparent disposition to injure me, is a proof that this poisonous serpent will molest no one unless first attacked—he was destroyed by the Indians, who appeared highly pleased with what they esteem a valuable acquisition, and of which they made a hearty breakfast!

About 10 the savages began to descend the mountain on the west side, which although of almost perpendicular ascent, and covered with a thick wood and briars, I descended with a less number of additional wounds and bruizes than could be reasonably expected;—from the bottom of the mountain oozed a stream of pure and most excellent water, of which the savages were partaking, when they were suddenly aroused by an Indian whoop, which seemed to proceed but from a short distance, and at the same instant an arrow buried itself in the limb of a tree just above their heads—they instantly gave the war-whoop, and seizing their weapons, lay flat on their bellies, having first secured me by hastily binding me to a tree in their rear—their enemies soon appeared, and with dismal and terrific yells, commenced the attack—the engagement soon became a close and bloody one, and did not terminate until six of the Indians (to whom I was a prisoner) were killed, and the only remaining three so secured that they could not make any further resistance. Although I perceived the issue of this engagement would place me in the hands of new masters, yet I could not conceive that any great advantage could result from such an exchange—the successful party were savages, and as I had been frequently told that there was not in the savage race, any material difference, but that to torture to death was their general characterestic, I could not reasonably expect any better treatment from my new savage masters than from my late ones.

While thus engaged in meditating on my wretched condition, I perceived one of the savages approaching me with his tomahawk, sending fourth a tremendous war whoop!—conceiving this as the certain harbinger of death, I concluded that this savage had been sent to put an end to my miserable existence! Indeed so confident was I, that I seized upon the moment (which I expected would be my last) to implore the forgiveness of that Being before whom I expected so shortly to appear!—as the savage approached with his tomahawk raised I inclined my head that he need not miss his mark, but dispatch me at a single blow!—he advanced and "grined a gaustly smile," at my pale appearance, and to my surprize, at the very moment that I expected to receive the fatal stroke, kissed my hand, as a token of friendship, and with his tomahawk cut away the withes that bound me to the tree!—Gracious Heaven! (thought I) is it possible, that I, who but one moment since thought myself on the brink of eternity, should in the next behold my deliverance, and in my deliverer, him, whom I thought would be my executioner! The savage perceiving by my looks that I doubted his sincerity, he broke from a bush a branch and presented me, as a further token of friendship—I was then conducted by him to where his companions were employed in digging a grave for two of their party who had been slain in the late engagement—they took but little notice of me until their funeral rites were over—having dug a hole of sufficient depth, in the bottom sticks were laid across, and the two bodied wrapped in skins and mats, were laid upon them—their arms and ornaments were deposited with them, and a mount of earth was raised upon the grave.

The dead bodies of the enemy that were killed lay shockingly mangled and scalped but a few feet from them, which were left a prey to wild beasts! having seated myself near one of their prisoners (who lay pinioned hand and foot) I was requested to move farther off—"for (said one of the savages who could speak a little broken English) they are your enemies as well as ours, and as they intended you as their victim when they arrived at their own town, but being unexpectedly disappointed, they would now knock out your brains with a stone, if they can get a chance to do it!" Here this Indian (taking me by the hand) made a long harrangue—in which he informed me that my countrymen (with whom they were at peace) were their brethren—but that the Indians to whom I had been a prisoner, were bad Indians and great enemies to white people, whose settlements they were continually attacking—that by sending out small parties they generally intercepted them on their return, and had liberated many white prisoners—that I was now no longer a prisoner, that they should take me to their settlement, where I might remain with them until I should find a favourable opportunity to return to my own country.

The savages now perceiving my hands and feet terribly cut and bruised, they applied to them the juice of a small weed,[1] which they extracted by bruizing in a small rag, between two stones, which gave me almost immediate relief—I next was supplied with a clean blanket and a pair of mocasons, thus equiping me, they late in the evening commenced their journey for their own settlement—these savages seemed to regard me as one of their own nation—whenever impeded in my course by thick bushes or briars, they were always ready to assist me, and when they ascended steep hills, they even carried me on their backs—one of their squaws with a young papoose perceiving me in a bad situation, in consequence of being deprived of my infant, kindly offered her's to perform the part which nature required.

The day ensuing, about noon, the savages arrived within sight of their settlement, when they made a halt to prepare their prisoners after their savage mode, which they did by painting their faces of various colours—they then dispatched three or four of their companions to their chief to acquaint him of the success that had attended their expedition, and of the number of prisoners that they had taken—in a few hours they were met by hundreds of their tribe, with their chief at their head—preparation was now made for a grand precession, of which their chief took the lead: then followed the sixteen warriors who had achieved the victory, and next the unhappy prisoners, pinioned, bearing the scalps of their unfortunate companions! while the remainder, composed of men, women and children, bro't up the rear—thus formed, they moved forward, every one of them setting up the most dismal yell!

As savages on such occasions (as well as when they are engaged in their funeral rites) never pay any attention to friendly strangers until the fate of their prisoners are determined: I hobbled after them far in their rear, unattended and quite unnoticed.

When they reached their town, they proceeded to a small square in its centre, where a council of their chief men were immediately assembled to decide the fate of the prisoners—it was determined that two of the prisoners should be sacrificed to atone for the loss of their two friends, who had fallen in the engagement; and that the remaining one should be adopted. A near connection of one of the slain, was now requested to select from among the prisoners the one that he would adopt; when, to my great satisfaction, I found that he pitched upon the old squaw, who had so kindly treated me in the tent—the other two I could willingly see put to death, as one of them was the identical savage, who, although I intreated for mercy, beat out the brains of my poor husband!—and from the other, I had received much savage treatment.

Things being thus concluded upon, the whole village set up the death-cry; when they began to make preparation for rioting in the most diabolical cruelty. They first stripped the prisoners, and fixing two posts in the ground, fastened to them two pieces from one to the other: one about a foot from the ground, the other six or seven feet higher; they then obliged the unhappy victims to mount upon the lower cross piece, they tied their legs to it a little asunder, and then in a similar way secured their hands to the upper piece; they next daubed their bodies with pitch. The whole village, men, women, and children, now assembled round them, when their torments began, every one torturing them in whatever manner they pleased, each apparently striving to exceed the other in cruelty—they first tore off their scalps, and then cut off their fingers and toes, joint by joint; they next dug out their eyes and filled their sockets with hot embers; and next drew out their tongues by the roots! until they were thus deprived of their speech, as extraordinary as it may appear, the prisoners, so far from uttering a complaint employed their whole strength in recounting their own exploits, informing their tormentors what cruelties they had inflicted upon their brethren, and the revenge that would attend their deaths! Brands of fire were now occasionally applied to the naked bodies of the prisoners, until life becoming nearly extinct, they beat out their brains with their tomahawks! in this situation they left them hanging in the frames, while the whole tribe joined in one general powwaw, which was attended with capering and singing and dancing to and fro around the wretched victims of their torture. I was invited to take a part with them in this barbarous revel, but declined, and what added much to my surprize was to see the adopted old squaw partaking cheerfully with them in all their hellish plans to torment her wretched companions! Such is the disposition of a savage!

The chief Sachem of the tribe becoming weary of their savage sport, now began to pay some attention to me, addressing me much after the manner of the Indian who first liberated me, assuring me that I had nothing to fear—that as he and my countrymen were at peace, the Good Spirit would be angry with them, and destroy their hunting and fishing, if they were to treat me ill—that I should receive kind treatment from him and his squaw and from his people until I should have an opportunity to return to my friends. To this Sachem's wigwam I was now conducted, where I was treated with all possible respect—well cooked dishes of wild fowl, flesh, &c. were presented me, and a convenient bed provided for me.

This Sachem, whose wigwam was now to become my home, could not speak a word of English, but there were three or four of his tribe who had been several times in New-Orleans, that could speak it tolerable well, they not only served as interpreters, but were serviceable to me in acquainting me with things of importance:—from them I learnt that they were the Akinsaw nation,[2] who were very numerous, and could raise six or seven hundred warriors; that their country was situated about 800 miles from New-Orleans, and 600 from any white settlement; that the Indians who took me prisoner were of the Saux nation, and that from the old squaw whose life they had preserved, they had learnt that I and my infant were to be tortured to death, provided they had succeeded in conveying us to their town, in retaliation for the loss of their companions that were killed by my husband!

With these Indians I had continued nearly three months, and with little prospect of ever again enjoying the society of a christian people, for these savages, although they profess great friendship for the whites, are unwilling to part with such as are so fortunate as to fall into their hands; when, I was informed by one of my interpreters (who had recently returned from an expedition) that among the Cowitas, a friendly nation, he had seen a white papoose, which they had taken from the Saux Indians six or eight weeks before; that he saw it at the hut of a Spanish trader, who had procured a squaw nurse for it, and who informed him that the mother was taken prisoner with it, but was drowned with a number of the Saux's, on their way to their settlement. [3]

As you may suppose, I concluded this child no other than my own, provided I could put any confidence in the story of the Indian. I hastened to the old sachem, to whom I related the story, and begged of him to permit me to go and ascertain whether it was, or was not my child. He listened to my interpreter with attention, but when he had done speaking, he shaking his head, observed that it would be imprudent for me to attempt such an excursion alone, as I might again fall into the hands of the enemy, and that he could not furnish any of his warriors to escort me short of six or eight weeks. I now attempted to flatter him, representing to him the valuable present that he would most probably receive for me from the Spanish trader. This plan had its desired effect, the Sachem now concluded to put up with a few inconveniences, and dispatch me the next morning, with forty warriors, to protect me on my route: and thought it wise to accompany me too in person! Such is the love for gold, even among the Savage race!

The distance was nearly 90 miles, and through an almost pathless wilderness, yet I can truly say, it seemed more like performing a journey through a pleasant country in a coach, than traversing a wild desert, escorted by forty frightful looking savages! As I was the object of the expedition, all attention was paid me; over steep hills and through every difficult pass, I was conveyed in their arms.

It was before we reached the place of our destination on the second day, that I, to my inexpressible joy, obtained confirmation of the story of my savage interpreter—we fell in with an Indian who was one of the number that made me prisoner, and who had been adopted. From him I learnt that they did not succeed in landing until near day, and then were so exhausted that they could not secure their boats; that my papoose would not have lived thro the day had they not fell in with a formidable body of the enemy soon after their landing, by whom they were attacked and totally defeated; that my papoose then had tender care taken of it, and a squaw nurse was procured for it.

A few hours now brought me at the door of the Spaniard's hut, which I entered without ceremony; in one corner of a small room sit the old Spaniard half dozing, with his pipe in his mouth; in another, his tawny mistress, wrapped in a blanket, dandling upon her knee my babe! Without further noticing the Spaniard, I hastened to that part of the room where the squaw sit, and clasping my infant, exclaimed—"MY CHILD!—MY POOR CHILD!" The afrighted babe screeched and clung to the breast of its new mother, who, too, alarmed at the sudden appearance of a white woman, set up a dismal yell! this alarmed the old Spaniard, who I believe would too have become panic struck, had not the Sachem with one of my friendly interpreters at this moment entered, and explained the whole business. The Spaniard appeared highly pleased at the recital of my miraculous escape; he related to me the particulars relative to my child, which he said he paid 10 dollars for, and calculated to take it with him the next week to New-Orleans, in hopes of discovering its friends. The generous Spaniard presented the Sachem with 50 dollars, and the next week was at the expence of conveying me, and my infant, to New-Orleans, from whence we reached home in a much better condition than could be expected."

ELIZA SWAN."

Notes

1. The weed used was probably comfrey, or perhaps a member of the mint family, such as hyssop, as each of these common wild plants has antiseptic, astringent, or demulcent properties that promote wound healing. Such medicinal plants were much used by Native Americans and early settlers.

2. The tribe was likely part of the band of Eastern Cherokee who, with permission of the Spanish governor, had moved west of the Mississippi prior to 1800, to a territory bounded by the Arkansas and White rivers.

3. There is no historical or ethnographic evidence of a Cowita tribe. It is probable that Swan refers here to the Kiowa tribe. A nomadic and raiding tribe, the Kiowa ranged in the western Montana and Black Hills areas in the early eighteenth century. Cheyenne and Sioux drove them from the Black Hills, and they were forced to move south into Comanche territory. A bloody war soon resulted in a peaceful coexistence with the Comanche, and, according to Lewis and Clark, by 1805 the Kiowa had settled on the North Platte River. Soon after this they occupied the Arkansas River area, which would certainly have placed them in possible contact with Mrs. Swan.

A Concise Narrative

of the

Barbarous Treatment

Experienced

by American Prisoners in

England and the West-Indies

At some point during 1816, known in Vermont as the "year without a summer," Danville's *North Star* editor, Ebenezer Eaton, published *A Concise Narrative of the Barbarous Treatment Experienced by American Prisoners*, a twenty-four-page narrative of an anonymous young man's ill treatment while in the hands of the British during the War of 1812.

Eaton, however, may have been not only the publisher but also the writer of this narrative. Born in Mansfield, Connecticut, on April 3, 1777, Eaton later moved to Danville, where he published the *North Star* and various pamphlets, chapbooks, and broadsides. Quite possibly, this Ebenezer Eaton was the same Ebenezer Eaton who was, between August 1799 and December 1800, a printer from Worcester, Massachusetts, and who then set up shop in Rome, New York, starting the *Columbian Patriotic Gazette*. Above all, this particular Eaton was also a brother of General William Eaton, a distinguished veteran in the war with Tripoli. With such a connection, and with such a print network, Eaton was probably better informed than most and in an enviable position to provide a growing reading public with the exciting and tantalizing tales of this new Republic, in particular with marketable stories of the recently resolved War of 1812.

That said, confusion persists over who the actual writer of this single-edition narrative is. The original Sabin entry lists no author for this narrative. Meanwhile, Evans lists *Barbarous Treatment* as having been written by Robert S. (Stevenson) Coffin, and there is evidence to suggest that Coffin was indeed the author. Confusing the issue still further is the fact that the *National Union Catalog*, an "Improved title" notice in Sabin, and the Library Company of Philadelphia each lists Simeon Coleman as the author. Danville records from the early part of the

nineteenth century indicate neither a Robert Stevenson Coffin nor a Simeon
Coleman as living in the town or the surrounding area anywhere near this time
period.

However, whether this is a firsthand account from a mysterious Coffin, or
Coleman, or whether it was cobbled together from various news reports through
an active imagination by Eaton himself, *Barbarous Treatment* does contain
enough verifiable information to lend some degree of credence to the narrative. While there are certainly fictive elements, such as the highly melodramatic
flogging scene and the detailed and imaginative response of a British housewife to
anti-British coconut art, the names and countries of origin—sometimes even the
existence—of the ships involved (nine British and one American) seem to match
up with British and American naval records. As a case in point, the narrative
claims the ship that transported the prisoners to England, the British frigate
La Pique, was commanded by Anthony Maitland and that Maitland had previously commanded the *Bellerophon* when she transported Bonaparte to Plymouth,
England. According to British naval records, a Commander F. W. (not Anthony)
Maitland did command the *Bellerophon* that took Bonaparte aboard on July 10,
1815. Theoretically, such a timeline would have given Maitland time to gather
a new ship once the *Bellerophon* was decommissioned and reach Barbados by
December 1815. As well, the mistake in Maitland's first name seems more likely
a lapse of memory as opposed to the error of someone working from direct
sources.

Whether fictive or not, this narrative is not just an entertaining captivity tale;
it is also a series of anecdotes designed to illustrate the themes of American
bravery and liberty alongside British cruelty and tyranny. On the whole, the
principal cruelty dealt with in this narrative is the continued imprisonment of
free men. The notorious and detested British practice of impressment had gone
on virtually unchecked for decades. Indeed, one of the great affronts committed in
this narrative is the continual attempt to force a freedom-loving American sailor to
"do his *duty*" by serving the British forces whereby, if he submitted, he would be
destined to "fight against his country." Such dealings were met with the strongest
rhetorical response throughout the narrative and reinforced the idea that for many
Americans the War of 1812 truly represented a second war of independence. The
narrative inculcates its American readers concerning acceptable behavior in the
face of cruel and barbarous British activities. Any true American, despite feeling
the "icy hand of death" from the sting of a British lash, knew death to be preferable
to forced servitude. At one point, the narrator recounts the adventures of several
"free-born tars of Columbia" who, after attempting to escape from their prison
ship—as the narrator exclaims—"knew too well the value of freedom" as they
were aware that "[a] day, an hour of virtuous liberty, / Was worth a whole eternity

of bondage." The narrative clearly depicts the British as a cruel oppressor and the enemy of freedom-loving Americans, thus destroying the notion that Great Britain could ever again be perceived as a "fond, loving mother."

While the narrative is clearly designed to further anti-British sentiment, it is also designed to boost American pride. On July 6, 1812, about two weeks after the war first began, Congress, under President Madison, passed an "Act for the Safe Keeping and Accommodation of Prisoners of War." *Barbarous Treatment* demonstrates a clear disregard for fair play on the part of the British. At one point, after peace had been declared, the commander of the British brig *Barossa* became a passenger of the *La Pique* carrying the Americans as "free" prisoners. Once he witnessed the cruel and barbaric treatment of the prisoners, he demanded that if the "tyrant" of a captain did not cease and desist he would be forced to remove himself at once to another vessel. He quitted the ship over Maitland's wretchedness and in the eyes of the narrator henceforth became "worthy the name AMERICAN." It was perhaps the highest compliment that could be paid to a British citizen as it reinforced the ideas of humanity and independence inherent in the emerging American vision of itself as a benevolent, freedom-loving country.

The narrative, as it depicts settings abroad, is also used as a discursive domain for ideas of liberty, citizenship, and independence at home. One of the offshoots of anti-British rhetoric in the narrative was the vehement attack on those who "style[d] [them]selves Federal Republicans" and who had "so often declared that 'England has done us no essential injury.'" No one, not even the most conservative Federalists, could accept the image of an "undaunted son of freedom lashed to the gangway" of a *"floating Bastille"* by *"licensed pirates."* No longer, this narrative claims, could Americans afford to consider themselves the "adopted" child of Britain and worthy of any gift of kindness as those "bestowed on her *legitimate* children."

On or about August 1, 1815, these prisoners of war returned to Boston harbor, having learned that despite how cruel a mistress the sea sometimes was, she was "less treacherous and cruel" than "a jealous and imperious Briton invested with power." The returning sailors came back to a cheering country where the tensions and fraction caused by the war were already beginning to mend—so much so that at war's end, on February 17, 1815, even the *Georgetown Federal Republican* had this to say: "O Thank God! we are still safe; we are still free; that we have gone thro' a bloody war, and have preserved our liberties entire."

SSB

A

CONCISE NARRATIVE

OF THE

BARBAROUS TREATMENT

EXPERIENCED BY AMERICAN PRISONERS IN
ENGLAND AND THE WEST-INDIES, &c.

WRITTEN BY A YOUNG MAN WHO WAS PRISONER
NEARLY SIX MONTHS IN THE ISLAND OF BAR-
BADOES, AND FIVE IN ENGLAND.

INTERSPERSED WITH

ANECDOTES, REMARKS, &c. &c.

TRUTH NEEDS NO ORNAMENT.

DANVILLE :
PRINTED BY EBENEZER EATON.

1816.

Title page of *A Concise Narrative of the Barbarous Treatment
Experienced by American Prisoners* (1816 edition; courtesy
of the American Antiquarian Society)

Narrative, &c

Sailed from Boston, (1814.) in a private armed Schooner, called the Dolphin, Johnson, commander, bound for the Island of St. Bartholomew, West Indies—spoke nothing on our passage, but saw a number of small vessels, supposed to be American privateers.[1] We had experienced but little bad weather, and nothing of importance occurred until the morning of the 14th day of our passage, (Sunday) having made the land the evening previous, when at day light the man at the mast head descried a sail. Our captain still kept the schooner on her course, until he could plainly discern the English colors flying at the peak of the man of war brig—as she afterwards proved to be;—he then ordered us to tack and stand before the wind, the brig also coming down, before the wind, with all sail set. The brig kept up the chase, and continued to gain upon us until 2 o'clock, P. M. when she fired several shot, which, however, fell short—she continued to fire at intervals, still gaining on us quite fast, for nearly an hour, when she had come so nigh that the shot from her long guns reached us, and in a few minutes after, she fired several shot from her carronades, which passed over us;—our captain now, with the advice of the crew, ordered the schooner to be hove to, which was immediately done; and our colors, not having been hoisted before, nor during the chase, were directly hoisted, and soon after struck to the British man of war brig Columbia.[2]

The 2d. Lieutenant of the brig and two Midshipmen came on board, and in an imperious tone demanded, "from whence are you?"—the reply was, "from Boston." He then ordered us to get our things ready to go on board the brig; but before we had time to pack up our dunnage, we were ordered into the boat, which leaked so much that she was half full of water before we reached the brig.—When on board, our bags, chests, &c. were searched, and some canvass taken from us.

The Commander of the brig had been—as he informed us—a prisoner in this country in the early part of the war, and was a Lieut. on board the JAVA when she was captured.[3] He spoke highly of the Americans—said they treated their prisoners well, and that we should be used accordingly. But although we fared as well as the crew of the brig, yea the most abject beggar in this country would think it an insult to his poverty, to be offered what this humane Englishman, doubtless, thought was a great *condescension* to allow us. I will only describe the bread—if so it ought be called;—it had been baked, to all appearance, at least *two years;* and had so long become the habitation of *worms* and *weevils*, that it resembled—except to the *taste*—an *honeycomb*, and was so extremely hard and compact, that I sincerely believe, were it converted into wagon-wheels, it would last nearly half as long as any kind of wood—except *Lignumvitae*—commonly used for that purpose. This bread we were obliged to break in pieces with a hammer or billet of wood, and then soak in our Cocoa or Chocolate; when it had become softened a little, the vermin would swim on top of the liquor, which we scum off and then satisfied as much as possible our empty stomachs with what little remained.

Here it is necessary to inform the reader, that I, though not then twenty years of age, had been a most strenuous supporter, so far as my abilities extended, of every act of injustice committed on our commerce and seamen by our fond, loving *"mother,"* Great Britain.—I had often heard of the *"roast beef and plumb puddings,"* which our "mother" so generously bestowed on her *legitimate* children, and therefore conceived myself entitled—though only an *adopted* child—to as large a slice as any of the rest, since I had come so far after it!—Indeed, so completely blinded was I by prejudice in favor of the English nation, that I even rejoiced before I was taken on board the brig, that I had been so *fortunate* as to fall into the hands of men, whose nation Gov. Strong had declared to be the *"Bulwark of our Religion"*—and how could I, having been resident among those *Knights of Christianity*, self-styled *"Silver Greys,"* for six years, and having always been taught to believe, that the federalists were the only champions of truth and virtue, doubt the word of the Oracle of Federalism—the then Chief Magistrate of Massachusetts?—I was also strong in the belief that there had been but ONE solitary instance of impressment from any of the sea ports in Massachusetts.—Poor, simple child!—I had often heard, before I went to sea, many a weather-beaten tar relate the hardships he had suffered on the ocean, and full often the cruel treatment received on board British men of war, after being impressed, because he refused to do duty, when by so doing he would be compelled not only to fight against his own country, but, perhaps, against relatives and friends. These stories, although I listened attentively to them, I conceived, at least, much exaggerated, if not altogether *false*. But alas! I have since found, that so far from being false or exaggerated, the picture needed colors of a much *darker* hue than the "Son of Ocean" had given it.

Picture to yourselves, ye who style yourself Federal Republicans, and have so often declared that "England has done us no essential injury," one of your own countrymen dragged from his own vessel by a set of *"licensed pirates,"* on board one of the *floating Bastiles* of the would-be "Mistress of the Seas"—view there this undaunted son of freedom lashed to the gangway—behold, on this side, the grinning fiend with his blood-stained lash, and on the other his inhuman commander—now he orders the fiend to inflict the dreadful punishment—the fiend obeys—the lash falls—the purple stream bursting from its channels flows to the deck—why sleeps thy vengeance heaven?—still his high-born soul disdains to yield—now the fiend pauses, and the lash for a moment ceases to fall—the petty tyrant advances—asks him if he will "do his *duty*," (which in time of war amounts to the same as if he had asked him, if he would *fight against his country*)—the son of the wave indignantly answers, No!—again with redoubled violence, the fiend renews his blows—already he feels the icy hand of death—still he consents not—at length nature sinks under the dreadful scourge—he dies!—he is committed to the deep.—And as he sunk,

> ——— "A hellish shout arose,
> So fare all Albion's REBEL Foes!"

But to return from my digression.—We remained on board the Brig three days—made the Island of Barbadoes about four hours before sunset of the second day.—This Island is remarkably healthy, the town being situated near the sea-shore, has the benefit of the sea-breeze, which springs up in the afternoon, and renders the remaining part of the day cool and agreeable.

The sun was just setting when we arrived here, and as its last rays were reflected on the yellow Orange, and different colored fruits of the Island, the scene appeared to me like the description Poets give of the heathen Paradise, Elysium.—We had now come to an anchor, and I beheld, a little distance from the shore, the place of our future residence—a Prison-ship. This Prison-ship had been a sloop of war, and was on our coast during the revolutionary war: she was a crazy, worm-eaten dirty old hulk; and was called the VESTAL, which name, however, we soon altered to a more appropriate one, viz: the BEASTIAL!

We were sent on board this Prison-ship in the afternoon of our arrival in port.—Although there were only about sixty prisoners on board when we came, yet before we left it, there were upwards of three hundred. Our situation became more distressing as the number of prisoners increased, being all crowded down on the birth deck at sun-set every night, in a very hot climate, without a single breath of air, except when we were allowed a wind-sail. This prison-ship was infested with innumerable *Cockroaches* and *Santapees*. The Cockroach is a large bug, sometimes weighing nearly an half ounce; they would eat our sugar, bread, &c. We dared not grease our boots or shoes, for if we did they would as certainly be eaten up by the Cockroaches during the night.—The *Santapee* is a most poisonous reptile, resembling a catterpillar, is from 6 to 8 inches in length, and has a large number of legs. There is but one remedy for its poison, and this, though seemingly paradoxical, is the poison itself; it is procured in the following manner:—two or three of these reptiles being caught, are immediately immersed in a vial of strong spirit; the spirit causes them great pain, and they eject their poison into the liquor; the wound being washed in this several times becomes gradually less painful, and in a short time is perfectly cured.

We remained on board the Prison-ship about five months. During the time of our tedious captivity here, many of the prisoners amused themselves with carving

Cocoa Nut-shells, and making Straw Hats. Some of these shells were polished and carved or engraved with great elegance and taste, having different inscriptions on them, most of which were satires on the English Navy, &c.—An American prisoner polished one of these shells in a most superb manner, and engraved under the bottom, the English Lion couching to the American Eagle, and round its sides different flowers, fruits, trees, &c. An English Officer happening to be near when the American had finished his shell, and was shewing it off to his fellow-prisoners, desired also to see it; and admiring its symetry and the beauty of the figures, (except those on the bottom which he did not then discover) offered the man 4 dollars for it, which he accepted. The officer immediately carried it on shore, to have it set in silver to present to his wife. When it was finished, he carried it home, doubtless in anticipation that the smiles of his dearly beloved would well reward him for so elegant though trifling a present. But, alas! how were his hopes frustrated, when his affectionate wife, like most other women, ever seeking to discover something new, espied the *British Lion couching to the American Eagle*, on the bottom of the cup! She immediately shew it to her generous husband, who, in a fit of rage, and exclaiming, d——n the yankee rascal, dashed it in pieces on the floor!

A scene occurred here, which, though not by any means new to English subjects, was nevertheless novel to us. It was what the British term "going through the fleet." The particulars of this horrid transaction were as follow;—A British seaman belonging to a frigate then lying in the harbor, for some disrespectful expression to an officer, was tried by a Court Martial, and sentenced to receive six hundred lashes, the boatswain of each man of war to inflict his proportionable number, until the whole was completed.

The criminal early in the morning was placed in one of the boats of the frigate to which he belonged, in which were also a guard of soldiers with fixed bayonets, and officers with drawn swords, also a Surgeon and Chaplain. This boat rowed away first, after which followed a procession of other boats;—the boats were rowed first to the Admiral's ship, where the criminal was lashed up to a triangular kind of *gallows*, and a prayer was made by the Chaplain, to the intent that he might be able to endure his punishment with *patience, fortitude* and *resignation*, and that it might be a warning to his shipmates from committing the like *crime*.—O Britain! thou blest "Bulwark of our Religion," how much is it to be regretted that all thy faithful subjects in this country could not *feel* the *cheering* INFLUENCE of thy *humanity*! But to proceed.—After the Chaplain had finished his mock-prayer, the boatswain of the Admiral's ship proceeded to inflict his proportionable part of the dreadful punishment. After he had done his duty, as the English express it, the boats again moved to the next man of war, where the same *ceremony* was performed, and so on alternately until the criminal had received his six hundred lashes!—We had an opportunity of witnessing nearly the whole of this heart-rending scene of barbarity; but for my own part I could not view the half of it—the tear "unbidden" stole down my cheek, and I turned my head aside. Indeed, there were but few American seamen upon whose rugged breasts the gem of sympathy did not glitter.

The men of British ships of war are *compelled* in all cases to witness this heart-rending spectacle of refined cruelty. If the criminal dies be[f]ore he has received the half of his punishment it makes no difference, he must receive the whole. The Doctor's duty (as I ought to have observed before) is to restore the criminal to *feeling* when he faints, and not a blow is inflicted while he remains insensible to feeling.

Now I would ask, is there a man in this country, so ignorant, or dead to feelings of humanity, who, being a spectator of the scene above described, and laying aside all party animosity, can place his hand on his heart, and assert in the face of heaven, that a Sovereign whose signature sanctions such scenes of cruelty, is a firm and sincere supporter of the mild religion we profess? No.—I believe that even GOV. STRONG, could he once witness a scene similar to the one just mentioned, would blush when he recalled to mind the assertion he had made that Great Britain was the "Bulwark of our Religion."

But to continue my narrative. Upwards of forty prisoners escaped from this prison-ship by getting out of the port holes, and swimming ashore, but were always taken and brought back. Fourteen made their escape in one night, by sawing off, with an old knife, the iron gratings of one of the stern ports. They travelled to Spikestown, (about 20 miles) that night, and concealed themselves the next day in a cane-patch—the evening following they ventured to the shore, where they found a small boat, which they took, and having supplied themselves with a quantity of bread and a small keg of water, embarked for the Island of Guadaloupe, belonging to the French;—but before they had proceeded three quarters of a mile, the boat sunk—and they with great exertions at length reached the place from whence they had taken the boat, when they were instantly seized by seventy or eighty negroes and some whites, armed with clubs, knives, &c. who had been informed of their escape from the Prison-ship, and the place where they had concealed themselves, by a slave who had discovered them in the cane-patch the afternoon previous. The whites permitted the negroes to rob the prisoners of their money, of which they had in the whole, from sixty to one hundred dollars.— The prisoners were taken the next day on board the Admiral's ship, probably to see if they would not rather enter, than be carried back to the Prison-ship; but in this the good Admiral was doubtless much disappointed—the free-born tars of Columbia knew too well the value of freedom—they knew

"A day, an hour of virtuous liberty,
Was worth a whole eternity of bondage."

The Admiral kept them on board his ship one night, and the next day sent them on board the Prison-ship, where they were kept in irons thirty days, and on short allowance.

Many of the prisoners had been here eight or ten months;—during this time several plans were formed for taking the ship, in order to gain their liberty—but none of these were put in execution—partly owing to the number of the guard being nearly equal to the number of prisoners, and partly from a story in circulation, that an American Cartel was shortly expected in to take them all to their native country.—A deep laid and last plan for liberating ourselves was devised, about a month before we received the news of peace between the United States and Great-Britain. It was arranged in this manner.

At the hour of sun-set, (the time we were counted down on the birth deck) two men before selected, were to place themselves near each sentry on the main deck—12 more were to stand near the quarter deck—these were to seize the arms of the guard who were then off duty, and reposing themselves in the gun-room—others were selected to secure the sentries on the gun and quarter decks, there being two sentries on each of these decks—six more were also appointed to seize the master and officer, who stood near the hatchway to superintend counting us down, &c. This plan, however, so far was frustrated, and we were again immured in our narrow dungeon. But we were not thus to give up all hopes of regaining our freedom. It was agreed that at eleven o'clock at night, when the watch-word* would be given, we should all rise at once—knock down, kill or secure the guard, officers, &c. and a number to swim to the Admiral's Tender, (a small but fast sailing schooner) seize or kill the watch on deck, fasten down the watch below, cut her cable, and bring her along side the Prison-ship, when the Americans were to embark and run out to sea—At this time there was but one armed vessel in the harbor, and she being a frigate half dismantled, could not have got ready to put to sea under two days at least—so that we should have been, with a good breeze, upwards of three hundred miles ahead, before the frigate could have got under way to come in chase of us. In fact, had we succeeded in taking the schooner, we should have been, in all probability, in 8 or 10 days afterwards safe in some harbor or other in the U. States. But heaven decreed it otherwise.

Just before the hour appointed for the execution of our plan, a prisoner was sent on deck to see if the guard, as was expected, and as they usually had been before, were carelessly reclining on their arms, or partly asleep on the deck; but what was our surprise when we were informed that so far from what we had anticipated, a double guard of soldiers were then on board the ship, besides several boats rowing guard, and upwards of two hundred soldiers stationed on the shore directly opposite!—Our feelings at this time I will not attempt to describe. Suffice it to say, that we who a few hours before had been indulging the

---

* The watchword was *"Lawrence"*

fond hope of again soon beholding our native country—and with the satisfaction too, of entering an American port, with an *English Admiral's Flag beneath our own*—for we had made an American Flag the night before—had nothing left now, but the gloomy prospect of languishing out the remainder of our imprisonment, perhaps life, in irons, and on short allowance!

It appeared evident that we had been betrayed—but by whom remained a mystery. It could not have been by the French or Spanish prisoners, for they knew nothing of the matter; suspicion therefore rested on some one of our countrymen. The traitor, however, was never satisfactorily discovered; but was supposed to be a Dutchman, who had been taken in an American Privateer, and who a few days after this affair, obtained his liberty, and went on board an English merchantman. Thus ended this last attempt to regain our liberty.

Sometime in February a sloop of war arrived here with despatches from the English Government, and bringing the welcome news of peace. We expected now to have been sent immediately home—but our cup of misery was not at this time full.

In a few days after the news of peace, we were ordered to prepare ourselves for a voyage to the "fast-anchored Isle" of the ocean.

The excuse made for this procedure was, that the Admiral had received strict orders to send all American prisoners in the West-Indies to England, previous to the receipt of despatches stating the conclusion of a treaty of peace between his Government and the Government of the U. States—and that these orders had not been countermanded. Whether this was the case or not, I will not pretend to determine.—However, fifty of us embarked on board the British frigate La Pique, Hon. Anthony Maitland Commander. This man, by what I have since learnt, afterwards commanded the Bellerophon, 74, in which Bonaparte was carried to England.[4] Capt. Maitland, to those unacquainted with him, has the appearance of being all benevolence, humanity and good nature—his eyes are remarkably bright, but mild—his features handsome, and his form straight and well proportioned;—a smile is generally seen to illumine his countenance, but it is the smile of a villain—for truly he could

"*Smile* and *murder* while he *smiled.*"

He was a most accomplished tyrant, so far as his power extended—was lost to all sense of shame, and delighted in sporting with the miseries of his fellow-mortals;—in fact he was

—— A *fiend* of *darkness*,
'Ray'd in the *light* of *heaven*.

Captain Maitland's inhuman treatment towards us during the whole passage to England, will prove this short sketch of his character correct.

After leaving Barbadoes, we touched at several Islands, for the purpose of convoying merchantmen to St. Thomas', from whence they were to proceed to different ports in England and Ireland.—We waited at this Island nearly a fort-night, when the fleet having all arrived—about 300 sail—we took our departure for the shores of Old England. This was in February.—After a few days sail, the weather became extremely cold, and most of us being destitute of warm clothing, would have rendered our situation miserable enough at best, had we been allowed the liberty of exercising ourselves on deck; but, alas! even this privilege was denied us.

Confined between two guns—a distance of about twenty feet in length, and 8 in width—with four sentries over us—the water continually pouring in upon us, having no place to sit down, except in the water, we had at this time but little relish left for life.

During the whole passage we were ordered down into the forehold at 4 o'clock, P. M. where we remained until 7 in the morning—and sometimes on days of punishment, till noon. Here we were necessitated to repose ourselves on the *soft side* of a water-cask, bundle of staves or iron hoops—and so crowded were we, that those who *first* laid down could not rise again without the consent of the *last*, whose bodies rested on the breasts or legs of the *first*.

Our allowance was but 3 gills of water per day, although there was plenty on board, and having nothing but salt beef or pork to eat, our thirst oftentimes became so extreme, that at night we have used an old handkerchief for want of a sponge, to soak up the putrid water remaining in old casks, and wrung it out and drank it!—This treatment, the reader will recollect, we received *after the news of peace was confirmed.*

The Commander of the British Brig Barossa, who came passenger in the La Pique, a very humane man, and who had ever treated American prisoners with the greatest lenity, took the liberty of telling the tyrant Maitland, that it was a shame and disgrace for him to treat, even criminals, in the manner he treated us; and at length told him plainly that unless he would consent to ameliorate our condition, he would not stay on board his vessel another day—Maitland refused—and the Capt. of the Barossa quit his ship the next morning, and went on board a brig.—Surely every candid mind must imagine our situation most distressing, when an *English* Commander quitted a frigate, in which he could have had every delicacy, and "fared sumptuously every day," to embark on board a small brig, merely because he could not view, without emotions of grief, such a scene of human wretchedness.—Was not the Commander of the Barossa worthy the name—AMERICAN?[5]

After our arrival in Portsmouth, (Eng.) we were put on board the Swiftsure, 74, on board of which vessel there was one hundred other prisoners, who had been sent from Barbadoes the same time we were. From Portsmouth we were trans-ported to Plymouth, and from thence in boats about five miles up the river, and put on board the Prison-ship Ganges, 84, where we remained about 4 months.[6]

Our allowance here was one pint of Cocoa—little better than warm greasy dish water—three quarters pound of fresh beef, without salt, and which after being boiled would shrink to five ounces, and three biscuit per day.

The soldiers on board this Prison-ship were not allowed any spirituous liquor, but as much small beer as they wished. The prisoners one night, by cutting a hole through the deck, found the head of a beer cask, which they tapped and drew off before morning. A Sergeant first discovered the trick, but seemed not at all angry about it. This Sergeant informed the prisoners that he had bought a cask of excellent beer, which if they would get in the same way they did the other, they were welcome to it.—The prisoners of course first endeavored to find where the cask was—which having discovered in a little room, forward of the galley, when the prisoners were to be counted down, some of them drew off the attention of the sentry, altho he then stood within 6 feet of the room, while others pryed the hinges from the door, and dug away the sand from under the cask, by which the Sergeant had raised it nearly three feet from the deck; then tacking the hinges on the door, were counted down as usual—They immediately went to work, and with their Jacknives, &c. soon cut through the deck, and drained this cask also. The Sergeant early the next morning discovering from the prisoners' smiles and whispers that all was not right, thought he would examine and see if his beer was safe—the cask, indeed was there, but, alas! the beer was fled! He then told us, in a jocular manner, that he should take good care not to give a yankee *leave* to steal his beer again!

We took our departure from England on the 5th June—this was the Queen's birth-day—and embarked in the English Cartel Brig Sovereign, for our beloved country—Nothing material occurred on our passage, except springing our bowsprit, which, however, was soon repaired. We had a tedious passage of 64 days, and our situation here was but little better than on board the La Pique—the Cartel being a small Brig, and having in the whole 256 prisoners on board, one third of which were Frenchmen and Spaniards—but the cheering prospect of soon beholding our native country, and embracing those we held dear, rendered even suffering a pleasure. We had, indeed, the winds and waves to combat, but experience had taught *us*, that even these were generally less treacherous and cruel, than a jealous and imperious Briton invested with power.

About the first of August, 1815, we all arrived at Boston, in health and safety—after an absence of nearly one year.

Note.—Many, perhaps, will doubt the truth of the foregoing Narrative, on account of the Authors name not having been prefixed to the title page—but the reason why he has withheld his name is, that he thought it would appear too much like vanity, to place it to so illiterate and short a performance.

The author is now resident at Danville, and pledges his honor for the truth of every statement contained in it. Suffice it to say, he had not wrote a line
"Which dying he would wish to blot."

The following Song was written by the author of this Narrative, on board the Prison-ship Vestal, in the West-Indies, December, 1814.

Song.

Columbia, Columbia, awake from thy sleep,
And hurl from his throne the proud king of the deep!
May thy sons, O Columbia, who toil on the waves,
Swear to heav'n they ne'er will submit to be slaves;
   For thy tars know not fear,
   Tho' death should be near,
And shew his grim face on the dark rolling waves.

Though the tyrant of England has tried once more,
To land his vile vassals on Freedom's blest shore,
Yet our Navy triumphant, shall soon let him know,
That we cringe not to tyrants, nor strike to a foe;—
   For our Seamen ne'er fear,
   Tho' death should be near,
And rivers of blood from their scuppers should flow.

Notes

1. Journals of the Continental Congress from Friday, June 27, 1788, discuss the monies to be awarded to Captain Samuel Nicholson and his crew of the *Dolphin* that had along with two other American ships, captured eight British vessels in 1777. It seems entirely possible that, thirty-seven years after the *Dolphin* first served her country, she, by this point in her career, had fallen into private hands and was a private armed schooner bound for St. Bartholomew on a nonmilitary mission.

2. The carronade, developed by a Scottish ironworks in 1778, was a short gun also referred to as a "Smasher." Supported by a sliding carriage and ropes to control recoil, the smasher could propel a weighty cannonball only a limited distance. No match for long guns, this limited range and its poor aim soon led to its disuse.

3. The French ship *Renommé*, renamed the *Java* (38), was captured May 20, 1812, off the coast of Madagascar by a British squadron commanded by Captain Charles Schomberg. The ship that captured the *Dolphin* was the British man-of-war *Columbia*. The commander of the *Columbia* states that he was captured by the Americans as a

lieutenant onboard the *Java* (*Java*, 38) during the early part of the war. On February 22, 1813, President James Madison, through his secretary Edward Coles, sent to the U.S. Senate and House of Representatives a letter "from Captain Bainbridge, now commanding the United States' Frigate the 'Constitution,' reporting his capture and destruction of the British frigate the Java." According to British naval records, her lieutenants at the time of capture included Henry Ducie Chads, William Allan Herringham, and George Buchanan, and her cargo consisted mainly of naval stores, including a large amount of copper sheeting to build a seventy-four-gun ship. All crew were returned from Brazil to England, where they were honorably acquitted at their court martial. On May 28 Lieutenant Chads was promoted into the *Columbia*, the boat that eventually captured the *Dolphin*. Although the narrative never names him, Chads would seem to be the commander in question. Interestingly, prior to her involvement in the war the *Java* seems to have imported a quantity of "Bandannah handkerchiefs" from Calcutta for the merchants of Salem, Massachusetts, who petitioned Congress November 12, 1807, for permission to receive this shipment.

4. After five months on board the *Vestal* and after peace had been declared, all the prisoners were transported to England aboard the British frigate *La Pique* with a commander by the name of Anthony Maitland. The *La Pique* has no British or American record. However, the narrative states that the British commander Maitland commanded the *Bellerophon* (74) as she transported Bonaparte to Plymouth, England. According to British records, a Commander F. W. (not Anthony) Maitland did command the *Bellerophon* that took aboard Bonaparte on July 10, 1815. Theoretically, such a timeline would have given Maitland time to gather a new ship and reach Barbados by December 1815. The *Bellerophon* was out of commission by 1816.

5. The *Barrosa* (not *Barossa*) was commanded at this time by a Captain John Maxwell and spent her last mission in the West Indies. She too was out of commission at Portsmouth by 1816. It is unclear why the commander of the *Barrosa* would need transport to England from the West Indies.

6. Once the prisoners arrived in England they were transported on the *Swiftsure* (74) to the prison ship *Ganges*. However, records indicate that the *Swiftsure* was serving her last tour in the West Indies during 1815 under Captain William Webley. *Swiftsure* too was out of commission at Portsmouth by 1816. Congressional records show that an American seventy-four-gun ship of war, *Ganges*, was seized by the French in 1798. After this point there are numerous records of a ship called the *Ganges* transporting goods from such places as Bengal and Calcutta to U.S. ports. The British also have record of a *Ganges* working with Lord Nelson in the early years of the nineteenth century. This *Ganges* was out of commission at Plymouth, England, in October 1811 and was classified at this point as a hulk. It seems entirely likely that she could have served as a prison ship from that point on.

An Affecting Narrative

of the

Captivity and Sufferings

of

Thomas Nicholson

...Who Was Six Years

a Prisoner

among the Algerines

An Affecting Narrative of the Captivity and Sufferings of Thomas Nicholson (1816) was published to stir up powerful feelings of outrage among readers of the early Republic. As a fictitious account of a Barbary captivity, the narrative was a textual commodity created to compete in Boston's literary marketplace. Published twice in Boston, by Henry Trumbull in 1816 and by Nathaniel Coverly in 1818, the text relates the six years Nicholson spent as a slave in Algiers. Like the more popular but equally fictitious narrative of Maria Martin, the Nicholson text is filled with sensational scenes of cruelty and servility.

Once captured by an "Algerine corsair" in the vicinity of Gibraltar, Nicholson—as he was depicted—was taken to Algiers, where he and other captured Americans were forced to grovel in front of the dey by "licking the dust as a token of our reverence and submission." Equally conventional, Nicholson was next taken to the "market place," where he was exposed with other "articles for sale." Purchased by an "austere man" who treated his slaves with "much severity," Nicholson was set to work carrying "large rocks and stones." Declaring that he preferred "death to such cruel slavery," he joined two other American captives in a "desperate plan to escape." The three were soon captured, however, and Nicholson watched as his two companions were impaled alive in a public spectacle of ritualized atrocity. For his part, he received a bastinado and was forced to wear a heavy "log yoke" for two years. After five years in "bitter bondage,"

Nicholson met a former shipmate, and the two escaped by swimming to a British ship in the harbor and hiding in a water cask until the vessel departed.

The conventional scenes and exclamations indicate that the writer was familiar with the Barbary genre. The narratives of Maria Martin and John Foss offer similar scenes and exclamations. To make the narrative more marketable, however, the writer added "A Concise Description of Algiers," adapted from James Wilson Stevens's *An Historical and Geographical Account of Algiers* (1797, 1800). An equally obvious marketing strategy was the inclusion of a brief narrative supplement concerning Stephen Decatur's 1815 voyage to subdue the Barbary powers. Decatur and his squadron were successful in forcing Algiers to sign a favorable treaty, and in 1816—the year the Nicholson text first appeared—he returned in triumph to the United States. Obviously, the writer of the Nicholson text intended to exploit the market value of both Decatur and the "barbarians" in Algiers who enslaved Americans.

In 1818 Nathaniel Coverly reprinted the Nicholson text, and a third printer, G. Walker, also produced a separate edition (most likely in 1816). The Nicholson text was later published in a compilation of several Barbary captivity texts, *Narratives of American Captives in Tripoli and Algiers* (ca. 1922). The copy text used in this anthology is the 1816 Trumbull text.

DW

The particulars of my birth, parentage and former adventures of my life, are deemed too unimportant to the public to record in this compendious journal of my late sufferings—let it suffice to say, that my parents (whom I have been informed were respectable, tho' poor) left me an orphan at five years of age—ever since which unhappy period misfortune has appeared to mark me as her own. At the age of 13 I turned my attention to the sea, which I have since followed for a livelihood;—on the 3d day of January 1809, I entered on board the brig Sally, of Philadelphia, bound up the Straits—on the 10th we set sail with a fair wind, and soon cleared the capes of the Deleware—nothing occurred during our passage worthy of record until the morning of the 4th February, when within sight of Giberaltar, we discovered a sail bearing down upon us, which proved to be an Algerine corsair!—as we had no large guns, and but few small arms, we were not in a situation to repel an attack, nor was there sufficient wind to favour our escape.[1] In a short time the Barbarians were along side, and although we hauled down our colours as a token of submission, they fired several shots into us, and then boarding us with sword in hand, commenced an outrageous attack upon our whole crew—for near a quarter of an hour they unmercifully beat and maimed us, and probably would have continued it much longer had we

AN
AFFECTING NARRATIVE
OF THE
CAPTIVITY & SUFFERINGS
OF
THOMAS NICHOLSON,
[A NATIVE OF NEW JERSEY.]
Who has been Six Years a PRISONER among the
ALGERINES,
And from whom he fortunately made his escape
a few months previous to Commodore DECA-
TURE's late Expedition.

TO WHICH IS ADDED,

A CONCISE DESCRIPTION OF
ALGIERS,
OF THE CUSTOMS, MANNERS, &c. OF THE
NATIVES,
AND SOME PARTICULARS OF
Com. Decatur's late Expedition
AGAINST THE BARBARY POWERS.

"There dwell the most forlorn of human kind
Immured though unaccused, condemned, untried,
Cruelly spared, and hopeless of escape."

BOSTON,
Printed by H. TRUMBULL.—1816.

Title page of *An Affecting Narrative of the Captivity and Sufferings of Thomas Nicholson* (1816 edition; courtesy of the American Antiquarian Society)

THOMAS NICHOLSON,

[A NATIVE OF NEW JERSEY.]

Who has been Six Years a Prisoner among the

ALGERINES,

Illustration from *An Affecting History of the Captivity and
Sufferings of Thomas Nicholson,* "Thomas Nicholson"
(1816 edition; courtesy of the American Antiquarian Society)

not sought refuge below;—the hatches were now closed upon us, and we were here confined forty-eight hours, without food of any kind and nothing on which to repose ourselves but the rolling casks. On the morning of the 3d day from that of our confinement, we were ordered on deck, and all of us conveyed on board of the corsair, which proceeded immediately for Algiers, within sight of which we arrived on the 10th—as the barbarians passed the castle which defends the harbour, they fired a salute, which the castle returned, we then entered the port. The prisoners, fifteen in number of us, were then conducted to the castle, where we were taken charge of by the Dey's troops, who confined us in a stinking and dismal apartment of the castle. The next day, we were conducted to a cleansing house, where our bodies were cleanly washed, and our heads and beards closely shaved; we were then cloathed in coarse linen drawers, a strait waistcoat of the same without sleeves, and a loose coat over the whole, with a pair of leather slippers upon our feet, and upon our heads a blue cotten cap—thus garbed we were informed that we were the next day to appear before the Dey, who in person was to select two from among our number, to which number he was entitled. The next morning we were accordingly paraded in front of the castle, the guards then formed a hollow square. We were all blind folded and followed by an immense rabble, who were permitted to pelt us with clubs and stones until we came to the palace of the Dey. Here the gates were unlocked and thrown open, and we were conducted into a spacious court yard, at one end of which the Dey was seated, upon a low stage covered with rich carpeting—he was surrounded by his principal officers, civil and military: and on each side about 1000 of his foot guards were drawn up in the form of a half moon.

The Dey appeared to be about sixty years of age, small in stature, with a long white beard. He was cloathed in a Turkish habit. We were directed by turns to approach the foot of the eminence—when within a few paces, we were made to throw ourselves upon the earth and creep towards the Dey, licking the dust as a token of reverence and submission. As each captive approached, he was commanded to rise, pull off his slippers, and stand in the most degrading posture with his face bowed to the ground. To some the Dey put questions by his drogaman, or interpreter, others were dismissed by a wave of the hand. After a few moments consultation among the officers, one of them came to where the prisoners were paraded and selected two from our number, who received the Dey's mark on their breasts. The remainder of us being considered as private property, another selection was made by the captain and owners of the corsair, and the few of us left were reserved for another fate.

On the next market day, we were stripped of the dress, in which we appeared at court. A narrow piece of cloath was wrapped round our loins, and a coarse cloak thrown over our shoulders. We were then exposed to public sale in the market place, a spacious square, enclosed by ranges of low buildings, in different sections of which were exposed the various articles intended for sale. Here were camels, mules, asses, goats, hares, dromedaries, women and men, and all other creatures, whether for appetite or use. The women slaves were concealed in a latticed shop, but the men were exposed in open view. The barbarians were very critical in their examination of our limbs, to see if they were free from any defect—they made us walk, run, lie down, and lift large stones of seventy pounds weight. I was purchased by a young man who lived in the interior, who compelled me to lie down in the street, and take his foot and place it upon my neck, as a token of submission and obedience to him. I was then pinioned and mounted upon a mule, and by three slaves conducted to the house of my new master. He was an austere man, and treated his slaves (of which he had a number) with much severity. Our constant employment was to dig out of the earth large rocks and stones, which we were compelled to convey to a considerable distance on our backs—I, unaccustomed to such kind of labour, sometimes became almost exhausted—my unfortunate fellow slaves, who had been longer in captivity than myself, and more habituated to hardship, often assisted me, and rendered my share of the labour less difficult to perform. As the whole of us had a certain proportion of work allotted us each day, my kind fellow-prisoners had it in their power to favour me, and would often perform a portion of my share of the task. We were at night confined in a dark and loathsome cell, where a few rotten branches were only allowed us on which to repose our wearied limbs—our food was inferior to that allowed their cattle, a few ounces of stinking meat, and a few rotten dates, composed our principal meals—this coarse fare, and constant fatigue soon reduced me to a skeleton, yet, I was enabled to perform my daily task, which I did for nearly two years, when an event happened that cost two of my unfortunate fellow captives their lives, and came very near depriving me of my own.[2]

Rather prefering death to such cruel slavery, and despairing of ever gaining our liberty by the interference of our countrymen, three of us formed a desperate plan to escape, which was to murder our overseer, and then make the best of our way to the city where we thought probable that we might be enabled to get safe on board of some European vessel. The day on which we were to put our plan into execution, at length arrived—at the instant our overseer was stooping to give some necessary directions with regard to the work, one of my companions struck him upon the head with a spade, which brought him to the ground, in which situation they bound him and threw him into a deep well situated but a short distance therefrom. We now bent our course toward the city, but we had not proceeded above five miles when we were pursued and overtaken. The overseer it appeared was not so much injured and disenabled as we conceived him to be, being only stunned by the blow which he received he soon recovered, and succeeded without any personal injury in extrecating himself from the well. I and my two wretched companions were now bound hand and foot and conveyed before a council of Mufties, to receive our sentence—the overseer was himself present and identified my two unfortunate fellow prisoners as the ones from whom he had received the injury, their awful sentence was consequently pronounced by the chief Mufti, which was—"to be impailed alive for attempting to take the life of their overseer!"—Early the ensuing morning we were all conducted to an extensive plain to witness the horrid spectacle. When we arrived at the plain, we found, surrounding a small enclosure, a large concourse of people, and among them great numbers who appeared to be slaves like ourselves. In the centre of the enclosure there was a frame erected, something resembling a gallows; on the centre of which a pole or strong stake was erected, sharpened at the end and pointed with steel. A band of music commenced playing, and at the very instant a party of armed guards approached the scaffold, accompanied by one of my late wretched companions, whom they compelled to mount upon the stage, with all the agonies of despair in his countenance.

To detail minutely the horrid proceedings of these merciless barbarians, would too much wound the sensibility of my humane readers—suffice it to say that, after they had stripped the sufferer naked, they inserted the iron pointed stake into the lower termination of the vertebrae, and thence forced it up near his back bone, until it appeared between his shoulders, avoiding the vital parts. The stake was then raised in the air, and the poor sufferer exposed to the view of the other slaves, writhing in all the contortions of insupportable agony. In this shocking situation he remained about half an hour, when he was taken down and beheaded—in the same manner did my other unfortunate companion next suffer—after which I was called to appear before the Muftis, to receive my sentence!—it was at this moment that I felt a cold chill run over my whole body!—I had witnessed the late cruel punishment inflicted upon my wretched fellow prisoners, with whom I had been concerned in their attempt to escape from slavery, nor could I expect otherwise than to meet with a similar fate!—but, contrary to my expectations, I soon found that as I was not implicated with my companions, in their attempt to destroy the life of the overseer, more lenity was to be shewn me, my life was to be spared!—but I was sentenced to undergo the bastinado, which are severe blows inflicted upon the feet with a broad strip of ass hide—in addition to which, I was sentenced to wear constantly upon my neck for the term of two years, a log yoke, of twenty pounds weight, and to toil with my head uncovered for the same length of time! [—See Plate.][3]

The bastinadoing was immediately inflicted upon me in presence of the other slaves, and the next day the yoke was affixed to my neck, and I, deprived of my cloth cap, was ordered out with the other slaves of my master to perform my daily task. My heavy yoke soon made my neck intolerable soar, which added to the acute pain which I constantly endured, in consequence of the powerful rays of the sun beating down upon my bare head, in a short time brought on a fit of sickness and rendered me unfit for labour. I was permitted to remain in my filthy apartment during my illness, but no attendance was allowed me, nor was my food different from that allowed the other slaves, nor could I obtain the removal of my yoke for a single hour, which continued to inflame my neck to a very great degree, nor was I without my apprehensions that a mortification would ensue—the pain occasioned thereby at length brought on me a settled fever which reduced me to a mere skeleton, and rendered me unable to raise my hand to my head. My only visitor was a renegado Turk, whose business it was to bury the dead—for several weeks he did not fail to call each day with his grave digging implements, expecting no doubt to find me dead—he indeed appeared so anxious to perform this last office for me, that on his entrance and finding that the breath of life had not yet become quit extinct, he would apparently in a rage toss me over with his spade, and after bestowing upon me a few of his Turkish epithets, he would quit me. When I came to my speech, I begged of him either to obtain the consent of my master to have my yoke removed for a few days, or to knock me on the head with his spade, and at once put an end to my sufferings—but I found my intreaties availed nothing with this flint hearted monster, who seemed pleased rather to increase than diminish my torments.

For nearly four months I remained in this distressing situation when I obtained sufficient strength to crawl upon my hands and knees a few rods from my hut, dragging my yoke after me like a dumb beast. As soon as I gained sufficient strength to walk on my feet, I was again ordered to accompany the other slaves, and to perform with them the task assigned me. To break hard rocks with heavy mauls, and transport large stones upon our backs up the craggy sides of the quarry were our common labours; and to drink stagnated water, and to eat black barley bread and stinking jerk beef, our daily fare; while the few hours, allotted to rest upon our filthy beds, were disturbed by the tormenting insects, with which the country abounds.

I had now been five years in bitter bondage, and I began to dispair of ever again visiting the happy shores of my native country, or of ever again enjoying my liberty—my countrymen at home it appeared to me, were either ignorant of my situation, or was unwilling to pay the price demanded for me by the Dey, indeed I knew not how to account for their remissness, as I had not then heard of the war between Great Britain and America. I now felt determined at all events to make one more desperate attempt to escape from these unprincipled barbarians, let the consequence be whatever it might. My master having removed to the city, there was indeed a better prospect of succeeding than before—there were frequently European vessels in the harbour, yet it was death for a slave to be caught boarding one of them, unless by permission of the Dey.

As I was one day passing through one of the public streets of the city, with a heavy load upon my back, I unexpectedly met the second mate of the brig, which was the first of my shipmates that I had seen since the day of our separation. We conversed but a few moments together, as christian slaves are forbidden upon peril of severe punishment, to hold any conversation with each other in the public streets—by him I was first informed of the late war between America and Great Britain, he having received his information from the mate of an English brig, then in the harbour—on board this brig, with the assistance of the mate, he had lain a plan to escape—which was to swim off to the brig the evening previous to her sailing, on board of which the mate had engaged to secret him—he pressed me hard to accompany him, observing that "even death was preferable to slavery—that if we let pass this opportunity, we might never meet with another;"—as I had myself formed the determination to make another attempt to escape the first opportunity that should offer, I did not hesitate to agree to the proposal of my fellow captive, whom I engaged to meet at the hour and place appointed.

Three days after I accordingly met my friend at eight in the evening—the brig was to sail the next morning—we succeeded in passing the centinels undiscovered, and reached the shore, where after stripping off the few rags attached to us, we plunged into the sea, determined either to perish therein, or to succeed in our attempts to reach the brig, which lie at anchor at the distance of one mile—we had both tide and surf against us, but although nearly exhausted, we both fortunately succeeded in reaching the brig—The mate who had been looking out for us with anxious expectation gladly received us on board, although as naked as when we entered the world—from the captain and all on board we received the kindest treatment, who after providing us with cloathes, food, liquor, &c. stowed us snugly away in a water cask, in the hold, as a place of the most safety, in case search should be made for us on board.

By the dawn of day the barbarians were along side in quest of us—they commenced a thorough search of every part of the brig, every cask, box, &c. in her hold was hoisted upon deck—as a discovery of our persons would have subjected us to a most cruel death, the reader, to judge correctly of our feelings at this moment, should imagine himself in a similar situation. After a strict search of two hours they quit us, and the captain was permitted to proceed to sea!—Happy moment!—in a few hours we were uncasked and called upon deck to take a final leave of the Barbary coast, which was then but just discernable. We had a short and pleasant passage to London, where I had the pleasure of once more walking on christian ground.—It was here that I was happy to hear that the war between America and Great Britain had terminated, and that the former was about fitting out an Expedition against the Barbary powers, to demand a release of her subjects.

A Concise Description of Algiers, &c.

Algiers is situated in the bay of that name, and built upon the sea shore, an eminence, which rises above it, and which naturally gave the distinction of the upper and lower city. Towards the sea, it is strengthened with vast fortifications, which are continued upon the mole, which secures the port from storms and assaults. It contains one hundred and sixty mosques, two hundred and fifty public baths, and innumerable coffee houses. The mosques are large stone buildings, not lofty in proportion to their extent on the ground, and have usually erected, upon their corners, small square towers or minarets, whence the inferiour priests call the people to prayers. The coffee houses or rooms are generally piazzas, with an opening over them, projecting from the front of the houses into the streets. Here the inhabitants delight to loll, to drink sherbet, sip coffee, and chew opium, or smoak tobacco, steeped in a decoction of this exhilarating drug.

The inhabitants say, Algiers contains twenty thousand houses, one hundred and sixty thousand believers, twenty one thousand Jews and six thousand christian slaves.

The men wear next their bodies a linen shirt, or rather chemise, and drawers of the same texture. Over their shirt a linen or silk gown, which is girded about their loins by a sash, in the choice of which they exhibit much fancy. In this dress their legs and lower extremity of their arms are bare. As an outer garment, a loose coat of coarser materials is thrown over the whole. They wear turbans, which are long pieces of muslin or silk curiously folded, so as to form a cap comfortable and ornamental. Slippers are usually worn, tho' the soldiers are provided with a sort of buskin, resembling our half boots. The dress of the women resembles that of the men, except that their drawers are longer, and their outside garment is like our old fashioned riding hoods. When the ladies walk the streets, they are muffled with bandages or handkerchiefs of muslin or silk over their faces, which conceals all but their eyes; and, if too nearly inspected, will let fall a large vail, which conceals them entirely. The men usually set cross legged upon mattresses, laid upon low seats at the sides of the room. They loll on cushions at their meals; and after their repasts, occasionally indulge with a short slumber. They cook their provisions to rags or pap, and eat it with their fingers, tho' the better sort use spoons. Their diversions consist in associating in the coffee houses, in the city, and, in the country under groves, where they smoke and chat, and drink cooling not inebriating liquors. Their more active amusements are riding and throwing the dart, at both which they are very expert. They sometimes play at chess and drafts, but never at games of chance or for money, these being expressly forbidden by the alcoran.

That extreme caution, which separates the sexes in elder life, is also attached to the youth. In Algiers, the young people never collect to dance, converse, or amuse themselves with the innocent gaieties of their age. Here are no theatres, balls, or concerts; and, even in the public duties of religion, the sexes never assemble together. An Algerine courtship would be as disagreeable to the hale youth of New-England, as our common courtships would be disgusting to the Musselman. The young Algerine never sees the face of his intended bride until after the nuptial ceremony is performed; and even some days after she has been brought home to his own house. The old people frequently make the match, or if it originates with the youth, he confides his wishes to his father or some respectable relation, who communicates the proposal to the lady's father. If he receives it favourably, the young couple are allowed to exchange some unmeaning messages, by an old nurse of the family. The bride's father or her next male kin, with the bridegroom, go before the Cadi and sign a contract of marriage, which is attested by the relatives on each side. The bridegroom then pays a stipulated sum to the bride's father; the nuptial ceremony is performed in private, and the bridegroom retires. After some days, the bride is richly arrayed, accompanied by females, and conveyed in a covered coach or waggon, gaudy with flowers, to her husband's house. Here she is immediately immured in the women's apartments, while the bridegroom and his friends share a convivial feast. After some trifling ceremonies, the bridegroom enters the women's apartment, and for the first time discovers whether his wife has a nose or eyes.

Within a limited time, the husband may break the contract, provided he will add another item to that already given, return his bride with all her paraphernalia; and, putting the holy alcoran to his breast, assert that he never benefited himself of the rights of an husband.

Notwithstanding the apparent restraint, the women are under, they are said to be attached to their husbands, and enjoy greater liberty than is generally conceived.

Their funerals are decent but not ostentatious. The corps, carried upon a bier, is preceded by the priests, chanting passages from the alcoran in a dolorous tone. Wherever the procession passes, the people join in this dirge. The relatives follow with the folds of their turbans loosened. The bodies of the rich are deposited in vaults, those of the poor, in graves. A pillar of marble is erected over them, with an unblown rose carved on the top for the unmarried.

At certain seasons, the women of the family join a procession in close habits, and proceed to the tomb or grave, and adorn it with garlands of flowers. When these processions pass, the slaves are obliged to throw themselves on the ground with their faces in the dust, and all, of whatever rank, cover their faces.

It is a question frequently asked in the United States, why the European Powers do not suppress the Algerine depredations? We answer, that this must be effected by a union of the European maratime powers with the Grand Seignior; by a combination among themselves; or by an individual exertion of some particular state. A union of the European powers with the Grand Seignior most probably would be attended with success; but this is not to be expected; as it never can be the interest of the sublime Porte to suppress them, as his dominion over them is little more than nominal, he is anxious to conciliate their favour by affording them his protection; considering prudently, that though intractable, they are still a branch of the Mussulman stock. Provoked by their insults, he has sometimes withdrawn his protection, as was the case, when he by treaty with the Venetians permitted their fleet to enter the Ottoman ports, for the express purpose of destroying the Algerine gallies; but, it is obvious the sublime Porte meant merely to chastise not to ruin them.

In the Grand Seignior's wars with the Europeans, the piratical states have rendered signal services, and he himself not unfrequently receives valuable presents for exerting his supposed influence over them, in favour of one or another of the contending powers of Europe. While the Grand Seignior reaps such solid advantages from them, it is absurd to predicate upon his cooperation against them; neither can a union of the European powers be more fully anticipated. But, if ever a confederacy of the European powers should be formed against the Algerines, experience affords us but slender hopes of its success.

The detail of the history of the Algerines evinces, that the arms of individual states can be attended with no decisive success. Indeed, the expense of an efficacious armament would defray the price of the Dey's friendship for years; and the powers of Europe submit to his insults and injuries from a principle of economy. An absolute conquest of the Algerine territory cannot be effected but by invasion from the interiour, through the co-operation of the Grand Seignior or the assistance of the other Barbary states. The former we have shewn cannot be predicated, and the latter, for obvious reasons, is as little to be expected. A permanent conquest of the city and port of Algiers cannot be effected, without the subjection of the interiour country. Temporary though spirited attacks upon that city and port, have never answered any salutary purpose. It should be considered, likewise, that the houses of the Algerines are built of slight and cheap materials; that upon the approach of an enemy, the rich effects of the inhabitants are easily removed inland, while nothing remains but heavy fortifications to batter, and buildings, which can be easily restored, to destroy. The following anecdote will shew how sensible the Algerines themselves are of these advantages. When the French vice admiral, the Marquis de Quesne, made his first attack on Algiers, he sent an officer with a flag on shore, who magnified the force of his commander, and threatened to lay the city in ashes, if the demands of the marquis were not immediately complied with. The Dey, who had upon the first approach of the enemy, removed the aged, the females and his richest effects, coolly enquired of the officer how much the levelling his city to ashes would cost. The officer thinking to encrease the Dey's admiration of the power of the Grand Monarch, answered two millions of livres. Tell your commander, said the Dey, if he will send me half the money I will burn the city myself!

Some Particulars of Com. Decatur's Late Expedition.

The Dey of Algiers having previous to our late war with Great Britain, declared war against the United States, by the aid of his piratical cruizers, many of our countrymen were so unfortunate as to fall into the merciless hands of the Barbarians, by whom they were doomed to the most abject slavery. The late unhappy contest between America and Great Britain, rendered it difficult for the former to afford her unhappy subjects that immediate assistance which she otherwise would have done;—but, as soon as the war was terminated the liberation of these unfortunate people occupied her immediate attention. An Expedition under the gallant DECATUR, was fitted out with all possible dispatch—which, comprised of the Frigate Guerriere, Com. DECATUR—Macedonian, capt. Jones—Constellation, capt. Gordon—Brig Epervier, lieut. Downs—Sloop Ontario, lieut. Elliot—Schooners, Torch, Chancey, and Spitfire, Dallas—sailed from New York in the month of May last—not for the degrading purpose of conveying a tribute to Algiers but for the noble purpose of demanding from the cannon's mouth, the liberation of their countrymen.

The squadron reached Gibraltar on the 13th and 14th June, in safety, although previously separated in a gale—they proceeded immediately on their destined expedition. At Gibraltar the Commodore obtained information of the Algerine squadron being out, a part of which he soon after fell in with and engaged—the result of the engagement was, the capture of two Algerine frigates, two sloops of war, and several smaller vessels—the Messoda, an Algerine frigate of 46 guns, 500 men, bearing the Admiral's flag, was fought by the Guerriere alone, to which she struck after an action of one hour, losing 24 men killed and a considerable number wounded—the Guerriere had 7 wounded only.

Commodore Decatur now proceeded for Algiers and anchored off the port, and was soon in readiness to commence a siege of the place—but the very name of DECATUR was sufficient to deter the Barbarians from any attempts of resistance—they expressed a wish to make a peace upon any terms that the Commodore should dictate, whom they politely invited on shore for the purpose—but the gallant Decatur refused to have the treaty concluded on shore, or on any other spot than the quarterdeck of the Guerriere! and it was there the Dey was compelled in person to sign a Treaty, in substance as follows:—All the American Prisoners to be given up, and all captured property restored—the Dey of Algiers to indemnify the American Government for the full expence of the Expedition—No tribute hereafter to be paid and American property to be respected. After the treaty had been concluded the Dey requested of the Commodore as a favour, to restore the vessels he had captured, stating that he (the Dey) was apprehensive of being assassinated by his own subjects should he refuse to give them up, from which circumstance the Commodore made a donation of them to the Dey. The Commodore sailed from Algiers on the 10th July, and arrived off Tripoli on the 15th, where he obtained restitution for an American prize (25,000 dolls.) and the freedom of the Christian slaves, with the promise of future good behaviour.[4]

Thus the Algerines and the Tripolitans have been reduced to humiliating terms by the gallant DECATUR. He has given them such an *electric shock* as was never before discharged from a christian battery. He demanded from the Barbarians, as a member of the christian family, a release "of all Christian prisoners," and obtained it.—This is a Glory, which never encircled the brows of a Roman Pontiff; nor blazed from an imperial diadem.

Notes

1. There is no historical record of an American brig *Sally* being taken by an Algerian corsair. The name, however, was plausible. *Betsy*, *Polly*, and *Eliza* were all ships taken by Barbary pirates. Algiers had declared war on the United States in 1785 and again nearly two decades later in 1814.

2. Stories of American captives forced to carry heavy loads were well known. Historically, many captured Americans were forced to carry stones from quarries outside the city to the harbor to help build sea walls and piers. For a similar account, see the narrative of John Foss.

3. Gruesome accounts of Barbary torture and execution had been commonly reported for over two centuries. Descriptions of impalements and burnings were particularly common. For similar descriptions, see the narratives of John Foss and Maria Martin included in this collection.

4. Stephen Decatur Jr. was one of the most illustrious and celebrated naval heroes from the early national period. In 1804 he had gained much fame for his daring raid to burn the captured ship *Philadelphia* in the Tripoli harbor. Although it contains some slight inaccuracies, Nicholson's account of the *Guerriere*'s victory over the *Meshuda* is generally correct. Negotiations with the new dey of Algiers, however, were carried out by both William Shaler, the new Barbary consul general, and Decatur. After his triumphant return late in 1815, Decatur was toasted at banquets and honored at commemorations throughout the United States. It seems likely that the writers of the Nicholson narrative wrote the text in an attempt to capitalize on Decatur's fame. For accounts of Decatur's exploits, see Allison and Wheelen.

A Journal

of the

Shipwreck and Sufferings

of

Daniel Foss

The writer or writers of *A Journal of the Shipwreck and Sufferings of Daniel Foss* (1816) would have us believe that it is a message in a bottle, the memoir of a castaway, lone survivor of the ship *Negociator*. And it is, in its way—like *Robinson Crusoe*—full of lessons of self-reliance, the trials of captivity, and the eventual joys of liberty. The text reproduced here, published by Nathaniel Coverly of Boston, claims that Daniel Foss, from Elkton, Maryland, was shipwrecked on November 26, 1809, and "lived five years on a small barren Island—during which he subsisted on Seals, and never saw the face of any human creature." It was published in 1816 and was apparently quite popular, for it was reproduced at least three more times that same year. All four printings were produced in Boston by other publishers and present similar texts and title pages, yet a Thomas Hazard edition lists Foss as from St. Mary's, Georgia, and the shipwreck date as November 26, 1811. It is as well the source for the engraving that features Foss displaying his wrought oar and sealskin clothes as evidence of his survival. This text has also been consulted in the case of a missing word or phrase in the Coverly edition. The text included in the present collection was reprinted in 1914 in *The Magazine of History with Notes and Queries* by W. Abbatt. The bulk of this tale was used by Jack London in his book *The Jacket (Star Rover)*, with interesting changes for a different reading public. As recently as 1990, the Foss narrative appeared in *Great Shipwrecks and Castaways: Authentic Accounts of Disaster at Sea*, originally published in 1980 by Dorsey, like Abbatt, in New York. In its most inventive incarnation, Foss's tale of survival has proved itself inspiration for a game entitled "Marooned" by Bruce Davis in the 2000 Interactive Fiction Competition.

The tale of Daniel Foss is highly entertaining, even if improbable. The crew of the *Negociator*, after her foundering, is in a bad way. The dingy is overfull, its residents underclothed, their rations precariously small. Exposure claims some, starvation others. Before land is hailed, the boat's last occupants must draw straws to see who will die for the benefit and sustenance of the remaining. In a desperate attempt to reach shore, Foss is the only passenger to reach dry ground, watching the others drown in the surf. His relief at reaching the island is short, for it is nothing but a pile of rocks, devoid of vegetation and fresh water. Deprived of the requirements for life, Foss descends into an animal state, similar to that of other captivity narratives: "Famine frequently leads men to the commission of the most horrible excesses—insensible, on such occasions, to the appeals of nature and reason, man assumes the character of a beast of prey." However, Providence is kind to our besieged castaway, and he is able to cheat death by eating a decaying seal and drinking rainwater. Against all odds, his luck holds out; he is able to endure on the flesh of seals, flying fish, and a beached whale alone for five years. And during this time, he constructs a house, a thirty-foot high wall, and a lookout tower completely from stone. However, his "improvements" to the island incomplete, Foss continues with his handicraft by grinding a water container out of stone and marking time and prayer on his only piece of wood, the steering oar from the lifeboat. Quite an accomplishment for a castaway armed only with a jack-knife. A notice on the title page assures us that it is not only possible but "truth," for the oar has been deposited in the Philadelphia Museum. The museum, when contacted, proved the suspicion that this fact was fiction, yet the narrative has endured.

With its gruesome details and familiar themes of conversion, captivity, and self-improvement, Foss's tale must have appealed greatly to early American audiences. The hero is able to tame the chaos of a deserted rock into a livable order. Out of the barest elements of existence—stone, flesh, and water—the maroon fashions a new world that reflects his needs and ingenuity. Simultaneously, he also masters his desire for society. Indeed, as Foss rises on the scale from subhuman to self-reliant solitary, he moves closer to an acceptance of God and his condition. "I was far more reconciled to my situation than thousand probably would have been," Foss states. "[U]pon this desolate island, where fate had placed me, I conceived myself far more happy than many, who, for ignominious crimes, were doomed to spin out their lives in solitary confinement."

The transformation of the Foss narrative in London's *The Jacket* is also noteworthy. In London's rendition, the psychological trials of the lonely survivor are enhanced to mirror the physical stress. Biblical symbolism, latent in the 1818 editions, are moved to the fore. This emphasis transforms Foss into a latter day Job, bereft of everything he once possessed—even his humanity. Connecting with the very beginnings of Christian mythology, Foss must conquer desires older than the castaway can understand: "It was the old Adam in me, I suppose—the taint of that first father who was the first rebel against God's commandments.

Most strange is man, ever insatiable, ever unsatisfied, never at peace with God or himself, his days filled with restlessness and useless endeavor, his nights a glut of vain dreams of desires willful and wrong. Yes, and also I was much annoyed by my craving for tobacco."

Jack London realized that Daniel Foss was a microcosm of the early Republic, the experience of an American Adam struggling for liberty against his desires and fears, pioneering regardless of the odds, and emerging victorious with the aid of God. Even over tobacco.

DB

On the 3d September, 1809, I sailed from Philadelphia, in the capacity of a Mariner on board the brig *Negociator*, JAMES NICOLL, master, bound to the North-West Coast, on a Sealing voyage—on the 20th October we touched at the Cape of Good Hope, from which we shaped our course for the Friendly Islands—as we proceeded north the weather became extremely cold, so that we were obliged to exchange our cloathing for such as were better calculated for the climate—on the 29th we passed several islands of ice, some of them nearly three miles in circuit, and sixty or seventy feet in height—this exhibited a view which for a few moments was pleasing to the eye; but when we reflected on the danger, the mind was filled with horror, for were a ship to get against the weather side of one of these islands when the sea runs high she would be dashed to pieces in a moment.

On the 25th November we experienced a severe snow storm the brig's sails and rigging were all hung with icicles—at twelve at night it blew a gale of wind and at half past two we struck an island of ice! The consternation we were thrown into by this unexpected shock—the fury of the storm—the darkness of night which surrounded us—the dashing of the waves against our stranded brig—and the prospect of an immediate death, which we was in momentary expectation of—created a scene of horror past description! As we found the brig in a sinking condition, we hastily threw into the long boat such articles of provision as could easily be got at, and embarked twenty-one of us in a small open boat, many hundred leagues from land, in a cold climate, and some without jackets, hats or shoes, myself having on only one thin jacket and a pair of trowsers—in five minutes after we left the brig, she went down.

At day-light the storm having somewhat abated, we had a chance to examine our little stock of provision, which was found small indeed for so great a number of us—it consisted of about 50 wt. of beef, half a barrel of pork, a barrel of water and a small keg of beer—we made such arrangements for the preservation of our lives as our miserable situation would admit of, every man was put on an

A

JOURNAL

OF THE

SHIPWRECK AND SUFFERINGS

OF

DANIEL FOSS,

[A Native of Elkton, Maryland.]

Who was the only person saved from on board the
brig *Negociator*, of PHILADELPHIA, which foundered in the Pacific Ocean, on the 26th Nov.
1809—and who lived five years on a small
barren Island—during which time he subsisted on Seals, and never saw the face
of any human creature.

☞ The public may rely on the truth of the proceeding narrative of the Shipwreck and Sufferings of D. Foss, who is now living with his
relatives in Elkton (Maryland) and has deposited in the Philadelphia Museum, the
OAR, which he so highly prized, and on
which he kept a reckoning of the
number of days he passed on the
dreary Island.

BOSTON—Printed for N, COVERLY, jr.—1816.

Title page of *A Journal of the Shipwreck and Sufferings
of Daniel Foss* (1816 Coverly edition; courtesy of the
American Antiquarian Society)

Illustration from *A Journal of the Shipwreck and Sufferings of Daniel Foss*, "Daniel Foss and his carved oar" (1816 Hazard edition; courtesy of the American Antiquarian Society)

allowance of provision and water, and an equal proportion of time allotted each to labour at the oars and to bail the boat, each being eager to claim his turn, as it was considered the only means to preserve our lives from the inclemency of the weather—but, these precautionary means did not avail, for in nine days from that of our leaving the brig, our number was reduced to eight, and four of these so severely frost bitten as to be unable to stand on their feet—to add to our misfortune, our water froze to a solid cake of ice, which we were obliged to cut off in small pieces, and dissolve it in our mouths.

As we had more to fear from the intense cold, than from the want of provision and water, our great object from the time of our leaving the brig, was to reach a warmer latitude, which on the 10th Jan. we succeeded in doing, but, alas! there were but three of us now remaining to experience a change of air, so eagerly wished for by my poor unfortunate companions. We continued to steer a South West course, but without the most distant prospect of discovering land, although five weeks had now passed since we left the brig—of our provisions we had eaten sparingly but we on the 20th consumed our last pound of pork!— death by starvation appeared now inevitable!—five days passed without being enabled to obtain any thing to satisfy the cravings of nature—we cut even our shoes in small pieces, which, after soaking in fresh water, we devoured with the keenest appetite.

We were now driven to the awful alternative of casting lots between us, to deter- mine who should die for the sustenance of the remaining two. Famine frequently leads men to the commission of the most horrible excesses—insensible, on such occasions, to the appeals of nature and reason, man assumes the character of a beast of prey; he is deaf to every representation, and cooly meditates the death of his fellow creature—fate had decreed that I should now myself take an active part in one of those shocking instances. Having cut a small piece of my jacket into three small detached pieces, one of which was marked with a brown thread, they were deposited in a hat, from which each with a trembling hand drew a piece—the unfortunate man on whom the lot fell had acted as Surgeon on board of the brig—he appeared perfectly resigned to his fate, "my friends," said he to us, "I am a native of Norfolk (Virg.) where I expect I have now a wife and three children living, the only favour that I have to request of you is, that should it please God to deliver either of you from your perilous situation, and should you be so fortunate as to reach once more your native country, that you would acquaint my unfortunate family with my wretched fate!"—he now requested of us a few moments to prepare himself for death, to which we could only reply with tears in our eyes, and which he employed in fervent prayer for himself, his family, and for our speedy deliverance. Having now informed us that he was ready to die, by his direction an incision was made in a vein of his left arm, while he caught and drank the blood which streamed from the wound!

We soon had the satisfaction to see our unfortunate companion expire without a struggle—the body we cut into small slices and dried as well as we could in the sun—such alone was our food for twelve days!—we must notwithstanding have perished ere this, had not the frequent rains supplied us with water, which we caught by wringing our cloathes when thoroughly wet, into a bucket, with which we bailed our boat—with this short allowance, which was rather tantalizing than sustaining in our comfortless condition, I and my only surviving companion now began to grow so feeble as to be unable to support ourselves long on our legs, and our cloathes being continually wet, our bodies were in many places, chafed into sores.

It was now nine weeks since the unfortunate night of our shipwreck—loathsome as our only food was, we had partaken of the last of it, when on the morning of the 5th March, we discovered breakers about two leagues ahead. We immediately shaped our course for them, and about noon discovered what we supposed to be land, which on our nearer approach proved to be a small island of about two miles in circumference, boardered with high craggy rocks, against which the sea broke with a tremendous roar. The next morning we approached the island as near as the surf would admit of, and rowed quite around it without discovering any place where we could attempt a landing with any degree of safety—this circumstance was borne by us with much impatience, for we had flattered ourselves that we should meet with fresh water at the first part of the land we might approach, and being thus disappointed, our hunger and thirst at length drove us to the extremity of even attempting a landing where there was indeed no small prospect of our being dashed to pieces.—Accordingly at half past four o'clock we steered the boat directly in for a point of rocks, but when within about an hundred yards of them, the surf upset our boat! at this critical juncture I was so fortunate as to seize an oar, with which I was enabled to buoy myself up until the swell of the sea carried me within reach of a shelving rock, which I was so fortunate as to ascend before the return of another sea—exhausted nature almost prevented my ascending the high and craggy rocks which lined the sea-broken shores of the whole island—having at length reached the summit, I looked around for my unfortunate companion, but, alas, nothing was discernable but broken fragments of the boat, which had been dashed into an hundred pieces by the surf, and which were now floating upon the foaming waves in all directions—thus did my dreary prospects become still more terrible when I beheld the last of my unfortunate shipmates perish in our most arduous struggle to preserve our existence!

As soon as I had recovered sufficient strength to walk, I proceeded in search of something to appease my hunger and thirst and to take a more minute view of the island—but, alas! what was my surprise, when I discovered that the island was barren of every thing that could serve to gratify the cravings of exhausted nature—not a shrub or plant did it produce of any kind, nor was there any appearance of springs of fresh water. This island, which had no appearance of having ever before been visited by any human creature, was about half a mile in length and a quarter in breadth, and composed wholly of rocks piled one upon another in all positions, as if tumbled together by the billows. As the succeeding night approached I sought a shelter beneath a large shelving rock, where on a little rock weed that I had collected, I attempted to repose my wearied limbs—in the night there was a heavy shower of rain, some of which I attempted to catch by spreading my jacket on the rocks, but in this I was disappointed, for it having been so frequently soaked with sea-water, that it had become quite impregnated with salt. Thus I had no other resource but to lie with my mouth open and catch the drops of rain as they fell. As soon as the day began to dawn I renewed my search for water, and found some in the holes of the rocks, but it was brackish, and not fit to drink—these holes I cleared out in hopes that I might thereby be enabled to obtain some fresh water, in case of another shower, which I earnestly prayed for. I was this day so fortunate as to find a few small shell fish of the size of snails, which I chewed to moisten my mouth. As night approached I again sought my lodging place, where I laid myself down, but with little expectation of ever again witnessing the rising sun—I had now been three days without food, and to add to my misery, my legs began to swell, and my whole body became so bloated, that notwithstanding the little flesh I had left, my fingers, with the smallest pressure upon my skin, sunk to the depth of an inch, and the impression remained for some moments afterwards—my eyes felt as if buried in deep cavities. It was at this moment that the recollection of the peaceful home and the fond parents whom I had left, at first uneasy on my account, anxiously expecting to hear from me; afterwards overwhelmed with grief at seeing the time elapse without receiving any intelligence; and at last condemned to bewail the loss of their son, during all the days of their old age. These serious reflections brought on such a fit of melancholly, that I lost all recollection for many hours. Toward morning I enjoyed for the first time upon the island an hour's sleep; perspiration took place, and I awoke as from a dream, free from delirium, but painfully alive to all the horrors that surrounded me.

As soon as I felt myself a little revived by the cheering rays of the sun, I once more crawled abroad in search of something to appease hunger and thirst, nor were my researches this day so fruitless as those on the preceding one—about noon I was so fortunate as to discover in the cavity of a rock, a dead Seal, which although in quite a putrid state, proved a most seasonable relief—without this discovery I must inevitably have perished.

Of my newly discovered food I had the precaution to eat sparingly, to avoid the dangerous consequences which might have resulted from my voracity in the debilitated state to which my stomach was reduced. Such parts of the carcase as remained I conveyed to my lodging place, and preserved for a future meal. The sun had now disappeared, and I should have enjoyed a tolerable night's rest, had not my insupportable thirst prevented it—but fortunately for me, the night proved a rainy one, which, although it was attended with heavy thunder and the sharpest lightning that I had ever before witnessed, yet as the rain fell in torrents it not only served to cool my parched tongue and lips, but enlivened my fondest hopes that the holes to the rocks, which I had cleared out for the purpose, would furnish me with a sufficient supply for present use.

Day light, which I awaited with great impatience, at length appeared. I has-tened to the several places which I had prepared for the reception of water and found them filled! "What a strange thing (as once said an object of wretchedness) is that called happiness!" How shall I express my extreme joy, when after being for three days deprived of a draught of sweet water, I was unexpectedly blessed with a sufficient quantity to last me, at least, ten days—"the fond lover (indeed) never rushed more eagerly to the arms of his bride; the famished tyger more ravenously on his prey, than I to partake of the reviving draught; I drank, rested, surveyed the precious liquid, drank again, and absolutely shed tears of pleasure!"[1]—and without once recollecting that I could not subsist on water alone, and that all the food that I had then the most distant prospect of ever obtaining, was the remaining part of the putrified carcase of the seal, which I had been so fortunate as to find the day preceding among the rocks.

I carefully covered over my rocky cisterns with flat stones, to secure their precious contents from the salt water, which would not unfrequently break with such fury upon the rocks, as to dash completely over the highest part of the island. Having done this, I again returned to the rock, which was the most comfortable shelter I could find on the island—I had here collected a considerable quantity of rock weed, which made me a tolerable bed. After partaking of a few mouthfulls of the seal (which was now nearly consumed) I stretched my self upon the bed, and attempted to gain that repose which nature required—but, those who have not experienced the irresistable power of sleep, after long watching and excessive fatigue, will scarcely believe that my repose was very short—this was nevertheless the case, my lodgings being of the most uncomfortable kind.

At daybreak I left my rocky cavern for the purpose of again searching among the rocks for something that might serve for food—a dead carcase in the most putrified state, would then have been considered by me of inestimable value. But what was my surprise, what my joy, to discover the rocks boardering upon the sea, covered with Seals, to the number as I judged of many thousands!—they appeared but little affrighted at my approach, but like a small fresh water turtle, creeped moderately into the sea as I advanced toward them. I ran directly for my OAR, which had once been the means of preserving my life, and which was now to be used as a principal instrument by which my food was to be obtained—indeed there was not another stick of wood of the smallest size upon the island. As I could easily approach them within reach of the oar, they fell an easy prey, a light blow upon the head was sufficient to stun them, so that they were easily taken. For the space of an hour I had fine sport, when they all (as if by a signal from their leader) instantly disappeared. With what a transport of pleasure did I now behold the rocks covered with their slain—judge reader if you can, what must have been the sensations of one nearly famished with hunger, who had for three days subsisted on the carcase of a seal, in a state of putrafaction, on beholding so unexpectedly before him, and at his disposal, such an immensity of (what was then indeed to me) good and wholesome food!

Fortunately for me, I had through my many hair breadth escapes, preserved my knife, with which I proceeded to cut the throats of the seals that they might bleed—their blood I drank as it oozed from their wounds, and thought it most delicious!—indeed I at this moment think that nothing could have been to me, in my then weak and emaciated state, more beneficial—nothing could have contributed more to my immediate relief—had I instead of thus satisfying myself with the blood, partook as heartily of the flesh, the effects might have proved fatal to me.

On numbering the Seals killed, I found them to exceed one hundred—a no inconsiderable quantity of provision indeed for the consumption of one man!—but so valuable did I esteem the acquisition, so sensible was I of the value of provision to me at this critical moment, that had the stay of the Seals and my strength admitted of it, it is probable that I should not have spared one of them—indeed I never made use of an eighth part of the number then destroyed.—Having skinned about a dozen of the largest of them, I cut them in thin pieces and spread them upon the rocks to dry—as I was not blessed with the priviledge of fire (the island producing nothing that could serve for fuel) the heat of the sun, which at mid-day was very powerful, I found a tolerable substitute, by the means of which my food was so far cooked as to render it tolerable palatable—and to add to my good fortune, in many of the hollows of the rocks, which in tempestuous weather had been filled by the surf, I found small quantities of salt, made by the evaporation of salt water.

Having been thus unexpectedly provided with provision and water (for which I did not forget to return thanks to that Being, through whose mercy I had been so meraculously preserved) a more comfortable shelter next demanded my attention. As I despaired of ever meeting with an opportunity that would enable me to quit this dreary island, I strove to reconcile myself to my situation as well as I could, and to employ my thoughts upon things that might serve to contribute to my convenience and comfort—I accordingly now projected a scheme of forming for myself as tolerable a dwelling as my situation, and the materials for building, would admit of.—I fixed upon a convenient spot upon the highest part of the island, being the only place inaccessible to the waves in tempestuous weather—as I had not yet fully recovered my strength, and as the building was to be constructed of such detached parts of rocks as I could manage, and they to be removed by bodily strength, I made but slow progress—it was indeed four weeks before I got my house completed, and rendered water proof—it was sufficiently spacious, containing three apartments, one for the deposit of provision, one to lodge in, and another an occasional retreat from foul weather or the heat of the sun by day—it was built in form of a sugar loaf, the walls of which were three feet thick, the whole of which I covered with dry rock wood.

Having thus completed my hut, I saw the importance of keeping some kind of reckoning of time, without which I was sensible that I should soon lose all knowledge of the day of the week, and not be enabled to distinguish one from another—but how was a reckoning to be kept, since I had neither pen, ink, or paper?—as I recollected that I possessed nothing brought with me but my jackknife and Oar, it occurred to my mind that with the assistance of the former, some kind of journal might be kept upon the latter—for this purpose I scraped the broad end of the oar and prepared it for the reception of such notches and characters as formed a kind of callander, by which I was enabled at all times to determine the day of the week and month—although I was thus doomed to spend my days in solitude, I never failed to pay due regard to the sabbath; and as the only mode of worship that I could adopt, I carved a short hymn, appropriate to my situation, on the oar, which I never failed to chaunt on the Sabbath.

The Seals whose unexpected appearance had afforded me such seasonable relief, and in a great measure dissipated my fears of starvation, I was happy to find were very frequently in the habit of visiting the island—not a week passed but I destroyed more or less of them.—As my cloathing had become much tattered and torn, I made me a complete suit of their skins; but for the want of proper management they became so dry and hard that I could wear them only occasionally—as I lost my hat in my attempt to effect a landing, of a part of my flannel shirt I made me a convenient cap.

The frequent rains continued to supply me with a sufficiency of water, which lodged in the holes of the rocks, of which there were many—but as they were subject to be filled with salt water, when there was a heavy sea, I found it necessary to prepare something for its reception in my hut—but how was a vessel to be formed, since I was in possession of no instrument by which one could be wrought?—as "necessity is the mother of invention," I at length hit upon a plan of forming a hallow in as large a stone as I could conveniently convey to my house, by means of other stones!—this was indeed an arduous task, but as "a continual dropping will wear a stone" so by an incessant pounding and grinding with smaller stones, in less than five weeks, I completely effected my object—I succeeded beyond my most sanguine expectations in forming a hallow that would contain four gallons of water. This stone vessel, of infinitely more value to me than a mere elegant piece of furniture, was carefully deposited in an apartment of my humble dwelling—but a smaller vessel to convey the water from the rocks to my jar, was still wanting, which I supplied myself with in a manner as above, but with less labour.

Thus I rendered my lonely situation as comfortable as could be expected—I had compleated me a snug and secure shelter, and as to provision, I had always on hand a six months supply, preserved by salting and drying—for these things so essential to preserve life, and which one could rarely have expected to have

obtained upon a barren island, I was sensible that I could not be too thankful.—
Although deprived of the priviledge of enjoying the society of even a single one
of my fellow-creatures, and with very little prospect of ever again seeing the face
of any human creature, I was far more reconciled to my situation than thousands
probably would have been—upon this desolate island, where fate had placed
me, I conceived myself far more happy than many, who, for ignominious crimes,
were doomed to spin out their lives in solitary confinement—however dreary
my prospects, I was not without hope that that providence which had cast me
upon these barren rocks, at the very moment when hunger threatened me with
dissolution, would finally direct some one to my relief.—If deprived of the society
of my fellow-creatures, and of the conveniences of life, I could not but reflect
that my forlorn situation was yet attended with some advantages—of the whole
island, tho small, I had a peaceable possession, and no one it was probable
would ever appear to dispute my claim, unless it was the amphibious animals
of the ocean!—as the island was almost inaccessible, at night my repose was not
disturbed by continual apprehensions of the approach of cannabels, or beasts
of prey!

After the first year I became still more reconciled to my wretched situation—I
continued to make such improvements in and about my dwelling as my helpless
situation would admit of—the second year I barricadoed my hut with a wall twenty
feet square, and ten feet in height—I was nearly two months in performing this
work, and as it completely defended my dwelling from the high winds, and the
spray of the sea, I did not conceive my time misspent.—I erected likewise near my
house, a pillar of rocks and stones, of about thirty feet in height—the foundation
was formed of as large rocks as I could conveniently work in, and upon these less
ones were laid, from which I made use of still smaller ones until I approached
the top.—The object of its erection was to enable me to discover from its peak
any vessel that might perchance pass the island—and that they might discover
me, I made a flag of my baze waistcoat,[2] which affixed to an end of the oar, I
occasionally erected from the summit of this rocky mass.

In the month of June, of the third year of my solitary confinement to the island,
I descryed a sail passing to the leeward, but at too great a distance to discover
me—the very appearance of this sail afforded me the greatest satisfaction—it
convinced me of a fact that I had before in a degree doubted (to wit.) that these
seas were sometimes visited by navigators, and that I might sometime or other
be so fortunate as to be discovered by them.

In the month of March, of the fourth year of my confinement, I experienced one
of the most tremendous storms, that perhaps was ever before witnessed by man—
it commenced at about nine in the evening, with the approach of black clouds
and a high wind from the south-west, which at ten increased to a hurricane—
attended with incessant peals of thunder and flashes of the sharpest lightning

that I had ever before witnessed—the sea, aggitated by the wind, dashed with such force against the island, that I was not without my apprehensions for its safety—over every part, except the little eminence on which my habitation was erected, it made a fair breach. It was now I saw the importance of the building which enclosed my lonely hut, without which, I am confident the latter could never have withstood the force of the wind, and I probably should have been crushed beneath its ruins, for had I attempted to have sought shelter elsewhere, I should have been swept into the sea.

It is frequently remarked, that the wind that blows no one any good is indeed an evil one—but in the present instance I was happy to find that this was not the case—as in the morning, the storm having subsided, I was not a little agreeably surprised to find the rocks covered with flying fish, among which there were many of the largest size!—this was indeed a treat to one who had been nearly four years confined to one particular kind of food—I picked six hundred of them up in less than half an hour, which I split and cured in the sun after the manner of cod. In visiting the south-west part of the island a few hours after, my surprise was again excited by the appearance of an enormous dead whale, which the sea had thrown high and dry upon the rocks—and what added to my astonishment, I discovered a harpoon (of the common form) buried in its bowels, with a few fathoms of new line attached thereto! Thus was my hopes again revived, that I should finally meet with an opportunity to quit the desolate island—the situation of the whale rendered it probable that these seas were frequented by whalemen, although this whale might have been struck many hundred leagues to windward.

As I had now made sure of at least a year's provision, I employed my time in sketching upon my oar, minutes of the most remarkable incidents that had attended me since I quit the peaceful shores of America—this I rendered as intelligible as possible, the letters being of the smallest kind, a dozen letters were a day's work for me.—And lest it should be my hard fortune never to meet with the long wished for opportunity, to return to my friends, the last year of my residence upon this island, I engraved or nitched upon the broad end of the oar, an account of my ill fate, &c. thinking that it might in some future day fall into the hands of some one, who might possibly visit the island, and who would give the information requested—the following is a copy of the engraving:—

"This is to acquaint the person into whose hands this Oar may fall, that DANIEL FOSS, a native of Elkton, in Maryland, one of the United States of America, and who sailed from the port of Philadelphia, in 1809, on board the brig Negociator, bound to the Friendly Islands, was cast upon this desolate island the February following, where he erected a hut, and lived a number of years, subsisting on seals—he being the last who survived of the crew of said brig, which ran foul of an island of ice, and foundered on the 25th Nov. 1809.

Said Foss earnestly requests that information of his fate and that of his ship-mates may be made known to their friends in America."

The Oar which had proved so serviceable to me in my destitute situation, and which now contained a record of my own fate and that of my shipmates, I spared no pains to preserve—as it was the only substitute for a flag staff that I could procure, to secure it from the weather, I made a covering of seal skins for it. When it could be spared, I never failed to keep it erected upon the summit of my rocky observatory, with the baze flag attached to it, that notice might be given to any vessel that might pass within view of the island, of its being inhabited—nor was this wise plan finally without its desired effect.

Having been considerably indisposed for two or three days previous to that of my happy deliverance, I did not arise until late in the morning, when, ascending my observatory, as I was accustomed to do, it is impossible for me to describe my feelings on discovering a ship with topsails a back, nearly within hail of the island!—That I might be discovered, I swung my cap in the air, and jumped from rock to rock, and soon had the satisfaction of seeing them looking at me with their spy glasses—I now made every motion I possibly could indicative of my distressed situation—which they answered by pointing to an extreme point of the island—thither I hastened and discovered their boat (which I had not before noticed) with three men attempting a landing, but were prevented by the surf.—After making several unsuccessful attempts, by their motions they signified to me that they must return to the ship without being enabled to effect their object!—But, at the greatest risk of my life, I was determined not to let this opportunity to quit the desolate island, pass unimproved. I seized my oar, and with it plunged headlong through the foaming surf, and was unaccountably successful in reaching the boat, which conveyed me immediately on board the ship!

The Ship proved to be the *Neptune*, Capt. Call, of New York, to which port she was bound from Batavia[3]—the captain declared that he should have passed the island unnoticed, had he not observed my flag, which he conceived erected as a signal of distress. By contrary winds the Neptune had been driven far out of her course, otherwise she would not have fell in with the island, which capt. C. could not find laid down in any map or chart whatever. My being finally relieved by a vessel bound to my own country, was indeed a fortunate circumstance—but from my very odd appearance, the captain and crew at first could hardly credit my being one of their countrymen—my cloathing was in a very tattered condition, and my beard more than a foot in length. My much regarded Oar, on which I had wrought so much, was viewed by all on board as a very great curiosity, which I have since my return presented to the keeper of the Philadelphia Museum, where it is lodged for the inspection of the curious. We had a quick and pleasant passage to New York, from whence I returned to my friends in Maryland, from whom I had been more than six years absent.

Notes

1. Quotes in this paragraph are taken from *The Life of Baron Frederick Trench: containing his adventure, his cruel and excessive sufferings, during ten years imprisonment, at the fortress of Magdeburg, by command of the late King of Prussia*, first published in Dublin in 1792 by T. Henshall, first American printing in 1793 by William Greenough of Boston and Peter Edes of Bangor, Maine. This was obviously a very popular text of the time, considering the number of printings during the next two decades.

2. *Baze*, also spelled *baize:* a loosely woven fabric napped to imitate felt.

3. In the nineteenth century, Batavia was the capital of the Netherlands Indies and headquarters of the Dutch East India Company. An important port in the region, it came to be known as Jakarta in modern Indonesia.

NARRATIVE

OF THE

TRAGICAL DEATH OF MR. DARIUS BARBER, AND HIS SEVEN CHILDREN, WHO WERE INHUMANLY BUTCHERED BY THE INDIANS

On December 8, 1829, in his first annual address to the Congress, President Andrew Jackson announced his policy of Indian "emigration," noting that extinction "surely awaits them if they remain within the limits of the states [and that] humanity and national honor demand that every effort should be made to avert so great a calamity." By December 3, 1833, in his fifth annual message, Jackson was less generous, contending that "those [eastern Indians] have neither the intelligence, the industry, the moral habits, nor the desire of improvement which are essential to any favorable change in their condition. Established in the midst of another and a superior race, and without appreciating the causes of their inferiority or seeking to control them, they must necessarily yield to the force of circumstances and ere long disappear." Yet long before he became president, Jackson had been working on the "Indian problem."

Jackson first began to work on the "Indian problem" as a frontier fighter. After the Creek War of 1814, during which he established himself as an effective and brutal Indian fighter, the Creeks began referring to him as "Long Knife." Soon after his defeat of the British at New Orleans, when his troops devastated Pakenham's British forces in a battle fought after the war had ended, Jackson was firmly propelled into the role of national hero.

On the heels of this, Jackson and the nation turned their collective gaze to the troublesome Georgia-Florida border, which had a long history of conflict between British and Spanish soldiers, Native Americans, settlers, slaves, and now American soldiers. Here too was an "Indian Problem." In 1816, while in pursuit of Seminoles who supposedly had scalped settlers, Jackson crossed into Spanish Florida, where he defeated bands of Seminoles in several skirmishes, burned several villages, and executed two British subjects whom he believed were inciting the Seminoles to attack settlers. As a result of the First Seminole War, Spain sold Florida to the United States.

Narratives such as the Barber text (1818) were published to justify the international, ethical, and moral lines that Jackson had crossed while pursuing the Seminoles. While obviously a print commodity created for consumers of popular narratives, the text helped explain Jackson's actions not only to the country but also to President Monroe, Spanish ministers bent on "suitable punishment" for the incursion, Secretary of State John Quincy Adams, Secretary of War John C. Calhoun, Kentucky's Henry Clay, and Secretary of the Treasury William H. Crawford, all of whom had an interest in Jackson's methods of handling the "Indian problem." The Barber narrative is as much about Jackson, a nation involved in a border war, expansion, and genocidal justification as it is about Eunice Barber, who in all probability was a fictitious representation of a peace-loving, freedom-loving American provoked to vengeance. Although Camden County records indicate numerous Barbers in the marriage records (1810–50) and census rolls (1810 and 1820), none verifies the existence of this particular family. The other players, however, are quite real. Francis, who is mentioned in the narrative, was a Maskókî medicine man hung by Jackson.

The narrative claims the Barbers were living in Camden County, the southeasternmost corner of Georgia, when they were seized and nearly all murdered by "thirty or forty . . . blood thirsty monsters." Eunice Barber is captured, decorated in "Indian mode," emotionally tortured, and made to "endure hardships," which, she states, "would have been impossible for many females to sustain." At times she is rendered nearly naked, goes out with a war party, and grasps the opportunity to pummel her cruel master with a tomahawk (as did the popularized figures of Hannah Dustan and Panther's Lady). Perhaps most crucially, for rhetorical purposes, Barber is privy to the secret machinations of the Mikisúkî (mistakenly called Creek) and Seminole leaders during a council of war, victory feasts, and their military preparations. Basically, Barber becomes a repository of insider information valuable to a country eager for details about what was happening at the edges of its expanding borders.

First published in 1818 in Boston for David Hazen, this twenty-four-page book carries a beautiful engraving nearly identical to the one found in the 1815 Eliza Swan narrative. The ax-wielding Indian and the assertive woman strike the same poses, while Swan's dying husband is replaced by the image of a foregrounded child. Each of these helpless figures, however, clearly seeks the protective power of the female figure. Hazen's 1818 edition was the only publication of this narrative in its entirety until it was included in volume 36 of the Garland Library of Narratives of North American Indian Captivities (1977). Also included in the Garland volume is the anonymously published 1818 broadside *Shocking Murder by the Savage!*, which is drawn from the Barber text. The *National Union Catalog* lists the twenty-four-page narrative as its single entry, while *Early American Imprints* lists a possible second twenty-four-page narrative. Only the first carries actual copy.

Although the narrative implies that it is the result of an epistle sent to "inform," it is never clearly stated in the text. The broadside, however, does include this information at the bottom of the page, declaring itself to be a "copy of a letter from a gentleman in Georgia, to his correspondent in New-York." Included in the broadside are excerpts from what it noted was a "more particular" forthcoming account. Excerpts include the slaughter of Barber's family, her capture, the wearing of Indian garments, notes on other captives, and her escape. Interestingly, over a third of this version is devoted to her solitary, one-week trek toward civilization. There is no mention of her bludgeoning to death her first Indian master or of the Indian's secret plans for the dispatching of General Jackson, both of which are described in the expanded narrative. It's possible that Hazen published the broadside as promotion for the expanded narrative. Equally likely, the broadside served either as a gauge of consumer interest or as the first draft of a tantalizing fiction not yet complete.

According to the narrative, Barber spent five weeks among the Indians and one week on a brutal trek back to civilization with a tale that would have fascinated the country with its hellish images. Such infernal images were shared by at least one U.S. soldier, who reportedly wrote home during the Seminole War: "If the Devil owned both Hell and Florida, he would rent out Florida and live in Hell!"

SSB

"In the evening of the 26th of January last, my husband (DARIUS BARBER, who resided near the line, in Camden county) having imprudently retired to bed, without taking the precaution to secure the doors of the house as usual, about eleven at night we were awakened by the horrid yell of savages who to the number of thirty or forty, to our inexpressible horror, we saw standing over us with uplifted tomahawks!—Mr. Barber jumped instantly out of bed and attempted to reach an extreme corner of the room, where his fire arms were deposited, but a dozen tomahawks aimed at him at once, brought him lifeless to the floor—they then seized me by my hair and drew me from the bed, brandishing their knives before me with frightful grimaces and a terrible shout, as if about to dispatch me—others

NARRATIVE

OF THE

TRAGICAL DEATH

OF MR.

DARIUS BARBER,

AND HIS

SEVEN CHILDREN,

WHO WERE INHUMANLY BUTCHERED BY THE

INDIANS,

IN CAMDEN COUNTY, GEORGIA, JANUARY 26, 1818.

To which is added an account of the Captivity and Sufferings of MRS. BARBER, who was carried away a
Captive by the SAVAGES, and from whom she fortunately made her escape six weeks afterwards.

☞ It may be a gratification to the reader, to learn that
the said tribe of SAVAGES have been since exterminated by the Brave and Intrepid

GEN. JACKSON,

And the Troops under his command.

BOSTON—Printed for DAVID HAZEN—Price 9d.

Title page of *Narrative of the Tragical Death of Mr. Darius Barber*
(1818 Hazen edition; the Beinecke Rare Book and Manuscript Library,
Yale University)

Illustration from *Narrative of the Tragical Death of
Mr. Darius Barber*, "Savage Barbarity. Mrs. Barber Intreating a
Bloodthirsty Savage to Spare the Life of Her Little Daughter"
(1818 Hazen edition; the Beinecke Rare Book and
Manuscript Library, Yale University)

tomahawked and scalped my poor children, as they lay in their bed unconcious of harm, in a room adjoining—a hired man who lodged in the chamber, and who attempted to make his escape by jumping out of the window, suffered a similar fate. Having completed their bloody work thus far, they led me nearly naked to a spot a little distance from the house, from which they bid me not to move on peril of my life. The Savage monsters now proceeded to pillage the house of every thing valuable, and in their researches, they discovered my only surviving child, my daughter of ten years of age, who during the awful butchery of my other children, had unperceived crept from her bed and secreted herself behind a desk—observing herself discovered, she broke through the savages and succeeded in reaching the door, when espying me at a little distance, she ran up to me and with the most plaintive accents, begged that I would interceed for her, and implore the savages to spare her life!—she was closely pursued by one of the blood thirsty monsters, of whom I begged that he would spare the life of my only surviving child! but my entreaties and lementations were of no avail, my poor child was tomahawked in my arms!!—heaven only knows what were my feelings at this moment.

The Savages loaded themselves with the most valuable contents of the house, and departed, compelling me to accompany them with a heavy load. They bent their course towards their own settlement, which they reached after a tedious travel of six days, over steep mountains and through almost impenetrable thickets and swamps. At the entrance of their village, they daubed my face and body with black and red paint, and dressed my head with feathers, in imitation of their own!—as soon as they had completed thus decorating my person, according to their Indian mode, they all set up a terrible yell, which was probably to announce their approach to their brethren in the village, as they were very soon met by two or three hundred of them to whom they, with an air of triumph, exhibited the bleeding scalps of my poor children which was viewed by the unfeeling wretches with much apparent satisfaction. While the older ones were employed in examining the articles of plunder which their brethren had brought with them! their children formed a circle around me, and were permitted to insult and torment me in whatever manner they pleased—sometimes presenting to my view the scalps of my poor husband and children, and then would mimic their dying groans!

The Savages having satisfied their curiosity, they conducted me to one of their wigwams, and left me in charge of an old Indian and his squaw—Here I found two more white captives, two lads of the age of 11 and 14—the poor youths informed me that they had been in captivity nearly four weeks; that they were from Camden county, that their house was attacked about midnight by the savages, who killed both their parents and older brother.

While I remained a prisoner with the Indians I was a witness of many of their brutal acts, and endured hardships, which it would have been impossible for many females to sustain! indeed, human imagination can hardly figure to itself a more deplorable situation. I became the property of an old, Savage and my place of abode was a filthy wigwam unfit for a shelter for dumb beasts.—My food was the offal of such wild animals as were destroyed in the chase, and my bedding no other than a few hemlock branches—with cloathing scarcely sufficient to cover me, and my arms, face and legs gashed with wounds and swollen with bruises, to have quit the world at this moment, would scarcely have cost a single pang—my thought was ultimately filled on a happier state of existence, beyond the tortures I endured—the bitterness of death, even of that death which is accompanied with the keenest agonies, was, in a manner, past. Nature, with a feeble struggle, seemed inclined to quit its last hold on sublunary things.

My savage master in one of his hunting excursions (unwilling to leave me behind) compelled me to accompany him.—During his rambles, I was frequently on the point of perishing with hunger, to allay which, a little Bear's meat was given me which I sucked through my teeth. My master having one morning wounded a Buck in such a manner as he supposed it could not escape, left it in my charge, but the animal soon recovering his strength and from my very weak state being unable to secure it, it escaped from me. When my master and his two savage companions returned they not only manifested their malevolence for the disappointment, by horrid grimaces and angry gestures, but declared they would *roast* me!—with this apparent intention they led me to a dark forest, stripped me naked, and bound me to a tree, and piled dry brush, with other fuel at a small distance in a small circle round me they accompanied their labour as if for my funeral dirge, with screams and sounds inimitable but by savage voices. I now concluded that my final hour was inevitably come—I summoned all my resolution and composed my mind as far as the circumstances could admit, to bid an eternal farewell to a troublesome world! but at the very moment that I expected that fire would be communicated to the fatal pile, my master approached and unbound me, and giving me a severe blow with the handle of his tomahawk, led me out of the thicket. I was now ordered to wrap an Indian blanket around me, and was loaded with as much of their game as could be piled upon me, strongly pinioned, and my wrists tied as close together as they could be pulled with a cord. After being compelled to march through no pleasant path, in this painful manner, for many a tedious mile, the party (who as well as myself were excessively fatigued) halted to breathe. My hands were now immoderately swelled from the tightness of the ligature, and the pain had become so intolerable—my feet were so much scratched that the blood dropped fast from them—exhausted with bearing a burden above my strength, and frantic with torments exquisit beyond endurance, I implored of my savage master to unbind me or to dispatch me at once and take my scalp!

Early one morning we fell in with nine more Indians (warriors) of the same tribe, who were in pursuit of a company of their Indian enemies, who a few days previous had surprized and plundered a number of their wigwams. It was soon agreed by both parties that we should join them in the pursuit; that I might be enabled to keep pace with them, my hands were unbound, and a pair of moccasons were allowed me, and I was permitted to march without any pack, or receiving any insult.

After a rapid march of three days over steep and ragged mountains, and through thick and pathless swamps, we came up with the objects of our pursuit— they were just the number of my conductors, and well armed; a warm contest was therefore to be expected. A tomahawk was put into my hands by my master, who ordered me to dispatch such of the wounded of the enemy as during the action I should discover attempting to make their escape (rather would I have sunk it into the head of this, the murderer of my dear husband and children.)

In a few moments a bloody conflict commenced, accompanied with frightful whoops, and horrid yells both parties were armed with muskets, knives and tomahawks, and both seemed determined on death or conquest. The action, though principally fought between man and man, soon grew intensely warm—it would be as difficult as useless to describe their irregular and ferocious mode of fighting; sometimes they fought aggregately in open view, and sometimes individually under cover; taking aim from behind the bodies of trees, and acting in a manner independent of each other.

Among the rest my master received a severe wound and fell, but raising himself upon his hands and knees, he was just enabled to creep unperceived by the enemy, into a thicket—not until this moment did it occur to me for what purpose the hatchet had been put into my hands—it was to dispatch a wounded enemy; and could I look upon one greater, than he who in the most barbarous manner deprived me of my innocent husband and children; for a moment I surveyed the unstrument yet crimsoned with the blood of the unhappy victims, and hastened to retaliate upon the wretch who was deaf to their entreaties for mercy! As I approached him as if sensible of my determination, he raised himself upon his knees in a supplicating attitude; but as I well knew that he who would not shew mercy to the defenseless, could not expect to receive it from others, I instantly aimed a blow at his head, and continued to repeat them until I was sure that he was quite dead—this I accomplished without being discovered by any of his brethren, who were too warmly engaged with their enemies to notice which of their party were slain.

After a bloody conflict of near two hours continuance, victory decided in favour of my captors, who having destroyed seven and wounded two of the enemy, put the others to flight. After the engagement, in numbering their own living, it was discovered that four had been slain and three wounded—my master was found in the thicket in the situation in which I left him, nor did they dream of his having fallen by any other hand than that of his Indian enemies. Their own killed they buried after their Indian mode on the spot, and scalped those of their enemies and suffered their bodies to lie above ground.

Having constructed an Indian litter, for the conveyance of their wounded, and of their prisoners, they set out on their return to their village, which they reached four days after—at the entrance, the prisoners were decorated with fine feathers, vermillion &c. as usual, and ordered to sing a death song—in a very few moments they were met by many hundreds of the villagers, men, women and children, who by way of savage triumph, caused the woods to resound with the whoops and yells—but, as soon as they were made acquainted with the number of their friends slain, their exulting airs and vociferations were changed & the most dreadful howlings and bitter lementations now rent the air; nor did they fail to reek their vengeance on their unfortunaet prisoners, whom they pelted with clubs and stones, so that they were hardly enabled to walk.

The conquering savages having lost three of their number killed, the fate of the two wounded prisoners was very soon determined; they were sentenced (in retaliation for the deaths of their friends) to be tortured after their Indian mode. The dreadful sentence was no sooner passed then the whole village set up the death-cry, preparatory to their rioting in the most diabolical cruelty.—The unhappy captives were first stripped, and bound to three posts that had been erected for the purpose, their bodies were next stuck from their necks to their waists with small pitch pine splinters, the blood gushing out at every puncture; all this the unfortunate victims sustained without a complaint!—in this situation they were compelled to remain for more than one hour, while the men, women and children of the whole village, were permitted and encouraged to torture them, in whatever manner they pleased, each striving to exceed the other in cruelty—the small splinters were then set on fire, which very soon placed the miserable sufferers beyond the reach of savage torture!

What is very extraordinary, not a groan, nor a sigh, nor a distortion of countenance escaped the victims during their torments—there indeed seemed during the whole distressing scene a contest between them, and their tormentors, which should out do the other, they in inflicting the most horrid pains, or the prisoners in enduring them!

During my captivity I almost daily saw hordes of savages returning from their expeditions against the white settlements, loaded with human scalps, and draging into captivity more or less of their defenceless inhabitants.—Among these unfeeling monsters I found too a number of wretched beings who had been much longer in captivity than myself—among these I became acquainted with one of my own sex, a Mrs. White, who had been nearly two years a prisoner among them, and whose history I am certain could not be read without emotion, if it could be written in the same affecting manner, in which she related it to me. She was still young and handsome as the troubles which she had experienced had taken somewhat from the original redundancy of her bloom, and added a softening paleness to her cheeks, rendered her appearance the more engaging. Her face, that seemed to have been formed for the assemblage of dimples and smiles, was clouded with care. The natural sweetness was not, however, soured by despondency and petulance; but chastened by humility and resignation. This unhappy woman looked as if she had known the day of prosperity, when serenity and gladness of soul were the inmates of her bosom. That day was past, and the once lively features, now assumed a tender melancholy, which witnessed her irreparable loss. She wedded not the customary weeds of mourning, or the fallacious pageantry of woe to prove her widowed state. Every thing conspired to confirm and to make her story interesting.—Her father was killed by the Indians at the time of St. Clair's defeat[1]—her mother and two of her sisters were taken captives by the savages soon after, and was never after heard of—her husband and three of her children were inhumanly butchered by the Indians on the night of the 10th May, 1815, and herself and the remainder of her children (five in number) led away into captivity! She was for some months held a prisoner by the clan of Savages who first took her, and during their rambles was often subjected to hardships seemingly intolerable to one of so delicate a frame. The Indians at length seperated, and carried off four of her youngest children into different tribes!—of no avail were the entreaties of their tender mother—a mother desolated by the loss of children, who were torn from her fond embraces, and removed many hundred miles from each other into the utmost recesses of the wild wilderness!

With them (could they have been kept together) she would most willingly have wandered to the extremities of the world, and accepted as a desirable portion the cruel lot of slavery for life. But, she was precluded from the sweet hope of ever beholding them again. The insufferable pangs of parting, and the idea of eternal seperation planted the sorrows of despair deep in her soul. This unfortunate woman begged of me, if I should ever be so fortunate first to gain my liberty and should be again restored to the arms of my christian friends, that I would beseech them to take measures to liberate her and her unfortunate children from cruel bondage—this I promised her I would do, nor have I failed to keep my promise—soon after my fortunate escape, I represented to the proper Authority the situation of this wretched woman, who, with the aid of government, are about to adopt measures to resque the fair prisoner from the hands of the barbarians.

As I obsereved while I was held prisoner by the savages, parties from 10 to 20 were almost constantly employed in expeditions against the christian settlements—their return to their village was always announced by whoops and yells, when the whole inhabitants of the village who had power to use their legs, hastened to meet them, and if their expedition had been a successful one, on their meeting, they united their voices with those of the captors, in their ejaculations of triumph.—But, if they had experienced a reverse of fortune, it was announced by dismal howls, and great lementations by those whose friends had been slain.—If a single prisoner was brought in, those who had lost a friend in the expedition, had the power to determine his fate, either to adopt him in the place of the deceased, or to doom him to savage torture—if they were disposed to save his life he was unbound, taken by the hands, led to the cabin of the person into whose family he was to be adopted, and received with all imaginable marks of kindness. He was then treated as a friend and a brother, and they appeared soon to love him with the same tenderness as if he stood in the place of their deceased friend. In short, he had no other marks of captivity, but his not being suffered to return to his own nation, for should he have attempted this, he would have been punished with death.—But, if the sentence be death, how different their conduct! these people, who behave with such disinterested affec[t]ion to each other, with such tenderness to those whom they adopt, here show that they are truly savages; the dreadful sentence is no sooner passed, than the whole village set up the death-cry; and, as there was no medium between the most generous friendship and the most inhuman cruelty; for the execution of him whom they had just before deliberated upon admitting into their tribe, is no longer deterred, than whilst they can make the nessary preparations for rioting in the most diabolical cruelty! preparations to destroy life by torture!—

Among those who held me in captivity there appeared to be many of the Creek Nation, who harboured great inveteracy against the American troops for depriving them of their lands, particularly their Commander in Chief, Gen. JACKSON, whom (as all the neighboring tribes had engaged to join them in the War against the whites) they vainly hoped soon to have in their power—so confident did they appear to be of this, that they had really held meetings of consultation to devise means how, and in what way they should inflict the most excruciating torture upon him—his heart, it was pretty generally agreed should be divided into as many detached pieces as there should be tribes engaged in the war, and a piece presented each, while his scalp, was to be the property of *Francis*, their distinguished leader! thus had they agreed to dispose of their much dreaded enemy, General JACKSON!—little thinking then, that this distinguished Commander was so soon to march fearlessly into the very heart of their village, lay their wigwams in ashes, and compel them to sue for peace, which he has actually since done![2]

A few weeks after I was taken prisoner, the Indians held a Council of War, at which my Indian master permitted me to be present—the Council was composed of the chiefs and heads of families, whose capacity had raised them to the same degree of consideration.—When they had assembled, the Chief Sachem first arose and taking up a tomahawk which lay by his side, with a stern voice enquired "Who among you will go and fight the white men? Who among you will bring captives from their settlements to replace our deceased friends, that our wrongs may be revenged and our name and our honour maintained, as long as the rivers flow, the grass grows, or the sun and moon shall endure?" upon which one of the principal warriors arose, and harrangued the whole assembly, and afterwards addressed himself to the young men, enquiring who among them would go along with him, and fight the white people; who thereupon all generally arose one after another, and fell in behind him, while he walked round the circle.

Their feast, which always attends their Council of War, now began on this occasion—there was a whole deer roasted, from which eash, as they consented to go to war, cut off a piece, and eating it, said, "Thus will I decour our white enemies!" This ceremony being performed, the war-dance began, each singing the war-song, which related to their intended expedition, and conquest, and to their own skill and dexterity in fighting, and the manner in which they would vanquish their enemies! Their expressions were strong and pathetic, attended with a tone that could not fail to inspire terror in a timid female.

The next week the warriors assembled to set out upon their intended expedition—their military appearance was odd and terrible—they cut off all their hair, except a spot on the crown of their head, and plucked out their eye-brows—the lock which they left upon their heads, they divided into several parcels, each of which they stiffened, and intermixed with beads and feathers of various shapes and colors, twisting and connecting the whole together. They painted themselves with red pigment, down to the eye-brows, which they sprinkled over with white down. They slit the gristle of their ears almost quite round, and hung them with ornaments that generally had the figure of some bird or beast, drawn upon them—their noses (which were bored) were likewise hung with beads, and their faces painted with various colors—on their breasts they wore a gorget or medal of brass or copper, and by a string around their necks was suspended that horrid weapon the scalping knife!

Thus equiped, they proceeded for the white settlements, singing their war-song until they lost sight of the village—they were attended by many of their squaws, who assisted them in carrying their baggage—they were to the number of nearly one hundred in the whole; but, it gave me inexpressible satisfaction to see but one half this number return 10 or 12 days afterward—the rest having been slain by the whites. While I inwardly exulted at their bad success, they seemed anxious to discover some object on whom they could retaliate, nor was I with out my fears that I should myself be selected as a victim on whom they might reek their vengeance—they did not however appear disposed to exercise more cruelty towards me than what they had previously done.

During the six weeks of my captivity, I am confident there were more than 50 prisoners (men, women and children) brought in by the Savages, beside many horses and other property to a very great amount. The particulars of many of the instances of barbarity exercised upon the prisoners of different ages, and sexes, and to which I was an eyewitness, are of too shocking a nature to be presented to the public—it is sufficient here to observe that the scalping knife and tomahawk, were the mildest instruments of death—that in many cases torture by fire, and other execrable means were used.

I remained nearly five weeks in charge of my Indian master, when being sent very late one evening for some water, I conceived it the most favourable opportunity that I should probably have to escape.—I proceeded without delay to a very thick swamp, where I concealed myself until it was quite dark & then proceeded in search of a tract, that might lead me to some white settlement, without the risk of being lost, and perishing with hunger. Taking a path leading in the direction of the settlement from which I had been taken, as I judged, about the break of day, three or four Indians passed within a few rods of me, without perceiving me!—these I concluded were probably my pursuers, and excited emotions of gratitude and thankfulness to divine providence for my deliverance. Being destitute of every kind of provision, and having no kind of instrument or weapon by which I might procure it, and being nearly as destitute of cloathing, and entirely unacquainted with the method of traveling through a wild wilderness, excited painful sensations—but certain death, either by hunger or wild beasts, seemed preferable rather than to be in the power of beings whose awful barbarity was still fresh in my mind. I addressed heaven for protection, & proceeded onward, sometimes penetrating thick and dismal swamps, at other times crossing high and craggy mountains, not marked with the footsteps of any human being. After travelling four days, my course was obstructed by a river—after proceeding up the same, for several days, I came to a prodigious water-fall, and numerous high craggy clifts along the water edge; that way seemed impassible, the mountain steep and difficult—however, I concluded that the latter way was the best. I therefore ascended for some time, but coming to a range of inaccessible rocks, I turned my course towards the foot of the mountain and the river side; after getting into a deep gully, and passing over several hish steep rocks, I reached the river side, where to my inexpressible affliction, I found that a perpendicular rock, or rather one that hung over, of 15 or 20 feet high, formed the bank. Here a solemn pause took place; I essayed to return, but the height of the steep rocks I had descended over, prevented me. I then returned to the edge of the precipice, and viewed the bottom of it, as the certain spot to end all my troubles, or remain on the top to pine away with hunger, or be devoured by wild beasts. After serious meditation, and devout exercises, I determined on leaping from the height, and accordingly jumped off. Although the place I had to alight on, was covered with uneven rocks, not a bone was broken; but, being exceedingly stunned with the fall, I remained unable to proceed for some space of time.

As five days had passed since I had received any other nourishment, but what the roots and bark of trees afforded, hunger, fatigue and grief, reduced me to a mere skeleton—as I was appsehensive that I should very soon fall a victim to one or the other, at times, I was ready to reproach myself for having attempted to effect my escape. After crossing the river, I travelled a south-east course for two days, but with as little prospect of reaching a friendly settlement—my spirits as well as strength began to fail me; I conceived myself the most wretched and forlorn of human beings! Altho' until now I had been enabled to support nature by chewing and swallowing the juice of young cane stocks, the roots and bark of sassafrass, &c. my hunger was too great to be any longer endured. About noon of the seventh day from my escape, as I was seated on the summit of a rock, upon a high hill, meditating on my wretched condition, the pleasing sound of the woodman's ax, (which proceeded from the valley below) met my ear! As I concluded this must be some friendly inhabitant employed in falling timber, I hastened to the spot, and to my inexpressible joy, found myself not mistaken—it was the christian friend by whom I was yesterday conducted to this village."

Thus, after remaining six weeks a prisoner among the cruel Savages, in which time I experienced every harship and cruelty which it was in the power of the inhuman monsters to inflict—by the interference of Divine Providence in my behalf, I was at length rescued from their hands—although bereaved of my kind husband and tender children, who all in one fatal night fell victims to savage barbarity, yet, I feel that I ought not to "charge the Almighty foolishly." I would rather acknowledge it right & just, that I have been afflicted.—God chastiseth him whom he loveth—it was his will and pleasure that I should be preserved amid the perils and dangers with which I have been surrounded—through his kind interposition was I saved from the tomahawk and scalping knife in the most exasperated moments of the Savages—He was my friend and protector, while a sojourner in the wilderness, and saved me from the ravenous jaws of the wild beasts—miserable must I have been had I been cut off in the midst of my transgressions!—Thanks to Him, who knows the impurity of every heart, that I have been spared yet a little while longer to repent of my manifold sins—may I improve the remaining precious moments of my life in such a way as will insure me permanent and uninterrupted happiness in the world to come.

EUNICE BARBER.

Notes

1. Arthur St. Clair, Revolutionary leader and governor of the Northwest Territory, was commissioned in 1791 to build a fort in order to thwart British influence on the Indian population. Unfortunately, this fort was to be built in the primary village of the Maumee (now Fort Wayne, Indiana) without consent of the Maumee. Several miles before the village, his troops were surprised by a predawn attack by the Mississagie that resulted in the deaths of over nine hundred of his men. Henry Rowe Schoolcraft's *History of the Indian Tribes of the United States* (1857) puts the number of total deaths at six hundred, half of the original twelve hundred men. According to Schoolcraft, it was a defeat that proved "most disastrous to the western settlements" in that "immigration was checked, and dismay prevailed along the entire frontier" (337).

2. Francis was a Maskókî medicine man hung by Andrew Jackson. This tribe is the Mikisúkî, mistakenly called Creek.

WORKS CITED

Allison, Robert. *The Crescent Obscured: The United States and the Muslim World, 1776–1815*. New York: Oxford University Press, 1995.

Appleby, Joyce. *Inheriting the Revolution: The First Generation of Americans*. Cambridge, Mass.: Harvard University Press, 2000.

———. Introduction. *Recollections of the Early Republic: Selected Autobiographies*. Boston: Northeastern University Press, 1994.

———. *Liberalism and Republicanism in the Historical Imagination*. Cambridge, Mass.: Harvard University Press, 1992.

Arch, Stephen Carl. *After Franklin: The Emergence of Autobiography in Post-Revolutionary America, 1780–1830*. Hanover, N.H.: University Press of New England, 2001.

Armstrong, Nancy, and Leonard Tennenhouse. "The American Origins of the English Novel." *American Literary History* 4.3 (Fall 1992): 386–410.

Baepler, Paul, ed. *White Slaves, African Masters: An Anthology of American Barbary Captivity Narratives*. Chicago: University of Chicago Press, 1999.

Bailyn, Bernard. *The Ideological Origins of the American Revolution*. 1967. Cambridge, Mass.: Harvard University Press, 1973.

Bailyn, Bernard, and John B. Hench. *The Press and the American Revolution*. Worcester: American Antiquarian Society, 1980.

Bakhtin, Mikhail M. *The Dialogic Imagination: Four Essays*. Ed. Michael Holquist. Trans. Caryl Emerson and Michael Holquist. Austin: University of Texas Press, 1981.

Banks, James Lennox. *David Sproat and the Naval Prisoners in the War of Revolution*. New York, 1909.

Bercovitch, Sacvan. *The American Jeremiad*. Madison: University of Wisconsin Press, 1978.

———. *The Puritan Origins of the American Self*. New Haven: Yale University Press, 1975.

Block, Ruth. "Gender and the Public/Private Dichotomy in American Revolutionary Thought." *Gender and Morality in Anglo-American Culture, 1650–1800*. Berkeley: University of California Press, 2003. 154–66.

———. "The Gendered Meanings of Virtue in Revolutionary America." *Signs: Journal of Women in Culture and Society* 13.1 (1987): 37–58.

Bowman, Larry G. *Captive Americans: Prisoners during the American Revolution*. Athens, Ohio: Ohio University Press, 1976.

Brown, Gillian. *The Consent of the Governed: The Lockean Legacy in Early American Culture*. Cambridge, Mass: Harvard University Press, 2001.

——. *Domestic Individualism: Imagining Self in Nineteenth Century America*. Vol. 14 of *The New Historicism*. Berkeley: University of California Press, 1990.

Brown, Richard D. *Knowledge Is Power: The Diffusion of Information in Early America, 1700–1865*. New York: Oxford University Press, 1989.

——. *Modernization: The Transformation of American Life, 1600–1865*. 1976. Prospects Heights, Ill.: Waveland Press, 1988.

Buell, Lawrence. *New England Literary Culture from Revolution through Renaissance*. New York: Cambridge University Press, 1986.

Burgett, Bruce. *Sentimental Bodies: Sex, Gender, and Citizenship in the Early Republic*. Princeton, N.J.: Princeton University Press, 1998.

Burnham, Michelle. *Captivity and Sentiment: Cultural Exchange in American Literature, 1682–1861*. Hanover, N.H.: University Press of New England, 1997.

Calloway, Colin G. *The American Revolution in Indian Country: Crisis and Diversity in Native American Communities*. New York: Cambridge University Press, 1995.

——. *New Worlds for All: Indians, Europeans, and the Re-making of Early America*. Baltimore: Johns Hopkins University Press, 1997.

Castiglia, Christopher. *Bound and Determined: Captivity, Culture-Crossing, and White Womanhood from Mary Rowlandson to Patty Hearst*. Chicago: University of Chicago Press, 1996.

Charvat, William. *The Profession of Authorship in America: 1800–1870*. Ed. Matthew J. Bruccoli. 2nd ed. New York: Columbia University Press, 1992.

Clark, J. C. D. *The Language of Liberty, 1660–1832: Political Discourse and Social Dynamics in the Anglo-American World*. New York: Cambridge University Press, 1994.

Cohen, Daniel A. *The Female Marine and Related Works: Narratives of Cross-Dressing and Urban Vice in America's Early Republic*. Amherst: University of Massachusetts Press, 1997.

Colley, Linda. *Captives*. New York: Pantheon, 2002.

Conway, Stephen. *The British Isles and the War of American Independence, 1775–1783*. New York: Oxford University Press, 1995.

Couser, G. Thomas. *Altered Egos: Authority in American Autobiography*. New York: Oxford University Press, 1989.

Danow, David K. *The Thought of Mikhail Bakhtin: From Word to Culture*. New York: St. Martin's Press, 1991.

Davidson, Cathy N. *Revolution and the Word: The Rise of the Novel in America*. New York: Oxford University Press, 1986.

Davis, Charles T., and Henry Louis Gates Jr. *The Slave's Narrative*. New York: Oxford University Press, 1985.

Davis, Lennard J. *Factual Fictions: The Origins of the English Novel*. New York: Columbia University Press, 1983.

Derounian-Stodola, Kathryn Zabelle, and James Arthur Levernier. *The Indian Captivity Narrative, 1550–1900*. Ed. Pattie Cowell. New York: Twayne, 1993.

Dillon, Elizabeth Maddock. *The Gender of Freedom: Fictions of Liberalism and the Literary Public Sphere*. Stanford: Stanford University Press, 2004.

Doyle, Robert C. *A Prisoner's Duty: Great Escapes in U.S. Military History*. Annapolis: Naval Institute Press, 1997.

————. *Voices from Captivity: Interpreting the American POW Narrative*. Lawrence, Kans.: University Press of Kansas, 1994.

Dudley, William S. *The Naval War of 1812: A Documentary History*. Washington: Naval Historical Center, Dept. of the Navy, 1985.

Dworetz, Steven D. *The Unvarnished Doctrine: Locke, Liberalism, and the American Revolution*. Durham: Duke University Press, 1990.

Ebersole, Gary L. *Captured by Texts: Puritan to Postmodern Images of Indian Captivity*. Charlottesville: University Press of Virginia, 1995.

Elkins, Stanley, M., and Eric McKitrick. *The Age of Federalism*. Oxford: Oxford University Press, 1993.

Ellis, Joseph J. *After the Revolution: Profiles of Early American Culture*. New York: Norton, 1979.

Eltis, David. "The Volume, Age/Sex Ratios, and African Impact of the Slave Trade: Some Refinements of Paul Lovejoy's *Review of the Literature*." *Journal of African History* 31 (1990): 485–92.

Epstein, William H. *Recognizing Biography*. Philadelphia: University of Pennsylvania, 1987.

Fabian, Ann. *The Unvarnished Truth: Personal Narratives in Nineteenth-Century America*. Berkeley: University of California Press, 2000.

Faery, Rebecca Blevins. *Cartographies of Desire: Captivity, Race, and Sex in the Shaping of an American Nation*. Norman: University of Oklahoma Press, 1999.

Ferguson, Robert A. *The American Enlightenment, 1750–1820*. Cambridge, Mass.: Harvard University Press, 1997.

————. *Reading the Early Republic*. Cambridge, Mass.: Harvard University Press, 2004.

Ferling, John. *Setting the World Ablaze: Washington, Adams, Jefferson, and the American Revolution*. Oxford: Oxford University Press, 2000.

Fitzpatrick, Tara. "The Figure of Captivity: The Cultural Work of the Puritan Captivity Narrative." *American Literary History* 3.1 (Spring 1991): 1–26.

Fleischaker, Samuel. *On Adam Smith's Wealth of Nations: A Philosophical Companion*. Princeton, N.J.: Princeton University Press, 2004.

Fliegelman, Jay. *Declaring Independence: Jefferson, Natural Language, and the Culture of Performance*. Stanford: Stanford University Press, 1993.

————. *Prodigals and Pilgrims: The American Revolution against Patriarchal Authority, 1750–1800*. New York: Cambridge University Press, 1982.

Fowler, William M. *Rebels under Sail: The American Navy during the Revolution*. New York: Charles Scribner's and Sons, 1976.

Geggus, David. "Sex Ratio, Age, and Ethnicity in the Atlantic Slave Trade: Data from French Shipping and Plantation Records." *Journal of African History* 30 (1989): 23–44.

Gilmore, William J. *Reading Becomes a Necessity of Life: Material and Cultural Life in Rural New England, 1780–1835*. Knoxville: University of Tennessee Press, 1989.

Gould, Philip. *Barbaric Traffic: Commerce and Antislavery in the Eighteenth-Century Atlantic World.* Cambridge, Mass.: Harvard University Press, 2003.

Habermas, Jürgen. *On the Pragmatics of Communication.* Trans. Maeve Cooke. Cambridge, Mass.: MIT Press, 1998.

———. *The Structural Transformation of the Public Sphere.* Trans. Thomas Burger. Cambridge, Mass.: MIT Press, 1989.

Haller, William. *Liberty and Reformation in the Puritan Revolution.* New York: Columbia University Press, 1955.

Hartman, James D. *Providence Tales and the Birth of American Literature.* Baltimore: The Johns Hopkins University Press, 1999.

Hatch, Nathan O. *The Sacred Cause of Liberty: Republican Thought and the Millennium in Revolutionary New England.* New Haven: Yale University Press, 1977.

Henretta, James. *The Evolution of American Society, 1700–1815.* Lexington: DC Heath, 1973.

Hickey, Donald R. *The War of 1812: A Forgotten Conflict.* Urbana: University of Illinois Press, 1989.

Holquist, Michael. *Dialogism: Bakhtin and His World.* London: Routledge, 1990.

Horsman, Reginald. *The New Republic: The United States of America, 1789–1815.* Vol. 1 of *The Longman History of America.* New York: Longman-Pearson, 2000.

Howe, Daniel Walker. *Making the American Self: Jonathan Edwards to Abraham Lincoln.* Cambridge, Mass.: Harvard University Press, 1997.

Howe, John. *Language and Political Meaning in Revolutionary America.* Amherst: University of Massachusetts Press, 2004.

Humphrey, Carol Sue. *The Press of the Young Republic, 1783–1833.* The History of American Journalism 2. Ed. James D. Startt and Wm. David Sloan. Westport, Conn.: Greenwood Press, 1996.

Imbarrato, Susan Claire. *Declarations of Independency in Eighteenth-Century American Autobiography.* Knoxville: University of Tennessee Press, 1998.

Isenberg, Gerald N. *Impossible Individuality: Romanticism, Revolution, and the Origins of Modern Selfhood, 1787–1802.* Princeton, N.J.: Princeton University Press, 1992.

Jay, Paul. *Being in the Text: Self-Representation from Wordsworth to Roland Barthes.* Ithaca: Cornell University Press, 1984.

Jordan, Winthrop D. *White over Black: American Attitudes toward the Negro, 1515–1812.* Chapel Hill: University of North Carolina Press, 1968.

Kerber, Linda. *Women in the Republic: Intellect and Ideology in Revolutionary War America.* University of North Carolina Press, 1997.

Kolodny, Annette. *The Land before Her: Fantasy and Experience of the American Frontiers, 1630–1860.* Chapel Hill: University of North Carolina Press, 1984.

———. "Turning the Lens on 'The Panther Captivity': A Feminist Exercise in Practical Criticism." *Writing and Sexual Difference.* Ed. Elizabeth Abel. Chicago: University of Chicago Press, 1982.

Kramnick, Isaac. *Republicanism and Bourgeois Radicalism: Political Ideology in Late Eighteenth-Century England and America.* Ithaca: Cornell University Press, 1990.

Lepore, Jill. *The Name of War: King Philip's War and the Origins of American Identity*. New York: Knopf, 1998.

Linebaugh, Peter, and Marcus Rediker. *The Many-Headed Hydra: The Hidden History of the Revolutionary Atlantic*. Boston: Beacon Press, 2000.

Looby, Christopher. *Voicing America: Language, Literary Form, and the Origins of the United States*. Chicago: University of Chicago Press, 1996.

Metzger, Charles H. *The Prisoners in the American Revolution*. Chicago: Loyola University Press, 1971.

Miller, J. Hillis. *Reading Narrative*. Norman: University of Oklahoma Press, 1998.

Morgan, Edmund S. *The Challenge of the American Revolution*. New York: W. W. Norton & Co., 1976.

————. *Inventing the People: The Rise of Popular Sovereignty in England and America*. New York: W. W. Norton & Co., 1989.

Morson, Gary Saul, ed. *Bakhtin: Essays and Dialogues on His Work*. Chicago: University of Chicago Press, 1996.

Mott, Frank Luther. *Golden Multitudes: The Story of Best Sellers in the United States*. New York: R. R. Bowker, 1947.

Namias, June. *White Captives: Gender and Ethnicity on the American Frontier*. Chapel Hill: University of North Carolina Press, 1993.

Nobles, Gregory H. *American Frontiers: Cultural Encounters and Continental Conquest*. New York: Hill and Wang, 1997.

Norton, Mary Beth. *Founding Mothers and Fathers: Gendered Power and the Forming of American Society*. New York: Knopf, 1996.

Novarr, David. *The Lines of Life: Theories of Biography, 1880–1970*. West Lafayette, Ind.: Purdue University Press, 1986.

O'Shaughnessy, A. J. *An Empire Divided: The American Revolution and the British Caribbean*. Philadelphia: University of Pennsylvania Press, 2000.

Patterson, Mark B. *Authority, Autonomy, and Representation in American Literature, 1776–1865*. Princeton, N.J.: Princeton University Press, 1988.

Pratt, Mary Louise. *Imperial Eyes: Travel Writing and Transculturation*. London: Routledge, 1992.

Purcell, Sarah J. *Sealed with Blood: War, Sacrifice, and Memory in Revolutionary America*. Philadelphia: University of Pennsylvania Press, 2002.

Reid, John Phillip. *The Concept of Liberty in the Age of the American Revolution*. Chicago: University of Chicago Press, 1998.

Rice, Grantland. *The Transformation of Authorship in America*. Chicago: University of Chicago Press, 1997.

Rogers, Daniel T. *Contested Truths: Key Words in American Politics since Independence*. New York: Basic Books, 1987.

Ruttenberg, Nancy. *Democratic Personality: Popular Voice and the Trial of American Authorship*. Stanford: Stanford University Press, 1998

Said, Edward. *Orientalism*. New York: Vintage, 1979.

Sayre, Gordon M. *American Captivity Narratives*. Boston: Houghton Mifflin, 2000.

Schoolcraft, Henry Rowe. *History of the Indian Tribes of the United States: Their Present Condition and Prospects and a Sketch of Their Ancient Status*. Philadelphia: Lippincott, 1857.

Sellers, Charles. *The Market Revolution: Jacksonian America, 1815–1846*. Oxford: Oxford University Press, 1991.

Sieminski, Greg. "The Puritan Captivity Narrative and the Politics of the American Revolution." *American Quarterly* 42.1 (March 1990): 35–56.

Silverman, Kenneth. *A Cultural History of the American Revolution*. New York: Columbia University Press, 1987.

Simpson, *The Politics of American English, 1776–1850*. New York: Oxford University Press, 1986.

Slotkin, Richard. *Regeneration through Violence: The Myth of the American Frontier, 1600–1860*. Norman: University of Oklahoma Press, 1973.

Smith, Adam. *An Inquiry into the Nature and Causes of the Wealth of Nations*. 1776. W. B. Todd, ed. Indianapolis: Liberty Classics, 1981.

Stedman, Raymond William. *Shadows of the Indian*. Norman: University of Oklahoma Press, 1982.

Stepto, Robert B. *From behind the Veil: A Study of Afro-American Narrative*. Urbana: University of Illinois Press, 1979.

Tebbel, John, and Sarah Miles Watts. *The Press and the Presidency: From George Washington to Ronald Reagan*. New York: Oxford University Press, 1985.

Tompkins, Jane. *Sensational Designs: The Cultural Work of American Fiction, 1790–1860*. New York: Oxford University Press, 1985.

Warner, Michael. *The Letters of the Republic: Publication and the Public Sphere in Eighteenth-Century America*. Cambridge, Mass.: Harvard University Press, 1990.

Wheelen, Joseph. *Jefferson's War: America's First War on Terror, 1801–1805*. New York: Carrol and Graf, 2003.

Wiebe, Robert H. *The Opening of American Society: From the Adoption of the Constitution to the Eve of Disunion*. New York: Knopf, 1984.

Wiegand, Wayne. *Print Culture in a Diverse America*. Urbana: University of Illinois Press, 1998.

Wood, Gordon S. *The Creation of the American Republic, 1776–1787*. New York: Vintage, 1998.

———. *The Radicalism of the American Revolution*. New York: Vintage, 1991.

Zboray, Ronald. *A Fictive People: Antebellum Economic Development and the American Reading Public*. New York: Oxford University Press, 1993.

INDEX

www.ingramcontent.com/pod-product-compliance
Lightning Source LLC
Chambersburg PA
CBHW060622100726
47907CB00006B/1731